The New Age in the Modern West

The New Age in the Modern West

Counterculture, Utopia and Prophecy
from the Late Eighteenth Century to
the Present Day

Nicholas Campion

Bloomsbury Academic
An imprint of Bloomsbury Publishing Plc

B L O O M S B U R Y
LONDON · OXFORD · NEW YORK · NEW DELHI · SYDNEY

Bloomsbury Academic

An imprint of Bloomsbury Publishing Plc

50 Bedford Square	1385 Broadway
London	New York
WC1B 3DP	NY 10018
UK	USA

www.bloomsbury.com

BLOOMSBURY and the Diana logo are trademarks of Bloomsbury Publishing Plc

First published 2016

British Library Cataloguing-in-Publication Data
A catalogue record for this book is available from the British Library.

ISBN: HB: 978-1-4725-2279-5
ePDF: 978-1-4725-2593-2
ePub: 978-1-4725-3237-4

Library of Congress Cataloging-in-Publication Data
A catalog record for this book is available from the Library of Congress.

Typeset by Integra Software Services Pvt. Ltd.
Printed and bound in Great Britain

To Wendy

Contents

Acknowledgements

I must acknowledge the influence of all my colleagues who have undertaken studies of New Age culture, particularly Marion Bowman and Michael York. Thanks are due to my colleagues and students at the University of Wales Trinity Saint David and all my former students at Bath Spa University. A series of great historians have also influenced my work: Norman Cohn, who launched the study of millenarian beliefs, Christopher Hill, who effectively illustrated the operation of Marxist theory in English history, R. G. Collingwood, who put such ideas into context in the history of ideas, and Geoffrey Elton, whose lectures I attended at Cambridge and whose constant advice was to stay close to the evidence. Personally, I am also indebted to my friends in the Soller Writers' Group and to Christina Black Rozei, who inspired me in the 1960s.

A Note on Capitalization

Throughout the text certain words and phrases are capitalized in some circumstances but not in others. Utopia should be with an initial capital – Utopia – when referring to Thomas More's Utopia. In all other uses it should be the generic utopia with a small 'u'. Golden Age is spelt with capitals when referring to *the* Golden Age but *a* golden age is lower case. Ideal and Idea have an initial capital when referring to Platonic Ideals and Ideas; and Nature, Progress and Imagination are capitalized when they refer to greater forces.

Introduction: Future Dreams

This book is about histories of the future. Modern western attitudes to time and history include two key ideas: one is utopian, the hope that a new and better world can be brought into existence; the other is dystopian, the fear that our own society, perhaps the entire planet, is doomed. Both are frequently linked to concepts of purpose, fate and destiny, in which history is propelled along a particular direction to a final, identifiable end. Often, time's arrow speeds us in a definite direction towards a recognizable end point. In some versions history moves in stages, oscillating between peaks of hope and troughs of despair. At the extreme, theories of eternal recurrence dictate that history is destined to repeat itself forever and ever, without end, sometimes down to the merest detail. But always, there is pattern, purpose and meaning.

I am concerned with certain kind of mentality – or mentalities.[1] It is about longing for the past, despair over the present and hope for the future. It is about people who believe that ideas, rather than events or socio-economic forces, shape the world. And it concerns the belief that time moves in patterns, sometimes forever, but often reaching a final end point. It is about a particular kind of what Hayden White called 'metahistory' – the idea of history as a single, all-embracing, underlying pattern.[2] History, in this sense, is directional, moving towards a certain destination no matter what people do.[3] As W. H. Auden put it, history is the operator, the great organizer of human affairs, time a flowing, refreshing river.[4]

My title, *The New Age in the Modern West*, defines my subject area: the belief that either as individuals or as a society, we are entering a new phase of history. My subtitle is 'Counterculture, Utopia and Prophecy', words with potent and contested meanings. The term 'counterculture' was first used as a description of the youthful rebellion of the 1960s, but it has since become a general term for networks of individuals with particular social or political grievances which are set up in deliberate opposition to mainstream culture. A utopia, meanwhile, is a society which is either perfect or aspires to perfection. It may be of this world or it may exist in the imagination, but it always aspires to perfection. Prophecy, my third key term, has a double meaning. One is divine revelation – to reveal the truth is what the classic Old Testament prophets did when they acted as mouthpieces for God. The second meaning is a particular function of revelation, to predict the future. The prophecy I am concerned with is the focus of my main title: the prediction of a future spiritual New Age, one when psyche, or soul, will take centre stage. We may call this New Ageism.

All four key terms are interlinked. Counterculturalism invariably involves an element of utopianism because people who challenge existing social and political norms search for better alternatives. New Agers tend to be both counterculturalists and utopians, as they hope to replace the current political and economic regime with a new spiritual, egalitarian dispensation. Utopianism involves a Prophecy of a perfect future, counterculturalism of a desirable one, and New Ageism of an inevitable one. And all are bound up with a complex of prophecies known collectively as millenarianism, or millennialism, at the heart of which is a deep concern with the return of Christ and the establishment of the Kingdom of God, as set out in the New Testament in the Book of Revelation.

In particular, I trace the history of one prophecy, closely associated with the coming New Age; that of the coming Aquarian Age. This was famously popularized in 1968–1969 by the song 'Aquarius (Let the Sunshine In)' from the hit musical *Hair*. 'This is the dawning of the Age of Aquarius', the song claimed, to much public fanfare.[5] The coming era was to be inaugurated when the planets were in the correct, auspicious alignment and would be one of love and peace, features borrowed from New Age beliefs. The Aquarian Age falls into a particular lineage of millenarian prediction in which astronomy provides a celestial timing mechanism for historical epochs. It offers what we may call a certain 'temporal integrity', which supposedly demonstrates beyond all doubt that the prediction of the coming period is true.[6]

The book as a whole is organized so that an underlying theme runs through every chapter – the modern application of the idea, derived from Plato, that history has a direction and that its driver is psychological. Further, the progression of history is a manifestation of the life of a World Soul. This notion reached its most notable form in the belief in a coming spiritual New Age. The general consensus is that this belief emerged in the 1970s as a consequence of the countercultural eruption of the 1960s. Critics of the New Age usually regard it as irrational, fringe and ridiculous. I examine both of these propositions by considering New Age thought within the wider history of ideas. Chapter 2 deals with the two key theories that history can or will reach an end point: millenarianism and utopianism.

Chapter 3 considers the eighteenth-century Enlightenment; Chapter 4 focuses on nineteenth-century Transcendentalism and Theosophy; Chapter 5 deals with the New Age teachers of the twentieth century to the beginning of the psychedelic era. Chapter 6 explores the 1960s, critically examining the nature of the counterculture, and Chapter 7 considers developments up to 2012, when prophecies of the end of the world as the Maya calendar supposedly came to an end prompted a media storm. Chapter 8 deals with perhaps the most important recent manifestation of Platonic historical theory in US neoconservatism. The conclusion is that New Age thought, being part of a much wider family of ideas, is manifestly not marginal and is no more ridiculous than many ideas which happen to be taken seriously.

The prophecy that a New Age of heightened spirituality is about to begin is one particular version of the wider family of millenarian ideologies, to use Wittgenstein's theory of family likenesses.[7] Just as some family members may have the same nose, and others the same eye brows, but not all have the same nose and eye brows, so theories of culture and history can share qualities but don't have to share them all. Millenarianism and utopianism therefore do not exist as fixed categories but as convenient categories of thought and behaviour. They are constructs from what Wittgenstein calls language games. The challenge to the notion of fixed historical periods was pioneered by Charles Webster, who demolished the notion of the 'Scientific Revolution' as a complete break with a superstitious past.[8] By looking at what the key protagonists actually said and did, he demonstrated that what had previously been thought to be a sudden revolution was actually a gradual evolution, displaying a great deal of continuity with previous eras, and not much in the way of discontinuity.

While New Age and countercultural ideas cross cultures, I have confined myself mainly to the United States and the UK for obvious reasons: while we find local conditions in each country, the common language shared by New Agers of the English-speaking world allows for the rapid exchange of ideas between them. The history of these ideas in Germany and France must await further work. That said, some of the main characters are European; Rousseau was French, H.P. Blavatsky was Russian, Rudolf Steiner was German and C.G. Jung was Swiss. I follow the idea of the New Age from its gestation in the eighteenth century in the wake of Isaac Newton's formulation of the modern universe, the optimism of the Enlightenment philosophers, the development of the theory of progress and the excitement of the French revolution. I conclude with two ostensibly very different cultural phenomena. One is the prophecy that the so-called end of the Maya calendar on 21 December 2012 was to be the focal point in the transition to a new spiritual age. The other is the ascendancy of US neoconservatism and its adoption of the belief that history is destined to end in the triumph of western values. In between I consider other aspects of the history of New Age thought, including its contribution to the counterculture of the 1960s. Central to my story is the question of what happened in the 1960s, a decade which has been mythologized more than most. The period was characterized by a remarkable eruption of youth culture which crossed the boundaries of fashion, style, politics and the arts and was intertwined with a belief that the world was entering a period of unprecedented change for the better; the final transition to paradise, for so long prophesied, was happening at last.

Three parallel narratives about history were developed after the 1750s, none of which was completely new but all of which acquired a new form. First, inspired by the Swedish visionary Emmanuel Swedenborg and popular amongst radicals and deists, it was believed that humanity was entering a spiritual new age. Second, drawing on Isaac Newton's discovery of the law of gravity, it was widely understood that the entire universe operates according to a single natural law, and earthly history must therefore also unfold in sequence with the orderly movements of the stars and planets. This is the basis of belief in the coming Age of Aquarius. And third, in the intellectual ferment in France in the 1780s and 1990s, as the revolution approached and climaxed, the theory of progress preached the perfectibility of humanity as history moved forward in time, independent of divine intervention. This period – from the eighteenth century to the present day – equates to Raymond Williams 'Long Revolution', characterized by a matrix of modernizing forces including, in his view, 'the struggle for democracy, the development of industry, the extension of communications, and … deep social and personal changes'.[9] New Age culture draws on and responds to the issues raised by Williams. It concerns itself with the struggle for democracy, reacts against industrialization, benefits from the extension of communications, and advocates deep social and personal change. It also includes a commitment to the idea of progress.

I have not dealt with Christian beliefs, which are dealt with well enough elsewhere; neither am I considering millennial theories in non-western cultures.[10] Both, it has to be said, are alive and politically potent. For example, Christian millenarianism continues to be as vibrant as ever and has gradually morphed into 'rapture culture', a term based on the doctrine that if the righteous suddenly ascend to Heaven as one, their absence will result in chaos for the remaining majority, the sinners.[11] In the Middle East are the fighters of what Richard Landes has called the 'enraged millennialism' of global jihad, violently epitomized by the so-called Islamic State's struggle to create the universal Caliphate, the final phase of their scheme of history, a combination of their version of Islam with the legacy of fascism and Marxist-Leninism.[12] In Iran, President Ahmadinejad was a devout believer in the imminent return of the Twelfth Imam and the institution of the Islamic end of history.[13]

The modern New Age movement, in spite of its presumed association with the 1960s, is millenarian in character and forms part of a broader cultural tradition which extends from the modern west back through Christian millenarianism to the ancient Near East.[14] The New Age is, in spite of the epithet 'new', part of a matrix of ideas which depend on the notion that the world, or just human society, is about to experience a cataclysmic transformation and which can be traced back to first millennium BCE. That this is so tends to be taken for granted but is rarely, if ever, examined. Equally neglected is New Age thought's debt to Plato, in which respect it is part of a current of ideas which pervades western culture. As Alfred North Whitehead wrote: 'The safest general characterization of the European philosophical tradition is that it consists of a series of footnotes to Plato.'[15] New Age thought is one such footnote.

New Age ideas are generally classed as part of an esoteric lineage in western culture. Like so many modern categories, the idea of 'esotericism' as an organized set of teachings is partly an academic construct.[16] That said, I will refer to esotericism as that set of beliefs which, drawing heavily on the Platonic strand of thought which pervades European civilization, asserts the primacy of consciousness over matter. It prioritizes the inner relation with the Divine on the grounds that the Divine itself has an inner existence within each person. To change, grow or discover God, all one needs to do is to look within. This is the essence of Gnosticism, the acquisition of gnosis – knowledge – directly from contact with the divine.[17] And to reform society, inner change is more important than revolution in institutions and power structures; the revolution will surely fail unless, it is believed, people first banish their inner demons.

Esotericism is so deeply embedded in western culture that we may talk about 'Westocericism', that long tradition of western esotericism that can be traced back through seventeenth-century Christian theosophy, medieval Jewish Kabbalah and late classical neoplatonism to Egyptian magic.[18] Esotericism inherits from Plato the belief that consciousness underpins matter, and that Ideas, with a capital 'I', are real. It stands in direct opposition to the materialist alternative set out by Karl Marx in his classic statement that 'man's consciousness changes with every change in the conditions of his material existence'.[19] Indeed Marxists were inclined to classify esotericists, along with adherents of all religions, as counter-revolutionaries.

The most influential medium for the transmission of esotericism into the modern world was theosophy. As a broad movement in western culture since the seventeenth century, theosophy is best understood through its Greek root as 'God-wisdom' or, perhaps, better as 'Divine-wisdom'. It finally achieved a potent institutional form in the foundation in 1875 in New York of the Theosophical Society, which was to play a huge and influential role in disseminating esoteric ideas, under its charismatic President, the Russian émigré Helena Petrovna Blavatsky. Discussion of esotericism's place in the modern world is often distorted by a general tendency to divide beliefs and activities into fringe and mainstream, in which case New Age is usually regarded as 'fringe'. Yet, as Benjamin Zeller has argued in his study of the Heaven's Gate UFO religion, the so-called fringe cannot be separated from the mainstream, and the apparently alternative may be a microcosm of the wider society.[20]

I am framing my period within Williams' 'Long Revolution', considering the Enlightenment and focusing on the question of the 1960s but we need to remain alert to the dangers of simple historical periodization. In this respect J. Milton Yinger's cautionary advice from his seminal article on contraculture is important: 'Carelessly used, our concepts can obscure the facts we seek to understand.'[21] The history of ideas is beset by the tendency to oversimplify and to identify periods which embody particular cultural movements, such as the Age of Reason, the Enlightenment, the Counter-Enlightenment, Modernism and Postmodernism. There is then a tendency to regard such phenomena as discrete, self-contained movements rather than aggregates of ideas, gathered together, often retrospectively by modern scholars, and to ignore subtleties, nuances and internal contradictions. The best we can say about such descriptions is that they are broad-gauged categorizations.[22] They are the results of the language games played by historians, who construct categories of ideas and behaviour, and the temptation is to imagine that they then have a reality other than as convenient descriptive categories.[23]

Such categories are also heuristic devices which provide a framework for analysing and contextualizing historical events. And, as such they are useful, but they are not absolutes: they do not exist independent of historian's constructions. The same cautionary advice applies to descriptions of New Ages. As Murray Rothbard, the veteran US libertarian pointed out, 'One problem with labelling ideological movements "old" or "new" is that inevitably, with the passage of time, the "new" becomes "old" and the markers get confusing.'[24] And as Stuart Hall asked, writing about the 1970s:

> How new are these 'new times'? Are they the dawn of a New Age or only the whisper of an old one? What is 'new' about them? How do we assess their contradictory tendencies – are they progressive or regressive? ... If we take the 'new times' idea apart, we find that it is an attempt to capture, within the confines of a single metaphor, a number of different facets of social change.[25]

Just as what is new to some people is old to others, so some see crisis where others see hope. Many people who express an opinion on the matter agree that New Age ideas are to be regarded with disdain. There is a widespread view, even amongst those who have no particular religious conviction, that some beliefs are inherently more intelligent than others. There is certainly a tendency amongst journalists at the highbrow end of the spectrum to affect a contempt for all things in the New Age. In 1996 the writer and TV chef Nigella Lawson argued that the established Church, which she viewed with respect, was being replaced by 'star-signs' and 'the cult of the clairvoyant', which she regarded with contempt, as 'the new religion'.[26] A few years later Derek Draper, a former adviser to the Labour government, asked: 'As religious belief dies in Britain, is it being replaced with a tendency towards superstition, magic or obscure cults?'[27] In 2005, Ken Goffman and Dan Joy, both enthusiasts of 1960s counterculture, wrote: 'The peculiarities and disasters of the New Age have been amply exposed, and particularly the authoritarian wing of that movement'.[28] George McKay, an admirer of many aspects of the New Age travellers who flourished in the 1980s, referred to the Hollywood actress Shirley MacLaine, who was well-known for her espousal of New Age ideas in the 1980s, as belonging to the 'wackier fringe' of Californian celebrities.[29] He also called occultism, to which many of the people he studied were attracted, 'the metaphysic of dunces'.[30] And, writing on the relationship between Theosophy, which stands at the heart of modern New Age culture, and the work of Dutch abstract artist Theo van Doesburg, the art critic Waldemar Januszczak wrote:

> The fact is, theosophy, founded by the fraudulent Madame Blavatsky in the 1870s, is embarrassing. If there is one thing you do not want your hardcore modernist to be, it is a member of an occult cult that believes in the essential unity of the cosmos, as proposed so battily by Madame Blavatsky. Theosophy takes art into Dan Brown territory. No serious student of art history wants to touch it.[31]

Even modern pagans regard New Agers as inferior in their supposed ephemeral superficiality and lacking the pagans' depth of commitment. As one pagan website recently disapprovingly observed: 'For many Pagans "New Age" is a dirty turn of phrase often dismissed as any sort of progressive Spirituality that comes with a large price tag'.[32] Yet, why such disdain? What is it that makes New Age ideas and culture ridiculous? What, we may ask, makes belief in the resurrection of Jesus Christ more sensible than belief in UFO visitations; the prophecy of the perfectibility of man more serious than the prediction of a coming New Age; or the notion that western values represent the highpoint of human civilization worth more consideration than that the Aquarian Age is dawning? New Age ideas and activities tend to become a focus of ridicule and are rarely regarded as a legitimate feature of modern western life. As the cultural commentator Jonathan Meades put it, succinctly: 'If you believe in fairies at the bottom of the garden you are deemed fit for the bin. If you believe in transubstantiation, parthenogenesis and the rest of it, you're deemed fit to run the country'.[33]

The question of why one set of ideas about the world which has no empirical support may be considered normal, while another, which has neither more nor less support, is somewhat problematic. Who decides what is normal? The question was first answered by Michel Foucault's influential argument that 'madness', as a category of behaviour, is largely an eighteenth-century construction.[34] This does not deny the existence of mental disturbance but challenges the manner in which it is diagnosed, categorized and treated. Another area where the issue has been considered, with considerable energy, is in the debates around physical disability. A significant contribution was made by Lennard J. Davis, who considered the process of 'enforcing normalcy' in the history of physical impairment, specifically in relation to deafness. He argued that, as modernity took root in the nineteenth-century west, the body became a utopian object, a perfect thing from which many people deviated, first as 'disability' was invented, and then as notions of marginality were universalized.[35] In this model, the nineteenth and twentieth centuries saw the development of binary notions of normal and abnormal psychologies, which were converted into culture as the distinction between 'mainstream' or normal on the one hand and 'fringe' or abnormal on the other. Davis' scheme draws obvious parallels between the development of ideas of disability and the racism and sexism inherent in the nineteenth-century proposition that the white man's body – and mind – represented the utopian ideal, while women and non-whites deviated in varying degrees, becoming progressively more marginal.

New Age culture is too often seen as a thing apart, an aberration divorced from modernity. This is a difficult proposition to sustain and is itself a product of the modernist myth that history inexorably moves in a particular direction, towards rationality, atheism and an acceptance of science as the one true source of knowledge. The consequence is that any manifestation of cultural practice or ideology which doesn't fit the modernist paradigm runs counter to the flow of time. As a result New Age beliefs become a kind of problem whose very existence in the modern world is in need of urgent explanation, which is usually that they are a consequence of ignorance or psychological inadequacy. Sometimes the hostile rhetoric on New Age matters suggests, implausibly, that there is a proper New Age as opposed to an inferior one. For example, looking back to a 1967 edition of the underground newspaper *International Times* (*IT*), the journalist Nigel Fountain wrote, 'the "New Age" promised in *IT* was still more to do with ley-lines and the "ecstatic return of everything blessed", as John Michel, the paper's fixture on UFOs, Britain's "holy places", and the "centres and lines of latent power in Britain", put it'; Fountain's dismissive tone is unmistakeable. 'Is this *all* the New Age had come to?', he asks.[36]

In spite of attacks on New Age culture, it continues to thrive. The magazine *Caduceus*, the glossiest of the English New Age publications, regularly carries features on alternative lifestyles, diet, medicine, science and self-awareness. In 2014, a special issue on the feminine to celebrate International Women's Day carried the optimistic news that: 'In 2014 we are fortunate to be in the period of transition to the Sixth Sun' (a reference to supposed Maya and Aztec millenarianism).[37] A second article added substance: 'We live in a culture when Spirit, Beauty, Meaning and the Mythology of the Divine tend to be repressed and suppressed by the predominant attitudes of science, materialism and free market economics'; but all is not lost and before despair sets in, a message of hope is offered: 'Things are changing, We are in the cusp of an age of synthesis. There is no doubt that over the next 10–20 years the wholeness vision will have become the dominant mind set in every aspect of human affairs, every profession and every academic discipline.'[38] Obvious in this statement is the certainty that history is moving in a certain direction, the conviction that the future will be better, the insistence on gender equality, the rejection of neo-liberal economics and the universalizing insistence that the new dispensation will be total, that nobody will be outside the new order.

The New Age emblem continues to have a considerable descriptive power in popular culture. In 2013 *The Daily Mail* carried a story about the environmental activist Daniel Hooper, who achieved fame in 1996 as 'Swampy', the anti-road protester.

> The 40-year-old lives with his four children in a yurt alongside 100 hippies, New Age travellers and nudists in a 200-acre stretch of farmland in the Welsh valleys. The assortment of characters in the camp live in tepees, caravans, yurts and mud houses. There is a communal tent, Big Lodge, where they gather for yoga sessions and meditation. The group, who appear almost entirely self-sufficient, even hold raves and full moon parties in the valley.[39]

As an example of an outsider's view of what constitutes New Age, this is typical. In media terms, New Age can be a powerful descriptor of an anti-modern, countercultural lifestyle.

The reasons why the esoteric strands in western culture are so consistently ignored by academics, outside a small circle, can be understood in relation to Herbert Gans' views on why popular culture has been traditionally regarded either as valueless or as a real problem. Conservatives, Gans argued, attacked popular culture because they regarded it as a threat, symptomatic of the rising power of the masses. Socialists, meanwhile, were simply disappointed with these same masses' failure to support politically correct solutions to the problems of society, and the way in which instead they were distracted by what was deemed to be the reactionary, hegemonic power of television, cinema and pop music.[40] The socialists followed Marx's dictum that mysticism distracted revolutionaries from an understanding of theory, and so from finding any practical solutions to political problems.[41] And, being intellectuals, the socialists paradoxically followed Antonio Gramsci's suspicion of intellectuals as agents of the ruling class's hegemonic power.[42] Theodor Adorno, notable amongst neo-Marxists and a major influence in cultural studies, categorized what we would call New Age culture (he didn't use the term) as evidence of fascist inclinations and believed that if only the proletariat would develop a true political consciousness, they would naturally reject such ideas as false.[43] Adorno's theories permeate writings on cultural studies, leaving little attention for the study of esoteric strands in popular culture. Most students of popular culture were influenced by the socialist critiques that Gans complained about, and for them, mysticism, as Roszak wrote, was 'one of the dirtiest words in the Marxist vocabulary'.[44] They therefore avoided all consideration of it.

In this way certain kinds of human activity have therefore tended to be considered taboo by some historians on the grounds that they conflict with modernity. In particular, esoteric and magical strands, being considered false, have largely been ignored.[45] The notion of a false ideology was written into modern political discourse by Karl Marx and Friedrich Engels, who in their famous statement declared that the ruling ideas of each historical era are those of the ruling class.[46] Such ideas are therefore necessarily or relevance only to a particular class at a particular time, and are therefore devoid of any underlying truth, the sole exception being Marx's own ideas. In Marxist taxonomy,

New Ageism, like all thought classified as esoteric or religious, is therefore necessarily classified as false, religion being compared to the opium of the people, designed to keep them in a state of stupefaction.[47] Gans was critical of the idea of hegemony, the belief that the ruling powers control the masses and prevent revolution not by terror but through fashion, style and the mass media, but it pervades the academic discipline of cultural studies.[48] However, the hegemonic argument has come under attack from several areas. For a start, in the 1960s television was a revolutionary force, one which altered the political and social fabric with stunning consequences; television coverage of the Vietnam War is universally considered to be a powerful factor in provoking opposition to the US military programme.[49] In addition, the public are not always gullible consumers of culture but are quite capable of generating cultures of resistance.[50] Popular millenarianism is one such culture.

Millenarian expectations cross political and religious boundaries to such an extent that they present a radical challenge to comfortable conventions concerning the border between such accepted dichotomies as the rational and the irrational, knowledge and belief, and alternative or mainstream ideas. The distinction between millenarian religion and politics was blurred by Norman Cohn when he argued that both Nazi and Communist hopes for a new world order were inherited from Christian belief in the coming heavenly kingdom.[51] Others have argued that Liberal humanist belief in the incremental struggles of the forward march of progress is essentially metaphysical and as superstitious as the expectation of imminent divine salvation.[52] Similarly, much criticism of modern utopias identifies socialism as the main modern carrier of the tradition.[53]

Utopianism is a universal feature of western political life. From the US neoconservatives to Tony Blair's New Labour, we saw evidence of major attempts to reconstruct society as the twenty-first century dawned. Utopianism also lurks in the academic world, particularly in sociology.[54] Many sociologists are driven by the desire not to understand the world but to understand it in order to change it and so take it to its final point of development. Indeed, the study of sociology was created specifically for this purpose, and it has never completely abandoned its belief in its own messianic mission.[55] This is Steve Fuller of the University of Warwick delivering the keynote talk at the British Sociological Association's 2014 conference: 'That's where I would see the empirical thrust of trying to see the extent to which these utopian visions can be realized. It would be through a kind of social experimentation.'[56] This is precisely the attitude satirized by Malcolm Bradbury in his 1975 novel, *The History Man*, the story of a left-wing sociologist who believes that he is on the side of history.[57]

Often, utopianism is regarded as automatically undesirable. And so some social democrats will assert the practicality of their aims by asserting that they are not utopian, as did Anthony Giddens, one of the architects of New Labour, in his discussion of his 'neoprogressive' Third Way, which argued for state intervention as a riposte to the economic deregulation of neoliberalism.[58] That Giddens should insist his work is not utopian speaks volumes about the disdain with which the word is often held. And, as applied to politics, 'utopian' is used as code for dangerous. In 2015, for example, the Green Party of England and Wales proposal for a flat-rate income for every person was criticized not just because it would hit the poor but precisely because it was 'utopian'.[59]

The Greek government's resistance to the EU-imposed austerity programme was similarly condemned by the *Times* with the harsh words: 'the road to a socialist utopia is always and everywhere a dead end'.[60]

Taken in isolation New Ageism is also often seen as ridiculous or bizarre and occupying the strange fringe of western thought. However, if we see it as part of a family of utopian and directional ideas of history, our perspective changes. For example, what about New Labour and Tony Blair's reimagining of the UK Labour Party that took place in the 1990s? Ruth Levitas has pointed out that concepts of 'social inclusion' (meaning inclusion in paid work), which she helped formulate and which were central to the UK New Labour project and are upheld throughout the European Union, are utopian. 'If New Labour's utopia is peculiar', she wrote, 'there is nothing peculiar about the fact that it has one. Such images of the good society are present in every political position'.[61] This is an astonishing claim, though no less true for that: every political position can be utopian, whether New Labour, New Right, neoconservative or neo-liberal. Millenarian and utopian beliefs are pervasive features of modern political discourse across the spectrum, from right to left and democratic to dictatorial. Even economic positions can be utopian: Keynesian economics pose a model of an eternally sustainable financial future.[62] In the 1980s, the marriage of neoliberalism and monetarism provided an alternative vision of a world of prosperity for all, a true utopia of financial deregulation and individual choice.[63] Seen in this context, the argument that New Age is necessarily bizarre becomes unsustainable. Instead it is deeply embedded in western culture.[64]

So where do we locate the history of New Age culture? Richard Evans raised the difficulties of locating such strands of modern history and made the bold assertion that:

> The great overarching narratives such as Marxism and modernisation theory have collapsed. Innovation has come above all from historians writing about the marginal, the bizarre. The individual, the small-scale. It seems reasonable to call these now-defunct metanarratives 'Modernist', as indeed many postmodernist writers on history do; and equally reasonable to call the new development 'postmodern', even if those who have pioneered it and participated in it would not regard themselves as postmodernist in any sense at all.[65]

Observing that the terms modernist and postmodernist can easily be exchanged, Evans leaves us with a conundrum as to where to place the history of New Age ideas. Many commentators have located New Age as postmodern, sometimes because they see it as appealing to individuals who are unable to cope with the pressures of modernity.[66] On the other hand, the great overarching New Age narrative of a universal, perfect utopia, survives. Unlike New Ageism, it has not collapsed, and neither has utopianism. Both preserve the belief in the progression of the world to a future which is universally benign.

This book is principally about ideology rather than social forms or political action; it is about the ideology of the New Age. Ideology is, of course, a complex word with multiple meanings, frequently dependent on context. Often, an ideology is something which other people have, a falsehood which is contrasted with our own 'truth'. As Terry

Eagleton wrote, 'Ideology, like halitosis, is in this sense, what the other person has'.[67] For many commentators, ideology is therefore an appropriate term for New Age thought which is so often deemed to be automatically false. To historians questions of the truth or falsity of any ideological position are irrelevant: ideologies are just ideologies and that's that. To talk about New Age ideology, then, is to explore New Age thought as a set of ideas which shape views of time and the place of the individual in history. Like other millenarian philosophies, New Ageism raises epistemological questions, largely due to the problem faced by believers of evaluating the truth of the prophecy of the coming crisis or paradise. But historians have no such problems. What matters is the context and consequences of the belief in coming word ages, not its truth.

As Roy Porter said, when considering arguments over the historical nature of the eighteenth-century Enlightenment, 'complex revisions mark our times'.[68] Such revisions extended the scope of history, first so that the working class were included in the historical narrative. Then came feminist history, Black history and queer history. In line with this revisionist spirit, this book is about the New Age and wider currents of historical thought.

2

End Times: Utopia and the Millennium

One of the deepest and most persistent features of western thought is a profound dissatisfaction with the world. There is an existential discontent; a sense that life is a constant struggle with want, disease, oppression and injustice. Max Scheler called it *ressentiment*.[1] But such despair is balanced by the hope that somewhere, perhaps in the future, a better place, a paradise, a heaven or a new golden age, is waiting for us, ready to save us from the world and from ourselves. There are two ideologies associated with this constant interplay of pessimism and optimism. One is millenarianism, the belief that, sometime in the future, the world will be born again. The other is utopianism, the notion that human beings can themselves construct a perfect future. Millenarianism and utopianism are not the same, but they are linked. Utopias can exist without the belief in a predetermined future which is central to millenarian dreams, but those dreams always look forward to a utopia. Millenarianism prophesies that we will be saved, while utopianism provides solutions by which we may save ourselves. Millenarianism can be other-worldly. It sometimes focuses on the spiritual world to come and believers may withdraw from the here-and-now. Yet it can as easily become this-worldly. The point about utopianism is that, in order to work, it has to be this-worldly.

Utopia is a contested concept. This does not mean simply that people disagree about what a utopia is, and about what the good society should be like. Rather the word changes its meaning depending on who is using it and whether they position themselves either for or against their chosen definition.[2] One person's utopia is another's nightmare. The notion of contested space has now become familiar in landscape studies, in which the same site may have completely different meanings and uses for different people.[3] Utopias are partly contested spaces, even when they have an imaginary location, but because they exist in the future, they exist within a contested timescape.

The term Utopia itself originated in Thomas More's account of the ideal republic, published in 1516, coincidentally the year before Martin Luther initiated the Reformation, perhaps the grandest attempt ever to reform the politics of Western Europe. More's work is no dreamy fantasy but a vehicle for discussing the practicalities of different political systems. He was concerned with the details of administration and how different systems might or might not work. For example, with remarkable prescience, he pointed out that communist system could never provide a decent standard of living because nobody would work hard enough.[4]

Yet the word utopia, in a generic sense, has achieved a persona beyond anything that More intended. It may exist in the past as a lost golden age, or in the future as an aspiration, as what we might call an 'ontology of the not yet', a knowledge of the unknown.[5] And, being the object of longing, utopia is defined partly by desire; it is bound up with psychology, with all humanity's hopes and dreams, as well as its fears. A utopia is a perfect society which may inspire humanity to self-improvement but, being perfect, is by definition impossible to achieve. If human beings are imperfect, then no human society can ever be perfect. In its absolute sense, the utopian project is doomed before it even starts. As a matter of principle, if the promised utopia is perfect, in extreme cases it will be impossible to realize. As Herbert Marcuse wrote, 'Utopia … refers to projects for change that are considered impossible'.[6]

Utopias draw their inspiration from two chief sources; the first is Plato's Heavenly City, and the second the Biblical New Jerusalem. The two came together in St. Paul's epistle to the Hebrews which, in the King James version reads, 'But now they desire a better country, that is, an heavenly one: wherefore God is not ashamed to be called their God: for he hath prepared for them a city'.[7] Plato himself straddled the boundary between the possible and the impossible. On the one hand he set out in great detail the rules and regulations by which his ideal republic could be managed by a virtuous, wise and self-aware elite in line with cosmological principles.[8] On the other his perfect city was an Idea, with a capital 'i', that was functionally impossible to realize because human beings, being imperfect, would always destroy it. 'The city whose home is the idea … can be found nowhere in earth …', he wrote, and exists only 'in a pattern … laid up in heaven for him who wishes to contemplate it'.[9] Plato established the enduring paradox according to which the perfect city can never exist; yet, implicitly, if we have to contemplate it, there must be a reason to do so, and this reason can only be to inspire us to improve society. Is it enough just to contemplate perfection, or should we try to implement it? And if perfection is unattainable is a compromise acceptable? Can we improve society by the very act of working to create a utopia which might itself be unattainable? That we can try is the foundation of social democracy.

Plato's utopia was contained within a philosophy now known as Idealism, after his theory that the origin of all things in our world are Ideas (later also known as archetypes) which emerge from the Creator, who he envisaged not as a personal God but as a supreme mind or consciousness.[10] There are a number of significant consequences of this theory. First is that consciousness is more important than matter and so at a fundamental level the way we think alters the material world. The material universe as a whole is embedded in a world soul, from the Latin *anima mundi*, a concept which found particular favour amongst eighteenth- and nineteenth-century Romantics and pervades modern New Age thought.[11] History itself, as the story of the development of the material world, is then imagined as contained within the unfolding of the world spirit, the *zeitgeist*. Second, as everything in this world is a pale imitation or a shadow, of its Ideal original, our world is inherently imperfect. Third, we can strive to return to perfection, and we can do this as individuals by practicing divine arts such as music or geometry, and by leading a virtuous lifestyle. By the second-century BCE the Platonic idea that the soul originates in, and returns to the stars, was codified in the texts which comprise the *Corpus Hermeticum*: it was thought that it was possible to ascend to the divine light of God by travelling upwards via the planets.[12] To return to perfection as a society is, however, impossible, because only a minority of people will ever manage the difficult task of reconnecting with the divine. The rest, the majority, who have not reconnected with their perfect selves, will inevitably sabotage any attempt to create a perfect state. Elitism was present from the beginning. As in some versions of Christianity, only some people will be saved: notably Revelation refers specifically to 144,000 saints.[13]

Millenarianism's power as a cultural force often lies in the paradoxes which run through its claims. The contradictions are in two distinct strands in Jewish eschatology: one prophesied the complete end of the world, the other its renewal. Jewish eschatology can then be described as 'a congress of beliefs and ideas which are marked by the expectation of a future event which is the effective End in the mind of the one using the term.'[14] One of millenarianism's central features is the interplay of endings and beginnings; death is followed by rebirth, destruction is necessary for the future to be built, and despair at the present is balanced by hope for the future. The paradoxes in millenarian time are contained within the two modes of Platonic time.[15] The original state of existence is Being, eternity, in which nothing ever changes so there is, in effect, no time. Being, being eternal, contains absolute truth, but Becoming, being in a state of constant change, contains only belief and opinion. One way to imagine it is that Being is outside of space and time, and Becoming is inside space and time. Becoming, the state of existence human beings experience as one of constant change, emerges out of Being, yet doesn't replace it. At one moment we can therefore slip from Becoming to Being and experience eternity. In this respect the golden age is no longer lost, and the coming new world is here already – and has existed since the beginning of time. Eternity, as Slavoj Žižek said, is the 'event' or 'cut' that opens up and sustains temporality.[16] The Greeks extended the paradox into two kinds of time: *chronos*, which measures the passage of events, and *kairos*, which reveals their changing qualities.[17] *Chronos* marks calendar dates as days, months and years follow each other, but *kairos* reveals the approach of the millennium.

Human beings have an innate tendency to struggle to return to pure Being, at the same time as they are simultaneously trapped in the physical world of Becoming. True perfection, though, is beyond their grasp. In practical politics this tension translates into a tension between the idealists, the utopians and seekers who hope for something better, and the conservatives, the lovers of stability, who are happy with the world as it is. And the clash between these two is the driving force of revolutionary movements in western culture. The neoconservative philosopher Daniel Bell summed up the situation in the 1950s:

> The chiliast and the anarchist live in crisis, at the edge of History, expecting the world
> to be changed in a flash. The Bolshevik identifies himself with History and confidently
> expects that the turn of the wheel will put him forward, replacing the old.[18]

Traditions of apocalyptic thought can be traced back to late third millennium BCE Mesopotamia and filtered through Babylon, Egypt, Persia and India to Gnostic, Jewish and Christian historical theories of pattern and meaning in history.[19] Christianity has given us a certain language associated with millenarian belief. From the Greek word *eschaton* (the end) derives the term eschatology, which literally means the study of ends, but is also used to imply actual belief in the end of the world. The word 'apocalyptic' (Greek for revelation) is now generally used less to mean a vision of the end than the violence which may precede the end. Although millenarianism has strictly Christian connotations, it may be applied to all beliefs that the world is about to enter a major new phase. In its looser definition, therefore, any political or religious movement or ideology which expects, prophesies, or fights for an imminent historical crisis and return to or inauguration of a golden age or state of purity can be described as millenarian.[20]

The individual actor in the millenarian process brings about a repetition in time in which, as in the moment of conversion, temporal existence and eternal existence meet. The fundamental incompatibility between the two encourages the tension of the millenarian moment: how can time pass and yet not pass at the same time? The effect is to change or undo the effects of eternity itself, and so open a new future.[21] Golden-age millenarianism plays a trick with time, creating the future in order to restore the past and the Christian longing for salvation draws its power as much from the final restoration of God's kingdom as from Eden, and past and future meet in an eternal present.[22] Reinforced by the Judeo-Christian expulsion from Eden and hope for a future Kingdom of David or New Jerusalem, the dual sense of loss of a perfect past and longing for a better future becomes the psychological skeleton on which so much western culture is based. Individual desire for release then becomes 'socially oriented' into collective utopian hope.[23]

The paradoxes inherent in millenarianism can be summed up in a series of dichotomies such as active–passive, rational–irrational, premillennial–postmillennial, prepolitical–political and conservative–radical.[24] So necessary is contradiction to millenarianism that even the failure of millennial prophecy can deepen the faith of the believer.[25] There is, though, always a tension between the realizable and the unrealizable, between compromise and the absolute, which was already evident in Plato's politics and later in Marx. More called his promised land Utopia, from the Greek *ou* (οὐ), 'not', and *topos* (τόπος), 'place'. Utopia is therefore nowhere. It exists as an ideal state which might never be achieved. At the same time, it is everywhere, in that its prescriptions for fair and just government are universal. Yet, the paradoxes can never be overcome and the very act of engaging in the politics necessary to create a utopia can corrupt that effort, a tension which haunts More's work.[26]

Given that utopianism is often associated with unattainable ideas, it comes in for some criticism and in its general usage, the term often means naive, ridiculous or fraudulent. Such attitudes inform popular views and, as Ruth Levitas put it: 'Lay understandings are generally either dismissive or hostile, seeing utopianism as at best impractical dreaming.'[27]

For W.H. Auden utopians were like the crew of a ship of fools, sailing blithely to a non-existent Atlantis.[28] Auden's Atlantis is unobtainable; to be glimpsed only in poetic visions; a comment on those people who are constantly led astray by utopias which they imagine are real but are actually no more than counterfeit models of the vision.

In its general usage, any vision of a better future can now be considered utopian in a general sense, in the same way that any prophecy of a future paradise can be called millenarian. As a compromise between the perfect Ideal and the flawed reality of human nature, a utopia is any society which is an improvement on the society we inhabit now. All utopianism is part of a family of ideas whose core is a belief in universal solutions to all human problems attained through human action.[29] Partly, such solutions are derived from divine knowledge, often mediated initially through saints and prophets but later interpreted by teachers trained in the correct understanding of such revelations: theologians, rabbis, mullahs and muftis. From classical Greece, the western world inherited a parallel tradition in which Reason, this time a matter of direct contact with the divine, might reveal the correct solutions. Plato veered towards the idea that only an elite might attain such knowledge, while the Stoics tended to believe that anyone who lived according to true reason might discover universal answers. The eighteenth-century French encyclopaedists gave new vigour to the notion of universality, enthused by the belief that the knowledge derived from the natural sciences, as well as from the great voyages of exploration, having banished superstition, would now lead to the creation of a fair, just and rational society.

The concept of utopia appears to be a standard feature of human society, as Ernest Bloch argued in his epic three-volume study, *The Principle of Hope*.[30] First published in 1954 at the height of the Cold War, it was inspired partly by Bloch's attempt to understand the clash between the two great utopianisms of the time, Soviet statism and western capitalism. Utopia, Bloch concluded, is a universal component of civilization. It is found in Native American culture, as well as Indian and Chinese and every other culture he examined. Recent studies have identified millenarian beliefs in so many non-western cultures that, like utopianism, the notion of the imminent ending or transformation appears to be a universal feature of human culture.[31]

Like utopianism, millenarianism – or millennialism – comes in different forms and has both narrow and wide definitions. The core characteristics of millenarianism are well recognized.[32] In the Judaeo-Christian version, the coming phase will be inaugurated by the appearance of a world saviour, messiah or son of God. The supposed authenticity of the Biblical messianic prophecy was reinforced by its occurrence in classical literature.[33] Strictly speaking, then, the millennium is the period identified in Revelation, the final book and dramatic climax of the Christian New Testament, which begins with the *parousia* (literally 'presence'), Christ's imminent return. The text provides an account of the vision of St. John of a coming thousand-year epoch which will culminate in the release from bondage of Satan, the lord of darkness, and a great, final battle between good and evil and a call for everyone to take sides; and there will certainly be a final release from current misery and a transition to paradise.[34] As Christ himself foretold:

> Nation will rise against nation, and kingdom against kingdom;
> there will be great earthquakes and pestilences;
> and there will be terrors and great signs from heaven.[35]

God's inevitable victory is to be followed by the arrival of a 'new heaven', a 'new earth' and a 'new Jerusalem'.[36] This final state would then complete the prophecy set out in Isaiah 66.22–23: 'For as the new heavens and the new earth which I will make shall remain before me.' In English translations of Matthew it is referred to as the 'age to come'.[37] Some Christian theologians retrospectively refer to this new era as 'the New Age'.[38] In the turbulent and excitable Christianity of the first and second centuries, the new era, the kingdom of God, was thought to be imminent. It might happen tomorrow or next year or in ten years, but it would undoubtedly be soon.[39] Many Evangelical Protestants and much of the Christian Right in the United States still expect Christ's return on a daily basis.

One feature of utopianism is its programmatic nature: when its rules and regulations are prescribed, and when its future inauguration is established by some system of numbers, or quirk of the calendar, or movement of the heavenly bodies, then the fantasy becomes locked into the 'real' world. The very reliance on external measuring devices means that the promised future will arrive. Endowing the future with reality in this way has been described as a kind of 'thaumaturgic' or magical prophecy; the act of making the prophecy is itself a means of bringing it into existence.[40] They provide what has been called a 'temporal integrity'.[41] The various constructions used to time the inauguration of the coming era, whether New Age, Aquarian Age, New Jerusalem, Kingdom of God or Dictatorship of the Proletariat, provide connectors between time and eternity, connecting them with the vital moments at which eternal recurrence becomes real instead of imaginary. The names under which the future age is known assume a magic power which encourages devotees to struggle for them to the point of self-sacrifice, even death. They are 'time-fetishes'.[42]

The psychological core is the interplay between pessimism, profound despair at the current state of the world, and optimism, a belief that salvation lies in the very near future, if not now. In the eighth century BCE, the Greek poet Hesiod prepared the literary foundation for all future depressives:

> I wish I were not of this race, that I
> Had died before, or had not yet been born.
> … Zeus will destroy this race of mortal men.[43]

A sense of the present crisis is invariably associated with the memory of a lost Eden or nostalgia for a vanished golden age, when the world was perfect. A Sumerian tablet from about 2000 BCE, perhaps our earliest surviving example, describes the blissful situation of the earth's earliest inhabitants, when peace and love ruled the earth.[44] Much later, Hesiod described the lifestyles of the lost golden race:

> like the gods they (men) lived with happy hearts …
> … ungrudgingly, the fertile land
> Gave up her fruits unasked. Happy to be
> At peace, they lived with every want supplied.[45]

Hesiod's era of the golden race became a golden age and entered European mythology. The desire to recreate the golden age is deeply embedded in nostalgia, a word constructed from *nostos* (home-coming) and *algos* (pain); in its mild form, nostalgia is a wistful yearning for the past, but when extreme it is pathologized as severe homesickness.[46] The Golden Age lies in an indeterminate past, close enough to remember but not to genuinely experience. Normally, we can never quite recapture it except in memories. When conceived personally, as in the golden age of childhood, it has certainly once been experienced but, in the present, exists only within the imagination. As a historical phase it is second hand, reported, and the individual who 'remembers' it was generally not present when it took place. In either case it can only be experienced again as a reconstructed memory.[47] Political golden ageism is concerned with the deployment of memory in order to influence the future, evoking images of past times to which we can return. To adapt Umberto Eco's discussion of memories of the Middle Ages, a golden age can be remembered in different forms, sometimes as an age of freedom but perhaps one of security; it is also, as Jean Baudrillard, agreeing with Eco, would have said, a simulacrum, a manifestation of the hyper-real.[48] A golden age is an image of a real past, false, yet indistinguishable from it; in effect, a truth in its own right.

However, millenarianism solves the problem of existential loss by promising to restore everything which has been lost, heal all current traumas and relieve the pain of nostalgic longing. It also resolves the internal contradictions in utopianism by transferring the collision between the ideal republic and human imperfection to a superior force, either time, history or God, whose task is then to enrol humanity in the new dispensation. The difficulties inherent in the construction of a utopia, including implementing laws, regulating social behaviour, and so on, are then replaced by the mere wish that the new state comes into being by itself. It is what we might now call a magic bullet in which time and history, or God working through time and history, steps in to save humanity from its suffering and restore the Golden Age. The faithful are called home and the pain of nostalgia is relieved. In Jewish and Christian mythologies, the coming age may be of this world, as in a restored Eden or Kingdom of David, or it may be supernatural, as in the Kingdom of God anticipated in Revelation. And it may be a utopia, a perfect civil society.

Between now and the restored paradise, though, there is usually a transitional phase. Normally this is supposed to be violent – or apocalyptic in the modern sense of the word. When the entry to the coming age is violent, whether natural, divinely inspired, a result of human activity or a combination of the three, we call this 'pre-millennialism', or 'catastrophic millenarianism'. This is the classic, violent form of Christian apocalypse described in the book of Revelation, inherited by revolutionary Marxism and now evident in the deep pessimism arising from fears of global collapse as a result of climate change. In this sense, the end of the world has been described as a 'hyperobject' – a future event which will exert a huge change to the world, forcing us into a new way of living.[49] If transition is peaceful, we call it post or progressive-millenarianism.[50] The coming era then arrives through a process of evolution rather than revolution.

The peaceful tradition traces its lineage to the thirteenth-century spiritual Franciscan Joachim of Fiore, whose apocalyptic prophecy envisioned a harmonious transition to the spiritual Age of the Holy Ghost, which he believed was to begin in 1260.[51] However, the violent and peaceful options are not self-contained binary opposites. Rather, they exist on a continuum and, except for the ultra-violent believers in extreme destruction, such as the Khmer Rouge or Islamic State, the reason for human engagement in the historical process is often to manage the transition in order to minimize disruption;

that the transition is imminent is self-evident from the moral and political decay of the current period. That is to say, the approaching historical trauma and the consequent return to the Golden Age must take place during the lifetime of the believer.[52] Translated into New Age prophecy, the claim is that the age is beginning 'now', not some time in the distant future. The result is then that the transitional phase itself becomes the dramatic focus. It's in the very nature of the millennium that it always lies in the future but the potential for its creation always exists in the present moment.

In many versions the approach of the millennium may be revealed through events in the sky, either through the orderly unfolding of celestial patterns or the occurrence of heavenly portents. The sky therefore provides a warning system which alerts us to deeper patterns of terrestrial disaster and recovery. One of the best-known passages of celestial omens is from Isaiah, who predicted that, as the 'Day of Yahweh' approached,

> … the stars of the Heavens
> and their constellations will not give their light;
> The Sun will be dark at its rising
> And the Moon will not shed its light.[53]

When the light of the sun is blocked out, so is the light of God and the light of wisdom. A different scenario, in which historical periods came to an end when the sun, moon, planets and stars simultaneously return to the point of their creation, was set out by Plato: 'The complete number of Time', he claimed, 'fulfils the Complete year when all the eight circuits with their relative speeds, finish together and come to a head.'[54] This long time period was later known as the Great Year. Because the cycle could begin again as soon as it had finished, some Platonists developed the ideas of eternal recurrence, in which each historical repeats the previous one.[55]

Plato's political astronomy scheme was adopted by the Persians who used the cycles of the two slowest moving of the known planets, Jupiter and Saturn, to create the idea of a historical period; each time the planets met in a significant location, a new period began.[56] It was believed that, from the rise and fall of states to the appearance of religious prophets, and the periodic birth and death of the entire universe, there is a system which, once understood, can provide a framework within which human affairs can be managed in order to maximize stability and minimize disruption. Indeed, the whole idea of a historical period originated with this system.[57] The Platonic scheme was popular in the classical world; became a commonplace in the Renaissance; and was given a fresh impetus by Isaac Newton in the eighteenth century.

But there was also an anti-prophetic, or anti-predictive, tradition in which the millennium most emphatically could not be forecast. Mark 13.32–3 recorded Christ's declaration of uncertainty: 'But of that day or hour no one knows, not even the angels in heaven, nor the Son, but only the Father. Take heed, watch, for you do not know when the time will come.'[58] More famous is the claim that 'the Lord will come like a thief' – when he is least expected.[59] That the date of the coming crisis cannot be forecast, though, does not mean that it is not inevitable. Karl Marx didn't know when the revolution would happen, but he knew with absolute certainty that it was inevitable.[60] But if the date of the coming transition of world ages is unknown, it could happen not sometime in an ill-defined future but tomorrow. In this case the pressure to prepare one's self, and one's soul, for the coming apocalypse is constant. In a Christian context, preparation has to be inward – to be sure of salvation when Christ returns one has to be free of sin and, given that sin can be a matter of unclean thought, it is necessary to understand one's own psychological dynamics.[61] The approach of God's kingdom therefore requires introspection as well as revolution. The central political priority must therefore be the inner revolution, to which the revolution in power structures and economic systems is only an adjunct or consequence. When I use the term anti-prophetic, it is in this anti-predictive sense, meaning that prediction of a coming millennial moment is irrelevant because salvation lies in the here and now.

Millenarianism depends on a metaphysic of time which assumes that the future already, to some extent, exists. In the fifth century, St. Augustine argued that past, present and future existed simultaneously in the mind of God, so everything that would happen in the future could already be thought to be happening; 'all things which he [God] knows', Augustine wrote, 'are present at the same time'.[62] It has been said that Marxism's metaphysics embraced past, present and future in a single 'creative breath'.[63] This is the logic of the certainty that a new period is to begin: it already exists. It follows that prophecy is a central feature of millenarianism, for it is essential to know just when the crisis – and the restored paradise – is coming. There are very obvious reasons why this should be so. One might wish to prepare one's soul or, at any event, be ready to cope with social and political collapse. As Matthew's gospel put it, 'Take therefore no thought for the morrow: for the morrow shall take thought for the things of itself.'[64]

Prophetic concerns aside, the belief that human affairs can and should be managed in the best interests of all is one foundation of utopianism as a political phenomenon. The idea finds its origins in both classical and scriptural tradition. In the Christian worldview, it is an obligation placed on every believer to prepare for the second coming through a combination of devout lifestyle and the conversion of unbelievers. The need for action is persistent and pervasive in all the major forms of millenarianism and points to a central paradox: the inevitable, imminent end of time provokes active participation in the historical process rather than, as we might expect, passive acceptance. God, or Time, manages the universe, but people are required to bring the inevitable crisis into manifestation. We are faced with the somewhat contradictory conception that knowledge of our fate may help us to influence this fate. Karl Popper defined the belief in an overarching historical destiny as historicism, while the active engagement with the historical process was dubbed 'activism'.[65] He saw both, manifested primarily through the historical theories of Plato and Marx. According to Popper, historicist theories have two central characteristics: they both take it for granted that historical change develops according to underlying laws, which suggest, in turn, a broadly predetermined pattern and a purposeful goal.[66] However, while history is predetermined, human beings paradoxically possess the capacity to make free choices. As Marx himself said, even though 'men are the products of circumstances and upbringing ... it is men that change circumstances', to which he added, 'the philosophers have only *interpreted* the word, in various ways; the point however, is to *change* it'.[67] The only free choice to be made in relation to history is to help it on its way and serve its greater purpose. The result is often seen in performance, in the great rituals, for example, of Christianity and the renewal of the world at Christmas and Easter; or in Marxist states in the now vanished May Day celebrations. The active-passive paradox extends to other forms of millenarianism. For example, the prophecy of the coming of the future 'Twelfth Imam' in Shia Islam inspires both great patience and revolutionary fervour.[68]

The tension between the possible and the impossible has driven utopian conflict. Trotskyism, for example, was denounced by Regis Debray in 1967 as a 'medieval metaphysic' which, although paved with good intentions, was based on the belief that people are perfect, containing a universal proletarian essence which is universal and cannot change with circumstances.[69] In Debray's sceptical version of Trotskyite cosmology, if revolutionary leaders set suitable, realizable objectives for the oppressed workers and peasants, they will automatically become aware of their essence, and socialism will immediately follow. As Debray pointed out, this was all so much theory, with no grounding in reality: his own revolutionary utopia was possible, he insisted, where the orthodox Trotskyite version was not.

The paradox by which human life is fated, yet personal development can alter fate is central to classical Stoicism. By willingly submitting to fate, the Stoic would be free and, if fate was coincident with nature, then the Stoic was required to live in harmony with nature.[70] This was well set out by Diogenes Laertius in his summary of Stoic opinions. 'All things happen by fate or destiny', he wrote.[71] At the same time, though, virtue can be taught and, once acquired, can lead to wisdom and freedom (although other statements suggest that one is either virtuous or not, and there is nothing that one can do about it). The wise man alone is free, Diogenes concluded, adding that 'freedom is the power of independent action'.[72] The paradox leads to the solution that freedom consists of doing what we would have done anyway or choosing what we ought to choose. So, education does not mean that we can become someone different to who we are, but we can be ourselves in a better sense than we were before. The psychological foundation of utopianism is the universal impulse to become one's self, to live one's unrealized potential. 'From early on we want to get to ourselves', Bloch wrote, and 'We have in us what we could become.'[73] 'I am. We are', he wrote in the aftermath of the First World War, and 'Now we have to begin.'[74] Life has become empty and it is our task not just to fill it but to fulfil it and, in so doing, initiate the future.[75]

The impact of Stoicism in western thought cannot be overestimated. It found its way into Hegel's Idealism, and from him to Marx, Engels and Lenin. This is Lenin's commentary on the Stoic paradox:

> Engels says: 'Hegel was the first to state correctly the relation between freedom and necessity. To him, freedom is the appreciation of necessity. "Necessity is *blind* only *in so far as it is not understood*".'[76]

The belief that we are on the side of history, then, dramatically simplifies our lives, including our politics. The way forward becomes obvious. The key psychological characteristic of the utopian is optimism. The utopian is not a cynic, resigned to an endless repetition of decay and decline. By the same token, a utopian is necessarily dissatisfied with prevailing conditions, otherwise there would be no reason for working to improve them. The quest is necessarily chaotic on account of a further unresolved tension between the idea of a utopia as grounded in human nature, in who we are, or in the potential for revolutionary transformation, so neither we nor society are the same.[77] It is this tension which tips utopianism into totalitarianism.

Utopianism is about 'reclaiming the future' by creating one's own reality instead of accepting someone else's.[78] Christian activism demands that the faithful evangelize the gospels to prepare for the second coming. Leninism requires the politically conscious elite to form a secretive, authoritarian, revolutionary vanguard to work for the revolution.[79] We have the idea of individual engagement with a wider process, which can be framed as a journey, which is why Norman Cohn titled his great book *The Pursuit of the Millennium*, while Isaiah Berlin, writing on utopias, spoke of 'The Pursuit of the Ideal' in his *Crooked Timber of Humanity*. The utopian millenarian is a striver, a seeker, a worker, a participant in time and history. The construction of an organized utopia out of the original impulse – the universal hope for a better future – is an operation which discloses the limits of our imagination of the future and, by providing limits and definition, allows us to create a structure and so make the future realizable.[80] In this case utopianism becomes less a dream of a possible future or ideal state, than a means of achieving that dream. It becomes a method for living and for engineering the future. It may even encourage great moral endeavour if the entry to the new world is matter of virtuous behaviour.[81] And from this basic impulse, we find the creation of utopian communities by millenarian groups in the nineteenth-century United States, and the ideal communities established in the UK by reformers such as Robert Owen.[82]

Millenarianism then also becomes revolutionary, inspiring political radicalism, but also transformation in a less confrontational manner, encouraging the faithful to work for a fairer and more just society, as in some sections of modern US evangelicalism.[83] Evangelical engagement with anti-slavery and social reform movements from the eighteenth century to the present provide sufficient testimony to the benign impact of the belief in the need to prepare for God's kingdom. Millenarianism and utopianism are both politically neutral and they can both take on either a gentle pluralism or strict authoritarianism in the same way just as they can be initiated through peace or war. As Ruth Levitas put it, 'the problem of totalitarianism is exactly that: a problem of totalitarianism, not one of utopianism'.[84]

The history of utopias prior to the Renaissance is largely one of religious communities in practice, and tales of fantastical lands in literature, with Eden as the lost Golden Age and the Kingdom of Christ as the coming paradise.[85] In the past, many Utopias occupied a physical location, even if, like the Garden of Eden, they were in the past.[86] There was always, though, the hope that they might really exist. The problem is partly one of language: can we find words to describe the boundary between the realizable and the not-realizable? The Islamic scholar and theosophist Henri Corbin, confronting the problem of whether or not the realm of Platonic archetypes was real, devised an impossible realm, which he named the 'imaginal':

> It was impossible for me, in what I had to translate or say, to be satisfied with the word *imaginary* ... we cannot prevent the term *imaginary*, in current usage that is not deliberate, from being equivalent to signifying unreal, something that is and remains outside of being and existence-in brief, something *utopian*.[87]

Recognizing that the imaginary utopia may be, by definition, impossible, Corbin altered his vocabulary, inventing a new dimension of consciousness, the imaginal, as a means of making the impossible possible. Drawing heavily on Plato, Corbin argued that on the one hand, the Ideal and Archetypal may exist in an unreachable, eternal state but, on the other, that it is in their very nature, as Plato insisted, to manifest in the material here and now. Corbin drew attention to the Persian notion of Na-koja-Abad, which he translated as a 'place outside of place, outside of where', literally identical in meaning to More's later Utopia and Samuel Butler's still later Erehwon, although metaphysically very different.[88] His Imaginal realm was a zone that mediated between Being and Becoming, allowing perfection to be realized.

Hope and optimism are the psychological foundations of utopian dreams, but the utopia itself is always a construct, an artifice.[89] Central to the psychology of utopianism, then, is the scarcity gap between socially constructed notions of what society should provide and what it does provide.[90] Utopianism deals with what should be, rather than what is, including what should happen in the future. At the core of utopianism is an activist metaphysics of time which allows the future to be altered. Yet, central to utopian confidence is the conviction that it 'will' be altered, so the uncertainty inherent in the proposition that the future is open to change is, paradoxically, balanced by the notion that such change must take place in a certain direction.

In addition, like any other cultural, social or political force, millenarianism constantly adapts to changing circumstances.[91] It is also cumulative in that later forms build on earlier ones and look back to them for authority.[92] As C.G. Jung put it, ancient 'mythological motifs frequently appear, but clothed in modern dress'.[93] Millenarianism innovates as time passes. It is improvisational, adapting to changing dogma and circumstances.[94] Psychology, though, is always mediated through social forms. It cannot be otherwise. 'The faces which turned in the utopian direction', Bloch wrote, 'have of course been different in every age ... (and) each individual case they believed what they saw'.[95] The direction is always the same but the goal, the *terminus*, shape-shifts, to use an analogy from science fiction. The goal may be psychological (happiness, freedom, non-alienation and a feeling of enchanted union with the cosmos) or physical (the Land of Milk and Honey, the New Jerusalem) or transcendent (God's heavenly kingdom, Platonic Being, the rise of the Eternal Feminine, the spiritual cosmos of the theosophists).

There is a direct continuity from the millenarianism of the ancient Near East down to the sixteenth century and the upheavals and excitement connected to the Reformation. And from there the flow of ideas leads to both Nazism and revolutionary Marxism, the most powerful political ideologies of twentieth-century Europe, both of which depended on the belief of a violent inauguration of a new Golden Age.[96] Marxism borrowed its historicist philosophy of time from the Idealist tradition via Hegel and therefore shares it with New Age philosophy. Marxism's apostolic descent from millenarian Christianity is now hardly a matter of debate. Slavoj Žižek even suggested that the two should form an alliance against less palatable ideologies.[97] The most pervasive form of secular millenarianism in the modern west, though, is belief in progress, the inevitable improvement of human conditions through time.[98] It is also the most insidious, mainly because it is so widely regarded as being absolute truth, rather than just another version of an old metaphysics.

For Isaiah Berlin, utopianism was one consequence of millenarianism and of the idea deeply embedded in western consciousness that a lost Eden could be recreated. Berlin wrote of the twentieth century: 'There are, in my view, two factors that, above all others, have shaped human history in this century. One is the development of the natural sciences and technology ... The other, without doubt, consists in the great ideological storms that have altered the lives of virtually all mankind.'[99] All the ideologies he identified were, in his view, destructive, intolerant and generally totalitarian: communism, Nazism, racism, virulent nationalism and religious bigotry. Of these, he categorized both communism and Nazism as variants of the long European tradition of millenarianism.

If utopianism is understood as both method and goal, then there is no necessary reason why it should be totalitarian.[100] A democratic utopia might be the expression of the social-revolutionary 'egalitarian' millenarianism which emerged in the fifteenth century and reached its full expression in the Reformation, particularly in the teachings of Thomas Muntzer, which held that Christ would be more likely to return to the world once social justice had been established.[101] Time is one problem. Another is place. Like a country, utopia constantly adapts and innovates and is marked by diversity: it may be tolerant or intolerant, exclusive or inclusive, industrial or anti-industrial, peaceful or brutal.[102]

In Berlin's diagnosis utopianism became totalitarian when it believed that the final stage is reached: 'Utopias have their value', he wrote, 'nothing so wonderfully expands the imaginative horizons of human potentialities – but as guides to conduct they can prove literally fatal. Heraclitus was right, things cannot stand still.'[103] The moment a true state of social being is found is the moment we encounter Lenin, Trotsky, Mao Tse-tung and Pol Pot, and the complete transformation of time inherent in the Khmer Rouge's resetting of the calendar to the Year Zero. All the ideologies identified by Berlin receive part of their power from the conviction that they are confronting an external threat. Communism set itself the task of wiping out its class enemies, while Nazism aimed to obliterate Jews and others whom it defined as sub-humans. Both owed a debt to religious fundamentalists whose task was to resist Satan and to extreme nationalists who struggle against their presumed alien oppressors. Berlin made the telling point, though, that 'these great movements began with ideas in people's heads: ideas about what relations between men have been, are, might be and should be; and to realize how they came to be transformed in the name of a vision of some supreme goal in the minds of the leaders'.[104] All the supposed external threats were fictions, whether a class, race, or national enemy or a metaphysical entity. They were illusions or, worse, delusions. They had no more existence, we may say, than goblins, demons, reds under the bed or, for that matter, the 'axis of evil' identified by George W. Bush in January 2002.[105]

The sheer range of possible futures, and the despair felt at the prospect of some of them, turns the least pleasant utopias into dystopias, in which, usually, the millennial upheaval, perhaps plague or nuclear war, has resulted not in a world reborn but a society condemned to murderous meaninglessness. Dystopian ideas emerged in science fiction with futurist films including Fritz Lang's 1927 masterpiece *Metropolis* and novels such as George Orwell's *Nineteen Eighty-Four*, published in 1949. Dystopianism became especially familiar in the 1970s as part of a fashionable but misplaced discussion about the 'end of utopia'.[106] If utopia is a 'vision of heaven on earth', then dystopia is 'an anticipation of hell'.[107] Dystopia is utopia's doppelganger, its dark twin, its Ahriman to its Ahura Mazda, its Satan to its Christ. Visions of a terrible future are rooted in the temporary disruption which takes place when the millennium arrives, before Christ's victory, and the permanent torture of those condemned to an eternity in Hell. They are secularized in such works as Thomas Malthus' *An Essay on the Principle of Population*, published in 1798. Malthus bucked the trend of late eighteenth-century optimism by predicting environmental catastrophe, providing a prehistory for late twentieth-century ecological millenarianism. He had considered all the arguments for human perfectibility and found them thoroughly unconvincing.[108] He didn't entirely disagree that great advances might lie in the future, but thought that catastrophe was equally likely.

Utopian and dystopian strands of thought are not entirely separate, but operate together like the interwoven strands of a kind of intellectual DNA. Often a dystopian phase is a necessary precursor to the promised utopian bliss. Sometimes, for example, the fear of global disaster only encourages the utopians to greater effort, as we see with the modern Green movement. And sometimes, as in the standard model of Christian millenarianism as foretold in the Book of Revelation, the coming utopia can only arrive after a period of war, plague and disaster on an epic scale. Both states of mind, the optimistic and the pessimistic, feed on the notion that the current time, the 'now' is somehow peculiarly subject to the forces of change as no previous age has been and that it has lost its faith, its soul and its myths, as humanity itself descends into a meaningless chaos. In modern terms, a 'paradigm shift' is coming which will release us from our current intellectual shackles and help us to save the world. We do not have to look too far to find examples. In 1829 Thomas Carlyle, one of the greatest political and social commentators of the Victorian era, believed that he was living at a time of unparalleled conflict between the Old and the New: he complained bitterly about the worship of the 'Mechanical' but found hope in what he saw as the importance of 'true religion' in the great reforming movements of the English and French revolutions.[109] Narratives of decline also have a certain constancy.[110] In his 1845 novel *Sybil*, Disraeli bemoaned the loss of community: 'Modern society acknowledges no neighbour', he wrote.[111] In 1995, a century and a half later, the US neoconservative Gertrud Himmelfarb declared that 'civil society has been infected by the same virus that has contaminated the entire culture: irresponsibility, incivility, a lack of self-discipline and self-control'.[112] Pessimism, like optimism, is a constant, and where some people see improvement, others interpret exactly the same circumstances through the lens of despair. The precise conditions seem to matter little to those people whose perspective is shaped by what they want to see. As Malthus pointed out in the 1790s, both sides adopt entrenched positions; neither pays any attention to empirical evidence; and both are therefore ultimately futile.[113]

Pragmatic dreams of the possible occur notably in the tradition epitomized by Machiavelli's *The Prince*. Machiavelli's proposition was that the perfect operation of society consists in doing what is possible in current circumstances but doing it better by recognizing nature, a category which includes the nature of the people.[114] Utopia is then not a matter of what can never be, however much we might wish for it, but what can be, if only we work for it. The potential for perfection is therefore already present and its potential is latent in current circumstances. If it is set in the future, it may consist merely of an improvement in current conditions and will be realizable through gradual change. Buckminster Fuller's eminently achievable version depends on the intelligent and comprehensive application of technology. Utopia then becomes a practical possibility. In 1969, surveying the upheavals around him, he wrote that 'Utopia is at least physically possible of human attainment.'[115] Even as the first warnings of environmental crisis were circulating, Fuller's pragmatic approach proposed an optimistic solution to what he clearly felt was a pessimistic context. He followed the traditions of nineteenth-century utilitarianism, in the sense that no problem lacks a practical remedy. For Jeremy Bentham, for example, the solution to all ills lies in the simple recognition of human nature's twin drives, pain and pleasure.[116] So, we see that utopians fall into two classes. First, there are the Realists for whom the better future works with human nature, and then, there are the Idealists for whom human nature is so flawed that a better society is impossible.

If there is a possibility of actually reaching utopia, then the quest for perfection itself may pass along a variety of paths. If it is enough for the utopia to exist as an alternative to mainstream society and in parallel with it, then true believers can find a promised land and start anew, as so many Europeans did when they colonized the United States, in which case we have a utopia of the willing. But, if it is the whole of society which must be transformed, then the situation becomes more complex, for the unwilling must be coerced. In such circumstances, utopians are not content to just hope for a better future or a final dispensation: they attempt to force everyone else to share their vision. But the willing and unwilling are united in a paradox which states that the unwilling must become willing. And then there are further options. In one, exemplified in Christian fundamentalism, divine intervention will necessarily result in a utopia of the saved and the damnation of everyone else. In another, familiar to victims of revolutionary terror from 1790 onwards, the unwilling must be killed or sometimes simply re-educated, as in Leninist Russia and Maoist China. Terror, as Frank Kermode observed, has long been a part of the millenarian mood.[117] The dream of perfection is never impossible and always realizable. There is therefore no limit on what millenarians and utopians can attempt. Like Stalin and Mao Tse-tung, they can set out to transform entire societies. Some terror lies in the future, reflected in fantasies of imminent destruction, and sometimes it is deliberately brought into being as witnessed in France in the 1790s and Cambodia in the 1970s.

Whilst the Platonic notion of the ideal commonwealth took hold of the Renaissance imagination, it became clear that a perfect society could also exist in a state of nature. A notable example was described in 'Of Cannibals', written by Michel de Montaigne (1533–1592) and published in the 1580s. Montaigne's starting point was the American New World, specifically Brazil. He considered classical antecedents, like Plato's account of Atlantis but concluded that America was a genuinely new, previously unknown continent. It is his account of the ideal society, though, which established a template for a major current of utopian thinking down to the present day. The debt owed by Montaigne to golden age literature going all the way back to Hesiod is clear. He even explicitly stated that the simple, close-to-nature quality of life in Brazil exceeded anything imagined by Plato or described in the poetry on the golden age.

These people have no trade of any kind, no acquaintance with writing, no knowledge of numbers, no terms for governor or political superior. No practice of subordination or of riches or poverty, no contracts, no inheritance, no divided estates, no occupation but leisure, no concern for kinship – except as is common to them all – no clothing, no agriculture, no metals, no use of wine or corn. Among them you hear no words for treachery, lying, cheating, treachery, avarice, backbiting or forgiveness.[118]

Montaigne's portrait of the honest, simple human, untouched by civilization was paraphrased and disseminated by Shakespeare in Gonzalo's famous speech in *The Tempest* that concluded with the words 'I would with such perfection govern, sir, To excel the golden age.'[119] It was Montaigne who established the modern concept of an ideal society as essentially pure and virtuous because it is based on being in harmony with nature, as opposed to the complex, alienating customs and institutions of European civilization. He established the idea that, if one lived in accord with nature, there would no longer be any need for political hierarchies, private wealth, agriculture or industry. And, having abolished such unnecessary burdens on the human condition, so the theory goes, individual behaviour would then naturally improve. Montaigne was deeply pessimistic about the condition of humanity in European civilization with all its laws, questionable philosophies and ephemeral fashions. He challenged those Christian views which regarded human nature as essentially flawed and, from now on, perfect societies could depend on less regulation rather than more; if people could be set free they might rediscover their lost innocence and the perfect state of nature would be restored. Ultimately, the state would wither.

Montaigne's is the first account of what was later to become the 'noble savage', the native whose life and values are actually superior to those of the Europeans. He explicitly rejected the prejudices of his time; denying that the savagery of the Brazilians meant that they were barbarous, he compared them to the deliciousness of a wild fruit as opposed to a cultivated one. The term 'noble savage' itself appears to have been invented around a century later – in 1673 – by the English playwright John Dryden, who also clearly admired the independent, pre-civilized man of the forest. Paraphrasing *The Tempest*'s Gonzalo he wrote:

But know, that I alone am King of me.
I am as free as Nature first made Man,
E're the base Laws of servitude began,
When wild in Woods the noble Savage ran.[120]

The idea of the pure, natural man achieved currency through its association with the opening lines of Rousseau's *Social Contract*, published a century later in 1762: 'Man is born free, and everywhere he is in chains.'[121] Rousseau elsewhere developed the idea that the decline of society began with private ownership of land; the decline of the child, he wrote, begins with rational education and the decline of society began with private ownership of land. He was not, though, against modern society in principle. His view was that the 'social contract', by which people had, sometime long ago, first agreed with each other and their rulers a set of fair political principles, had become corrupted. Echoing Plato and qualifying Montaigne, Rousseau argued that people were the problem: his great work on education, *Emile*, which he completed in 1760, opened with the words 'God makes all things good; man meddles with them.'[122] Rousseau's utopia was one in which men would always be put first, instead of the old feudal and aristocratic interests of land and advantages of birth; in the future, equality would be guaranteed by the regulation of the state according to natural law.[123] Yet he was too cautious about human nature to advocate a simple return to Eden or to an imagined primitive idyll, and his prescription was social and political reform, leading to the creation of a representative democracy.[124] Rousseau's argument that humanity is naturally good was a counterblast to the idea most closely associated with Thomas Hobbes, that people are essentially self-interested. Hobbes, the originator of the concept of the 'social contract', believed, like Rousseau, that people are born equal but that, fatally, they were equal in their selfish ambition. As a remedy, he prescribed a combination of a firm governing authority and adherence to the rule of law. The crucial passage occurs in his chapter on 'the Natural Condition of Mankind' in *Leviathan*, published in 1651. Like Shakespeare, Hobbes glossed Montaigne, summarizing the state of nature as being one in which there is no agriculture, trade, arts and learning but warned that, far from being idyllic, in the natural state 'the life of man [is] solitary, poore, nasty, brutish and short', and consumed by a 'continuall feare, and danger of violent death'.[125] The state of nature in Hobbes' universe was the original dystopia. By contrast, society would improve, in Rousseau's view, when people truly behaved in harmony with nature, expressing the better sides of their own nature, shunning the world in which knowledge of facts, possession of wealth or the exercise of power over others were the measures of one's humanity.[126] In *The Confessions*, which he completed in 1770, Rousseau wrote with admiration of his female companion whose mind remained so much as Nature made it that she could neither read properly nor tell the time.[127] His admiration for the primitive state of nature mirrored Montaigne's, although his solutions to the problems of eighteenth-century Europe were pragmatic and forward-looking. Above all, his utopia was realizable. But it required hard work: it was not enough merely to tear down the old and expect history to step in as the guarantor of future bliss.

Montaigne and Rousseau had opened a fracture in the utopian dream between those who followed Plato and the Bible, for whom the Heavenly City and the New Jerusalem might literally be an urban space, on the one hand, and those, on the other, for whom the city is essentially threatening and salvation is to be found in nature.[128] The way is then clear to the late twentieth century, and to a choice of utopias between two options – either Le Corbusier's modernist legacy, the high-rise cityscape of concrete and glass, or the quest for the natural and escape to rural communes. The Hobbes-Rousseau dichotomy became one of the guiding frameworks of all western politics: to what extent should individual rights trump government authority? All people had inherent natural rights derived from the fundamental law of the universe, as Thomas Paine wrote in 1791, but civil rights were reached as part of the contract between government and governed and had to be enshrined in law.[129] There was a compromise between the absolute freedom promised by natural rights and the need to regulate civil society. How to strike the right balance between authority and civil rights was to be one of the key concerns of John Stuart Mill's great work *On Liberty*, published in 1859.[130] The debate between those who believe that human beings can manage their own affairs and those who think that they need to be subject to firm control featured prominently in the utopian literature of the late nineteenth century. The anti-government line is evident in William Morris' 1890 utopian fantasy, *News from Nowhere*. Morris positioned himself firmly in the world of revolutionary socialism, believing profoundly in the virtues of social and political transformation: yet the whole point of his art and craft was spiritual elevation.[131] His belief in the inspirational effects of medieval imagery gave him an identity not so far removed from the esotericism of the Romantics. In one exchange, in a short chapter entitled 'Concerning Politics', the question is posed 'How do you manage with politics?', to which the answer is given, 'we are very well off as to politics, – because we have none'.[132] In the next chapter, 'How Matters are Managed', we are told that the state itself has disappeared and that while cultural distinctions retain all their former diversity, they are no longer tied to the existence of the nation state and, contrary to Hobbes, all disputes are settled peacefully. Much the same spirit was articulated by Oscar Wilde in 1891 in his enthusiastic exposition of a form of Christian socialism in which the goal was the liberation of the individual in line with what he said was the message of Christ: to 'be thyself'.[133] In Wilde's new Renaissance, which he hoped would restore all that was best in the Hellenistic world, morality was to be determined by the absolute freedom to do what one wished while respecting everyone else's right to do as they wished. And in his opinion, everyone who lived by this code could be an artist, which he thought was the highest calling.

H.G. Wells echoed Morris and Wilde with his *A Modern Utopia*, published in 1905. Wells was a realist, his utopianism pragmatic, and his view of past utopias recognized the collision between pluralism and authority, favouring Rousseau with a touch of Malthusian caution: in short, he rejected revolution in favour of gradualism and reform.[134] Crucially, he recognized that a utopia is not necessarily a better form of society in any absolute sense but is better in the mind of the person who imagines it; however, one person's perfect utopia can perfectly well be oppressive to another. 'Would this new sort of Utopian state', he asks, 'be any less forbidding?'[135] Like Morris, Wells imagined a universal state, governed by toleration, consent and cooperation, but he inclines to Hobbes in his recognition of the need for law:

> A socialism or a communism is not necessarily a slavery, and there is no freedom under Anarchy. Consider how much liberty we gain by the loss of common liberty to kill.[136]

Did utopia's perfection lie in the recognition of human difference and individual rights or in the system itself, to which all people should submit? Morris and Wells were both preceded by Samuel Butler's remarkably prescient *Erewhon*, a satire in the surreal tradition of Jonathan Swift's *Gulliver's Travels*. Butler's true opinions are as difficult to identify as Plato's. However, the issues Butler raised between 1863, when he published his essay on 'Darwin Amongst the Machines', and 1872, when *Erewhon* appeared, permeate modern environmentalism. In swift succession, Butler applied the prospect of a coming evolution of consciousness (anticipating the Nietzsche and Theosophical

Society) to the development of consciousness in machines as well as the rest of the biological world; this included not just animal rights but also, he mischievously suggested, the rights of vegetables.[137]

Montaigne's natural paradise was sustained in the US imagination by a continuous tradition of rural communes and lone frontiersmen. Eventually, the naturalism of hippy culture was to find literary expression in the imaginative future of 'Ecotopia', a mid-1970s vision extrapolated from attitudes and ideologies in mid-1960s California. In the Ecotopian account, 'the meadow sustains itself on a steady-state basis – unless men come along and mess it up'.[138] In this sense, human society exists in opposition to nature. However, individuals who have renounced the world of conventional, materialist, capitalist and suburban United States, through whatever means, are freed from their alienation from nature and return to their pure condition:

> Ecotopians, both male and female, have a secure sense of themselves as animals. At the Cove, they lie about utterly relaxed, curled up on couches or floor … They stretch, rearrange themselves, do mysterious yoga-like exercises, and just seem to enjoy their bodies.[139]

Aside from its natural attitudes to sex (shared with many previous utopias), Ecotopia was the very embodiment of small town United States, with wooden houses, independent stores instead of supermarkets, and workshops in place of factories. Callenbach's vision is rooted in More's original utopia, with its emphasis on a self-supporting sustainable economy in which manufacturing is devoted to durability rather than short-term profit, and the accumulation of profit is unknown.[140] It is also the inspiration for hundreds of green visions of modern living, down to the current concept of the 'transition town' with its gradual, pragmatic construction of communities living in harmony with nature and outside the world of corporate capitalism.[141] Transition utopias depend not on withdrawal from society but on the setting up of alternative structures within them as an evolutionary progressive manifestation of the millennium. At one extreme, ecotopias can dispense with humans altogether; 'anti-humanist' utopias are glimpsed when urban life reverts to nature, as happened in Chernobyl after the 1985 accident in the nuclear reactor.[142] The end result is 'ecologism', what we might call the 'anti-utopian' the doctrine whereby nature matters so much that humanity matters hardly at all: ecologist utopias need no human beings at all.[143]

Human beings will have wished not just the present world but themselves, out of existence and Nature, then, can now proceed happily without Rousseau's selfish humanity to corrupt it. Dreams slip unto the world of virtual reality. It is as easy to have virtual utopias as actual, physical ones, as claims that the Internet, or cyberspace, can inaugurate a new utopia of global connectedness demonstrated.[144] Sixties hippy utopianism directly fed into the development of the Internet and the idea of a utopia of computer networks.[145] Unnoticed by Berlin and Gray and the disillusioned anti-utopians, swimming in the eddies at the margins of wider idealistic current were other more harmless ideologies, which also fit securely into the broad millenarian trope.

One of the most recent of millenarian eruptions manifested in the so-called counterculture of the 1960s.[146] The etymology of the word can be dealt with quite briefly. The favoured term of countercultural activists of the time was 'Underground', a word used by those close enough in age to the Second World War to evoke notions of networks of resistance running through what was then known as 'straight' society, but also possibly derived from Kerouac's use of the term in his novel, *On the Road*.[147] The term 'counterculture' appeared in the so-called 'underground' press in 1968, in an article by Joseph Berke, in which it was equated with the 'alternative society', using arguments which were elaborated the next year in a book.[148] Berke's counterculture challenged the perceived ills of the time – the consumer society, centralized, bureaucratic government and the misuse of technology – and proposed replacing them by a fairer distribution of wealth, participatory democracy and the use of technology for human benefit. He used the voguish word revolution and the language of Marxism – the withering of the bourgeois state – but he was advocating evolution. In terms of Marxist periodization, his counterculture was the equivalent of the dictatorship of the proletariat, the penultimate stage of history prior to communism, the end of history. His revolutionaries were the young dropouts who turned against their parents, exposing the contradictions in bourgeois society. Theodore Roszak's *The Making of a Counter Culture*, published like Berke's in 1969, established the term as a general metaphor for youthful rebellion, being the first substantial academic book on the on the utopian fever that swept parts of the western world's youth in the 1960s.

In order to counter a culture one needs to know what culture one is countering. Culture, though, is a complex word, especially now that notions of high and low culture have been so comprehensively questioned.[149] One of the most effective definitions is Clifford Geertz's: culture, he wrote, is 'an historically transmitted pattern of meanings embodied in symbols, a system of inherited conceptions expressed in symbolic form'.[150] Images, words and ideas take on symbolic forms in flags, monuments and names for gods and goddesses, and people then use them to build and challenge political systems and, ultimately, go to war over them. Time and again, struggles are not concerned with real oppression but symbolic oppression. The signs people send through flags, emblems, clothes and hair become the battle ground, as they did in the 1960s.

The etymological ancestry of the term 'counterculture' lies in the development of the idea of 'subculture' as a culture within a culture. This idea gained popularity in the 1950s with sociological attempts to understand what were seen as delinquent or deviant aspects of youthful behaviour. A subculture has to somehow involve a clash with the dominant culture and is usually looked down on by it.[151] The use of the term 'sub' automatically suggested that a subculture is automatically below the main culture, hierarchically, and therefore may be in a state of tension with it.[152] Any revolutionary millenarian group may therefore, in principle, constitute a subculture. Finding the simple culture versus subculture typology inadequate, J. Milton Yinger, the sociologist of religion, identified a different kind of subculture, which he defined as 'contraculture'.[153] Yinger's logic was clear. Some subcultures, he realized, had no necessary connection with the wider culture, in that they could be understood on their own terms. This didn't mean that members of the subculture were not part of the wider culture, just that no general attitude was taken to that wider culture. A contraculture, though, has one distinctive psychological feature: its anger against, and rejection of, norms accepted by the wider culture. Socio-economic factors alone can therefore not explain the anger and rejection which characterizes contracultures as opposed to other subcultures. 'Culture and personality are always empirically tied together', Yinger observed, so a 'social-psychological approach is necessary'.[154] Sociology, he argued, cannot explain such phenomena without an understanding of psychology. He asked, simply: why should one person be happy with their condition but another from the same socio-economic background reject it? As a cause of historical movements, socio-economic factors are often limited. Millenarian, utopian, apocalyptic and New Age ideas are driven by emotions – by hope, fear, desire, longing, regret, nostalgia and other feelings. At an extreme level this issue seriously concerns our understanding of terrorism. A standard sociological model sees terrorism as driven by economic deprivation or political oppression, a view contradicted by examples of terrorists – or other revolutionaries – from privileged or bourgeois backgrounds. Osama bin Laden comes to mind, as do the Symbionese Liberation Army, the Angry Brigade, and the Red Army Faction, the middle-class revolutionaries of the United States, the UK and Germany, who briefly emerged into public consciousness as the 1960s turned to the 1970s. The comfortable children of the middle-class resent not their material oppression or political freedom but the fact that it denied them the authenticity of experiencing genuine oppression: the society they rejected was described as 'straight' and condemned as 'plastic', code for alienation from nature, lacking in feeling and spirit.

However, a subculture is not necessarily a counterculture.[155] The terms 'contra' and 'counterculture' have a slightly different feel to subculture, removing the notion of subordination or subsumption within a larger whole and emphasizing a self-conscious challenge to whatever is perceived as the mainstream or dominant culture. Part of the motive may be negative, which is precisely what 'contra' and 'counter' suggest. George McKay used the term 'culture of resistance', particularly in relation to the 1970s, suggesting a more coherent and rebellious attitude.[156] We might also use literary critic Lionel Trilling's phrase, 'adversary culture'.[157] Maffesoli speaks of 'avoidance' lifestyles.[158] Yet, where utopianism comes into play, positive alternatives always complement the rejection of existing norms.

The important feature of countercultures is that they issue an explicit challenge to what is seen as a conformist, outmoded society. And the challenge is issued not just because it is thought that society should be reformed, but because it is believed that it *can* be reformed. And usually there is a teleology, a metaphysic of time, which assumes that society will be reformed, that the success of the reformers is inevitable. This is the source of the remarkable confidence of self-proclaimed 'progressive' politicians and parties that they are automatically right, good and on the side of history.

Originally, counterculture was discussed as a single phenomenon confined to student protest/hippy culture of the 1960s, but by the 1970s the conversation moved in to the discussion of many countercultures.[159] A 'counterculture' in the generic sense consists of a group of people who self-consciously set themselves up in opposition to what they perceive as mainstream or dominant culture. Any oppositional culture can be a counterculture. For example, following the inauguration of the Hanoverian dynasty in Great Britain in 1714, the Jacobites, supporters of the deposed Stuarts, constituted a 'counterculture'.[160] They were reactionaries, Roman Catholics and supporters of the divine right of kings, a combination which prompts the hypothetical question: was the Counter Enlightenment a counterculture? Like millenarianism and utopianism, the concept of counterculture has now been universalized. Timothy Leary, the 1960s Harvard psychologist and premier psychedelic evangelist, claimed that counterculture is a perennial phenomenon, 'possibly as old as culture itself', he thought.[161] And as an ideology, it sets itself up as an alternative to what it defines as the dominant ideology.[162] A dialectical process then emerges: culture produces counterculture and the interaction between the two results in a final reconciliation before the process begins again. Leary defined counterculture in terms of artistic and lifestyle experimentation rather than organized politics.

> Counterculture blooms wherever and whenever a few members of a society choose lifestyles, artistic expressions, and ways of thinking and being that wholeheartedly embrace the ancient axiom that the only true constant is change itself. The mark of counterculture is not a particular form or structure, but rather the evanescence of forms and structures, the dazzling rapidity and flexibility with which they appear, mutate and morph into one another and disappear.[163]

Leary's counterculture encompasses the unconventional anti-nomianism of improvisational millenarianism and its capacity to change over time as it morphs from one form to another. His perspective was documented and detailed by Ken Goffman and Dan Joy, who identified six qualities which define a counterculture: 'breakthrough and innovation across culture, in art, science, spirituality and lifestyle; diversity; authentic, open communication and profound interpersonal contact'; 'generosity and the democratic sharing of tools'; persecution by mainstream culture; and 'exile or dropping out'.[164] Such codification has obvious weaknesses: why should a counterculture include authentic, open communication and profound interpersonal contact, and why can't it be totalitarian? Was National Socialism not a counterculture which set itself in opposition to the aspiring pluralism of the Weimar Republic? At its core, then, a counterculture, like a utopia, has no fixed qualities.

There is no boundary between the heightened emotional awareness characteristic of millenarian groups and the normal run of social dissidents, only the 'comparative graceful rise of curves of expectation'.[165] It is indeed, when individual hopes coalesce to provide what Catherine Albanese called a 'culture of expectation', that people find the power to manifest their hopes for the future in constructing utopias.[166] The difference, then, between millenarianism and utopianism is clear: millenarianism requires the destruction of an existing order while utopianism does not. The utopian may be a millenarian but does not have to be. The utopias of Plato and More are rational constructs, derived from a level-headed assessment of what is required of the ideal Republic, considering the, in their view, often unpleasant nature of human beings.

In the 1970s, a particular variety of millenarian prophecy came to academic and public attention. This was the belief that a New Age of peace, love and heightened spirituality is beginning. There is a small but thorough academic literature on New Age culture of the 1970s and onwards which locate it as a species of alternative religion or new religious movement. The most substantial academic work on the New Age movement was published in the mid-1990s in three books by Michael York, Paul Heelas and Wouter Hanegraaff, respectively.[167] Most work since then has elaborated the foundations that they laid.

Everyone now knows what New Age means. For example, when the US *Library Journal* reviewed the memoir of Helen Weaver, who met the Beat writer Jack Kerouac in 1956 and became his lover, it knew exactly what the constituent ideas of New Age thought were: 'ideas like Native American spirituality, goddess worship, witchcraft, and astrology'.[168] However, the term New Age has a double meaning.[169] It is both the future spiritual era and the culture which has been promoted by the prophets of the coming era or which has coalesced around their followers; it is both a historical period and a state of mind. It has a narrow meaning as the coming spiritual age but a wider association with a range of ideas and activities that are said to be associated with the coming age. Wouter Hanegraaff characterized these two levels of New Age activity and affiliation: New Age *sensu stricto* – the strict, or narrow, sense – and New Age *sensu lato* – the broad sense.[170] The New Age *sensu stricto* is concerned with the coming historical transition and the resulting urgent need to find means of spiritual transformation in order to prepare for the coming of the World Teacher, ameliorate any violent potential in the approaching crisis and serve the needs of cosmic evolution. The wider associations of the New Age *sensu lato* range from a belief in Hindu concepts such as karma and reincarnation, to divinatory and healing practices including yoga, tai chi, homeopathy, acupuncture and the *I Ching*.[171] All are connected by their Idealism, their belief that consciousness is more important than matter and that thoughts are real, and; exist within the western esoteric tradition. There is also some debate about whether New Age culture constitutes a 'movement' and whether, if it is not, it is a network.[172] It is actually a counterculture which has set itself up in specific opposition to the religious and political mainstream – to organized Christianity, capitalism and the politics of parties and state institutions – all of which it hopes will soon disappear.

New Age utopias have a particular lineage within the genre, inherited from theosophical and gnostic traditions traceable at least to the flowering of Islamic scholarship after the eighth century. The modern New Age movement has roots in classical esotericism but began to achieve its recognizable modern form in the eighteenth century. Most commentators agree that it is a contemporary millenarian movement, an argument set out by evangelical critics and taken for granted by academic commentators.[173] As a millenarian phenomenon, the New Age movement shares common roots with other movements which may have millenarian characteristics and includes Marxism, progress theory and evolutionary Darwinism. Such specific characterizations of something which is transcendent and which therefore cannot be characterized represent the 'fetishization of hope'.[174] As the magician may project intention on to an icon, image or talisman, so time is fetishized in the naming of the future utopia. The millenarian prophet who conjures up a future scriptural, numerological or astrological rationale for the coming transformation is creating a fetish, an abstract talisman, which provides a focus, an object for contemplation which facilitates the dawn of the new era.

And because all true knowledge in the esoteric worldview is gained from inner exploration, personal experience becomes the key to all truth.[175]

There are three modes by which the New Age might come about: firstly, external supernatural intervention; secondly, inner, spiritual work; and, thirdly, social and political action. However, while the believer in the coming New Age is required to prepare spiritually, and so practice Feng Shui, homeopathy or yoga, the practitioner of those things does not need to believe in the imminent transition to a new world. There are two distinct meanings to the word New Age: the wider culture (sensu lato) and the narrow prophetic tradition (sensu stricto).[176] I am concerned primarily with the narrow prophetic tradition, defined by Michael York as:

> the vision of radical mystical transformation on both the personal and collective levels. In fact, the awakening to the potential abilities of the human self – one's individual psychic powers and the capability for physical and/or psychological healing – is the New Age springboard for the quantum leap of collective consciousness which is to bring about and constitute the New Age itself.[177]

The coming New Age is a utopia. It is a not a civil society as defined by Plato or More but a spiritual kingdom as described in the Book of Revelation. Like utopianism, it can function as a method which focuses the believer on the need for self-improvement; Michael York described New Age prophecy as a 'mnemonic device', and for Steven Sutcliffe it is a 'millennialist' or 'apocalyptic' emblem.[178] Wouter Hanegraaff's opinion is that 'New Age' is 'a label' which can be 'attached indiscriminately to whatever seems to fit it'.[179] Like the great millenarian movements, it stresses the need for active engagement in the historical process. William Bloom, a key New Age author, identified four key practices which assist the inauguration of the New Age: new science (including new forms of healing), ecology, new psychology and spiritual dynamics.[180]

> What unites all New Agers, however, is the vision of radical mystical transformation on both the personal and collective levels. In fact, the awakening to the potential abilities of the human self – one's individual psychic powers and the capability for physical and/or psychological healing – is the New Age springboard for the quantum leap of collective consciousness which is to bring about and constitute the New Age itself.[181]

Some argue that New Age culture is also secular. This idea was developed by Hanegraaff, who argued that the New Age is 'characterised by a popular western culture criticism expressed in terms of a secularised esotericism'.[182] Others agree – as Joscelyn Godwin has pointed out, Blavatsky's theosophy was as much a product of the Enlightenment as a reaction against it.[183] Elsewhere Aquarian Age devotees have been described as 'humanists' on the grounds that the key to the prophecy concerns 'long-term prospects for man' rather than, as traditional millenarianism would have it, the inauguration of the kingdom of God.[184] The Christian writer Elliot Miller argued that New Age prophecy is broadly descended from Enlightenment secularism, especially in its humanism, naturalism and existentialism, albeit in a 'spiritualized' form.[185] And for Paul Heelas it is 'a highly optimistic, celebratory, utopian and spiritual form of humanism'.[186]

There has been a recent, fashionable, argument the fiction that utopia has died out, as proclaimed by Herbert Marcuse in 1970.[187] 'What seems important today', Krishan Kumar concluded in 2000, 'is to understand why it is so difficult for us to contemplate utopia.'[188] In 2007 John Gray thought that utopianism had suffered a crushing blow with the failure of the neoconservative attempt to export US-style democracy following the 2003 invasion of Iraq.[189] But theories of the 'end of utopia' have more no substance than do those on the 'end of history'.[190] And one of the forms in which utopianism flourishes is New Ageism. In the New Age utopia is not a result of divine intervention by the Christian God, or the Marxist seizure of the means of production, but in increase in self-understanding and self-awareness in the minds of every willing individual. This is the prevailing dogma amongst those who believe in the coming New Age. One feature of historicism, Popper noted, is that it constantly reinvents itself, craving novelty.[191] And so, what is the return of Christ or arrival of the twelfth imam to one person is the communist revolution or Aquarian Age to another.

Utopias provide a relational ontology that links space and time: they exist in the future and are often mapped, sometimes visually, other times as literary descriptions. They are both the map and the journey. As Oscar Wilde wrote in 1891:

A map of the world that does not include Utopia is not worth even glancing at, for it leaves out the country at which Humanity is always landing. And when Humanity lands there, it looks out, and, seeing a better country, sets sail. Progress is the realisation of Utopias.[192]

If the new world, the utopian millennium, is a state to be pursued and to be arrived at after a process or a journey, how do we know when it has been achieved? And how do we know when the New Age has arrived? As Gabriel García Márquez wrote: 'I have always thought that each version of a story is better than the one before. How do we know, then, which is the final version? In the same way that a cook knows when the soup is ready, this is a trade secret which does not obey the laws of reason but the magic of instinct.'[193]

Enlightenment and Progress
in the Eighteenth Century

Prior to the early seventeenth century, it had been almost universally taken for granted that every person had a unique, personal connection with the totality of the environment, which is synonymous with the entire universe. Every single human being was locked into an intricate web of relationships with everything in the world, from the smallest to the greatest and from the most material to the most intangible, from plants to planets and from the physical body to feelings, thoughts and dreams. The name later given to this all-encompassing system was the Great Chain of Being.[1] Individual lives were bound to the existence of the state as the 'Body Politic' and the state was perfectly integrated with the natural world below and the heavens above. As Jean-Jacques Rousseau imagined it, the state as a Body Politic was 'a simple entity, an individual'.[2]

However, between Galileo's publication of his telescopic observations in 1610 (which for the first time allowed people to see the solar system free of angels) and Newton's formulation of gravity in 1687 (which confirmed that the planets could move without any need to be pushed by divine beings) in his *Philosophiae naturalis principia mathematica*, the cosmos was stripped of its personality.[3] One of the most substantial features of the changes brought about by the intellectual revolution of the seventeenth and eighteenth centuries was the depersonalization of nature, or 'disenchantment' to use Max Weber's phrase.[4] The movements of planets like Venus and Mars across the night sky still offered visible evidence of an underlying order, but Venus was no longer the goddess of love and Mars lost its role as the bringer of war. Only mathematical formulae were left. God survived, but now he spoke through the laws of physics.

The new universe gripped the imagination of many of the eighteenth century's leading thinkers, for whom the laws of astronomy were thought to contain the clues to a true understanding of human society. 'The *philosophes*', Graeme Garrard wrote, 'wished above all to extend the scientific and philosophical revolution inaugurated by Galileo...Newton...and [Francis] Bacon, into society and politics.'[5] More than any other astronomer or natural philosopher, Isaac Newton gave the eighteenth century its new, reformed cosmology of unity, predictability and order and his discovery of gravity provided a single universal rule for the entire universe – one formula according to which all existence might be understood.[6]

Newton's *Principia* was widely read. In fact, it was essential reading for all educated people and was to exert a particularly powerful impact on the European world view. The application of Newton's astronomy to the service of an atheist, mechanical, determinist universe governed by one single law has been termed Newtonianism.[7] The emerging idea of universal rights was embedded in the logic of what I call 'Political Newtonianism'. The core principle held that just as one single law governs the entire universe, so human society must also be governed by the same single law: no king should be above the law anymore than any commoner, and the arbitrary exercise of political power was condemned as contrary to natural law.[8] The political implications were profoundly radical and were articulated in what came to be known as Natural Rights philosophy: life, liberty and the pursuit of happiness were to be proclaimed natural and tyranny unnatural. This was the version of universal truth which inspired the founding fathers of the United States, providing a scientific framework for their quest for political equality.[9] For Thomas Paine, who did so much to persuade the Americans to break with Britain, the perfect order of the planets was a profound demonstration of the truth of God's natural creation, and, quoting the radical French aristocrat the Marquis de Lafayette, he wrote how the truths which Nature had engraved on the heart of every citizen carried an innate love of liberty.[10] Natural rights belong to people through the fact of existence and freedom is the default position of the Newtonian universe.[11] And the force which manages society for the best, Paine said in 1776, paraphrasing Newton in the very year that US independence was declared, is like a 'gravitating power'.[12] It is irresistible: it must succeed.

Newtonianism emphasized order, stability, regularity and the rule of a law under which all men were, in theory, equal. The universe was, above all, organized, and God's withdrawal, promoted by the Deists, from an intimate relationship with every individual to a distant, impersonal, role meant that the universe now was essentially self-regulating. But Newton's philosophy also held out the possibility that the current state of political disharmony, embodied in the arbitrary exercise of monarchical power, could be replaced by peace, freedom and harmony. Humanity, with the benefit of knowledge of the true working of the universe, was now perfectible – a revelation which was to underpin both the theory of progress and the development of science. Above all, though, the emotion associated with the *philosophes* was optimism, borne of the belief that, finally, a way had been found to make a better world with no outside agency: no God and no angels. At last, the dream of the Renaissance humanists was fulfilled: human beings, it was hoped, would finally stand on their own feet.

If the eighteenth century had a secular god, it was Newton. As the poet Alexander Pope wrote: 'Nature and Nature's Laws lay hid in Night; God said "Let Newton be!" and All was Light'.[13] Precisely because the law of gravitation was universal, there was, in principle, no sphere of human behaviour which was free from its influence. It was in 1728, just one year after Newton's death, that the natural philosopher John Theophilus Desaguliers wrote the earliest known manifesto of Newtonian political theory, applying the new astronomy to the management of the state in a work whose title could not have set out his intention more clearly, *The Newtonian System of the World: the Best Model of Government, an Allegorical Poem*:

> What made the Planets in such Order move,
> He said, was Harmony and mutual Love.[14]

Desaguliers' reference, as any classical scholar knew, was to the sixth-century BCE philosopher Empedocles' belief that the universe was governed by two great forces in the universe, love and strife.[15] This did not lessen the revolutionary impact of Newtonian ideology. Rather, it elevated Newton's stature by presenting him as the genius who completed what the ancient philosophers had begun. Voltaire (1694–1778) argued in similar fashion that the lessons of astronomy should be applied to politics. He revered astronomers such as Galileo and Johannes Kepler but saved his greatest praise for Newton, whom he elevated to a semi-divine status. His praise was ecstatic: 'if true Greatness consists in having receiv'd from Heaven a mighty Genius, and in having employed it to enlighten our Minds and that of others; a Man like Sir Isaac Newton, whose equal is hastily found in a thousand Years, is the truly great Man'.[16]

The myth of Newton the divine scientist became such a familiar part of conventional wisdom that the Count de Saint-Simon (1760–1825), one of the first socialist theorists, spoke of universities in his ideal state in religious terms as 'temples of Newton'.[17] Saint-Simon's secretary and disciple, Auguste Comte (1798–1857), the founder of sociology, was to elevate Kepler, Galileo and Newton together as a divine trinity, symbolizing in their combined careers one manifestation of the universal 'law of three' in human society.[18] Sociology, as an academic discipline, then originated as an attempt to identify the operation of the same mathematical laws that moved the planets in the movement of people. It remains the ultimate expression of Newtonianism in the micro-management of human society.

The world into which Newton was born in 1643 was awash with millenarian fervour, which reached fever pitch in the turbulent period of the civil war and Republic of 1642–1660. The belief in a coming paradise, whether a return to Eden, restored Kingdom of David or a New Jerusalem, was a common-place of the time.[19] And so it continued throughout the eighteenth century, with many groups, such as the French Prophets, encouraging the descent of the Holy Spirit through ecstatic worship.[20] Newton, as is now well-accepted, prized his alchemical experiments and his theological investigations as much as he did his scientific inquiries. In fact, the distinction between these different kinds of inquiry is a modern one which would never have occurred to him. For many years he worked on a system of chronology in which major historical events could be matched against the movement of the stars in order to illustrate the unfolding of God's mathematical plan in history, work he published in 1724. Newton was fascinated by number as the manifestation of God's law, which was revealed astronomically in the shift of the stars in relation to the sun's location on the spring equinox – 21 March – of one degree every seventy-two years. The complete cycle takes slightly less than 26,000 years. As an example of his method, Newton placed the construction of the ship Argo, in which the hero Jason set out to search for the Golden Fleece, in 939 BCE. This was when, according to his reckoning, the Sun's location was 15 degrees of Aries, the sign of the Ram. So, according to Newton, the Ram's position in the sky equated to the appearance of the ram in one of the most famous events in classical history.[21] Newton's historical theory was widely noticed at the time. In particular it was greeted enthusiastically by Voltaire for what he judged to be the advance it represented on previous efforts to understand historical time.[22] Newton's mathematical system was not perfect, and he believed that, from time to time, God in the shape of Providence had to step in and recalibrate the mechanics in order to prevent a collapse in the entire system.[23] This was precisely why it was so important to understand exactly how the universe operated, history included.

Newton himself was also deeply familiar with classical concepts of the sun as the transmitter of the divine light of heaven as well as the physical light of the world. Salvation from the ignorance of the material world therefore lay in enlightenment: 'for in you too', the *Corpus Hermeticum* asserted, 'the word is son, and the mind is father of the word … Now fix your thought upon the Light … and learn to know it'.[24] Further: 'He who has recognised himself', that is, acknowledged the divinity within, then 'enters into the Good'.[25] The idea of the divine sun had featured in the opening lines of Nicolaus Copernicus' *De Revolutionibus*, the work which began the astronomical revolution by arguing that the Sun was the centre of the universe, rather than the Earth, as had been previously thought.[26] Newton's experiments in optics need to be understood in this context – as another facet of his attempt to identify the details of God's influence on the world. By extension there are implications for the notions of words such as 'illumination' and 'enlightenment' as having spiritual qualities.[27] Central to the mythology that has been constructed around Newton is his pivotal role in a scientific revolution of the seventeenth and eighteenth centuries, which represented a radical break with the superstitious and ignorant past. Charles Webster demonstrated in 1982 that this version of events is a fiction and that the scientific revolution was not a sudden break with old ideas but an evolution in which the ideas about the nature of the world developed gradually, not by rejecting the past but by building on it.[28] Newton himself was deeply immersed in the esoteric notions of the time. In particular he saw the sun as the channel by which life and inspiration passed from heaven to earth. He was well aware of the Hermetic texts, which were composed originally around the second century BCE, and had a huge impact on the Renaissance world after they were translated into Latin in the mid-fifteenth century. Newton himself made his own translation of one of the most famous Hermetic texts, the *Tabula Smaragdina*, or Emerald Tablet. We now know that this was written in Arabic around the eighth century, but in Newton's time it was thought to be one of the foundations of ancient wisdom. His translation expresses with great clarity his belief in the unity of heaven and earth, with the sun and moon, metaphorically speaking, in parental roles.

> That wch is below is like that wch is above & that wch
> is above is like yt wch is below to do ye miracles of one
> only thing
> And as all things have been & arose from one by ye
> mediation of one: so all things have their birth from this
> one thing by adaptation.
> The Sun is its father, the moon its mother.[29]

The standard English translation of the entire *Corpus Hermeticum* at the time was John Everard's, published in 1650, which included the following lines equating the mind with God and the light of the sun:

> The Mind therefore is not cut off, or divided from the essentiality of God, but united as the light of the sun.
> And this mind in men, is God, and therefore are some men Divine, and their Humanity is near Divinity. [30]

And from the King James version of the New Testament, the standard English translation of the time, Newton knew that 'the light shineth in darkness; and the darkness comprehended it not.'[31] Newton may have provided the framework by which God was dethroned as lord of all in favour of science, but his own faith was deep. Along with every devout Christian, he knew one of the best known verses in John's Gospel, in which Christ declares that 'I am the light of the world: he that followeth me shall not walk in darkness, but shall have the light of life.'[32]

By the beginning of the eighteenth century, light had become a metaphor for the triumph of the west, then represented by the beginnings of the English, Dutch and French colonial empires; the expansion of global trade; and the technical innovations which were laying the foundations of the Industrial Revolution. In 1706 the Earl of Shaftsbury, the greatest of the English Whig peers, wrote, 'There is a mighty Light which spreads itself over the world, especially in those two free Nations of England and Holland.'[33] But what exactly was this light? In 1750 Anne-Robert-Jacques Turgot (1727–1781) published *A Philosophical Review of the Successive Advances of the Human Mind*, one of the foundations of the theory of progress and a seminal work on cultural and intellectual evolution. Turgot spoke of 'the enlightenment of man on the subject of the Divinity' and of the Christian faith which saved Europe from barbarism after the end of the Roman Empire.[34] Enlightenment, for Turgot, was synonymous with the triumph of Christian, that is, European civilization. History was coming to an end and the New Jerusalem was no longer a supernatural fantasy but to be found in the salons of Paris. Turgot's optimism shines from every page. 'The Time has come. Issue forth, Europe, from the darkness which covered thee', he proclaimed.[35] And it was Newton, Turgot insisted, who had shown the way:

> One man, Newton, has subjected the infinite to the calculus, has revealed the properties of light which in illuminating everything seemed to conceal itself, and has put into balance the stars, the earth and all the forces of nature.[36]

The whole world was a model of the rotation of stars, an idea Turgot could have taken from Plato as much as Newton. But it was Newton who had explained one of the supreme mysteries of God's creation, implicitly raising himself, in the eyes of his admirers, to divine status. It was reasonable for Turgot, then, to conclude that all events, both social and political, move inexorably towards the same ends as do the stars:

> Different events take place in different countries of the world and all of them, as if by so many separate paths, at length come together to contribute to the same end,

to raise up once again the ruins of the human spirit. Thus, in the night, we see the stars rise one after the other; they move forward, each in its own orbit; they seem in their common revolution to bear along with them the whole celestial sphere and to bring in for us the day which follows them.[37]

Newtonianism replaced one God with another – Nature.[38] And if, as John Locke argued in his *Essay Concerning Human Understanding*, all knowledge was derived from sense perceptions (completely rejecting the Platonic belief in innate Ideas), then the highest aspiration was to harmonize one's self with nature, a concept which then provides the basis for the Heavenly City of the Enlightenment philosophers.[39]

The Enlightenment itself, as a historical era, separate from concepts of the acquisition of wisdom divine light, has assumed a mythical status as the foundation of modern European civilization. Even as a historical phenomenon, the term Enlightenment has a double meaning. One is as a historical period, in which sense it appears to have been first used in English in 1894.[40] The other is as a worldview, a set of opinions about the way that people should behave and society should operate which represent a qualitative improvement on all previous worldviews. The identification of the Enlightenment as a single benign movement promoting human betterment through progress, universal rights and political freedom has led to the notion of 'Enlightenment Values' as a coherent set of principles that provide the foundation for modern western civilization, as well as a road-map for the ideal direction of non-western culture.[41] This idea is embodied in the recent notion of an 'Enlightenment Project', a concept which was critiqued almost as soon as it was proposed.[42] There is, supposedly, in the modern world, a Manichaean, global struggle between two great powers, reason and unreason, or science and superstition, we might say. Repeatedly, the protagonists of modern liberal secularity announce themselves as defenders of 'Enlightenment values', in which science and reason provide a bulwark against the irrational forces which would destroy civilization. Such conversations have become more prevalent with the rise of both militant Islam and what is often identified as a strand of dogmatic, intolerant, secularism in the west.[43]

The Enlightenment is simultaneously attacked for its supposed legacy in western arrogance and cultural imperialism on the one hand but defended on the grounds that such behaviour is an abdication of Enlightenment values rather than their genuine expression, on the other.[44] In the eighteenth century, though, itself the issue was not Enlightenment, but *philosophie*. This was the interest, concern, worldview and activities of the *philosophes*, the small circle of philosophers who questioned the current state of European politics, religion and knowledge, all of which they considered somewhat backward and in need of reform. The *philosophes* especially disliked the absolutist aspirations of various monarchies, of which the worst offender was the French, and the Catholic Church's attempted stranglehold on knowledge. The philosophers were united by a belief that all knowledge about the world, independent of scripture, could be contained in one book – or series of books – hence the compilation of the *Encyclopédie, ou dictionnaire raisonné des sciences, des arts et des métiers* between 1751 and 1772. The *Encyclopédie*'s tone was materialistic, naturalistic and sceptical of what were now being distinguished and discredited as supernatural claims. The Encyclopaedists gave new vigour to the familiar Stoic notion of universality, enthused by the belief that the knowledge derived from the natural sciences, as well as from the great voyages of exploration, would now lead to the creation of a fair, just and rational society. The *Encyclopédie*'s two editors, Denis Diderot and Jean-Baptiste le Rond d'Alembert, along with key contributors, such as Montesquieu, Rousseau and Voltaire, became identified as the key Enlightenment thinkers, although Rousseau was later, anachronistically, reallocated to the 'Counter-Enlightenment'.

The Enlightenment's core qualities are normally identified as respect for human equality, the intelligibility of the universe, and the universal values of, respectively, modern science, democracy, individual rights, liberalism, atheism, secularism and toleration.[45] It is also said to be the origin of the modern notion of the 'cosmopolitanism' of the global society. It is generally these ideas that are meant when people talk collectively about 'Enlightenment values'. We might call this the standard model. And the idea that the Enlightenment represented a revolutionary break with the past is also deeply held: Ernest Cassirer spoke of 'the triumphal march of the modern analytical spirit' which 'in the course of barely a century and a half had conquered all reality'.[46] However, the notion of Enlightenment values as an unambiguous ancestor of benign modern liberalism and secularism is a myth, which I call Enlightenmentism, after Simon Schaffer's Newtonianism.[47]

That the Enlightenment had a well-defined character is often taken for granted, but like all other broad-gauge generalizations, it tends to collapse under close scrutiny, and in recent decades it has become increasingly contested.[48] Ironically the struggle over the identity of the Enlightenment was, as Anthony Pagden has observed, a feature of the Enlightenment itself. It is inevitable, we might conclude, that an intellectual movement based on free inquiry must generate its own internal arguments, and the debate began back in the late eighteenth century. One of the first to enter the fray was the theologian and educational reformer Johann Zöllner. In an article published in 1783 he answered his own question, 'What is Enlightenment?' by responding, 'this question... should indeed be answered before one begins enlightening. And I have never found it answered!'[49]

There have been substantial critiques of the standard model of the Enlightenment from a number of directions, all rooted in eighteenth-century criticisms.[50] Even the retrospective construction of the Enlightenment as a single movement is in large measure a result of an attack on the *philosophes* during the French revolution: the enemies of *philosophie* blamed it for what they saw as the evil consequences of excessive rationalism and identified the *philosophes* as a single, coherent threat to order.[51] The major problem for the standard view of the Enlightenment as automatically benign is the awkward fact of the revolutionary terror in 1790s France. Was systematic murder an aberration, a deviation from true Enlightenment values, as believers in the Enlightenment claim?[52] Or was it a logical consequence of Enlightenment rationalism (in the sense that it is perfectly rational to kill people who have no role in the coming historical order)? The latter argument was first posed by Joseph de Maistre (1753–1821), a notable defender of monarchy and an enemy of the Encyclopaedists.[53] The Enlightenment, in other words, was the basis of Jacobin terror, the execution of the king was the logical result of criticism on absolute monarchy, and the slaughter of priests was the end result of attacks on the Church.

The accusation that, through Robespierre and the Jacobins, the Enlightenment generated a totalitarian utopia was argued persuasively by Isaiah Berlin. For Berlin the Enlightenment was a kind of utopia, and one which encompassed all the intolerant, authoritarian instincts which he saw as inherent in utopianism. He witnessed what he saw as its consequences, via the savagery of the French terror, in the horrors of Nazism and Stalinism. For Berlin, the totalitarianism spawned by Enlightenment thinking was no accident but was a direct consequence of the movement's utopianism, its belief that it could satisfy all human needs and create the final stage of history, based in the universal values which it had discovered.[54] And that totalitarianism may be 'enlightened' makes it no less brutal.[55] John Gray has taken Berlin's critique further, denouncing what he sees as the Enlightenment's superstitious belief in the automatic superiority of modern science and the resulting assumption that it has the right to denigrate all other forms of knowledge.[56] The Enlightenment was then hypocritical, inconsistent and the ancestor not of liberal democracy but of twentieth-century tyranny. In truth, like utopianism, the Enlightenment is neither essentially democratic nor tyrannical. It can equally be both.

The problem of defining the Enlightenment has prompted a proliferation of other kinds of Enlightenment. Chief is the 'Counter-Enlightenment', a term popularized by Isaiah Berlin in 1973, although not coined by him, in order to describe reactionary and irrational opposition to the *philosophes*.[57] There was indeed genuine and strident opposition to the *philosophes* in the eighteenth century from critics such as de Maistre, but the Counter-Enlightenment's origins are now commonly associated with Rousseau and his admiration for nature.[58] According to this theory, there is simple binary opposition which pits Rousseau's admiration for nature against the Enlightenment regard for civilization, and Rousseau must therefore represent the Counter-Enlightenment. Following Berlin, the notion of the Counter-Enlightenment itself has achieved some currency as the origin of all that is undesirable in modern thought. It is said to be, for example, the ancestor of the intellectual weaknesses of postmodernism's malign rejection of universal values, and the flirtation of too many twentieth-century intellectuals with fascism.[59] Added to which, because New Age thought is normally identified as post-modern, it must therefore be a dangerous product of the Counter-Enlightenment and inimical to civilized values.[60] In this model, totalitarianism is a descendant of the Counter-Enlightenment rather than an aberration of the Enlightenment and the Enlightenment then retains its position as the ancestor of, and authority for, modern secular liberalism; the Enlightenment then becomes a time fetish, a golden age.

Under such pressures, the need to save the standard model of the rational Enlightenment has thrown up several solutions. One is the move away from a single, all-encompassing Enlightenment, and instead the identification of multiple Enlightenments and a series of Counter-Enlightenments, which constituted successive challenges to the Enlightenment.[61] We may therefore have a 'Radical Enlightenment', which is the ancestor of modern liberalism, leaving the French terror as a 'Rousseaueste' aberration.[62] Then there is a 'Low Counter-Enlightenment' of popular polemics, attacking the *philosophes*, for their anti-religious tendencies.[63]

The abandonment of a singular 'Enlightenment' in favour of plural 'Enlightenments' parallels the recognition of multiple 'countercultures'.[64] So we are left with the following position: there was a group of philosophers, mainly in France, who believed in liberty of though, argued that the world could be understood empirically and as a natural process, and tended to be anti-monarchical and anti-ecclesiastical. They were elite counterculturalists, challenging authoritarian political systems and religious dogmas of their time. But there is no necessary connection between such principles and a range of political ideologies, beyond opposition to absolute monarchy.

The *philosophes*' rejection of Christianity with its own notions of equality amongst the descendants of Adam and Eve, it is argued, opened the way to the inherently unequal notions of modern racism. For example, Voltaire, the icon of Enlightenment rationalism, regarded the African Negro as belonging to a different and inherently inferior species to the European, in fact, more like an elephant or a monkey than a Frenchman;

> THE NEGRO race is a species of men as different from ours as the breed of spaniels is from that of greyhounds ... if their understanding is not of a different nature from ours, it is at least greatly inferior. They are not capable of any great application or association of ideas, and seem formed neither for the advantages nor abuses of our philosophy. They are a race peculiar to that part of Africa, the same as elephants and monkeys.[65]

Here, starkly, is Voltaire, perhaps the greatest Enlightenment philosopher, applying free thought, empirical evidence and reason to lay the foundation for European racism. Once the notion of the Enlightenment has been sufficiently deconstructed, what is left? Christian Delacampagne suggested that the final, underlying feature which underpins all the strands of thought potentially described as Enlightenment is 'the will to emancipate human life (including knowledge) from the tutelage of religion'.[66] However, even this minimalist assertion hinges on the problematic definition of religion. According to modern definitions of religion, there was nothing which was necessarily anti-religious about the Enlightenment.[67] For example Clifford Geertz defines religion as:

> a system of symbols which acts to establish powerful, pervasive, and long-lasting moods and motivations in men by formulating conceptions of a general order of existence and clothing these conceptions with such an aura of factuality that the moods and motivations seem uniquely realistic.[68]

The Enlightenment, and the positions we take in relation to its character, are pervaded by symbols. The *Encyclopédie* itself has become a symbol of the eighteenth century as a time of knowledge and reason. We should substitute anti-church for anti-religious and we would be nearer the mark. The *philosophes*' problem was with the standard Christianity of the Catholic church and its Protestant offshoots: belief in a single personal God, oppressive and complex doctrines which claimed to hold the key to all human questions, and an authoritarian ecclesiastical structure which attempted to control the flow of knowledge. In Geertz's sense there was an Enlightenment religion, it was Newtonian and its cardinal doctrine was the belief in a single natural law which controlled the entire universe; it was embedded in the fabric of the universe itself; it was not ordained by a creator God; and it could be understood through reason and experiment. The archaic, Platonic sense of Reason, with a capital 'R', as a means of accessing divine wisdom was sidelined, leaving reason with a small 'r' as dependent on logic and evidence-based empirical observation.

The radical attitude to religion was summarized brilliantly by Thomas Paine in 1794. The Christian church, he argued, was just a fraudulent perversion of true religion, which was founded in reason, nature and reverence for God's creation; to stand before nature is to be in awe of God.[69] Rational belief, as Paine called it, was Deist, and God was the pure, divine mind and universal consciousness envisioned by Plato, not the capricious, selfish, God of the Jewish and Christian scriptures. To adapt Paine, to be enlightened meant to use one's reason. This might be reason as logic or it might be Reason as a path to divine wisdom. In either case, it provided a valuable purpose: it was 'enlightened reason', Rousseau argued, which fulfilled a vital function in curbing rash judgements.[70] The simplest definition of Enlightenment therefore has to be Kant's, written in 1784 in response to the question 'What is Enlightenment?'. 'Enlightenment', Kant wrote, 'is man's emergence from his self-incurred immaturity. Immaturity is the inability to use one's own understanding without the guidance of another'.[71] Kant then sets other conditions, such as the requirement for freedom in order to exercise one's understanding. But this was his opinion. Voltaire's was quite clearly that Africans were incapable of exercising either understanding or freedom, a principle which the Jacobins extended to enemies of the Revolution. So if we stay with Kant's core definition, Enlightenment becomes a state of mind rather than a historical period. He was absolutely clear that the inner and outer worlds are intimately connected. In 1788 he wrote:

> Two things fill the mind with ever new and increasing admiration and awe, the oftener and the more steadily we reflect on them: *the starry heavens above and the moral law within*. I have not to search for them as though they were veiled in darkness or were in the transcendent reason beyond my horizon; I see them before me and connect them directly with the consciousness of my existence.[72]

Kant's argument was not with the Platonic integration of consciousness and matter, or with morality and the stars, but with occultists who claimed that the truth was hidden. The feature of Kant's Enlightenment is that the truth is apparent to all who care to look. And this is the key to the mentality of the *philosophes*. It is not that religion is wrong and science correct but that all people should have an equal right to explore the wonders of the universe free from interference by church and state.

Roy Porter, considering the debates, moves the concept of Enlightenment away from exaggerated attention on an elite group of philosophers towards society as a whole, seeing the period as 'a ferment of new thinking amongst the reading public at large', diffused via the entire scope of available literature, including novels, newspapers, prints and pornography, adding up to a 'living language, a revolution in mood, a blaze of slogans, delivering the shock of the new'.[73] The key to the *philosophes*' worldview then becomes newness; the old world which is being rejected is that of the established church and monarchical power. The legacy of the Enlightenment is then no longer necessarily a rejection of all religion or all authoritarian government. In addition, interest in the occult, which might often be termed irrational or counter-enlightenment by modern critics, may be driven by the same experimental respect for empiricism, discovery and a drive to extend the boundaries of human knowledge as motivated the *philosophes*.[74]

This then leaves us with the problem of Romanticism, which is normally presented as a rejection of the Enlightenment of rational empiricism. The nature of Romanticism was described by Isaiah Berlin who said that the Romantic

> creates, he does not copy. He does not imitate; he does not follow rules; he makes them. Values are not discovered, they are created; not found, but made by an act of imaginative, creative will, as works of art, as policies, plans, patterns of life are created. By whose imagination, whose will?[75]

But the creative impulse was not purely personal: the individual provided the vehicle for the expression of transcendental reality, the eighteenth-century descendant of the Platonic world soul. Berlin spoke dramatically of Romanticism as 'a shift in consciousness... which cracked the backbone of European thought'.[76] The art critic Edward Lucie-Smith, who adopted Berlin's orthodox view, argued that 'Essentially the broken back-bone was reason, or, rather, the long-standing belief in the power of human reason to govern all actions and solve all problems'.[77] The new anti-rational Romantic ideology, Lucie-Smith believed, featured the triumph of subjectivity and the imagination, summed up in the dictum that 'Men now looked within themselves for guidance'.[78] What is important is the emphasis on the inner, the concept that true knowledge comes from esotericism, from looking within, rather than an empirical study of the natural world. The two do not have to be mutually exclusive, but there is a difference of emphasis. Lucie-Smith's description of Romanticism is perfectly balanced: what is at issue is an apocalyptic model of European history in which Reason, as defined above, first triumphed over superstition and then, in its turn, was overthrown: in a linear progression, one dominant mode of thought being replaced another.

Berlin, who remains so crucial to our understanding of the history of ideas, then draws a different consequence from Newtonianism, challenging the standard Enlightenment view that he had demonstrated absolute order. Berlin saw that Newton had destroyed the old, carefully structured medieval cosmos in which everything occupied a place in the divinely ordered hierarchy.[79] He described the Romantic consequence of the astronomical revolution in distinctly countercultural terms:

> the extreme expression of which is the self-assertion of the individual creative personality as the marker of its own universe; we are in the world of rebels, against convention, of the free artists, the Satanic outlaws, the Byronic outcasts, the 'pale and fevered generation' celebrated by German and French romantic writers of the early nineteenth century, the stormy Promethean heroes who reject the laws of their society, determined to achieve self-realization and free self-expression against whatever odds.[80]

The Enlightenment versus Romantic dichotomy may therefore have a certain value as a distinction between families of ideas. But it is misleading to characterize some individuals, ideas or movements as inherently 'Enlightenment' and others as essentially 'Romantic', when they may partake of both. Both, for example, share an abiding belief in human autonomy. The best solution is to treat such categories as 'Enlightenment', 'Counter-Enlightenment' and 'Romantic' not as descriptions of well-defined historical periods or movements but as heuristic tools, providing an interpretative framework for analysing historical trends.[81] The fixed binary distinctions according to which 'reason', 'science' and 'secularism' might be allocated to the 'Enlightenment' and 'irrationality', 'superstition' and 'religion' are bracketed as belonging to the 'Counter-Enlightenment' or 'Romanticism' therefore breaks down in individual cases. As a form of utopianism, the notion of Enlightenment can also function as method, a means of galvanizing its supporters to political action, providing confidence and a conviction that history is in their side, so they are bound to be successful.

Such confidence was provided by Turgot's theory of progress, which was elaborated by the Marquis de Condorcet in the 1790s.[82] Condorcet was Turgot's biographer and was deeply familiar with his arguments in favour of the improvement of society. He was elected first to the Commune of Paris when the revolution broke out in 1789; then to the Legislative Assembly in 1791, eventually becoming its President; and serving on a sub-committee of the Committee of Public Safety along with Robespierre. Condorcet became a controversial figure: he was 'for the enemies of the Enlightenment, on both the extreme left and far right, one of the worst exponents of the confidence in human rationality, which had supposedly made the revolution possible'.[83] In 1794 the revolution itself devoured Condorcet; having opposed the execution of the king and the new Jacobin constitution of 1793, he was arrested and subsequently died in his prison cell. However, while hiding from the authorities in Paris he had composed his great manifesto on progress, published in 1795. Condorcet did not invent the idea of the betterment of humanity: Voltaire and Rousseau provide obvious precedents, as does Turgot. There was also Adam Smith, whose masterpiece, *The Wealth of Nations*, published in 1776, developed the idea of the perfection of society through free trade.

> The uniform, constant, and uninterrupted effort of every man to better his condition, the principle from which public and national, as well as private opulence is originally derived, is frequently powerful enough to maintain the natural progress of things towards improvement, in spite both of the extravagance of government and the greatest errors of administration.[84]

But Condorcet's experience of the revolution inspired him with the exhilaration of the moment, the blissful experience of a world reborn, quite unlike Turgot's gradualism.[85] Like others who experienced the Revolution, Condorcet saw how the world could change in a few days. He was a Newtonian, convinced that the entire universe operated according to a single set of laws, as evident amongst people as in the movement of the planets. 'The sole foundation for belief in the natural sciences', Condorcet wrote, 'is this idea, that the general laws directing the phenomena of the universe, known or unknown, are necessary and constant. Why should this principle be any less true for the intellectual and moral faculties of men than for the other operations of nature?'[86] Time was historical, social and ceremonial, and manipulation of its symbols educated the masses in the ideals of the revolution. But his assumption that the timing of political and intellectual progress is tied to the revolution of the planets, suggests that history must follow its own course and can neither speed up nor slow down. Paradoxically, human action is therefore limited in what it can achieve, beyond assisting history on its way. In spite of his own personal situation – on the run from the Jacobins – Condorcet was an incurable optimist:

> Our hopes for the future state of the human species may be summed up in three important points: the elimination of the inequality between nations; progress in equality within the same peoples; and finally the real perfection of mankind.[87]

Condorcet's utopia is essentially a utopia of the unwilling in the sense that the logic of history dictates that all people must participate. On the other hand, true to the paradox that underpins all utopian hopes, the involuntary participation of the unwilling will be driven by the realization that progress is in the best interests of all humanity. Progress theory offers a fine example of improvisational millenarianism, and Condorcet took the Christian model of a finite world with a definite ending, removed God, and turned it into an account of humanity's ascent from barbarism to perfection with no need for divine intervention.

In Condorcet's scheme, history passed through ten phases. The final, the most civilized, he thought, had already been reached by the French and Americans in the creation of the United States, ideas later taken up and disseminated in the United States by Alexis de Tocqueville.[88] Condorcet believed that it was the duty of more advanced nations to civilize the more primitive through education, free trade and the export of democracy. Above all, though, the process was inevitable and could not be resisted, even in countries which tried to obstruct it. Isaiah Berlin, who disapproved of Progress as a form of totalitarian metaphysics summarized Condorcet's system:

> There was historical development, continuous change; human horizons altered with each new step in the evolutionary ladder; history was a drama with many acts; it was moved by conflicts and forces in the realms of both ideas and reality, sometimes called dialectical, which took the form of wars, revolutions, violent upheavals of nations, classes, cultures, movements. Yet after inevitable setbacks, failures, relapses, returns to barbarism, Condorcet's dream would come true. The drama would have a happy ending.[89]

Krishan Kumar identified the foundation of determinism which underpinned self-referential progressive theories of the logic of industrialization in the twentieth century. Western society, he argued had moved from agriculture to industry, it was observed, and therefore all societies should follow this model, as if history had an evolutionist logic which would inexorably climax in a world which was entirely western in character.[90] Progress theory was far more than a mere academic model of social and biological development. It was a political ideology whose function was vital to the development of European culture from the eighteenth to the twentieth centuries. It became a method in which possible futures – utopias – can be constructed on the basis of how far they reflect presumed Enlightenment values. And, given that progress is inevitable, its metaphysics decree that one cannot stand in its way. Further, significantly for the future of tyranny, the interests of those who stand in the way of history's benign trajectory should be disregarded. Scepticism about progress was evident even amongst those who opposed tyranny. For example, in 1859 John Stuart Mill, a resolute defender of liberty, considered that while progressive parties are a necessary part of a balanced political system, progress itself 'only substitutes on partial and incomplete truth for another'.[91] Belief in progress had a certain value in encouraging social reformers but not to the exclusion of other considerations.

Absolutely central to the belief in progress was the unquestioned assumption that contemporary European civilization was superior to that of all other cultures, past and present. This superiority might be moral, it might be intellectual and it might be technological, but that it was superior, there was no doubt. Progress theory proper requires development from an original point which is considered quantitatively worse, lower or (in biological evolutionism), less complex than the end point of history which is qualitatively higher, better and more complex. When value judgements are added, what is simple or primitive becomes morally inferior to that which is more complex and sophisticated.

Progress mythology's main function was to unify the potentially different world views of the various emerging sciences, including geology, palaeontology, archaeology and biological evolutionism in order to present them as representatives not just of a growth in knowledge but an inexorable and benign trajectory in history. Its main practical question was 'how to predict the future course of society'.[92] Its goal, simply, was to prophesy for the future, which it could do by observing the ordered trajectory of time and so assist in the ordered management of history. Progress theory was to exert a huge impact on emerging ideas that the way to the future lay in science and reason, finding its culmination in materialistic forms of late twentieth-century modernism and the metaphysical belief in the triumph of technology. However, it also had an immediate impact in contemporary Platonic Idealism. Notably the German Idealist Johann Fichte (1762–1814) adopted a form of periodization in which the world soul manifested in successive cultures or empires. The fundamental attitude to time was expressed by Fichte in a characteristically Platonic-Stoic mode:

> The comprehension of Universal Time, like all philosophical comprehension, again presupposes a fundamental Idea of Time, an Idea of a fore-ordered, although only gradually unfolding, accomplishment of Time, in which each successive period is determined by the preceding; or to express this more shortly – it presupposes a World Plan, which in its primitive unity may be clearly comprehended, and from which may be correctly deduced all the great Epochs of human life on Earth, so that they may be distinctly understood both in their origin and in their connection with each other. The former, the World plan, is the fundamental Idea of the entire life of Man on earth; the latter, the chief Epochs of this life, are the fundamental Idea of particular Ages.[93]

Largely through Fichte, progress theory fed into nineteenth-century German Romanticism. Fichte's contemporary and fellow Idealist George Friedrich Hegel (1770–1831) was perhaps the most important of the Newtonian solarizers. His Idealism embedded his work firmly in the same traditions as theosophy, and his theories of mind have been described as 'theosophical pietism'.[94] He accepted the interrelationship of the spiritual and material worlds: 'Secular life', he wrote, 'is the positive and definite embodiment of the Spiritual Kingdom'.[95] In Hegel's historical scheme, the Platonic World Soul became manifest in a succession of four great cultural epochs, corresponding to a cultural progression from east to west, following the sun's daily journey from dawn to dusk.[96] For Hegel, the sun was more than a metaphor – it was the physical embodiment of the supreme Mind, embodied in Light. His belief that those aspects of the world soul which had been alienated from itself were to be reunited echoed the Joachite hope for an age of the spirit, and he prophesied that the final age would inaugurate 'the unity of the divine nature and the human, the reconciliation of objective truth and freedom appearing within self-consciousness and subjectivity'.[97] History, he believed, was the progressive embodiment of light in civilization; this was the true meaning of enlightenment:

> In the geographical survey, the course of the World's History has been marked out in its general features. The Sun – the Light – rises in the East. Light is a simply self-involved existence; but through possessing thus in itself universality, it exists at the same time as an individuality in the Sun. Imagination has often pictured to itself the emotions of a blind man suddenly becoming possessed of sight, beholding the bright glimmering of the dawn, the growing light, and the flaming glory of the ascending Sun'.[98]

However, as is so often the case, we have to draw a distinction between the philosopher and the appropriation of his work. Hegelianism often adopts a deterministic view of a goal-oriented history which is bound to arrive at a final destination. Hegel himself was somewhat more equivocal, for while there is an end and a purpose, its precise form is unknown.[99] The final state may be Germany, or it may be the United States, but this is for individual Hegelians to decide and doesn't matter as long as it is the advanced, industrial regions of the white, Protestant, Anglo-Saxon world. Either way, the Hegelian utopia lies at the end of history. According to Gruner, Hegel 'belonged to a tradition which began in late antiquity, and continued with ideas to the effect that all reality is an emanation from a divine prime ground, that the one has released the Many out of itself, that it has left itself, but will return to itself once more'.[100] Hegel's Platonic Idealism proved particularly enduring and found a recent manifestation in US neoconservatism. But it also had a significant influence on Marx, who despised Hegel's belief in the world soul, and in consciousness as having independent existence, but applied Hegel's deterministic version of dialectical history (in which an original state, the thesis, produces its opposite, the antithesis, and the two then react to produce the third state, the synthesis) to his own materialistic philosophy.[101]

While Fichte and Hegel took Romantic Idealism in a literary direction in the visual arts, one of the leading English Romantics was the painter J.M.W. Turner (1775–1851).

According to Turner's biographer, John Ruskin, just a few weeks before he died the painter had remarked 'the Sun is God'.[102] Turner was well-versed in classical mythology, had studied Hinduism and was aware that the Christianized imagery of the west was just one way of representing the sky as an allegory. He may have picked up this idea from Alexander Dow's 1768 *History of Hindostan* or from Payne Knight's essay in comparative religion, the sensational *Account of the remains of the Worship of Priapus lately existing in Isernia*, published in 1786. Knight, for whom Turner worked in 1808, was deeply anti-religious but the orientalist William Jones, who greatly influenced Turner, was both a devout Christian and respectful of Hinduism. Jones' work on oriental languages which spanned the years 1770–1794 stated that there must be a relationship between the Hindu and classical Greek Pantheons and that both were fundamentally expressions of the sun. He concluded,

> It seems a well-founded opinion that the whole crowd of gods and goddesses in ancient Rome and modern Varanes [Varanasi], mean only the powers of nature, and principally those of the SUN, expressed in a variety of ways, and by a multitude of fanciful names.[103]

The idea that all male gods and heroes are descended from an original solar deity was later given academic credibility by the orientalist Max Muller.[104] But for the previous century it had been a commonplace amongst anti-Christian propagandists. From Turner's statement, 'the Sun is God', I have developed the phrase the 'sun-as-god', to describe the theory that all major male deities originated as solar gods.[105] We could also use the term 'solar myth'.[106] Joscelyn Godwin has written of an eighteenth-century 'cult of the sun'.[107] And we could talk of 'solarism' as the idea that the sun provided a metanarrative against which all great movements in history and politics could be understood.

The solar philosophies of Turner and Hegel were deeply symbolic and were both influences by the Hermetic belief that the Sun's light was the visible form of God, its movement the passage of history. Separately, though, a group of French radicals developed Newton's idea, outlined in the *Chronology of Ancient Kingdoms*, that the 2,160-year cycle of the stars in relation to the Sun's location at the spring equinox – 21 March – corresponded exactly to make stages in human history. Three radical thinkers took up the challenge set by Newton in 1724: to identify broader patterns in history by relating it to astronomy. The first was Jean Sylvain Bailly (1736–1793), notable as one of the most important figures in the early stages of the Revolution. He was elected to the States-General in 1789, became leader of the Third Estate and administered the Tennis Court Oath, the key moment at which the Third Estate challenged the power of the king. He subsequently became President of the National Assembly and Mayor of Paris, although having been criticized by Jean-Paul Marat and the Jacobins for being too conservative, he suffered the same fate as Condorcet and was guillotined in 1793. Bailly was then joined by the lawyer, Professor of Rhetoric and, following the Terror, member of the National Convention, Charles François Dupuis (1742–1809).[108] The third member of the trio was François Henri Stanislas Delaunaye (1739–1830).

Bailly expounded his arguments on the astronomical origin of the forms of religious worship in two major works, *Histoire de l'astronomie ancienne*, published in 1775, and the *Traite de l'astronomie indienne et orientale*, which appeared in 1787. Dupuis' *Mémoire sur l'origine des constellations, et sur l'explication de la fable*, published in 1781, extended the argument. Bailly's idea that a complex scientific civilization had existed before the Deluge, which he outlined in the *Traite de l'astronomie indienne*, proved influential. He had previously discussed the theory with Voltaire who himself thought it quite likely that 'long before the empires of China and India, there had been nations cultured, learned, and powerful', an opinion later cited approvingly by H.P. Blavatsky, the founder of the Theosophical Society.[109] His message was reinforced by his second major work, the three volume *L'Origine de tous les Cultes, ou Religion universelle*, published in 1795 and summarized for the less hardy in a one volume abridgement in 1798. The overall target was the classic Enlightenment one: the Church. By establishing a common origin to all religion in the worship of the sun, Christianity's claim to unique status could be disproved beyond all reasonable doubt.[110] Popular millenarianism was as vibrant as ever and provided a revolutionary backdrop for events in France.[111] The revolutionaries' real target was not religion as a whole but false religion, as opposed to their radical new faith of 'universal ... austere new secular moralisme'.[112] But then Dupuis, Bailly and Delaunaye were creating a model of history based on order, process and pattern, rather than enthusiasm for Christ's coming kingdom. Their goal was the Newtonianization of history, the demonstration that historical processes followed a natural path; that astronomy could demonstrate the harmonization of human affairs with nature as a whole; and that history had one way forward – their way. Dupuis' work proved to be an international sensation. His attack on scriptural chronology paralleled the abandonment of the Christian calendar and the systematic de-Christianization encouraged by the Jacobins, although he opposed their extremism. In 1786, he was invited to Berlin by Frederick the Great, the greatest political patron of Enlightenment thought, although unfortunately Frederick died before Dupuis could accept the offer. After 1789, liberated by the revolution from the need to explain his date for the invention of the zodiac in a Catholic context, Dupuis was free to mix his classical erudition with overt anti-clerical polemic, and he set out his belief that God is the Platonic world soul, the animating force in nature and the universe. Even though the paganizing tendencies of the revolutionary era came to an end with Napoleon's coup in October 1795, Dupuis' theories persisted. Dupuis' work was sufficiently well known in England by 1797 to attract a violent rebuttal, although it did not actually appear in English until abridged versions were published in 1857 and 1873.

It was Delaunaye who completed what Newton had begun and tabulated for the first time a complete theory of history in which astronomical, and hence religious iconography, evolved with the long-term cycles of the stars. His 1791 work, *L'Histore générale at particulière des religions et du Culte*, was an attempt to establish the foundation of religion in astral worship. His scheme concluded with the sun rising for the first time in Aquarius at the spring equinox of 1726. As to what this meant, he wrote simply 'Plus de changements'.[113] We could translate this as 'more changes', but another reading might be 'enough change', meaning that there will be no more change because the final stage of history has been reached. At any rate, by the 1960s, the notion of 'many changes' was to become popularly associated with the coming of the Age of Aquarius.

The construction of history based on vast, astronomically derived historical periods was paralleled in the daily management of the state by the calendar reform, which designated 22 September (the autumn equinox) 1792 as the beginning of Year One (the inspiration for the Khmer Rouge 'Year Zero' in 1975) of the new revolutionary era, and an intensified concern with accurate time-keeping.[114] Much technological effort was devoted to chronological accuracy but the enterprise was not a scientific one in any narrow sense. This much is evident from a series of festivals intended to reinforce revolutionary virtue, culminating in Robespierre's festival of the Supreme Being. The theatrical culmination of the revolutionary attempt to create a religion based on nature, the festival was celebrated with pagan pomp on 8 June 1794 and was to be one of the greatest examples of radical politics as performance and the use of grand symbols to keep the revolutionary spirit alive. For Mona Ozouf, 'the men of the Revolution' believed that 'man (is) defined by his quality of being, a being of sense...led not by principles but by objects, spectacles, images'.[115] And at the time this new world was greeted by like-minded people across Europe with extraordinary enthusiasm, bordering on messianic fervour.[116] In England William Wordsworth wrote 'Bliss was it in that dawn to be alive, But to be young was very heaven!' [117] In Germany, Hegel said 'this was a glorious dawn...a sense of exaltation reigned...and enthusiasm of the spirit thrilled through the world as if the actual reconciliation of the divine with the world had now for the first time come to pass'.[118] Even the resolutely cautious Thomas Malthus wrote that 'the French Revolution, which, like a blazing comet, seems destined, to inspire with fresh life and vigour' and, combined with recent advances in natural philosophy and technology suggested that 'we were touching on a period big with the most decisive changes, changes that would in some measure be decisive in the future history of mankind'.[119] He added the rider that disaster was equally likely!

The French astronomers were not ivory-tower philosophers but shared the *philosophes'* crusading spirit, recovering 'the holy places of the religion of humanity from Christian philosophy and the infamous things that supported it'.[120] The challenge to Christianity was far more effective if an alternative was put in its place, and the emergence of Aquarian Age thinking between the 1780s and 1990s did precisely this. As Gregory Claeys wrote, the coming of the French revolution represented a fundamental shift in the terms in which utopian writing was conceived as 'Heavenly and lunar words now descended to earth'.[121] The sentiment is a little overstated, given the long standing of previous political astronomy, but the point is well made.

The Theosophical Enlightenment in the Nineteenth Century

The United States possessed a thriving network of utopian communities throughout the nineteenth century. Many were heir to the theosophical and Neoplatonic traditions of European millenarianism, a culture of expectation which had been embedded first in the minds of many of the colonists and then the founders of the independent United States.[1] While the United States offered more opportunities to establish utopian communities than did the UK, purely because of its available space, the two nations shared a common culture of concern about spiritual evolution, esoteric teachings, coming spiritual eras and transcendental hope. This mindset was so deeply entrenched that it has been referred to in its own right as an enlightenment – 'the Theosophical Enlightenment'.[2] This esoteric enlightenment held true to the principles of enlightenment as spiritual illumination and, being profoundly influenced by Platonism, saw the use of Reason, with a capital 'R', as entirely compatible with spiritual exploration, as opposed to reason, with a small 'r' which came to mean the opposite as logical, critical, sceptical and designed to challenge superstition.

There was a constant flow of utopian tracts throughout the eighteenth century, often with millenarian associations, pleading for universal charity and the equality of all people.[3] Some millenarian movements, such as Methodism, were outstandingly successful, to judge by its survival to the present day. Other utopian experiments remained in the minds of those who dreamt them up: in June 1794, inspired by the boundless opportunities offered by the New World, the poets Samuel Coleridge and Robert Southey met in Oxford to draft a plan for a utopian community in the United States, 'an ideal community where twelve young men with their twelve wives were to conduct an experiment in human perfectibility'.[4] America, being virgin land, manifested the Rousseauesque dream of creating a society which was uncorrupted by past human weaknesses and failings. But the poets' dream of a new life in a new world never took off. However, by the 1790s others had established more enduring ideas.

The modern concept of the New Age utopia as specifically one of spiritual enlightenment is directly derived from the teachings of the Swedish Christian reformer and scientist, Emmanuel Swedenborg (1688–1782).[5] One of the leading mathematicians and engineers of his day, Swedenborg became increasingly concerned about the relationship between spirit and matter. In the context of the time this was not unusual. What was different about Swedenborg was his visionary experience of journeys to other planets and his conversations with the spirit beings who inhabited them, as a result of which he devoted the rest of his life to his theological theories. Swedenborg's celestial journeys provided the link between a traditional Christian view of celestial beings as angels and the modern idea of extraterrestrials as spiritually advanced beings.

Swedenborg's major contribution to millenarian cosmology lay in his claim that the *parousia*, the restoration of Christ's presence on Earth through the Second Coming, had actually occurred in 1757. However, he insisted that this was an individual, inner, spiritual event rather than a historical one, which meant that one had to have a certain level of spiritual awareness in order to perceive it.[6] 'The new heaven, the new earth, and the New Jerusalem', Swedenborg wrote, 'does not exist on the earth, but in the spiritual world.'[7] And, if we follow Kant's definition of Enlightenment, the new era also becomes more a state of mind, rather than a historical period. Kant disliked Swedenborg but his view that Enlightenment represents the maturing of humanity can encompass Swedenborg's claim that the New Jerusalem consists of the development of one's inner, psychological state. The conclusion, as Swedenborg pointed out, was that there was no date to the beginning of the new spiritual era and no historical entry to the New Jerusalem. True, the spiritual transformation to the 'Kingdom of God' had occurred in 1757, but there was to be no earthly equivalent and therefore no point in waiting around for it. Instead, any willing individual could gain access to the spiritual world at any moment, purely as a result of inner change:

> In heaven there is one single influx which is received by every individual according to his own disposition...and although there is one influx only, everything nevertheless conforms and follows as one. And this comes about through the mutual love shared by everyone in heaven.[8]

As the Swedenborgian devotee Richard Clarke wrote in 1772: 'In our own inner man, lies the foundation of the new Jerusalem.'[9] Swedenborg's followers in London formed themselves into 'The Theosophical Society Instituted for the Purpose of Promoting the Heavenly Doctrines of the New Jerusalem' and, after 1787, the 'New Church', explicitly emphasizing notions of newness and novelty. This was to be no traditional church but an entirely new way of relating to the Christian revelation. The New Church broke with the rules of standard millenarianism in its anti-prophetic, in the sense of anti-predictive, attitude to time: there was no point in predicting a future which had already arrived. And, by making the entry to the Kingdom of God personal rather than collective, it left the beginning of the new era to individual choice, effectively making the transitional period between ages of unlimited duration. In addition, the Swedenborgian utopia had no physical location; it existed purely in the mind. Swedenborg's emphasis on the inner world is fundamental to the modern New Age movement. It continues to engage New Age evangelists such as David Spangler, who claimed in 1977 that 'For each of us the New Age is here now. It has always been here.'[10] The spiritual New Age then constitutes an eternal present which is removed from the world of time and material change much as, in Plato's cosmogony, 'Being' was a pure, unchanging condition which underlay the constantly shifting uncertainty of 'Becoming', the material world.

For a while, Swedenborg's vision of a new world aroused considerable enthusiasm and his followers thrived briefly in the millenarian context of late eighteenth-century England in which, as Clarke Garrett put it: 'Spiritual enlightenment and human regeneration would come about through events on this earth, including both natural and political, until the wicked had been defeated.'[11] The emphasis on the inner world did not require a complete renunciation of political action. Prominent amongst the English Swedenborgians was Joseph Priestley, the famous scientist, who wrote in 1791: 'This kingdom of Christ, and consequently Swedenborg's doctrine, is speedily to prevail over the whole world, and to continue forever.'[12] Being a scientist (he isolated oxygen in 1774) or, more properly in the language of the time, a natural philosopher, Priestley believed that knowledge of the natural world would promote human progress and so encourage the fulfilment of Christ's kingdom.

Although the New Church's peak of popularity passed quickly, Swedenborg himself was to become a profoundly influential figure in esoteric circles.[13] His credibility amongst the *philosophes* had suffered a blow in 1766 when Emanuel Kant publicly mocked him in his *Dreams of a Spirit Seer*, but such criticism had no impact amongst theosophists.[14] Blavatsky later wrote that she regarded him as, if not an adept, at least 'the greatest among modern seers', although she cautiously kept an open mind on his precise proclamation of the New Jerusalem.[15] Discussing the anthropomorphizing of God, a phenomenon which she regarded as distancing humanity from a real understanding of the divine, she cited Swedenborg's solution – that, rather than making God in his own image, 'man imagines God after his own image' and then forgets that 'he has set up his own reflection for worship'.[16] And in this way, the humanism of the *philosophes* made its way into the emerging New Age movement.

The term New Age itself appeared in the 1790s, although no absolute first use has been traced. It certainly occurred in one of the popular polemics on political philosophy of the French revolution, Constantin François de Volney's *Les ruins des empires*, published in 1791. Volney (1757–1820) was an aristocratic radical, having been elected to the National Assembly in 1789, and *Les ruins* was his account of the problems inherent in the European political system, accompanied by his suggested solutions. In particular, Volney proposed the creation of a new egalitarian world to be based on the recognition of the universal, natural order of all things. His language was marked by triumphant enthusiasm: 'Yet another day – a little more reflection', he proclaimed, 'and an immense agitation will begin; a new-born age will open! an age of astonishment to vulgar minds, of terror to tyrants, of freedom to a great nation, and of hope to the human race!'[17] Volney's brief chapter entitled 'The New Age' consisted mainly of a dialogue between people, who questioned the existence of all traditional authority and their Civil Governors, who represented the old order. Right, and the future, Volney made clear, were on the side of the people, and his New Age, as Rousseau had proposed, was to be ushered in by democratic legislation, all properly proposed, drafted and voted on, not by Swedenborgian inner transformation, a concept in which he had no interest whatsoever.

Volney's *Les Ruins* was translated into English in 1795, as was his argument in favour of natural religion, *The Law of Nature, or Catechism of a French citizen*, published in 1793. Volney became one of the most influential free thinkers in the English- and French-speaking worlds; according to Joscelyn Godwin: 'The *Ruins* became one of the foundational works of free thought in the English-speaking world, causing its author's name to be coupled with that of Voltaire as religion's greatest foe.'[18] Voltaire's reputation has, if anything, grown, over time, but the obscurity in which Volney now languishes would have been surprising to the revolutionaries of the 1790s.

Volney's New Age was to be new but was free of the metaphysical overtones employed by the English radical and artist, William Blake (1757–1827). For Blake, the late eighteenth century was in dire need of rescue from the effects of over-rationalization. 'Perhaps there never was a period', he wrote, 'in any Age of the World, which required a Vindication and Elucidation of the Divine Providence of the Lord, more than the present.'[19] Full of fervour, and perhaps influenced by Volney, he issued the following inspirational challenge to the nation's youth in 1804: 'Rouze up, O Young Men of the New Age!'[20] In his great poem 'Jerusalem', he expanded his expectations of the coming world: people would gaze out to explore 'Eternal Worlds', he hoped, even as they turned inwards to discover new 'Worlds of Thought'; finally, simultaneously pursuing the inner and outer quests, they would unite, through the Imagination, with the God of Love.[21]

Blake's use of the phrase 'New Age' was influenced by his knowledge of Swedenborg's writings – as well as by Volney's. He certainly had contact with Swedenborgians in London, although claims that he was a member of the New Church are almost certainly exaggerated, for he was far too independent-spirited to join other people's organizations. He actually took a violent dislike to Swedenborg's work on two grounds.[22] First was that Swedenborg's supposedly new ideas were not new at all but rehashed millennial esotericism. Even his journeys to other planets had a deep lineage in magic and esotericism dating back to the ancient world.[23] In *The Marriage of Heaven and Hell*, Blake referred to Swedenborg as a fraud, as a man living amongst monkeys; wiser than the monkeys, certainly, but no more so than any other wise man. 'Thus Swedenborg', Blake wrote, 'boasts that what he writes is new; though it is only the Contents and Index of already published books'.[24] Blake was undoubtedly a fellow traveller, captivated by the notion of inner transformation as a necessary precondition for social revolution but on the detail, he insisted, Swedenborg was plain wrong. Secondly, Blake complained, Swedenborg only spoke to angels, as a result of which he received only partial truths. The Swedenborgian New Age followed Hermetic teachings that the cosmos is essentially benign and that humanity is evolving to the light and to a state of blessed spirituality. Blake took a radically different view: one cannot know Heaven, he insisted, unless one knows Hell and has talked with the Devil. Blake's view was to remain a minority one amongst esotericists until it was introduced into the psychedelic culture of the 1960s by the writers Allen Ginsberg and Aldous Huxley.

The quest for the light was to be a dominant motif, especially in the United States, where the Swedenborgian church retained an influential presence. It contributed to what has been referred to as a 'golden age' of American utopianism from the 1810s to 1840s; the theosophical, pietist Christian communities established at the time ranged from the Society of Separatists at Zoar in Ohio, founded in 1817, to the Bishop Hill community in Illinois, which was established in 1846.[25] The background to this so-called golden age lay in traditions of millenarian Christianity which recurred in waves of renewal, beginning with the English Civil War and Republican period of the 1640s–1650s and continuing throughout the eighteenth century.[26]

We now talk of successive periods of evangelical, millenarian enthusiasm as 'Awakenings'. Conventional wisdom identifies a 'First Great Awakening' that occurred in England and America in the 1730s and 1740s, led by the charismatic preachers John Wesley and George Whitfield in England and Jonathan Edwards in the American colonies.[27] The Second Great Awakening supposedly occurred in the United States from 1800 to 1845.[28] A third Awakening lasted from the mid-nineteenth century to the 1900s, and a fourth began in the 1960s.

The notion of distinct Awakenings is actually an artefact of an overeager tendency to identify neat historical periods, all with clearly defined beginnings and endings, playing down evidence for continuity. Rather, there is a constant flow of biblical preachers exhorting all people, both sinners and the faithful, to cleanse their souls and prepare for the coming Kingdom of God. Such evangelical movements are essentially democratic, driven by whoever is the most effective preacher of the moment, judged by whoever can muster the greatest popular following. Improvisational millenarianism pays little heed to authorized theology and breaks rules wherever it finds them. The attempt to draw tight demarcating chronological lines between successive Awakenings is ultimately doomed, for the strands of thought and belief that were predicated on Christ's imminent return never disappear. The prophecies in the Book of Revelation are perpetual; they always exist in the present and are applicable to any circumstances.[29]

The feelings stirred up by millenarian preachers were reported by the poet and Quaker John Whittier in his highly censorious survey of 'supernatural' groups in New England in 1847. Whittier's disapproval aside, his work is a valuable record of a culture which was deeply syncretic, drawing indiscriminately on a wide range of beliefs and practices, from Native American to Christian. Whittier was no fonder of corrupt, capitalist, secular America than of corrupt, devout, religious United States. But he saved most of his righteous anger for the latter. He discovered what he called 'a spiritual activity – an undercurrent of intense, earnest thought…a capacity of faith in its most transcendental possibilities', of which he approved, but also 'no infrequent traces of the Old Superstition – that dark theory of the Invisible World, in which our Puritan ancestors had united the wild extravagance of Indian tradition with the familiar and common fantasies of their native land…'[30] Whittier painted a vivid picture of nineteenth-century rapture culture. He observed the hysteria of the Millerites, who attracted huge support in the 1840s after their leader, William Miller, predicted Christ's second coming for 22 October 1844, waiting for the apocalypse at Boston's 'Temple of the Second Advent'.[31] He saw alongside the Millerites the devotion of the Transcendentalists, who awaited the millennium at 'nightly gatherings of the "Disciples of Newness"'; both Millerites and Transcendentalists, Miller noted, longed for the 'down-rushing of the fiery mystery of the Apocalypse'.[32] The Millerites sprang out of a Christian tradition while the Transcendentalists were Platonists; yet for Whittier, what they shared was far more important than what separated them. And anyone, Whittier noted, could announce themselves as a prophet of the End Times. Quoting lines from an unnamed poem to make his point, he wrote that we can all:

Listen to our own fond thoughts
Until they seem no more as Fancy's children;
Yea, put them on a prophet's robe, endow them
With prophet-voices;[33]

Whittier could equally have travelled in England where he could have encountered Mary Ann Girling. She was born in Suffolk in 1827 and died in 1886 after a prophetic career which took her from her original revelation in 1858 to involvement with the 'Peculiar People' and the 'New Forest Shakers'.[34] Communal living, ecstatic worship and disregard for authority was familiar: the evangelical world was democratic, spontaneous and offered ordinary people a route to self-assertion in a world in which most still had no political rights. The poor, the farmers and the labourers could all find a voice to protest against their oppression by framing their opposition to the political order in the language of Biblical prophecy.

There was no binary opposition between Christian and non-Christian forms of millenarian thought.[35] Esotericism is itself descended in part from the Platonic-influenced free-thinking Lutherans of the sixteenth to seventeenth centuries as well as from deeply embedded Gnostic traditions in which the individual's personal relationship with God trumps all official theology and hierarchies.[36] There was also, throughout the esoteric world, a deep respect for the 'cosmic Christ' – the non-human Christ seen as one of a series of prophetic manifestations of the divine. Liberated by the Reformation, Gnostic conceptions of the direct, inner relationship with God once again began to flourish.

In this context the 'Awakening' of the early nineteenth century included an additional significant esoteric current already noted by Whittier – Transcendentalism. This philosophy was most closely associated with Ralph Waldo Emerson and Henry Thoreau, and began in 1836 as a reforming movement within Unitarian Christianity.[37] The term Transcendentalist was initially used in a critical attack on the new movement, but has become the accepted description, partly because Emerson himself adopted it in 1842, at the same time as he identified the movement's principal inspiration as Kant's Idealism.[38] Like the Swedenborgians, the Transcendentalists themselves often used other terms which were deliberately intended to convey novelty, including the 'New School' or 'Disciples of Newness'. Transcendentalist doctrine was announced in Emerson's manifesto, *Nature*, published in 1849. He opened with his Romantic proclamation of a new world:

Our age is retrospective. It builds the sepulchres of the fathers... The foregoing generations beheld God and nature face to face; we, through their eyes. Why should not we also enjoy an original relation to the universe? Why should not we have a poetry and philosophy of insight and not of tradition, and a religion by revelation to us, and not the history of theirs? Embosomed for a season in nature, whose floods of life stream around and through us, and invite us by the powers they supply, to action proportioned to nature, why should we grope among the dry bones of the past, or put the living generation into masquerade out of its faded wardrobe? The sun shines to-day also. There is more wool and flax in the fields. There are new lands, new men, new thoughts. Let us demand our own works and laws and worship.[39]

Emerson's Christian Platonism was theosophical with a small 't' in that Christ was seen as one great prophet amongst many, and inclined to Stoicism in the sense that Nature and Spirit were considered pretty much coincident. The individual was therefore fully integrated with the life-world, a perfect combination of nature and spirit, a tiny part of the grand totality of the universe. There is more than a touch of Thomas Paine in the way he talks about nature: 'it never wears a mean appearance', he wrote, and 'never becomes a toy to a wise spirit'.[40] In both Platonic and Stoic philosophies, as Emerson understood, the cosmos is 'a living being, rational, animate and intelligent'.[41] One of the Transcendentalists' central religious duties was to live in harmony with Nature and so be fit to express its Spirit through Reason and the imagination. Emerson and his friends had no concern with the prophecy of a coming era. Rather, they believed the world was already perfect; all one had to do, they thought, was wake up and realize its beauty. Entry into paradise was therefore a Swedenborgian matter of individual choice rather than historical necessity. If 'Thought' with a capital 'T' was the cardinal principle of Transcendentalism, then all improvement in the world proceeded from an ability to truly think.[42] The revolution began with the self and would then spread to the whole of society. This did not mean, though, that the Transcendentalists withdrew from political activity. Far from it: Emerson was a passionate abolitionist. But it did mean that political action for its own sake, devoid of inner change, was essentially pointless.

The term 'new age', in lower case, is a commonplace which need not imply an approaching spiritual paradise. Esler records a student revolutionary looking back on the upheavals of 1815 in Göttingen, recalling, in terms which Volney would have understood that 'A new age was about to begin', but without any necessity for this to be one of the spirit.[43] By the middle of the nineteenth century, the use of the term New Age had crossed the boundaries between mainstream Christianity, Swedenborgianism, spiritualism and psychical research and theosophy. The term New Age, with capital letters, was first heavily promoted by Warren Felt Evans (1817–1889). Evans began his pastoral career as a Methodist minister but joined the Swedenborgian Church of the New Jerusalem in 1863. He also became deeply involved in the New Thought movement, which flourished in the United States from the mid-nineteenth century.[44] New Thought saw itself partly as a Christian reforming movement, restoring the purity of the early, pre-Constantinian church and considered God to be universal and imminent. And, if matter is permeated with divinity, the conclusion is that the cure to all medical problems lies in divine healing – hence Mary Baker Eddy's Christian Science, which emerged as an offshoot of New Thought and which argued that as all disease is of spiritual origin, so is the cure. Her Platonism was quite clear: 'God is incorporeal, divine, supreme, infinite Mind, Spirit, Soul, Principle, Life, Truth, Love', and, with italics for emphasis, '*God is Mind, and God is infinite; hence all is Mind*'.[45] Significant for

New Thought, as for all New Age thought, is the composition of the Platonic cosmos primarily of psyche, which we may translate as soul or, better, as consciousness. Like Transcendentalism, New Thought took the view that inner transformation could be combined with political activism; its overwhelmingly white, middle-class advocates drifted towards anti-capitalist socialist politics and social activism, engaging with such issues as homelessness and reform of the legal system.[46]

The term New Age achieved its first major outing in esoteric circles when Evans launched his spiritualist paper, appropriately called *The New Age* in the 1850s, followed by a short book, *The New Age and Its Message,* in 1864.[47] This was both a manifesto for the coming era and a handy introduction for the curious seeker. Evans located the New Age in the double meaning of enlightenment – first, as a blessing of the spiritual sun and second, of the enlightenment of the intellect via science.[48] He presented Swedenborg as a mainstream Christian reformer, with the New Age as the Joachite third, spiritual, peaceful Age, that of the Holy Ghost; the evidence of its approach was the current state of moral darkness which he saw all around him: the world was in a state of pre-millennial crisis. The coming transformation, he forecast, would be political but only in that political authorities the world over will acknowledge the authority of the new dispensation:

> The kings of the earth shall contribute their spiritual wealth to the New Jerusalem.
> In all churches there are stray beams of light that came from the sun of the New Age.[49]

While New Age ideology was being developed by the Transcendentalists in the United States, in the UK, meanwhile, the work of the French radicals Dupuis, Bailly and Delaunaye found a ready audience. Dupuis' work finally appeared in English translation as *Was Christ a person or the sun? An argument from Dupuis* (1857), *Christianity a form of the great solar myth* (1873) and *On the connection of Christianity with solar worship* (trans. T.E. Partridge, 1877). The first of Dupuis' English translations appeared in the aftermath of the row over Robert Chambers' *Vestiges of the Natural History,* which challenged creationist theories that the Earth was only 6,000 years old.[50] It appeared just two years before Darwin's *Origin of Species* (published in 1859) and provided a scientific foundation for evolution. Dupuis' work therefore played a very small part in the much wider controversy over who had the right to speak about the age of the Earth. Chambers had encountered serious criticism from contemporary Christian millenarians, who objected to a scientist dealing with matters – the beginning and end of the Earth – which were the preserve of theologians.[51] Various divines and preachers who believed that the End Times were appearing in 1840s saw *Vestiges* as part of an atheist attempt to establish the sciences as independent of scripture and so challenge Biblical prophecies of Christ's return.[52]

Dupuis himself considered that conventional religion's fundamental error was to mistake astronomical allegory for religious truth. He claimed that ancient fables were 'a veil thrown over the operations of nature', in which anthropomorphic deities obscured the natural phenomena which were worshipped by the earliest people.[53] In the distant past, he wrote, people had revered the sun for its life-bringing qualities, its light and heat, but later, male sun gods were created, one of whom was Christ. The veil metaphor was to prove particularly attractive with its attendant notions of secrecy and occult knowledge and passed to H.B. Blavatsky's *Isis Unveiled*, published in 1877, via Godfrey Higgins' *Anacalypsis* (from the Greek 'unveiling'), published between 1833 and 1836, J.C. Colquhoun's *Isis Revelata*, which appeared in 1836, and W. Winwoode Reade's *The Veil of Isis*, published in 1861. This is classic occultism, resting in the belief that true knowledge is hidden from view but can be discovered by adepts with sufficient spiritual or intellectual capacity. The veil is pierced only by the inner quest, via introspection, meditation, divination or ritual magic. Knowledge of history and of the coming era is therefore also available via esoteric revelation, even if supported by, mainly Christian, sacred texts.

Dupuis' ideas were propagated by his English followers. The anticlerical deist (and former Tory MP and diplomat), Sir William Drummond (1770?–1828), published his summary of Dupuis' theories in his best-known work, *The Oedipus Judaicus*, published in 1811. He was followed by the antiquarian Samson Arnold Mackey who, in 1822, published the *Mythological Astronomy of the Ancients Demonstrated*, in which he expounded at great length on the mythological significance of changes in the stars' location.[54] Whereas Drummond and Mackey avoided causing offence to established religion, the Reverend Robert Taylor (1784–1844), took a radical and confrontational line. Taylor was a convinced anti-Christian deist who discovered Dupuis' work in 1829 on his release from prison after serving a sentence for blasphemy. Twenty-eight years later, he gathered many of his sermons into a collection under the title *The Devil's Pulpit: or Astro-theological Sermons*. In this he reproduced his sermon on Easter Sunday 1831, in which he had enacted a parody of the Eucharist and claimed that the blood of Christ represented the sun's loss of power at the Autumn equinox. For this offence Taylor was returned to gaol on further blasphemy charges. Taylor did not mince his words. In his sermon on the Star of Bethlehem, which he had delivered on 7 November 1830 in the Rotunda on London's Blackfriars Road, he denounced the Bible as an astronomical/zodiacal allegory and Christianity, as 'stupid' and 'ignorant' for failing to recognize its own origins.[55] Elaborating on William Jones, the orientalist whose views in the origin of religion had influenced Turner, he wrote:

> Sun and Day were found in the first primitives, not of a particular language, but of the most ancient and universal ever uttered by men. San, pronounced Zan, Zon, Son, and Zun, that is, with every vowel, and every mode of uttering the initial, that the tongue could encompass, like Gad, Gid, Ged, God and Gud, was, like the word, the common Ammonian name, for the Sun and Jupiter.[56]

Once it was recognized that all deities were solar, Taylor argued, and that Christ was the same as all other solar gods, including Heracles, Bacchus, Mithras, Apollo, Krishna and Vishnu, Christianity would finally collapse.

Taylor, in turn, was followed by another radical deist and a keen supporter of Bailly, Dupuis and Drummond, Godfrey Higgins (1772–1833).[57] Higgins thought that the pre-millennial crisis was near; he worried that 'perhaps man is near his end', but he looked forward to a coming 'new aera'.[58] His significance lay in the sheer size and reach of his work in the huge two-volume *Anacalypsis*. Published in 1836, it became the well-known standard work on the solar origins of religion and the developing ideas of the stars' relationship to history: paraphrasing Taylor, he wrote, 'the history of the sun is the history of Jesus Christ'.[59] He then began to put into place a key idea of what was to become an unquestioned feature of Aquarian Age ideology – that forms of solar worship change with the astrological ages. When the sun was in Taurus, the sign of the Bull, at the spring equinox, from 4700 BCE onwards, he wrote, gods were worshipped as Bulls; when it entered Aries, ram-headed gods were in vogue, while Christianity, symbolized by the Fish, was connected with Pisces.[60] The shift in thought that is taking place here is interesting. The argument that all religions are equally meaningless because they are all mistaken expressions of astronomical motions gradually alters into the belief that in their essence they are all equally meaningful.

The unification of New Age millenarianism with Aquarian Age historiography took place via the Theosophical Society.[61] The Society's foundation in 1875 in New York by Petrovna Blavatsky (1831–1891) and the former Unionist army officer Henry Steel Olcott (1832–1907) marked a seminal moment in the history of the modern New Age movement. For the first time all previous esoteric and millenarian strands of thought, with their competing theories of inner revolution and historical change, were brought together in 1875 in a single institution. The Society's ancestry also lay in a solid tradition of utopian activism and it constituted a moment of Awakening as substantial as any of the more conventional evangelical Christian movements: the key to spiritual development, Blavatsky argued, following Mary Baker Eddy's Gnostic Platonism, is the 'awakening of the inner man'.[62] Blavatsky's influence proved more enduring than Olcott's, mainly because she composed the Society's manifesto in her two substantial works, *Isis Unveiled* and *The Secret Doctrine*, so she remains the better known of the two.[63] Blavatsky's political goal was spelled out very clearly. She wished to form a body of people who, by studying and practicing ancient wisdom, could prepare the world for the imminent shift into a new historical era. The Society provided an institutional framework which attracted like-minded thinkers from across the esoteric, occult and magical worlds of the late nineteenth century. It established branches, known after the Masonic custom as Lodges, in every country it reached, from the United States in the west, to most European states, and India in the east, all linked together in a federal structure. It was democratic, emphasized gender equality and encouraged scholarly study and so appealed to all those middle-class people who craved education, social reform and the right to self-determination and hoped that the world might become a better place, but rejected revolutionary socialism. In Theodor Adorno's phrase, her followers were 'semi-erudite'; they loved learning; were self-taught; were usually unable to go to university for reasons of money or social status; and frequently deviated from orthodox scholarly opinion.[64]

Blavatsky's genius lay in her synthesis of western occulture, to use Christopher Partridge's phrase, from its ancient philosophical – Neoplatonic – and magical traditions to more recent ones, such as spiritualism, with eastern, especially Indian, teachings. Her way had been prepared by the networks already established by the Swedenborgians, Christian Scientists and Transcendentalists, who had stimulated the thirst for the new, the mysterious and the spiritual but, as Robert Ellwood pointed out, had failed to completely satisfied it.[65] The Society brought together various undercurrents which were already thriving in the middle of the century, including esoteric Christianity, millennial belief, fascination for the orient and spiritualism, which seemed to offer proof of survival after death.

It is difficult to identify any originality in Blavatsky's thought. She was a synthesizer, skilled in what Claude Lévi-Strauss defined as bricolage, the recycling of ideas, images and objects to create a new mythological synthesis.[66] The Society's influence resided in Blavatsky's skill as a performer; her creation of a system which seemed to contain all one need know about the self and the soul; and the nature of time, history and the universe. She popularized two principles. First, the universe is Idealistic, in a Platonic sense, seeing consciousness rather than matter as the primary substance of the universe. Second, the current period of history is the low point of an outgoing phase, the Indian *kali yuga*, and we stand on the brink of a new era of heightened spiritualty.

Blavatsky's historical theory was influenced by the French radicals, and she had read Volney, Bailey and Dupuis, as well as Plato.[67] Citing Hegel, whose theories of history, Blavatsky noted, had 'their application in the teachings of Occult science', she set out her theory of cyclical history, in which complex patterns of cycles regulate a cosmos in which physical evolution is dependent on spiritual evolution.[68] In her own words:

> The revolution of the physical world, according to the ancient doctrine, is attended by a like revolution in the world of intellect – the spiritual evolution of the world proceeding in cycles, like the physical one.
>
> Thus we see in history a regular alternation of ebb and flow in the tide of human progress.

Blavatsky set out the broad structure of history in *Isis Unveiled*. Following Hindu cosmology, she argued for an infinite series of universes, punctuated by points of destruction and rebirth. The cyclical process involves an initial descent from a state of pure spirituality to the current phase of gross materiality, followed by a return to pure spirit, the beginning of which is imminent. When the cycle of existence finally climaxes, the entire universe will dissolve. All humans will either escape from the cycle of existence into nirvana or will commence a 'new cycle of transformations', each of which is so profound as to practically constitute an entry into 'a new world'.[69] The Theosophical utopia, like ecologism, wishes human beings out of existence, prophesying that eventually they will exist only as pure spirit. And like Nietzsche's philosophy, it follows the Stoic doctrine of eternal recurrence, in which history never comes to an end. Or, rather, as it ends, so it begins again. Nietzsche's examination of eternal recurrence in *Thus Sprach Zarathustra* was written in 1883–1885, midway between *Isis Unveiled* and *The Secret Doctrine*. He was inspired by Persian ideas and veers into nihilism and despair, in contrast to Blavatsky's message of hope, but his effect was to reinforce notions of historical cycles as so impossibly huge and inevitable that the individual has no choice but to assist history on its way. People and the universe being one and the same, our fate is sealed. 'All these years resemble one another', he wrote, 'so that we resemble ourselves in each great year'.[70]

Blavatsky, by popularizing the drift of the millenarian experience towards inner transformation, satisfied emerging ideas of the self. Her contribution to culture, pretty much laying the foundations for New Ageism as a movement, was to provide an institutional framework for study, lectures and publishing. In 1900, there were around seventy-one branches of the Theosophical Society in the United States, and the international network extended across Europe and into India. Its membership was never great – it peaked at around 45,000 in 1929. But its influence was spread via its members and fellow travellers, including the classical scholar G.R.S. Mead, the poet W.B. Yeats and the abstract artists, Wassily Kandinsky, Paul Klee and Piet Mondrian.

Blavatsky was writing within a much wider utopian context, which included such towering figures as Leo Tolstoy. Isaiah Berlin described the European-wide phenomenon sympathetically:

> Their approach seemed to me essentially moral: they were most concerned with what was responsible for injustice, oppression, falsity in human relations, imprisonment whether by stone walls of conformism – unprotesting submission to man-made yokes – moral blindness, egoism, cruelty, humiliation, servility, poverty, helplessness, bitter indignation, despair, on the part of so many ... And conversely they wished to know what would bring about the opposite of those, a reign of truth, love honesty, justice, security, personal relations based on the possibility of human dignity, decency, independence, freedom, spiritual fulfilment.[71]

Blavatsky had nothing to say about the Aquarian Age, preferring Hindu ages. It was up to her contemporary, the poet, Chartist and spiritualist Gerald Massey (1828–1907), whom she much admired, to take Higgins' work forward and for the first time develop the Age's meaning and character.[72] Massey was as bitterly anti-Christian as the French radicals and held true to their anticlerical principles. By distorting its true astronomical nature, he argued, Christianity had turned the sun from a symbol of life to one of death. In his opinion, paraphrasing Dupuis, and with an obvious reference to Darwin:

> The Christian religion is responsible for enthroning the cross of death in heaven ... (and had) taught man to believe that the vilest spirit may be washed white, in the atoning blood of the purest, offered up as a bribe to an avenging God. The Christian Cult has fanatically fought for its false theory and waged incessant warfare against Nature and Evolution.[73]

Massey set out his ideas in detail in three books. In *The Coming Struggle* (1873), he discussed the contemporary meaning of the apocalyptic texts in Ezekiel and Daniel, and in *The Natural Genesis* (1883) and *The Hebrew and Other Creations* (1887), he set out a theory of history which combined the French radicals with Plato's Great Year and Blavatsky's belief in successions of world saviours. He claimed that each time the sun rose at the spring equinox in a new zodiac sign, which happened around every 2,000 years, a prophet appeared who took on the qualities of that sign – a Taurean prophet under Taurus, an Arien one under Aries and so on.[74] And then he added the prophecy that a new messiah will be born again who 'will be … fulfilled when the Equinox enters the sign of the Waterman [Aquarius] around the end of this century'.[75] This, in 1887, just ninety-five years after Delaunaye's work was published, marks the beginning of belief in the coming Aquarian Age as one of religious reform.

The Theosophical Society's unifying tendencies produced their own internal contradictions as different groups struggled to make their voices heard. From the outset, the late 1870s and early 1880s witnessed a tension in the Society between the 'easterners', for whom Indian teachings were paramount, and the 'westerners', who placed a higher value in western wisdom, including esoteric Christianity.[76] In 1879, Blavatsky and Olcott moved to India and in 1880 they converted to Buddhism, both of which decisions greatly discomforted the western-leaning members of the Society. The westerners initiated a series of schisms that eventually debilitated the Society itself, but in the process they revitalized the developing New Age movement. The western counter-movements were not hostile to the East per se but argued that the western tradition, to which they owed their allegiance, should not be subservient to it. The three most significant western organizations were the Hermetic Society, founded by Anna Kingsford and Edward Maitland in 1884; the Hermetic Brotherhood of Luxor which assumed a public role in the same year; and the Hermetic Order of the Golden Dawn, which was established in 1888. Kingsford and Maitland in particular shared a sense of millenarian longing and set about the task of disseminating esoteric wisdom with an urgency derived from their belief that the coming era, 'The Age of Michael', which was associated with the Aquarian Age, had been inaugurated in 1880–1881. The definitive description of the Age of Michael, which directly links nineteenth-century ideas to Renaissance Hermeticism, was given in a text issued to its members by the Hermetic Brotherhood of Luxor. The Brotherhood's revolutionary intent was clear: the 'Age of Michael'

> will be a period of Imperial Greatness, Empires will shine full of glory, the Human intellect will have full play and all Churches, Religious Creeds and Ecclesiastical Dogmas will fall to the ground and become things of the past. Parsons, Vicars and Bishops will have to work in different fields if they mean to obtain an honest livelihood. Yes, I repeat this prophecy. The Churches and Chapels will fall with a terrible crash, and be destroyed. But from their ashes, Phoenix-like, shall arise a new Religion, whose shining Motto will be: Veritas Excelsior, Truth Above. This era shall proclaim the rights of man. It is essentially the age of reason dreamed of by [Giordano Bruno] Bruno and Thomas Paine.[77]

Aside from the prophecy of Imperial greatness, which was somewhat at odds with the Age of Aquarius' normal egalitarian character but coincided comfortably with European powers 'scramble for Africa', the manifesto's Jacobin tone is unmistakeable and its claim to the legacy of the Age of Reason clear. The Hermetic Brotherhood's statement set the model for all future descriptions of the Aquarian Age as one of religious and spiritual revolution. Although the Hermetic Brotherhood's prophecy envisaged the destruction of the old church, the new religion was heavily influenced by Swedenborgian, Christian esotericism.

The theosophical prophecy that a new period of history was imminent required, within the framework of Popperian activism, a social and political programme which would facilitate its smooth inauguration. The culture of expectation they embodied produced in their followers a devout belief in the coming historical transformation. From the moment of its foundation in 1875, The Theosophical Society fulfilled this purpose, having a clear mission to prepare for the coming of the New Age through organized activity, primarily spiritual activity and education. The Theosophists and their fellow esotericists constituted an adversary culture, a counterculture whose aim was to hasten the end of the power structures of the entire world. They formed a revolutionary vanguard, a cohort of spiritual Bolsheviks committed to the foundation of their paradise, which would be for all people, not just the proletariat. Better, it required no violence nor personal sacrifice, only personal meditation and study.

New Age and Transcendence
in the Twentieth Century

The passage from the nineteenth to the twentieth century was a time of self-conscious awareness of the transition from one time to another. The calendar assumed a metaphysical quality and the last years of the nineteenth century brought a sense, not of the winding down of the old, as might be expected, but an excited anticipation of the future. The 1890s were mythologized while they were actually happening as years which combined social upheaval, political radicalism and artistic experimentation, much of which was overlaid with a self-conscious decadence and an overwhelming sense of the new.[1] The term fin de siècle itself was coined in 1888 and initially was widely to taken to indicate a sense of decline, of lamentation for the end of progress and fear of the future.[2]

Many who considered themselves part of the avant-garde were aware that they were living at a special time, and fin de siècleism as an 'ism' was in general use by 1894, before the decade was even half-way through. The myth of the 1890s as a transformational decade is apparent from the description by Jackson Holbrook, one of the period's foremost cultural commentators:

> It was an era of hope and action. People thought anything might happen; and, for the young, anything sufficiently new was good … It was a time of experiment. Dissatisfied with the long ages of convention … many set about testing life for themselves. The new man wished to be himself, the new woman threatened to live her own life … young men and maidens were suddenly inspired to develop their own souls and personalities. Never, indeed was there a time when the young were so young or the old so old.[3]

The culture of hope and expectation identified by Jackson in the 1890s continued into the 1900s and beyond, carried by the esoteric millenarianism disseminated by various theosophical and esoteric movements.[4] Just over a century after the French revolution, the legacy of Baily, Dupuis and Delaunaye merged seamlessly with Swedenborg's, in the recognizably modern, self-confident New Age movement. The emphasis, inherited from nineteenth-century millenarianism, tended to be strongly

Christian to the extent that it may be considered an 'Awakening': the main propagandists clearly saw their task as to awaken humanity from its materialistic slumber.

The slaughter of the First World War from 1914 to 1918 was a shattering event in European culture as a whole, but New Age ideas seem to have continued undisturbed, perhaps because the millenarian mentality incorporates catastrophe into its expectations. In 1919 Horatio Dresser, the New Thought writer, referred to the war's impact: 'The great war', he wrote, 'came as a vivid reminder that we live in a new age ... one of various signs of a new dispensation.'[5] The war, he added, provided a salutary lesson that the naïve optimism that was prevalent before 1914 was no longer sufficient. Instead, he advocated a renewed emphasis on the use of science only for moral purposes and the development of the higher – psychic and psychological – sciences. This never happened, though, and in practice there appears to have been little change in New Age belief or behaviour from the pre-war to the post-war world.

The mood in the 1920s, much like that in the 1890s and 1900s, remained conducive to notions of new worlds.[6] Theosophy and its related esoteric and magical currents were firmly embedded in a wider 'alternative' culture which combined Bohemian lifestyles, a belief in self-development and such ethical choices as vegetarianism, on which Theosophists were especially keen. As Virginia Nicholson wrote in her study of British Bohemians: '(Vegetarianism) was further propagated in the 1920s by the influential New Agers of the day, the Theosophists and Transcendentalists' who believed it was essential for both health and enlightenment.[7]

Theosophical hope flourished within a wider context, and optimism for a better future came in a variety of forms. We might look further for evidence of millenarian hope: Eric Hobsbaum considered the case of the Marxist-inclined 'red scientists' whose enthusiasm and intellectual quest was all the more convincing because 'they knew themselves to be living in times of extraordinary change'.[8] Those of a millenarian disposition could make their choice between different methods of overthrowing capitalism. They could either support an extension of the Bolshevik revolution across Europe or line up behind Mussolini's Fascists or, later, the Nazis. A third choice, the New Age option, required inner transformation and with no overt challenge to the institutions of state and economic power. The numbers actively engaged in groups such as the Theosophical Society were small (a peak of 45,000 around the world in 1929), and in magical groups like the Golden Dawn, were negligible. Yet they punched well above their weight in the arts, so their cultural significance is greater than one might expect and deserved more of a mention than Jackson gave them.

The range of prophetic emblems employed to designate the transition into the new world was inherited from nineteenth-century esotericism: the Aquarian Age, the Age of the Archangel Michael or the Indian Yugas, the great ages of Hindu mythology. Around 1925–1928, W.B. Yeats put substance to the Theosophical version with his own elaborate version mathematically regulated and vision of eternal recurrence as analogous to the phases of the moon.[9] Earlier he had appeared to lose hope in his poem 'The Second Coming', written in the wake of the war:

> Things fall apart; the centre cannot hold;
> Mere anarchy is loosed upon the world.[10]

The early twentieth century was to see a series of charismatic teachers develop these millenarian motifs, chiefly Rudolf Steiner (1861–1925), Carl Gustav Jung (1875–1961) and Alice Bailey (1880–1949). The first, though, was Aleister Crowley, often known as the century's most infamous occultist. Crowley was born in 1875, the year that the Theosophical Society was founded, and died in 1947, but his popularity has remained persistently high. His ongoing fame is due in part to his supposed notoriety (summed up in the title of the 1971 biography by John Symonds, *The Great Beast*), accompanied by his own accounts of orgiastic and drug-fuelled behaviour but also to his forthright opinions and the lucid, uncluttered nature of much of his writing.[11] Crowley's inclinations directly clashed with the sobriety of the Theosophical Society and its followers. However, his vision of a new global religion; his understanding of all great prophets as manifestations of a single essence; and his desire to restore the west by teaching the east to the west mark him out as an heir to Blavatsky. He also established his own organization, the Ordo Templi Orientis, or OTO, in order to propagate his teachings. He exerted a peculiar fascination for the decadent rock and roll world of the 1960s, appeared on the cover of the Beatles' *Sgt. Pepper's Lonely Hearts Club Band* in 1967 and, looking back from 1980, the psychedelic proselytiser Timothy Leary identified his own work in preparing the world for cosmic consciousness as an extension of Crowley's beliefs.[12]

Crowley's esotericism was by and large unoriginal. However, his most important contribution to New Age thought was to provide a statement of universal rights. He first formulated his famous aphorism 'Do what thou wilt shall be the whole of the law', followed by the rider 'Love is the law, love under will', in 1904.[13] But then, in 1941, seven years before the United Nations composed its own Universal Declaration of Human Rights, he asserted the following non-negotiable rights: to live, work, play, die, eat, travel, write, speak and love without restriction.[14] Crowley's challenge to a world dominated by imperialism and dictatorship was clear. Fascism was to be rejected, as were all forms of socialism and communism, along with the great European empires. The state in its entirety was ruled illegitimate. He argued for complete freedom of travel and of expression and anticipated much later arguments for gay rights and the right to die. The militant, and somewhat jarring, conclusion to his list of natural rights was the right to kill anyone who repressed one's own rights. Having painted a picture of a gentle world of peace and love, Crowley then legitimized revolutionary violence. His utopia might easily slip from pluralism to totalitarianism, and his contribution to Enlightenment thought could encompass Jacobin terror with only a slight adjustment. However, Crowleyites in general ignore the legitimization of murder and tend to emphasize love rather than hate: there are no known examples of Crowleyites killing those who stood in their way, unless we include the possible OTO associations of Charles Manson.[15]

Crowley's own new age, which he Hellenized as the 'New Aeon', was revealed to him in Cairo on 8–10 April 1904 by a 'superior being' – not an ordinary human – whom he called 'Aiwass'. The coming period was to last for 2,000 years and just as he rejected the pacific connotations of the New Age in favour of his own New Aeon, so he named his new world the 'Age of Horus', after the saviour and solar deity of ancient Egyptian religion, rather than the more familiar Aquarian Age.[16] In the premillennial spirit of apocalyptic Christianity, Crowley forecast that the transition to the New Aeon was to be marked by war and violence. But, once that phase was over, the New Aeon was to be one of Wildean individuality. Cultural relativity was to be the order of the day, with one person's beliefs and behaviour to be the equal of all others provided that they didn't interfere with each other. Crowley, along with Oscar Wilde and other hyper-individualists, laid the foundation for the New Age 'self-ethic' – the idea that the individual was the source of all moral authority, constrained only by the higher power of love.[17] If there was such a thing as the 'Century of the Self', as the film-maker Adam Curtis has described in his documentary of the same name, it owes as much to Crowley as to Sigmund Freud.[18] However, whereas Freud saw uninhibited sexual behaviour as problematic, Crowley celebrated it. For Crowley, the boundary between liberty and licence was invisible.

The paradoxes in Crowley's philosophy were described by his disciple J.F.C. Fuller, one of the UK's leading military theorists, as 'Crowleyanity'; he summarized them as, among other things, 'Sceptical Transcendentalism ... the conscious communion with God on the part of an Atheist.'[19] Crowley's appeal was partly based on the paradoxical sense that one could believe and not believe, both take magic seriously and yet recognize the world's essential absurdity; he anticipated surrealism and Dada and has influenced, both directly and indirectly, every subsequent western magical order. He was a cultural revolutionary of the first order, taking the self-conscious decadence of the fin de siècle and turning it into a religious creed, endowing self-indulgence with divine approval.

Initially, though, Crowley was just one aspiring magician and guru in a crowded field. Commenting on the time Crowley spent in Paris in the early 1920s, John Symonds wrote: 'The world had never seen anything so amazing. The Russian Ballet and Russian bolshevism, psychoanalysis, Dadaism, were the new currents everyone wanted to talk about, not the Great Revelation in Cairo and the divinity of Aleister Crowley.'[20] Nevertheless, Crowley soon gathered around him a network of radical artists. The Argentinian painter Xul Solar is a case in point. Solar met the painter Austin Osman Spare, later described as the father of English surrealism in London in 1913.[21] Spare then introduced Solar to Crowley's *Astrum Argentinum* order and, after a period of activity in the Theosophical Society, around 1919, Solar was personally initiated by Crowley in Paris in 1924; he later went on to become a national hero in Argentina, where his memory is still revered.[22]

Apart from his promise of higher wisdom and magical power, the appeal of Crowley's system for his followers was his certainty that they were part of a new period of history. Yet the claim that this period has already begun leads to a certain anti-prophetic mentality. The full flowering of the New Aeon may still be to come, but its beginning, as with Swedenborg's New Jerusalem, now lies in the past. And, in that case, historical preparations are less important than developing one's self in order to harmonize with the new era. The lack of interest in New Age as a prophetic discourse was reflected in wider anti-prophetic trends in esoteric culture. These are represented largely by two Russian teachers, Georges Ivanovitch Gurdjieff (1866–1949) and his one-time partner, Peter D. Ouspensky (1878–1947). Gurdjieff began teaching in Russia in 1912, moved west after the revolution and acquired a circle of wealthy and well-connected students, including Countess Rothermere, wife of the UK newspaper magnate Lord Rothermere, and the writer Katherine Mansfield.

Ouspensky's major work was published in Russia between 1909 and 1917 in three books; *The Fourth Dimension, Tertium Organum* and *A New Model of the Universe*, and his work began to appear in English from around 1911. By the early 1920s he was lecturing in London; in 1924 he separated from Gurdjieff and then continued as an independent teacher until his death in England in 1947. His lectures were attended by the young writers Aldous Huxley (1894–1963), later the author of the utopian satire *Brave New World* – and the utopian *Island* – and Gerald Heard (1889–1971) who was later to be the founder of Alcoholics Anonymous. Like Blavatsky, Gurdjieff and Ouspensky promoted themselves as the heirs to a continuous tradition of secret esoteric schools and teachings which could be traced back to the ancient world. Gurdjieff despised the prophetic mysticism of the Theosophists, whom he contemptuously called 'pseudo-esotericists'.[23] And millenarianism – global transformation – was an error, he insisted: 'There is no evolution of masses', he declared, 'only of individuals'.[24]

Ouspensky, like so many utopians at the time, was also deeply influenced by Nietzchean concepts of eternal recurrence and the superman. For Ouspensky, there was little point in getting excited about the coming of a new age, as one era simply led to another in an endless sequence.[25] The crucial transformation, he said, is to be personal, not collective, and the millennial moment is now; 'A new type of man is being formed now and amongst us'.[26] Only the most backward and degenerate races were to be excused from this evolutionary transformation but, in a reversal of the normal preconceptions, he considered that it was the most advanced races, the Europeans and Americans, who were actually the most degenerate. He condemned those 'completely involved in pseudo-culture', the intelligentsia of Europe and America, those who accept blindly the claims of materialistic science and progress.[27] We would not be far off the mark if we described Ouspenskeyanism as consciously countercultural, setting itself up in explicit opposition to what was perceived as a dominant culture which had lost its soul.

The core of the Gurdjieffian system, then, was the experience of a form of enlightenment in which the individual becomes aware of their true, eternal, cosmic nature, and the stultifying, trivial, irrelevance of ordinary life is revealed.[28] And only then can a new life begin. Gurdjieff and Ouspensky both asserted their difference with Theosophy through their insistence on the primacy of individual transformation irrespective of historic change. Like Swedenborg, they believed that the new world, however defined, was to be an individual experience, and utopia could only exist wherever small groups of enlightened individuals gathered. In Theosophy, however, individual transformation was necessary in order to facilitate the inauguration of the new spiritual era; it was inclusive, egalitarian and, even though it inevitably threw up leaders, anti-elitist.

The term New Age, with capital letters, achieved wide currency, beyond the rarefied circles of the advocates of New Thought, in the aftermath of the 1890s, with the founding of the reforming socialist journal *The New Age*. The magazine itself was launched in 1907 by two independent-minded socialists, Alfred Orage and Holbrook Jackson, and published until 1938. Orage, who left in 1922 in order to join Gurdjieff's institute in Fontainebleau, was quite a figure in the literary and socialist circles of the time, to the extent that, after he went to the United States, London, it was said, lost most of its savour.[29] He was deeply familiar with all the varieties of utopianism at the time; he employed H.G. Wells as a contributor to *The New Age* and, out of a deep unease with the collective vision of state socialism, he also promoted the interests of Guild Socialism (socialism based on craft guilds, inspired by the medieval model, and promoted by William Morris) as a model for economic and industrial organization.

Announcing itself as 'an independent socialist review of politics, literature, and art', *The New Age* was firmly aligned with the Fabian Society and became the core publication for those British intellectual socialists and social reformers whose interests extended beyond politics to wider culture, the arts and literature. Its content was described as 'eclectic, provocative, often apparently inconsistent, and sometimes infuriating'.[30] Ezra Pound, then a rising star, was an early and regular contributor, and the magazine played a major role in introducing the UK to the works of Epstein, Gaudier-Brzeska, Wyndham Lewis and Pablo Picasso.[31] Esoteric and magical content was only visible at the margins via contributors such as Florence Farr, the West End actress and women's rights activist. Farr was also the mistress of George Bernard Shaw, a friend of W.B. Yeats and a leading member of the Hermetic Order of the Golden Dawn, in which role she encountered Aleister Crowley. Crowley noted Farr's critical review of J.F.C. Fuller's book *The Star of the West*, on the grounds that at least it would increase sales.[32] Crowley and Orage represented extreme poles of the New Age movement: both believed in inner transformation as an essential ingredient for the inauguration of the new dawn, but Orage believed in collective action and social justice. He supported a reform of the social contract as much Crowley rejected the concept altogether.

The New Age may have been to all intents and purposes an orthodox socialist publication of its time, but Orage's understanding of the term New Age was as esoteric as it was exoteric.[33] Orage was essentially an independent thinker. He was a long-term student of Plato, introduced Gurdjieff to the United States and was a follower of Nietzsche, but neither Theosophy, nor socialism nor the theories of Gurdjieff held complete answers for him. He had briefly been a regular lecturer for the Theosophical Society, which published his book *Consciousness* in 1907, just as *The New Age* was being launched. As Jackson put it delicately, first Orage 'fluttered the dovecotes of Theosophy', and then he distanced himself from the Society when he founded the magazine. [34] Yet he managed to find common ground in Blavatsky, Nietzche and Gurdjieff in his vision of the development of the superior human being, the transcendental Nietzchean 'superman' or the Theosophical 'seed-man', who would one day flourish in a world of political equality, economic justice and spiritual enlightenment.[35] As Jackson later recalled: 'We all developed supermania.'[36] Much later, Gerald Heard, who was around in supermaniac circles, coined the phrase 'Leptoid Man', from the Greek word *lepsis* 'to leap', to describe the new, super-evolved individual.[37]

Nietzche's übermensch is interpreted in various ways, largely because his language is often phrased in riddles.[38] He rejected transcendence and other worldly solutions to the world's problems, which means he despised theosophy. More important than what he intended, though, is the way in which his work was received in the English-speaking world as reinforcement for the idea that humanity was about to experience a leap in consciousness. At the point at which socialism and esotericism merged, there were two different conceptions of consciousness raising. While the Platonic, esoteric standpoint holds that consciousness is an entity in itself, out of which matter emerges, the Marxist, materialist, perspective is that consciousness is shaped by both biology and socio-economic circumstances, and that consciousness raising is possible but directed solely towards understanding one's political and historical circumstances, prior to becoming a true revolutionary.[39]

Two years after Holbrook and Jackson launched *The New Age*, The Theosophical Society announced that the new era was finally about to arrive. In 1909 one of the Society's leading figures, Charles Webster Leadbeater, discovered a young Brahmin, Jiddu Krishnamurti, at Adyar, the Theosophical Society's headquarters in India. Leadbeater proclaimed Krishnamurti the herald of the New Age, the prophet of the coming of the World Teacher, the Baptist to the coming Christ. Krishnamurti rapidly became the focus of a global cult. A brief-lived organization, the Order of the Rising Sun, was set up to promote him, in 1910 and replaced a year later by the much more successful Order of the Star in the East. The announcement of the Order's founding studiously avoided the use of the term 'New Age', or any of the familiar timing measures for its beginning, whether the Ages of Aquarius or Michael or the end of the Kali Yuga. Instead there was a fixation on the messianic figure of the Teacher, accompanied by the constant repetition of the word 'new'. Everything had to be new. And the success of newness centred on spiritual renewal driven by one imperative – love:

> The dawning age is one of Brotherhood. The great Teacher Himself comes to inaugurate that age. Even therefore, upon the question of His coming, there should be gentleness as tolerance shown, and not their opposites. The first propagandist in the world is love … And so, in this age as in all others, the very alphabet of the spiritual life has to be learnt anew – how hatred disappears not by hatred, but by love alone.[40]

The mood was very much one of apocalyptic revivalism. In 1911 Krishnamurti was taken to lecture in London, and by 1913 the Order had 15,000 members worldwide and was attracting media coverage. The Great War came and went and, as 1925 approached, there was a fever of anticipation that the Teacher himself was about to appear. However, the Society's messianic fervour was to inflict serious damage on it from which it has never fully recovered. The first blow came in 1912 when Rudolf Steiner, the leader of the German Theosophical Society resigned in protest at the promotion of an Indian to messianic status. Steiner founded his own organization, the Anthroposophical Society, in 1913, to carry theosophical principles forward within a western framework.[41] The second blow came ten years later when Krishnamurti himself, who was now based in Ojai in California, developed doubts about the Theosophical Society's rigid and simplistic dogma and the messianic role which the Society had foisted on him. In 1929, he helped destroy the Society as an institutional force by appearing at the Order's annual Star Camp in the Netherlands, on 3 August 1929. Promoting his aphorism 'Truth is a Pathless Land', Krishnamurti proclaimed his intention 'to make men unconditionally free' and declared that all dogma and institutions were automatically inimical to the goal of spiritual self-realization.[42]

Krishnamurti's personal charisma guaranteed him a role as one of the most important spiritual teachers of the twentieth century until his death in 1986, in spite of his own rejection of his messianic mission. He gathered a circle of friends and fellow seekers, most notably, in terms of subsequent countercultural history, Aldous Huxley, whom he met in 1938. Krishnamurti's rejection of all religious institutions, teachers and teachings included the Theosophical Society and all its offshoots, but he retained its tendency to withdraw from the world and emphasize inner change. His repeated emphasis of the word 'revolution' in his 1934 essay 'A Dynamic Society' is somewhat in tune with the fashionable communism of the time, but his insistence that only the inner revolution mattered and that political change would naturally follow was uncompromising.[43] Krishnamurti's key cultural reference was essentially Buddhist: Enlightenment, he thought, is available right here and now. In the perpetual tension between time as *kairos* (quality) and time as *chronos* (quantity), or between Being and Becoming, it was Being that mattered. Therefore, Krishnamurti concluded that in the eternal present, transformation is only possible in the now, not as time passes and not in the future.[44] In which case, millennial prophecy therefore becomes completely redundant, and belief in the New Age, the Aquarian Age and the New Jerusalem is as oppressive as belief in the Kingdom of God or the Dictatorship of the Proletariat. He completely rejected the fetishization of time evident in such notions. Krishnamurti took Swedenborg's anti-prophetic view of history but was even more militant. For Krishnamurti, the structures of millenarian prophecy did not promise freedom in the future but destroyed it in the present, and utopia, paradise and the golden age could only exist in the present as personal experience.

The new, optimistic utopian dispensation was announced by a series of other charismatic teachers. They included representatives of the Third Awakening's porous boundary between protestant millenarianism and transcendentalism, such as Levi Dowling (1844–1911), a preacher with the evangelical 'Disciples of Christ'; Emmet Fox (1886–1951), who began his career as a healer and preacher in London, moved to the United States and, in 1931, became the pastor of The Church of the Healing Christ in New York City; and the Theosophist Frank Homer Curtiss (d. 1946). Curtiss himself was an exponent of New Thought, founded the Order of Christian Mystics in 1908 and served as a minister of successive churches in Santa Barbara and Los Angeles, until he completed his career in the 1960s as head of 'the Unity Church of Dallas where he ministered to thousands from the pulpit and through his regular radio and television programs'.[45]

Whereas Dowling, Fox and Curtiss expressed their vision through churches, with an appeal to the mainstream, others preferred more informal Christian affiliations. Edgar Cayce (1877–1945), the clairvoyant and former Sunday School teacher eschewed any organizational framework and relied instead solely on the distribution of his psychic readings.[46] The German emigré Max Heindel (1865–1919) made his contribution to California's esoteric culture by founding his own organization, the Rosicrucian Fellowship, near San Diego. Alice Bailey, Steiner's equal as an enduring New Age icon, had a background in evangelical Christianity before she moved to the United States and joined the Theosophical Society in 1917. She fell out with the Society and established her own vigorous publishing and teaching outlets, the Lucis Trust in 1922, and the Arcane School in 1923. One of the most significant of the Aquarian Age millenarians, though, was Carl Gustav Jung (1875–1961) the former pupil and protégé of Sigmund Freud and, founder of Analytical Psychology. Jung's influence on the modern world is immense. Although, with the exception of lectures he delivered in his lifetime, he is almost completely ignored in the world of academic psychology, Jung's is the most significant of all the non-academic schools of counselling and psychotherapy, largely on account of his insistence that the inner life was meaningful, relevant and absolutely central to individual well-being and social stability. In particular, his theory of the collective unconscious was to provide a fresh understanding of the role of the individual in history, in the sense that great historical movements might be manifestations of disturbances in the psychic links between all members of a society. Jung's earliest brief published reference to the astrological ages was in the 1916 edition of his *Psychology of the Unconscious*, originally published in German in 1912, the same year that he split with his mentor, Sigmund Freud.[47] Millenarian optimism was in the air and it was also in 1912 that Steiner elaborated on Blavatsky's system of world ages in a series of lectures given in Helsinki in 1912, originally laid out in his *Occult Science*, published in German in 1909.[48]

The New Age movement of the 1910s and 1920s was active, vigorous and had an ability to reach those sections of the population who dissented from the current political and religious establishment but had no fondness for socialism. The figures tell the story. The Aquarian Foundation, a utopian community set up by the charismatic leader (and fraudster), Edward Wilson, also known as Brother XII, in British Columbia, had 8,000 devoted members.[49] In the 1930s, crowds of reputedly over 4,000 people packed Emmet Fox's Sunday morning lectures at the Hippodrome Theatre, the Manhattan Opera House and Carnegie Hall. Alice Bailey never counted the numbers who passed through the Arcane School, but in 1951 she estimated that 30,000 people had passed through the school and that there were 'many hundreds ... still with us'.[50] And what many of them had was the fervour born of a discovery of the truth. One of Bailey's followers was the philosopher and composer, Dane Rudhyar (1895–1985), who himself became a prolific author. Born in France, he emigrated to the United States in 1916, discovered Theosophy in 1920 and spent the rest of his life in California.[51] In 1938, Rudhyar had opened his second book with an apocalyptic proclamation of the change of the ages written in the style of a charismatic preacher:

> Today is a new birthday for the ancient gods. New men call for new symbols. Their cry rises, beyond their logical intellects ashamed of mystical longings, for new gods to worship and to use in order to integrate their harrowing mental confusion and to stabilize their uprooted souls. Young gods, fresh and radiant with the sunshine of a new dawn, glorified with the 'golden light' of a new Sun of Power, ecstatic with virgin potentialities after the banishment of ancient nightmares.[52]

Thirty years later, in the summer of 1968, Rudhyar debated the date for the beginning of the Age of Aquarius with veteran San Francisco astrologer Gavin Arthur in San Francisco's Glide Memorial Church, an event which was to mark hippy culture's mass introduction to his ideas.[53]

The New and Aquarian Age evangelists were united by their prodigious energy and literary output. Emmet Fox, for example, was a prolific author, writing around fifty books on subjects ranging from yoga and magic to the Bible and prayer. Edgar Cayce produced thousands of readings obtained in trance states from 1923 until his death, concerning the state of the universe. These were recorded and interpreted by his friend Arthur Lammers, who cast them in the framework of the Aquarian Age.[54] Rudolf Steiner and Alice Bailey also kept up a constant stream of publications and lectures throughout their lives, which were disseminated through their own publishing houses and networks of followers. It was the sheer volume of correspondence generated by her first three books – *Initiation Human and Solar* and *Letters on Occult Meditation*, both published in 1922 and *The Consciousness of the Atom*, and her classes on Blavatsky's *Secret Doctrine* – that resulted in the formation of the Arcane School in April 1923.

All the Aquarian Age teachers believed that they had a message of vital importance for humanity and their duty was to spread it. As Jung wrote in 1951: 'My conscience as a psychiatrist bids me fulfil my duty and prepare those few who will hear me for coming events which are in accord with the end of an era.'[55] There was also a definite sense of the need to create a revolutionary vanguard. Steiner's foundational lectures for the Anthroposophical Society in 1923–1924 made it clear, on behalf of the society's new members, that their purpose was to 'dedicate ourselves in selfless cultivation of the spiritual life' at the current 'turning-point of worlds'.[56] Alice Bailey's work began in earnest in 1921 when she and her husband Foster, who was secretary of the Theosophical Association of New York, formed a small meditation group 'to discuss the Plan of the Masters of the Wisdom and to meditate for a while on our part in it'.[57] There are fundamentally two groups within this wider cohort, Bailey argued. Key to her historical mission was – and still are – her own revolutionary vanguard, the New Group of World Servers, those who 'conceal and nurture the germ or seed of the new civilisation of the Aquarian Age'.[58]

The Aquarian Age is fairly simply defined as a period when humanity is due to mature. One view, from 1925, is remarkably similar to Kant's description of the Enlightenment in 1784:

> Briefly, the new age means the coming of age of the peoples of the earth, when by coordinated action, they enter their inheritance of a greater freedom of harmonious effort and individual expression.[59]

An essential part of the New Age's appeal was its imminent approach: it is necessary for the believer to live in the transitional phase.[60] Looming over everything, though, is the threat of global catastrophe. In 1925 the society clairvoyant Count Louis Hamon, writing under the pseudonym Cheiro, forecast a violent combination of political revolution, global war and natural catastrophe that would be sufficient to destroy the known world.[61] Predictions of environmental crisis considerably predate late twentieth-century concerns with climate change. However, Cheiro stressed, disaster was only inevitable if people failed to act. And this brings us to the whole point of the New Age movement: to avert global crisis through individual transformation.

For Bailey personal transformation begins with the recognition of the inner Christ, psychologized as 'master teacher', a kind of psychological 'Christ-Will', existing simultaneously inside every person and throughout the entire cosmos. When enough people contact Christ through heightened self-awareness, there will be a psychological transformation.[62] The threatened apocalyptic violence of the premillennial crisis will then be converted into postmillennial harmony, and the transition to the New Age will be peaceful. For Max Heindel, influenced by Nietzche, like Orage and Ouspensky, 'the Son of Man is the Super-Man'.[63]

At the moment at which the state of harmonious transition is reached, all distinctions between the feminine and masculine aspects of divinity are resolved. At this point, all struggle will cease, and the political competition between men and women is brought to an end.[64] For Jung, following in the spirit of William Blake, the reconciliation of opposite went wider than the end of the struggle between the feminine and the masculine. He thought that the wider metaphysical solution to the world's ills lay in the recognition that because apparent opposites share an underlying unity, good is not distinct from evil.[65] Once this is understood, human beings can begin to become self-directed, self-aware individuals, no longer at the mercy of unconscious forces. Humanity will attain a state of maturity in which collective action destined to achieve harmony between society and nature is perfectly coordinated with the development of individual expression. Curtiss forecast that 'Man should reach a point where he no longer acts like a mere child (but)...will reach a point of intellectual and spiritual development which today is reached only by a few'.[66] This democratic, evolutionary, esoteric Christian optimism set the tone for future works and such ideas, explicitly equating the Aquarian and New Ages, quickly became a commonplace in the following decades.

Political action begins with personal change. As Edgar Cayce said 'Concern yourself with the world inside you. And you will have little to concern you in the world outside you'.[67] Jung deliberately couched the question of political engagement in millenarian terms:

> This problem can be recognised neither by philosophy, nor by economics, nor by politics, but only by the individual being, via his experience of the loving spirit, whose fire descended upon Joachim.[68]

Love is part of the solution. 'Individuation', Jung's own term for the goal of his psychological system in the creation of the self-aware individual, is another.[69] Put these two together and the world will be transformed.

Emmet Fox's thoughts on the New Age were published in 1933, based on a lecture given at Victoria Hall in London on 6 September.

> The new age upon which we have now entered is called Aquarius – the Man with the Water Pot – and the Aquarian Age is going to be a completely new chapter in the history of mankind ... As a matter of fact, we are, within the not very far distant future, going to change everything in the outer world around us. Our political, social, and ecclesiastical institutions, our methods of doing our daily work, our relationships with one another, our manifold instruments of self-expression and self-discovery – all will undergo a change, a radical change, and for the better.[70]

As soon as enhanced spirituality and self-awareness had promoted the promised evolutionary leap in consciousness, the Aquarian Age was to see a complete breakdown of the current financial and political system: capitalism and national boundaries would completely disappear.[71] As William Morris proposed, the state itself will disappear and, while cultural distinctions retain all their former diversity, they will no longer be tied to the existence of the nation state.[72] And, contrary to Hobbes' brutal realism, all disputes in the future will automatically be settled peacefully. In Marxist terms, the state will wither and humanity will enter its final, communist phase of existence. Only Crowley, always the contrarian, struck an occasional ambiguous note. For example, he appeared to speak of imperialism as a natural feature of the human condition.[73] He, though, was far from typical and completely out of step with the generally egalitarian, radical tone, as well as with his own declaration of universal rights.

Aside from the changing face of religion, a number of other radical developments were to greet the dawning of the Aquarian Age, including the development of new forms of technology, the erosion of national boundaries, individualism, female emancipation and the rights of children.[74] The utopian agenda was clearly anti-imperialistic, individualistic, egalitarian and rights-driven, offering an explicit alternative to the confrontational, collectivism and totalitarianism of Marxism. The message of inner revolution was further circulated through the networks of the Swedenborgians, theosophists, spiritualists and other oppositional groups, who longed for an end to the inequality and brutalism of imperialism, capitalism and industrialization, but were not attracted to visions of class struggle and the dictatorship of the proletariat. Their millenarianism was Joachite, spiritual and based on the premise that there would be no true revolution unless people changed. Otherwise, any new order would merely replicate the old one.

While some, such as Alice Bailey, evangelized amongst their followers, Emmet Fox preached the Aquarian message to large audiences in London and New York at a time when the Soviet utopia was still regarded as a serious rival to western capitalism.

Aquarian Age thinking spread through the esoteric world. In France, Paul le Cour published his *L'Ere du Verseau* in 1937. Le Cour's historiography was by then the standard version: political and social history begins with the evolution of human consciousness, which in turn is tied to the shift of the constellations.[75] In 1947, just ten years later, The Grande Fraternité Universelle began to merge Aquarian Age ideas with theories about the history of the Americas before the arrival of the Spanish, spreading the word of the coming era though Latin America.[76] Interestingly, L. Ron Hubbard, the founder of Scientology, who was drawn into Crowley's circle in 1945, was interested in establishing this New Aeon.[77] In 1939 Olga Fröbe-Kapteyn, the founder of the Eranos meetings, lectured on the Aquarian Age at the Analytical Club in New York, one of the centres of Jungian activity in the United States.[78] Fröbe-Kapteyn was closely connected with the Theosophical Society, knew both Annie Besant, the Society's President, and Jiddu Krishnamurti, briefly the Society's prophet, and was a friend of Alice Bailey.[79] She was also closely associated with Jung, who himself was convinced that the world was experiencing unprecedented crisis, which might be standard millenarian thinking but is reasonable given his time frame – the 1930s. He alluded to the 'Utopian mass-psychoses of our time', by which he meant communism and, most likely Nazism, the psychic causes of which he had addressed in his 1936 essay 'Wotan'.[80] Like Isaiah Berlin and Karl Popper, Jung saw utopianism as a cause of humanity's ills, being essentially totalitarian and unwilling to admit alternatives.

Jung's work had an appeal to an intellectual constituency in the late twentieth century, whereas Blavatsky's was sometimes regarded as old fashioned. Jung's general appeal overlapped substantially with the theosophists' yet the general scholarly tone of his work exposed a new constituency to neo-platonic esotericism. 'If we now try to cover our nakedness with the gorgeous trappings of the East, as the theosophists do', Jung wrote, 'we would be playing our own history false'.[81] In spite of his dislike of the theosophists, his work paralleled theirs: he took the western, esoteric tradition, descended largely from Plato – and combined it with large elements of non-western teachings to produce a synthesis which claimed a universal, cosmic validity. Jung was distinguished from the theosophists by the nature of his writing. Like Blavatsky, he made extensive use of classical and renaissance sources, but with the exception of his recently published 'Red Book', he made no reference to the communication with higher intelligences which characterized so much theosophical literature. He did, however, develop his own post-Nietzchean version of the übermensch, or the Theosophical 'seed man', in an essay originally published in 1931. Jung's 'modern man' has far left behind the 'primitives', or the dismal mass of westerners and has reached such a state of consciousness that 'he stands before the Nothing out of which All may grow'.[82] His utter contempt for those who have failed to reach this advanced state is evident.

Jung's ideas were disseminated in the United States partly through a series of six visits. The first was with Freud in 1909, as one of his protégés, during which the two promoted their theory of the unconscious as the location of deep significance for the understanding of daily life. His influence on the avant-garde was reinforced by the major exhibition on 'Indian Art of the United States' in 1941 which, for the first time, promoted indigenous art on a par with the products of European culture. Jung's impact amongst artists and freethinkers in the United States in the 1930s and 1940s was substantial. His respect for non-western ways of seeing the world endeared him to critics of modern materialism, and his theory of the collective unconscious provided verification that spontaneous creativity in art could produce matter of genuine relevance to a much wider audience. For example, the painter Jackson Pollock entered Jungian analysis in 1939 and is said to have declared in 1950 that, while everyone – by which he meant all artists – was a Freudian, he had long been a Jungian.[83]

Jung's most complete work on the Aquarian Age was contained in *Aion*, the major application of psychology to history. The text was conceived between 1944 and 1947, written in 1950 and published the following year, in the shadow of the Second World War and during the critical, opening phase of the Cold War.[84] He elaborated the by now familiar idea that Christianity was the religion of the Piscean Age by arguing that the shift into Aquarius would see the internalization of the Christ-symbol.[85] In Gnostic terms, human and divine would be reunited.

Jung began work on *Aion*, five years after Fröbe-Kapteyn's speech in New York, but it was not his final thought on the matter. In 1959, he published his ideas on the then relatively new UFO phenomenon in his essay on 'Flying Saucers'. His ideas subsequently appeared in English in his Collected Works in 1964. He concluded that the question of whether they were extra-terrestrial craft was the wrong one to ask. Rather, he described their appearance as 'manifestations of psychic changes which always occur at the end of one Platonic month and the beginning of another' consisting of disturbances in what he called 'the constellation of psychic dominants or the archetypes of "gods"' arising at the beginning of the Aquarian Age.[86] This, he added was exactly what had happened in ancient Egypt, when one astrological era had given way to another. By a simple move Jung had taken Swedenborg's concept of spiritual planetary entities, married it with the current interest in flying saucers and merged the Aquarian Age with the space age. His attempt to relocate the phenomenon as a kind of psychic projection was to have a strong appeal amongst the users of psychedelic drugs from the 1960s onwards, for whom the boundary between the material and the psychic became blurred but literalism persisted. In 1964 George King, founder of the Aetherius Society, exhorted his followers to prepare for the New Age, on the basis of advice received from extra-terrestrials.[87]

Jung was a westerner, an esoteric Christian, but he engendered a huge interest in eastern teachings partly through his respect for the teachings of Buddhists and Hindus. He made a major contribution largely on account of his study of the *I Ching*, the Chinese oracle, for which he provided a mechanism 'synchronicity', or simultaneous psychic connection – or meaningful coincidence.[88] By this he meant that two events can be linked because they take place at the same time rather than because one causes the other. He added that the synchronous connection only acquired significance when it was observed, precisely the kind of claim which appealed to that species of New Age ideology which placed the individual at the centre of the universe.

In the magical milieu of the early 1960s the similarities between Jung, the high-minded esoteric Christian, and Crowley, the drug-taking, sexually promiscuous magician, counted for more than their differences. The indiscriminate application of Jung's work in 1960s 'occulture' is evident in the activities of the Esalen Institute, which was established at Big Sur in 1962, just under a three hour drive south of San Francisco. Esalen's mission, which has proved highly effective, was – and remains – to encourage self-awareness through the study and practice of eastern and western esoterica and humanistic, non-psychiatric forms of psychotherapy and analysis. In the early days this included the use of psychedelics.[89] Similarities between competing theories tended to be treated as more important than differences and the fact that Freud and Jung both advocated the exploration of the unconscious was far more important than that their views radically diverged in detail. The core mission was personal liberation.

It is difficult to disentangle Jung's influence from Bailey's, Steiner's or Crowley's, precisely because they all rationalized their historical teachings by a shared reference to varieties of Aquarian Age thinking. Crowley's lineage, at the heart of which was his proclamation of the New Aeon, was carried into Californian culture by a succession of enthusiasts through the inter war years. Notable was John Whiteside, 'Jack', Parsons, who is distinguished as one of the founders of the US space programme.[90] Parsons joined Aleister Crowley's OTO in 1941 and became master of the Agapé Lodge, based in a mansion in Pasadena which acted as a commune for Parsons and his close associates. He fell out with Crowley in 1946 and also had a brief friendship – and falling out – with L. Ron Hubbard, the founder of Scientology.[91] Parsons described the condition of humanity at the end of the Age of Osiris in despairing terms: 'Feeling himself unloved and unknowing of the way to live, Western man moves in a sterile wasteland of the mind, lacking the knowledge, understanding and will to save himself by an act of love.' All this, he hoped, was to change with the arrival of the imminent 'Age of Horus' and the inauguration of a new age religion of love. A new and better world was to come about through psychological revolution, through the self-aware recognition, and full expression, by each individual of their dual male/female nature.[92]

Parsons died in 1952, the victim of an explosion of the rocket fuel he was mixing, but he had succeeded in bringing together an assortment of artists, writers and occultists for whom Crowleyism provided a religious context which legitimized experimentation with drugs and sex. More than that, the conviction that the New Aeon was arriving supported a conviction that such behaviour was historically ordained and therefore right. The motley crew gathered around Parsons included the young student and film-maker Kenneth Anger, who was to be instrumental in carrying Crowley's religion into the decadent circles of 1960s rock musicians, including the Rolling Stones (Mick Jagger composed a sound track for Anger's film, *Lucifer Rising*).[93] When Anger moved briefly to London in 1968, he was greeted with reverence, having known Parsons and experimented with mind-altering drugs way before they were made illegal.

The Crowleyites were one small counterculture. They overlapped in time and drug use with another, the Beats. Countercultural generations succeed each other in a smooth transition. The first countercultural generation in the post-First World War United States were the hipsters who Stephenson traces to the jazz clubs of Harlem in the late 1920s. He recorded their distinctive dress code, liberal attitudes to sex and drugs and an affected of lack of concern with the affairs of the world qualities, all qualities based on 'a code, a way of life that … was in direct opposition to the predominantly puritanical, Anglo-Saxon ethic of the society around it'.[94] By the 1940s the hipsters had absorbed avant-garde and bohemian groups and ideas, becoming by around the middle of the decade, 'a sort of cultural underground throughout the United States with international affiliations'.[95] The hipsters, in turn, existed alongside the 'Lost Generation', a group which included radical, disillusioned writers such as Ernest Hemingway and F. Scott Fitzgerald, whose nihilist world view was shaped by the First World War. Of course, most people were neither hipsters nor Lost. But this is how the stereotypes run.

The Beats owed a debt both to hipster exuberance and Lost Generation despair, along with a dose of bohemianism, political radicalism and, from the art world, Dadaism and surrealism. Their intellectual ancestors included Crowley-esque artists such as Austin Osman Spare and theosophical abstractionists, including Mondrian and Kandinsky. They also espoused an openness to new ideas and the prophetic, shamanistic, 'ecstatic self-transcendence' that resulted from creating or listening to jazz music.[96] All of these might also be considered key characteristics, say, of the 1960s.

It was Jack Kerouac who originally named the Beat Generation in a conversation with his friend, the writer John Clellon Holmes in 1948.[97] In 1969 he recalled meeting Hipsters in New York in 1944 and became aware, as Gregory Stephenson put it, that 'some new consciousness was being born'.[98] One told Kerouac that '"I'm beat" with radiant light shining out of his despairing eyes'.[99] In Kerouac's own words: 'Anyway, the hipsters, whose music was bop, they looked like criminals but they kept talking about the same things I liked, long outlines of personal experience and vision, nightlong confessions full of hope that had become illicit and repressed by war, stirrings, rumblings of a new soul (that same old human soul).[100]

Kerouac himself used the word 'beat' in his novel, *On the Road*, which he wrote in 1951, describing Dean Moriarty, the central character as 'BEAT – the root, the soul of Beatific'.[101] At that moment Moriarty was a physical wreck but possessed, Kerouac imagined, some deep knowledge. Kerouac also used 'beat' in the sense of exhausted, so the word contains its own mythical narrative in which, when one is worn out by the conventional world, one can begin to perceive realities which are otherwise hidden. The analogy is with William Blake. One has to experience rock-bottom, to pass through Hell, before one can develop higher consciousness and evolve towards a true, integrated wholeness. The essence of 'beat' was a Romantic turning inwards, away from the conventions of the material world. This is how Allen Ginsberg used the word. Writing of his poem 'Howl', which Roszak described as 'a founding document of the counter culture', Ginsberg said 'for I'd had a beatific illumination years before during which I'd heard Blake's ancient voice and saw the universe unfold in my brain'.[102] There was, arising from such experience, an optimistic sense of possibility. Kerouac recorded how the Beats (Moriarty and his friends) were 'rising from the underground, the sordid hipsters of America, a new beat generation that I was slowly joining'.[103]

The Beats could be inward-looking, aesthetic, rebellious and transgressive.[104] John Clellon Holmes listed the key characteristics and ideology of the 'beat' or 'hipster', most of which were negative: anti-materialism, alienation from mainstream politics, resistance to social norms, use of marijuana, individualism and resistance to the requirements of corporate America.[105] The Beats clearly constituted a self-conscious counterculture and their deliberate nihilism created a powerful impression. In 1953 the conservative philosopher Robert Nisbet discussed what he saw as the overwhelming pessimism of so many modern writers and concluded, 'The outstanding characteristic of contemporary thought on men and society is the preoccupation with personal alienation and cultural disintegration'.[106] However, those who identify existential problems in modern society may be the same people who propose solutions. They may be reformers, the awakeners of their generation. This is the essence of the Blakeian proposal that one has to experience the bad in order to know the good: dystopia and utopia then become inseparable allies rather than irreconcilable opposites. Hedonism is combined effortlessly with idealism, cynicism with hope. And the result, as William Burroughs claimed, was that the Beats 'wrote a worldwide cultural revolution'.[107] The Beats' despair, which Nisbet observed, was inseparable from hope and their belief that they themselves represented a better future.

The problem of the inner life, and its emptiness in 1950s America, preoccupied the Beats. In 1949 Allen Ginsberg wrote to Jack Kerouac that he had received 'a mad long letter from Holmes – asking me about my soul…'.[108] And in 1952 Holmes stated, echoing Jung, that 'the problem of modern life is essentially a spiritual problem'.[109] When the Beats engaged with politics, they opened a second revolutionary front to more orthodox political agitation, proposing 'a revolt of the soul, a revolution of the spirit'.[110] 'Like all youth cultures', William Fowler wrote, the Beats 'held exciting new ideas in their excited hearts and minds, and with them came the dynamic indeterminacy that worried the parents and guardians of the day'.[111]

For William Burroughs, perhaps the Beat writer with the most enduringly outrageous reputation, after he accidentally shot and killed his wife in 1951, any magical affiliation was less important than the power of the artist to speak on behalf of alternate realities and deeper truths.[112] Burroughs was to be as much a hero in the 1960s as was Ginsberg; his 1959 novel *The Naked Lunch* has been described as 'the plat du jour of Sixties counter culture'.[113] He was a compulsive drug user and alcoholic, but he was perhaps the first of the modern seekers to use the psychedelic yagé, or ayahuasca, which was to become the drug of choice for mystical voyagers during the 1980s and 1990s. Burroughs anticipated all future hallucinogenic seekers: 'Maybe I will find in yagé what I was looking for in junk and weed and coke', he wrote in 1953, adding, 'Yagé may be the final fix'.[114] He immortalized his experience in the *Yagé Letters*, which he composed in 1953 in Ginsberg's flat in New York, although they were not published for a further ten years. The deconstruction of any residual notions of normality was evident in his letter to Ginsberg of 21 June 1960 in which he replied to the statement 'Your AYUASKA consciousness is more valid than "Normal" Consciousness', with the rhetorical question 'Whose "Normal Consciousness"?'[115]

Burroughs' experimentation with the occult spanned his time in Morocco from 1954 to 1958. He spent much of his time smoking kif and, under the inspiration of the surrealist Brion Gysin, discovering cut-up writing, which he later interpreted as a magical act, a kind of sorcery.[116] Gysin thought that the future leaked through the rearranged words, or even that they could determine the future, like magic spells.[117] Gysin didn't actually invent cut-up. In a similar exercise in 1897, the symbolist poet Stéphane Mallarmé had redistributed the words of one of his short poems. But Burroughs, for whom cut-up represented the intervention of apparently random events in life, named it, gave it form and transported it into the Sixties.[118] And then it became a means for applying the deconstructive effects of psychedelic drugs in the arts, in order to represent the new world revealed by hallucinations. Gysin's own creativity was drawn from a combination of the spontaneous voice of his inner world, hashish, and the authentic magic of Morocco. Then there was the occasional dash of classical Gnosticism, as in his use of the opening verses of John's Gospel:

I talk a new language, I talk about the springs and traps of inspiration.
IN SPIRATION – what you breathe in. You breathe in words. Words breathe you in...
In the beginning was the Word – been in You for a too long time
Music from the Moroccan hills proves the great god Pan not dead.
I cast spells: all spells are sentences spelling out the word-lock that is you.
In the beginning, Word. You in the word and the word in You-Time.[119]

For Burroughs, art was itself magical both in its origins in ancient ceremonial rituals which were designed to create effects in consciousness, and in its current purpose, to make something 'happen in the mind of the viewer'.[120] This was much more than metaphor for Burroughs, who believed in the reality of psychic forces, and he was convinced that the fatal shooting of his wife was caused by possession by an evil spirit. In 1959, during a psychic experiment at the Beat Hotel in Paris, Gysin, in a semi-trance, revealed that the spirit was called the 'Ugly Spirit' and, after being haunted for over thirty years, in 1992, Burroughs underwent exorcism by a Navajo shaman.[121] Being influenced by positive scientific research into psychic phenomena, he saw no boundary between the mundane and the magical, the individual psyche and the collective, dreams and daily life, present and future. However, his universe was 'random, Godless and meaningless'.[122] Burroughs had no New Age in the accepted spiritual sense, no prescription for utopia, nor any overt belief in a better future. What James Grauerholz called the 'Burroughs mythos', the primary appeal of which was the sense that the whole world was a mystery, later took hold in the Sixties.[123] There was only the self, Burroughs held, and only the here and now. Predictions of coming world ages, therefore become redundant. However, this did not rule out a certain evolutionary perspective: the psychedelic experience necessarily suggests something which is beyond the material here and now, and space travel provided inspiration for ideas about the next great leap. Considering the astral, or dream body, and punning on the word 'light', he wrote in the 1980s, 'The human body is much too dense for space conditions…This lighter body, "a body of light", as Crowley called it, is much more suited to space conditions'.[124] Gysin clarified the thought in *The Process*: 'The answer to the Riddle of the Ages has actually been out in the street since the First Step in Space…What are we here for? We are here to go!'.[125] And as Ginsberg said in 1953, 'Yage is space time travel'.[126]

Among the Sixties pioneers, the Beats took their inspiration more directly from Indian influences than from the filter of Theosophy. Gysin mentioned Alice Bailey but only dismissively. Drugs rather than Christ consciousness were the beats' path to enlightenment. Neverthless, in an interview in 1960 Kerouac said that he became a Buddhist in 1954 after reading a discussion by Henry Thoreau about Hindu philosophy.[127] It was Kerouac who introduced Ginsberg to Buddhism.[128] In June 1954 Ginsberg wrote to Kerouac, 'it is clear that your heavenly duty, your Buddha balloon, is to write, and that your unhappiness is undeserved in a way that only acceptance can make clear'.[129] In September Ginsberg followed up with the question, 'When you send me your essay on Buddha? I read it with pleasure'.[130] Kerouac's Buddhism, though, was tinged with Catholic roots that remained persistent until his death. Helen Weaver, Kerouac's partner, described him as

> one of a small band of pioneers who set out to map unknown territory of spiritual life, but he lacked the tools to explore it…The Buddhist idea that all is an illusion wasn't a good enough crutch for Jack. Theoretically, if all is an illusion, then suffering is illusion too, and shouldn't be a problem, but that syllogism didn't work for Kerouac.[131]

Around the same time, in 1954, Kerouac's friends, the poet Neal Cassady and his wife Carolyn, became firm followers of Edgar Cayce.[132] Kerouac disliked Cayce's theories although the claim that 'it drove (him) mad to hear Neal Cassady, his All-American hero, babbling on about the Akashic – spiritual – records of Atlantis and second sight' is probably a little strong. The accounts Kerouac gave to Ginsberg have a somewhat softer, if still dismissive tone. Kerouac was seized by all the fervour of the convert.

His Buddhism had prompted him to doubt the value of his entire previous existence, including poetry, but particularly the kind of absolute claims made by Cayce, which concerned him because of Cassady's new faith in them. In March 1954 Kerouac wrote to Ginsberg that I 'have long since realised that only am I the Messiah deceived but you too, and Neal [Cassady] too' and then, paraphrasing Cassady's beliefs,

> From the ten quarters of the universe it is said that they come and lay radiant hands in a wheel on your brow. This is in appearance, like the moths of light, and that Atlantis radar machine we saw in the sky over the New School when you said it had been there since the beginning of eternity anyway, and now Neal claims they had atomic power in Atlantis and Gurdjieff and Ouspensky and Bill Keck and all the social details so drearsome come flooding in to repeat what we know has already happened and will happen again.[133]

In retrospect 1954 was a seminal year. Kerouac discovered eastern esotericism in the form of Buddhism, Cassady tapped into the western apocalyptic tradition, and Allen Ginsberg set off to explore the Maya temples in Mexico. On 18 January 1954 he wrote to Kerouac with news of a woman whom he had met in the ruins of Palenque. He stayed with her for the next week during which, Ginsberg reported, she 'told me all sorts of secrets, beginning with outline of Maya metaphysics and mystical lore and history and symbolism'.[134] Later, Ginsberg described a vision to Kerouac: 'On codeine on the bus up to Veracruz and image, as in a Giotto painting, likeness of a heavenly file of female saints ascending a starry gold stairway winding up into the sky ... Salvation! It's true, as simple as this picture'.[135] Ginsberg then set out what he called his 'CREDO', which would from then on be his personal theology, and which he was to carry into the 1960s:

1. The weight of the world is love.
2. The mind images all visions.
3. Man is as far divine as his imagination.
4. We go create a world of divine love as much as we can image.[136]

Later, in 1960, an ayahuasca trip induced a profound experience of eternal recurrence, which Ginsberg described in a letter to Burroughs:

> The ringing sound in all the senses
> Of everything that has ever been Created
> All the combinations recurring over and
> Over again as before.[137]

Everything, Ginsberg realized, had always existed and would always exist, and human life consisted of experiencing the patterns in which the cosmos manifested itself. He could never go back, he said, having glimpsed 'a Changed Universe permanently changed'.[138] Between them, the three friends engaged with three of the principal narratives of the New Age ideology of the time. Kerouac, who was also absorbing Taoism, responded to Ginsberg,

I won't quote you or the Tao, or make demands or impositions or go into detail about what I been doing, except to mention, as you'll hear from Edgar Cayce, Cassady and Carolyn, my discovery and espousal of sweet Buddha ... I always did suspect that life was a dream, now I am assured by the most brilliant man whoever lived, that it is indeed so. Consequently I don't want to do anything any more, no writing, no sex, no nothing ... I would ... live in $4 a month dobe cottage where with my Buddha Bibles and bean stews I would live life full of mendicant thinker in this humble earth dream ... As for all your latest Mayan discoveries and poems, I want to hear every word of it if you want to transmit it, or tell it when we meet, but don't expect me to get excited by anything anymore.[139]

The philosophical dispute between Cassady and Kerouac paralleled on a personal level the collective collision that Joscelyn Godwin observed between eastern and western theosophists, as played out between Rudolf Steiner and the followers of Krishnamurti. Neither did Kerouac's Buddhism convert into unqualified delight in 1960s hippy culture. This is in spite of the reverence within which he was generally held and his influence on such musical icons as Bob Dylan and the Grateful Dead. Ginsberg, though, made the easy transition from Beat ideologue to Hippie metaphysician as the 1950s segued into the 1960s.

The key link between the early twentieth-century New Age and theosophical currents on the one hand, and the use of drugs as a path to enlightenment on the other, was Aldous Huxley, the author of *Brave New World*, one of the best-known dystopian novels of the twentieth century. Huxley had a childhood interest in theosophy, which he studied while at school.[140] He moved to California in the 1930s and immersed himself in the theosophical milieu and became a firm friend of Krishnamurti, whom he met in 1938. He was associated with the leading Hindu organization, the Vedanta Society of Southern California, up to around 1960, and wrote for its journal, *Vedanta and the West*, for many years. His eastern inclinations were evident in the 1950s when there was talk of he, Igor Stravinsky and the dancer Martha Graham collaborating on a ballet based on *The Tibetan Book of the Dead*.[141] He was also friends with the Russian philosopher Nicholas Berdiaeff, whose anti-utopian views were quoted at the beginning of a recent edition of *Brave New World*: 'Perhaps a new age is to begin, an age when intellectuals and the educated classes will reflect on means of avoiding utopias and of returning to a society that is not utopian, less perfect, and freer'.[142] In books such as the pacifist *Ends and Means*, published in 1937, Huxley set out a political programme for the more sensible ordering of society using Stoic, Hindu, Buddhist and Taoist ideas of non-attachment as a starting point.[143] More influentially, in *The Perennial Philosophy*, which appeared in 1945, he introduced to the literary audience who were already reading his books, the notion of a universal teaching underpinning all world religions to the literary audience who were already reading his books. 'The Universe' he wrote, borrowing from Stoic and Platonic sources, and paraphrasing Augustine, 'is an everlasting succession of events, but its ground ... is the timeless now of the divine spirit'.[144]

Huxley's introduction to the drug mescaline in May 1953, and his account of his experience the following year in *The Doors of Perception*, provides the literary foundation for all future descriptions of the psychedelic experience as a fast track to enlightenment. To make sense of his trip, he referenced it back to his intellectual schooling in the teachings of east and west, including Platonism, Christian mysticism – 'Words like Grace and Transfiguration came to my mind' – and 'the Dharma Body of the Buddha', which itself he described as 'Mind, Suchness, the Void, the Godhead'.[145] Locating the common denominator in the other-worldly components of Plato, Meister Eckhart and Buddha, he spoke of entering a state of 'Being-Awareness-Bliss'. He followed the Taoists and Zen Buddhists in looking beyond the world of everyday things to the 'Void', the true 'objective reality'.[146] To paraphrase Žižek, mescaline was the 'event' or 'cut' that pierced time and revealed eternity.[147] And in eternity all world ages exist simultaneously. The drug offered proof of the universalism of the 'Perennial Philosophy':

> Every mescalin experience, every vision arising under hypnosis is unique, but all recognizably belong to same species. The landscapes, the architectures, the clustering gems, the brilliant and intricate patterns – these, in their atmosphere of praeternatural light, praeternatural colour and praeternatural significance, are the stuff of which the mind's antipodes are made.[148]

Of the world of mundane reality, though, of 'brightly coloured, constantly changing structures that seemed to be made or plastic of enamelled tin', he wrote 'all this shoddiness existed in a close, cramped universe'.[149] Modern technology, he called a 'devaluating' influence on the material world.[150] Most western philosophy, he concluded, including 'Christian, Marxist, Freudo-Physicalist' schemes, and the over-verbalized, excessive rationalism of the western academic system, is as nothing compared to the transcendental wisdom of the Indian peasant.[151] Huxley did not entirely decry the standard verbalist model (by which he meant an overdependence on words), but he did regard it as producing only ignorance without the non-verbal, irrational, 'unsystematic… direct perception of the inner and outer worlds' available through transcendental experiences, such as that induced by mescaline and meditation.[152]

Huxley's mescaline was administered by his friend, Humphrey Osmond, and it was Osmond whose name for the visionary, hallucinatory class of drug – psychedelic – was widely adopted. From the Greek *psyche* (mind) and *delein* (to manifest), Osmond established the identity of psychedelic drugs as mind-expanding. In a culture which revered Romantic notions of individual creativity, one primed by the previous century of psychological exploration, these substances were regarded as necessarily benign. Huxley's psychedelic utopia was of the mind, and partook of Corbin's imaginal realm, poised between the stillness of eternity and the relentless ticking of time. Huxley's revelation was fuelled by Krishnamurti's belief in an individual rather than collective entry to Enlightenment, and a Gnostic state of direct communication with the Ultimate. Like his friend Krishnamurti, Huxley was an anti-millenarian. Hope for him, was in the here and now, and required no utopian city. His utopia lay in the mystical bliss which he saw realized in the psychedelic experience. In one of his articles for *Vedanta and the West*, he had written, 'whenever well-intentioned contemplatives have turned from the marginal activities appropriate to spiritual leaders and have tried to use large-scale action to force an entire society ... into the Kingdom of Heaven, they have always failed. The business of a seer is to see'.[153] Huxley's influence was immense, thanks to his status as the author of *Brave New World*. When he presented a series of lectures at the Massachusetts Institute of Technology in 1960, the Boston police department reputedly had to bring in extra forces to control the crowds.[154] Huxley stood in that line of theosophical thought, with a small 't', which rejected the historical determinism of Theosophical Society dogma. But he created the script for the psychedelic utopians' vision of a new world based on individual perception of universal truths, and was to be a hero of the counterculture in the 1960s, in which role he was promoted by Timothy Leary.

Leary wrote to Huxley in March 1961, inviting him to the fourteenth International Congress of Applied Psychology in Copenhagen. The letter had a reverential tone and invoked Huxley's old friend and fellow Vedantist, Gerald Heard, Albert Hoffman, the discoverer of lysergic acid diethylamide (LSD), and Alan Watts, the Buddhist, to give the invitation credibility.[155] Huxley attended the conference and liked Leary, whom he had met in November 1960, as a person, but regarded him as a fool for his advocacy of the unregulated use of LSD.[156] Nevertheless, Huxley's influence in the emerging psychedelic culture was immense precisely because Leary used him in order to promote his own credibility.[157] In a letter to Arthur Koestler, probably written in 1961, Leary told Koestler that he was 'working with' Huxley, a claim hardly borne out by Huxley's own dismissive comments.[158] By then, Leary himself had already embarked on what, in the same letter he called his 'cosmic crusade', writing to Koestler that he had heard of 'housewives' who, thanks to psychedelics, were 'understanding, experiencing satori describing it – who have never heard of Zen'.[159] Leary's ambition, as a psychiatrist, was not, primarily to set people free, in which case they might develop in was that he disapproved of, but to change them in ways which were for the better in his view.[160]

There were two important currents of New Age prophecy in the twentieth-century west until the 1950s. One was embedded in the theosophical and esoteric tradition, promoted by Alice Bailey, Rudolf Steiner and Carl Jung, and emphasized esoteric Christianity and moral rectitude. The other was magical, promoted by Aleister Crowley, and emphasized paganism and decadence. But there is a further distinction. On the one hand there is a reliance on prophecy of a future age, as promoted by Crowley, Bailey, Steiner and Jung; on the other were the anti-prophetic but equally utopian teachings of Gurdjieff, Ouspensky, Krishnamurti and their followers, which argued that the new era was personal, here and now. By the end of the decade, a new factor entered the millennial milieu: psychedelic drugs as the path to enlightenment, a short cut to utopia, bypassing the difficult transition to the millennium.

Myth and the Millennium in the Sixties

Few decades have been so mythologized as the 1960s. Whether characterized as hedonism or political upheaval, the decade is seen as having a particular and unique quality as one of hope that a new world was being born. In the western industrialized world, it was certainly a rare period, combining social revolution, radical politics and youthful idealism. The marriage of the arts with pop music, style and fashion added to the mix, as did rising wealth and the unprecedented use of recreational psychedelic drugs. And the whole was underpinned by the belief that the world – or just parts of the west – was experiencing extraordinary change for the better. Hope and utopianism were in the air, at least, for some people; the millennium was beginning, a new world was dawning and the counterculture was born. The myth of a uniquely special period of history is still maintained by twenty-first-century journalism. In 2011, UK television featured a series on the Sixties with the headline which emphasized outrageous hedonism, 'Sex, Drugs and Rock "N" Roll: the 60s Revealed', while in 2014 the UKTV – Yesterday series 'The Sixties' was accompanied by the claim 'A decade that history will never forget'.[1] This 'Sixties' of the media is a mythical period which coincides with the calendrical 1960s but not exactly. The calendar is based on time as *chronos*, as the counting of dates, to use the Greek term, whereas mythical moments evoke time as *kairos*, as quality. *Chronos* and *kairos* may coincide but not necessarily, and the Sixties should best be seen as *kairos*, as an epic narrative in recent history. When we refer to the Sixties it is to this mythical construct, which does not include a great deal of what else was happening in the west in the 1960s, especially the continuing mundane lives of most people, their families, jobs and daily routines. Similarly terms like the Fifties and the Seventies – and the Roaring Twenties – describe a *zeitgeist*, not a decade.

As a decade the 1960s were strung together with a series of potent moments: John F. Kennedy's inauguration as US President in January 1960; the peak period of the 1950s Civil Rights movement in America from 1960 to 1964; Beatlemania in 1963 and the group's arrival in the United States in 1964; the anti-Vietnam War protests which began in 1965 and climaxed in 1969–1970; the 'Human Be-in' in San Francisco's Golden Gate Park in January 1967, which launched the 'Summer of Love' in Haight-Ashbury and San Francisco; the riots in Paris in 1968; the clashes in Chicago at the Democrat Party convention in 1969; and the Woodstock festival in the same year. All were concerned with a popular revolt against the orthodoxy and conformity of the past and, together, they present an interwoven series of moments of peculiar dramatic power. The phrase 'counterculture' was invented by those at the heart of such events and was to become the emblem by which many of the decade's developments are known; mainstream culture was consciously countered by a new, vibrant alternative.

There is also a wider mythology which embraces such events as the CIA-run invasion of Cuba at the Bay of Pigs in 1961, Kennedy's assassination in 1963, the US bombing of Vietnam, and the Apollo moon landing in 1969. Most of these events were part of a mainstream culture of American expansion and military adventurism, a continuum which extends from the 1950s and earlier to the 1970s and later, undisturbed by popular waves of revolutionary hope. The attempt to build a new, 'alternative' society, on the other hand, was countercultural on account of its explicit opposition to what it considered the political and economic mainstream. The term 'counterculture' in the singular, though, is misleading, suggesting that there was just one such culture. There were actually a series of competing and sometimes contradictory countercultures.

Everybody who comments on the Sixties has his or her favourite view of when it supposedly began and ended. Attempts to date the beginning of the Sixties, which range from 1960 to 1965, or the end, which run from 1967 to 1969 right up to 1974, all depend on an arbitrary selection of events based on competing views of what the decade was, whether a time of peace and love, of protest, or of experimentation in style, fashion and music. Did the Sixties begin in 1960? David Eisenhower, son of the outgoing president, recalled the excitement that greeted Kennedy's inauguration in January of that year.[2] Or was 1963 the year that the 1960s began? It is certainly a popular choice, being the year when, according to Philip Larkin's poem 'Annus Mirabilis', sexual intercourse began and the Beatles' first LP was released.[3] It was also the year when the assassination of President Kennedy shattered the Camelot myth that had already generated a belief that the United States *was* entering a new dawn: one dream ends but results in the beginning of another; the king was dead and now it was up to the people to build a better world. Or we might choose 1965 when, as Theodore Roszak wrote, 'the project which the Beats of the early fifties had set themselves – the task of remodelling their inner selves, their way of life, their perceptions and sensitivities – rapidly takes precedence over the public task of changing institutions or policies'.[4] For José Argüelles, who subsequently did so much to promote the belief that the world was to be transformed as the Maya calendar came to an end in 2012, the Sixties was centred on a brief 'psychedelic revolution' which began around the middle of the decade, entered a phase of violent upheaval by 1968 and was over by the early 1970s.[5] This view is not untypical but tells a partial story in which history is linear, moving from one phase to another in a sequence, from hope to crisis and disillusion, not unlike the classic structure of Greek tragedy. As Aristotle wrote:

> It is clear that plots, as in tragedy, should be constructed dramatically, that is, around a single whole, and complete action, with beginning, middle and end, so that epic, like a single and whole animal, may produce the pleasure proper to it. Its structures should not be like histories…[6]

Following Aristotle's stricture that a good plot should extract a partial narrative and use it to create a drama which does not rely on chronology, analysis and causation, the Sixties is dramatic extract from the 1960s, a *kairos* extracted from the *chronos*. Misleading as it is, the narrative of growth, decline and loss is a popular one in which the Sixties then becomes a golden age, a lost land which can be the subject of nostalgic longing.

To identify any decade as unique, self-contained and completely distinct from those preceding and succeeding it is bound to result in over simplification. The world is far too messy and, besides, every decade can have what we might call its 'moment of myth'.[7] In the UK the 1960s followed in turn a series of previous mythologized events and movements, including the alienated Angry Young Men and Beatniks of the 1950s, the 'Dunkirk Spirit' and cheery resilience in the face of the London Blitz in the 1940s and the insurrectionary Jarrow marchers of the 1930s. We could return further to the 1920s, with their decadent jazz age, surrealist art, rejection of war and widespread enthusiasm for the coming world socialist order. And we might also include the self-consciousness cultural innovation of the 1890s' avant-garde or the 1840s, when Europe was swept by revolution.[8] To identify the 1960s, then, as entirely without precedent is misleading.[9] And, like the 1890s, the 1960s were mythologized while they were actually happening, thanks to a self-conscious awareness of the combination of social transformation, political radicalism, artistic experimentation and playful decadence, overlaid with a profound sense of newness. On 3 December 1967, the *Observer* devoted an entire issue of its colour magazine to events in London:

> Something Is Going On Underground. If you are under 25 you are certain that It's All Happening. A curious alliance has been struck between teenagers, the hippies, commercial pop and the young intellectuals. Somehow all have crystallised into a separate society or 'scene'. At its centre, the authentic full-time hippies, young, serious, flamboyant in dress, claim to have taken an analytical look at the adult world, experienced a violent revulsion at what they saw, and decided that the only honourable course is to detach themselves, or 'drop out'.[10]

The Underground, the article continued, was lively, vibrant, diverse, separated from 'grey' society by its use of LSD and marijuana, and united only in support for human rights and opposition to the war in Vietnam.

There is also a widespread belief that what was initially a vague and unformed longing for a new and better world in the 1960s gave rise to the New Age Movement of the 1970s. According to this version of events, when the psychedelic culture of 1965 onwards lost its sense of transcendental hope, it acquired a need for structure; this was then satisfied by the development of New Age ideas and practices which provided a means for self-transformation free from the unpredictable and chaotic consequences of drug use. The New Age movement, it was claimed with remarkable precision, began in 1971.[11] This claim is not true but is particularly persistent, has become accepted wisdom, and pervades the academic literature. The wider narrative, simply put, is that part of the western world was swept by an unprecedented wave of euphoria in the 1960s which then began to crystallize into a series of precisely focused post-countercultural movements, of which the New Age movement was just one, the other chief examples being second-wave feminism and the environmental movement.[12] Most commentators, whether academic or otherwise, take it as a given that this is true. It is undoubtedly the case that second-wave feminism and environmentalism – and gay liberation – achieved a huge public profile as the 1960s gave way to the 1970s, but attempts to portray them as consequences of the Sixties fail simply because all have roots in the early 1960s, if not earlier. Rather, such movements were part of the same radicalism that produced the Sixties and, in turn, they achieved a huge public profile and a fresh constituency of youthful supporters as the decade closed. The same goes for the New Age Movement, which contributed to the Sixties as much as it benefitted from it. But there was no linear, causal sequence.

In 1961, as the decade began, Raymond Williams wrote that:

> There is a certain perpetual tendency evident in the modern world for each generation to announce the completion of the revolution, and to be bewildered and angry when the new young generation asserts that the revolution has after all not occurred.[13]

Williams' words proved remarkably prophetic in view of what was about to occur. He observed the unexpected tension between the obvious accomplishment of the goals for which so many generations had fought. In the UK the dreams of early utopian socialists, such as William Morris and H.G. Wells, mediated largely through the Labour Party, had resulted in free education and healthcare and massively better housing. In both the United States and the UK, adult suffrage and unprecedented rising material living standards secured consent for the prevailing economic and political system from the majority but, in a clearly dialectical process, generated a sense of existential frustration and alienation amongst the generation born in the 1940s. Just as material satisfaction had been achieved, so spiritual dissatisfaction set in and was manifested in the reaction of middle-class youth against what was perceived as the sterility and conservatism of middle-class life.[14] The problem came not from poverty and oppression but from freedom and wealth and from a society which had sacrificed spiritual values in favour of consumerism, an issue previously raised by Jung in his *Modern Man in Search of a Soul*, first published in 1933.[15]

Sociologically and institutionally, the Sixties were completely unplanned. Nobody at the end of the 1950s ever suggested that so many people were about to rebel against conformity. Eruptions of popular excitement are, after all, notoriously difficult to predict, and the central quality of the Sixties was a feeling of euphoric hope. This was described in 1965 by Irving Kristol, the leading neoconservative theorist, who identified the single most important feature of the burgeoning protest culture as passion:

> One thing is fairly clear: the teach-ins, the sit-ins, the lay-downs, the mass-picketing and all the rest are not merely about Vietnam, or civil rights … there is, transparently, a passion behind the protests which refuses to be satisfied by the various topics which incite it.[16]

His conclusion was that the youth revolt was essentially apolitical in that it could propose no legislation or constructive solutions and was 'existential' not in the sense that it was occurring because things were bad for the students in reality but because the students experienced their lives as difficult. It was all about passion. Spontaneity was the key, as in so many genuine revolutionary movements, which, like the Russian Revolution in 1917, the East European uprisings of 1989 or the Arab Spring in 2011, take the revolutionaries themselves by surprise. Lenin noticed the tautology by which spontaneity is spontaneous.[17] Such is the unplanned, unpredictable nature of such eruptions, he argued, that their hopes are bound to fail unless managed by a secretive, disciplined revolutionary vanguard. As populist eruptions they unavoidably disappoint.[18] 'The psychedelic movement', Timothy Leary recalled, 'was to develop without organisation, without leaders, without dogmatic doctrines.'[19] This was not entirely true. While the hope for a renaissance was genuine, the youthful revolution was not exactly free from leaders. The rebels were actually in search of leaders as much as anyone else, which is precisely the demand that Bob Dylan was constantly rejecting, when people asked him, 'you show us the way'.[20] In the absence of institutions, though, the leaders' power arose from consensus and charisma rather than election, as did Ken Kesey's role in the Merry Pranksters.[21] But there were leaders nonetheless, who could extract massive obedience from their followers.

The key feature of the Sixties was a remarkable upsurge of the optimism that, as Bloch observed, underpins utopian movements. One common metaphor has the black-and-white Fifties replaced by the technicolour Sixties.[22] In 1962, the journalist Anthony Sampson's analysis of UK life created quite a stir with its description of the country as demotivated, drifting and directionless, suffering 'a loss of dynamic and purpose and a general bewilderment'.[23] Sampson, of course, may have been prey to the common notion that one's own time is always worse than the previous era. But whether or not Sampson overstated his case, he presented a popular view of the times. We find similar opinions in the United States. The conservative philosopher Robert Nisbet observed what he saw as the overwhelming pessimism of so many modern writers and concluded in 1953: 'The outstanding characteristic of contemporary thought on men and society is the preoccupation with personal alienation and cultural disintegration.'[24] The 1950s, in this version, were a time of grim austerity in the UK and McCartheyite-enforced conformity in the United States.

Recollections of the apparent excitement in London in the early 1960s are legion. The film director Guy Hamilton recalled: 'In 1961 I returned from a stint of film making in Israel to a rather exciting London. The Beatles had not yet arrived but there was something going on. A trip down the King's Road, the clothes, the hairstyles, music: there was a feeling that a youthful revolution was in the air.'[25] According to another typical account: 'When I arrived (in London) in '60 it still felt like after the war: it was very grey and conservative... When I came back in '64 something had started to happen ...'[26] We should not be entirely taken in by the notion of an unprecedented eruption into colour from an era of grey, though. In 2000, the writer Alan Bennett recalled his excitement at visiting the site of the Festival of Britain in 1951 when he had been 'a raw provincial schoolboy, famished for colour ... [and] captivated' by the light, airy, adventurous of the bold, modern architecture.[27] Still, the Festival appears to have represented a false start and, in any case, was directed to the modernism and science and technology which was to be regarded with distrust or distaste by the romantic currents in Sixties thinking.

The wave of optimism that was a hallmark of the Sixties is dated by some to the beginning of the decade. David Eisenhower, son of the former President, later wrote that:

> Many, perhaps most people my age look back on 1960 on the Kennedy promise as the beginning of something very exciting. That year marked a rite of passage for many of us – the first real awareness of a political campaign, of being able to take sides. This awareness coincided with a mood: in Kennedy's words the passing of the torch to a new generation.[28]

It is often remarked that Kennedy was the first Roman Catholic President. What was truly significant about his election, though, was that it brought to an end to two and a half centuries in which Roman Catholics were not regarded as proper Americans.[29] The abandonment of one of Anglo-Saxon America's founding taboos prompted a cascade of freedoms in which other restrictions fell like dominoes. Not even the shock of Kennedy's assassination could dent the excitement, and within a few years every conceivable boundary in American culture had been crossed.

In October 1965, following the Free Speech movement in Berkeley, Allen Ginsberg recalled: 'There was an air of expectation and apocalyptic demand which was quite beautiful and at the same time unrealistic. I remember one kid kept climbing on the window of my poetry class demanding a revolution. He was demanding that I lead an immediate revolution right then and there, and he wasn't able to define it.'[30] Looking back, the UK disc-jockey John Peel recalled: 'I believed absolutely, without question ... we were going to change the world ... there was huge excitement because you felt you were the vanguard of something, that things genuinely were going to change.'[31] Robert Stone remembered: 'It embraced risk in an attitude of faith that looked forward to the advancement of everything within us that was nobler, more generous and more just ... In our time, we were clamorous and vain ... We wanted it all.'[32] Such passion was typical of the 'enthusiasm' which had been identified as a characteristic of seventeenth- and eighteenth-century millenarians – and a dangerous one at that. John Locke had considered that enthusiasts were subject to nothing but the fantasies of their own brains.[33] That was his sceptical view. Yet neither truth nor accuracy have ever been requirements of millenarian utopian hope or millenarian fever. The primeval root of all utopianism was everywhere, residing in the tendency to spontaneous revolution which Lenin observed in the nineteenth century. As Bloch wrote: 'From the bare inside something reaches forth. The urging expresses itself first as "striving", craving to go anywhere. When the striving is felt, it becomes "longing", the only honest state in all men ... (and then) "searching".'[34] And so the Sixties was characterized by the search for something new, better, different and deeper.

For some, idealism was as nothing compared to hedonism. The jazz musician George Melly's 1974 obituary for the 1960s summed up the alternative culture as consisting of 'love, dope, sounds, macrobiotic food, tripping, instinctive anarchism, youth, the new life-style'.[35] There is in such sentiments an obvious direct transmission of the truncated version of Crowley's commandment 'Do what thou wilt shall be the whole of the law' into unrestrained hedonism. However, not everyone believed in a complete absence of limits. Timothy Leary's individualism was Gnostic in inspiration and, in spite of his libertarian tendencies, did not necessarily imply that one could behave exactly as one wished, for personal behaviour must be constrained by family duty; he disseminated this idea via his own lectures and the underground press in 1966–1967: 'First, nothing you do outside is important unless you're centred within. Secondly, you must center your life around your family...Each country has its own laws and we urge our communicants to obey the law of Caesar...but we will not let that law interfere with the Kingdom of Heaven which is within.'[36]

Jim Haynes, founder of the London Arts Lab, described the coming new world in highly individualistic terms:

> First and foremost it was going to be a world of mutual respect, mutual acceptance. No more prejudice: you could worship who you wanted to worship, how you wanted to worship, wear the clothes you wanted to wear, have the sexual attitudes you wanted, eat what you wanted to eat, drink, smoke, whatever you wanted to do – mutual acceptance. You were a human being and you had the right to do that. And I had the obligation to respect that, because that's what you wanted.[37]

And herein lies the basis of cultural relativism: that if you can't criticize my culture because it's mine, then I can't criticize yours precisely because it's yours. The sense of uninhibited libertarianism and cultural relativism was epitomized by Richard Neville in his book, *Playpower*.[38] Later Neville recalled: 'The aim of the alternative culture was...to break down barriers not only between sexes and races...it was also to have a good time, it was to enlarge the element of fun...to abolish this work/play situation.'[39] But to play one must destroy that which prevents one acting exactly as one wishes. As one anonymous inhabitant of the Haight-Ashbury said, 'In order to act with freedom, one must not be constrained by the oppressive systems of orientation and the selfish meaningless goals that were learned while a member of the uptight, plastic society.'[40] There is no liberality here, no toleration, just an absolute contempt for those who do not share the new vision of a better world.

All conversations about the Sixties tend to be responsible for a fundamental misconception: that there was a single youth movement, one counterculture, an identifiable revolt against conformity. There were instead three distinct strands of behaviour, or taste cultures, which overlapped, yet still had their own identities.[41] The first two, which we may label for convenience respectively as the New Left and the hippies, represented competing utopian traditions, each possessing an expectation of dramatic social and political change. The third represented a generational crisis, with no political framework, and this might better be described as an ordinary subculture rather than a counterculture. The three are best understood as ideal types, abstract categories of behaviour which were rarely represented in the lives of particular individuals. Most youthful rebels could move between the three.

The first of the countercultures was the overtly political culture dominated by the New Left, a coalition of civil rights activists and anti-war protesters, anarchists, libertarians and feminists, plus some socialists and black nationalists, and including both pacifists and advocates of violence. Borne partly out of disillusion with the orthodox Marxism of the 1950s, which was itself still based in the old dogma of the pre-war years, the New Left found its voice in 1960 with the foundation of Students for a Democratic Society (SDS) by Tom Hayden. The SDS's manifesto, the Port Huron Statement, named after the city in which it was drafted, was composed in a mood of optimistic euphoria in 1962: the world, it was believed, was on the brink of a momentous change. The Statement called for a 'New Left', and a democratic revolution which was to be based on respect for the individual, not the state. Marxism's revolutionary fervour survived in the New Left's self-confident sense of its own destiny, but the old left's materialism and collectivism were roundly rejected. The clash between the Port Huron radicals and the conservative Marxists, that mixture of Stalinists, Trotskyites and socialists, was not so much a debate about ideas but as what Hayden himself characterized as 'two very different kinds of consciousness staring at each other, an uncomprehending conflict'.[42] The SDS's view of humanity was idealistic and its place in the millenarian tradition was Joachite: 'We regard men as infinitely precious', the Port Huron Statement proclaimed, 'and possessed of unfulfilled capacities for reason, freedom, and love'.[43] In the New Left vision, humanity was perfectible because, left to itself, it was, as Montaigne believed, perfect.

The New Left rejected previous models of progressive political activity but maintained fairly orthodox views that the struggle for social justice and economic and racial equality was the key to creating a new society. The simplest distinction between the radicals of the New Left and the hippies was the radicals' emphasis on a challenge to the institutions of state and economic power. By contrast, the second main countercultural group, the hippies, were distinguished from the New Left mainly because they put such an emphasis on individual rights that collective action, with rare examples, was considered redundant. In this sense, the collective consisted solely of individuals and collective action only occurred when the actions of sufficient individuals coincided. Personal experience was everything, and if sufficient people had the right kind of experience, it was believed, a new and better world would inevitably and swiftly follow. The influence of the early twentieth-century esotericists was clear and the hippies believed that change must come from within. Hippyism conforms to New Age 'self-spirituality', and the 'self-ethic', in which the individual is the source of all moral authority, constrained only by the higher power of love.[44]

The term hippy – or hippie – is problematic because, by the early 1970s, it came to be widely understood as indicative of helpless and naive idealism, much in the way that the New Age is now often regarded. As Levin and Spates wrote: 'The hippy problem becomes distinctly ideological'.[45] The label hippy, or hippie, appeared around 1965–1966 as a derivation of hipster. The term 'hep-cat' or 'hip-cat' was in use around 1965. Ron Thelin, one of the prime movers in Haight-Ashbury in 1966–1967, described the alternative community as 'hip'.[46] And by 1966, one could be 'hippier' in the sense of more hip than another hip individual.[47] But this was to be hip in the sense of wearing the right clothes and listening to the right music, to be at the forefront of the fashion trends.

The designation hippy expanded into the description of an entire, utopian worldview. But it is a loose term and there was no official definition and no organized movement. Within general hippy culture, there might then be radically different assumptions about life-style, the balance between personal freedom and social responsibility and historical change. From outer appearances, a hippy was someone who had long hair and wore colourful clothes. Long hair for men and flowing clothes for women, together with sex outside marriage and public nudity, became the ritual, taboo-breaking challenge to the old world. Such was the antinomianism – the law-breaking – typical of millenarian movements.[48] And it was this rampant libertarianism that gave rise to what became known as the 'permissive society'.[49] Everything was permitted and nothing was forbidden and Aleister Crowley's dream was manifested. Even sex between adults and children, which was to be reclassified in the early twenty-first century as one of the most heinous crimes imaginable, could be regarded as benign.

So what were the hippies responding to? Perhaps it was to the disenchantment, the banishment of magic from the world, experienced in response to secularization and modernity discussed by Max Weber.[50] One answer to this problem of alienation, for Robert Nisbet, was community.[51] This is precisely what the hippies experienced by gathering at Golden Gate Park in 1967 or at Woodstock in 1969, enacting the home-coming which Bloch saw as the end point of utopian psychology: 'Once he has grasped himself and established what is his, without expropriation and alienation, in real democracy, there arises in the world something which shines into the childhood of all and in which no one has yet been: homeland.'[52] Much about hippy culture was an exercise in nostalgia, an attempt to live close to nature, like one of Montaigne's natives or the inhabitants of Hesiod's golden age. And one could only achieve this by being free of the spiritually smothering culture of suburban United States.

To an extent, hippy style can appear to be no more than a fashion statement which set out to confront the conformity of the 1950s. Yet, in the mid-1960s, choice in what one wore was a profound assertion of individual freedom. And if individuality was the revolution's goal, then dress was the means by which it might be accomplished. Did hippy culture constitute a form of religiosity? It seemed so to some people at the time. The 'ideal' hippy was characterized by a number of existential qualities, listed by Jack Levin and James Spates. First, he or she was 'tuned in to the cosmic affinity of man'.[53] Such an affinity was to be achieved partly through the use of LSD and marijuana, locating hippy culture in a line of descent from Aldous Huxley's Gnosticism. Second, hippies were obliged to love all people, to subscribe to the 'love ethic'.[54] For many, love was the key: peace and love ideology reached its most public and visible form with the release of the Beatles' single 'All You Need Is Love' as part of the first ever global television broadcast on 25 June 1967. The pacifist, nature-oriented political ideology, which emerged from the belief in love as the cure-all for the world's ills was quickly named 'flower-power', a term which originated with Allen Ginsberg's advocacy of the use of flowers as a symbol of peace in protest performance.[55] There are echoes here of Joachim via Alice Bailey. The ascent to the light also became a familiar metaphor. Ron Thelin described the purpose of his underground newspapers as 'to provide an organ for the hip community, an evolution of communications, consciousness and the miracles of light in this community'.[56] In 1967, the UK underground magazine *Oz* reported, with a hint of sarcasm, that:

> The Utopian sentiments of the hippies were not to be put down lightly. Hippies
> have a clear vision of the ideal community – a psychedelic community to be sure –
> where everyone is turned on and beautiful and loving and happy and floating
> free.[57]

Similar scepticism pervaded UK alternative culture. George Melly, for example,
described flower power as 'crippled from the off', having become 'a national joke', by
the end of 1967, and mocked its often fey, coy music as 'nursery surrealism'.[58] Levis
and Spates' list of hippy qualities was correct as far as it went but they had bought
into the propaganda fiction, propagated by the media, that hippyism could only be
peaceful. True, 'flower-power' ideology, with its core mantra of peace and love, was a
feature of the counterculture, but only a feature, and the so-called 'summer of love' was
largely a media event.[59] Gentle, back-to-the garden utopianism was promoted by Scott
MacKenzie's hit record 'San Francisco' and its evocative subtitle 'Be Sure to Wear Some
Flowers in your Hair', which was released in May 1967 and, more than anything else,
brought the summer of love to a wide audience, although was derided by some.[60] In
reality, some veterans of the San Francisco underground were already deeply alarmed
by the corruption of Haight-Ashbury by the influx of drug-taking young men and
exploitable young women, compounded by what they saw as the commercialization
of their ideals. Haight-Ashbury had become a kind of vast sanatorium, offering a
'therapeutic regime of drugs and good vibes, rather than mountain air and mineral
springs', and by early 1966 it was home to an estimated 15,000 hippies.[61] The numbers
grew rapidly and the problems generated by so many young people in search of
salvation featured on the agenda of an extraordinary summit meeting of leaders of
the hippy subculture (the term 'counterculture' was not used) of Haight-Ashbury in
1967. Emmet Grogan, one of the most prominent of the San Francisco Diggers and 'the
closest thing the hippies of Haight-Ashbury had to a real live hero', gave as an example
what he described as the starving to death of a 15-year-old girl's unborn baby.[62] Such
was the disillusion that, on 6 October 1967, the deep-insiders in San Francisco hippy
culture called an end to the phenomenon at a mock funeral, 'The Death of Hippy'.[63] It
was clear by then that utopia could not be achieved just by wishing it into existence.
It was not enough to reject the mainstream in the vague hope that something better
would take its place. One actually had to build an alternative as, of course, many, such
as the San Francisco Diggers, already knew.

Despite their differences, both New Left and hippyism shared some common
attitudes. Hippy politics, like those of the New Left, could be revolutionary, advocating
what the Californian journalist Warren Hinckle described in 1967 as the 'reduction
of private property, rejection of violence (and) creativity before consumption'.[64] And
yet, Hinckle continued, were it not for their long hair and tattered clothes, the hippies'
sentiments resembled those of young Republicans, even of the John Birch Society, in
a number of key respects. First was the sanctity of the individual, an idea inherited
from the Beats. William Burroughs, writing in the 1980s and summing up the spirit of
the 1960s, said: 'It's every artist his own movement now.'[65] As Margaret Thatcher later
said, 'society as such does not exist except as a concept. Society is made up of people.
It is people who have duties and beliefs and resolve. It is people who get things done.'[66]

Second was resistance to government, in which hippies shared an essential anti-state conservatism with their more sober compatriots in the SDS. For the SDS's part, the Port Huron Statement's aspirational tone clearly read like a call for the restoration of those American values which had been abandoned in the pursuit of materialism; the Port Huron radicals, Hayden himself wrote, were 'straight out of the mainstream'.[67] There was a strong feeling amongst the rebels and radicals that they represented the ideals of the founding fathers of 1776 and the true legacy of the frontier spirit and the utopian experiments of the early nineteenth century. Hinckle linked contemporary developments directly to the early nineteenth century. He remarked that:

> It is not improbable, that after a few more mountain seminars by these purposeful young men wearing beads, that Haight Ashbury may spawn the first Utopian collectivist community since Brook Farm.[68]

In this sense, the counterculture was a reforming movement, one which rejected a modern world whose love affair with materialism, consumption and technology, it believed, had resulted in a sacrifice of the United States' founding values. That the counterculture should have a strong strand of conservatism was entirely consistent with the millenarian desire to recreate a lost golden age, a time of simplicity, honesty and virtue, to return to the blissful simplicity recalled by Hesiod, and to the state of nature praised by Montaigne. The fictionalized encounter between the hippy bikers played by Peter Fonda and Dennis Hopper and various rural communards in the 1969 film *Easy Rider* borders on satire, but the impulse to return to spiritual intimacy with the Earth was deep and genuine.[69] Joni Mitchell's 1970 song 'Woodstock', for example, lacks the ambiguity of the film and is an entirely sincere evocation of the idea of the festival goer as a child of god, made of stardust, and returning to a restored garden of Eden.[70]

In the absence of material deprivation or political tyranny, the only restriction can be on our ability to express our inner selves at any cost. Spates identified the core quality of the hippy utopia as what Morris Zeldetch called 'expressivism'.[71] Notions of protest as performance invite direct comparisons with the most dramatic single event of the Sixties in Western Europe: the May Days of 1968 in Paris. It briefly looked as if the French government would collapse before a wave of protests which, when challenged by the police, turned as violent as anything seen in the United States. This is from the testimony of Jean-Jacques Lebel, who was both a participant and commentator:

> The May uprising was theatrical in that it was a gigantic fiesta, a revelatory and sensuous explosion outside the 'normal' pattern of politics ... Desire was no longer negated but openly expressed in its wildest and most radical forms. Slavery was abolished in its greatest stronghold: people's heads. Self-management and self-government were in the air. The subconscious needs of the people began to break through the ever present backbone of capitalism ... The first things revolutions do away with are sadness and boredom and the alienation of the body.[72]

In November 1965 one of the earliest anti-war demonstrations in San Francisco was conceived as theatre in order to manifest peace, in order to get away from the negativity implied by protest.[73] Jerry Rubin wanted Bob Dylan to lead it, but Dylan's Dadaist suggestions – to carry signs with the names of pictures of fruit or other random objects – failed to impress the organizers and he didn't take part. Ginsberg's diagnosis was that the marchers were too much into their own anger and not enough into theatre.[74] As Roszak noted, what Allen Ginsberg described as his 'Angelic Ravings' would 'never quite fit to the adamantly secular mould of the Old Left'.[75] Yet, for Abbie Hoffman, theatre could provide the link between competing New Left and hippy wings of the underground. He drew on sources from Leary's politics of ecstasy to Lévy Bruhl's participation mystique to create an 'action-theatre' and construct 'a vast myth' which he hoped would assist in the development of a true alternative society.[76] Lebel's notion of 'fiesta' was likewise far-removed from the activities of the Old Left. Politics were combined with theatre, leaders were seen as no different from followers and, in artistic terms, the artist and the audience were the same, and the consumers participated on equal terms with the producers: the whole event was performance.[77] This was the essence of a 'Happening'. And at the extreme was the sexual boundary-pushing of such avant-garde performers as the Living Theatre, with their emphasis on nudity and audience participation, where the political and the personal blended in spontaneous self-expression.[78] And what expressivism did was provide the medium for revolutionary transformation of the inner world, and the individual rather than the state. A poster of Bob Dylan from 1967 put it well, converting the words of the song 'Blowin' in the Wind' to the slogan 'Blowin' in the Mind'.[79]

The third strand to the counterculture might be better described as a taste culture or subculture on account of its lack of any overt ideology or concern with wider historical transformation. This was the much wider youth culture in which individual freedom was a matter of the right to wear what one wanted, in which the revolution consisted of short skirts and short hair for women and brightly coloured clothes and long hair for men. Its revolution was that of style, fashion and music, and it was not at all hostile to aspects of established culture, such as capitalist business: one of its icons was a shop, the legendary boutique, Biba.[80] As the singer Cilla Black recalled in 2014, 'What the Sixties was all about was fashion'.[81] It was marked, though, by a self-conscious knowingness, a sense of being part of something bigger and brighter, unlike the normal unconscious nature of popular culture in which action is pursued for its own sake.[82] In England, an inventive sense of fashion and freedom generated the iconography of swinging London, a term coined by *Time* magazine on 15 April 1966: 'In a decade dominated by youth', the magazine enthused, 'London has burst into bloom. It swings; it is the scene.'[83] Swinging London was not a place of protest, but of flowers, greenery, colourful fashions, uninhibited behaviour and wild pop music, in which there was no conflict between the old and the new, but rather a playful interaction between the two. It consisted of a series of 'urban tribes' such as the mods, based around clubs, clothes and pop groups.[84] Swinging London was a happy place but, like the summer of love, it was a journalistic creation.[85]

Youth culture in general should properly be considered a subculture on the grounds that its challenge to the dominant culture was ephemeral. It wished to assert itself but did not demand wholesale changes to the economic and political structures as a counterculture should, nor a transformation of consciousness.[86] But we can still identify in it a utopian quality. As Ernest Bloch said, the impulse which leads to utopianism includes 'the girl who adorns herself for the special boy she does not know'.[87] It was also rich in meaning.[88] It asserted freedom, independence and individuality, a visual challenge to old-style politics represented by conservative fashion. The fashion revolution which swept the west from around 1962 onwards is no less a utopian manifestation than were the revolutionary hopes of the New Left or the dreams of the psychedelic evangelists. In this version of utopia-as-method, the new world was to be inaugurated by the freedom to look and dress as one pleased; all, in Ernest Bloch's terms, were manifestations of young people's desire to be special, to become themselves, to live out their potential and so, in their way, transform society. It was, in its way, revolutionary; Diana Vreeland, editor of *Vogue*, referred to it as a 'youthquake'.[89] For the first time, it was thought, class and age were no longer bars to a better life.

Gans' notion of 'taste cultures' tends to remove the distinction between levels of commitment.[90] Whatever kind of counterculturalist one was, whether a militant revolutionary, a radical artist, a drug-taking musician or a hippy romantic, it was all a matter of taste and personal preference. We might even present the difference between the dedicated commune-dweller and the 'weekend hippy' who retained a weekday job as less a matter of countercultural commitment than a matter of taste. Utopia became a consumer choice.

Attempts to locate causes for the Sixties exclusively in external, material developments alone fail to convince. For example, that the upsurge of utopian fervour in the Sixties coincided with a 'remarkable rise in the middle-class availability of the "means of publication"' meant that radicals *could* communicate, but it didn't say *why* they wanted communicate or *what* they wanted to communicate.[91] Explanations for the flowering of youth culture in the 1960s tend to focus on such factors as the rise of financial independence in a generation born during or immediately after the Second World War, who reacted against the perceived conservatism and materialism of post-war society. Some argue that there was a response by young people to a crisis in their social status, borne of two factors: the first was deindustrialization, which destroyed old working patterns, and the second was the huge rise in college attendance, coupled with a decline in the status of, and hence respect commanded by, further education.[92] Francis Fukuyama saw the youthful revolutionaries of the French *événements* of 1968 as the pampered offspring of the bourgeoisie who had no reason to rebel other than that their comfortable middle-class lives deprived them of any sense of struggle.[93] The impulse, he thought, was not dissimilar to the need for community and togetherness which prompted enthusiastic demonstrations at the outset of the Great War in 1914.[94] As Hegel, Fukuyama wrote, had realized, the 'peace and prosperity' of the former age was not enough, for these conditions would breed complacency and decay.[95] The youthful rebel rejects the comfortable materialism of suburban life in order to live on the street in Haight-Ashbury or hurl petrol bombs in Paris. He is the classic rebel identified by Raymond Williams, committed to replacing the entire current social structure, believing it cannot be saved.[96] But the rebel, in a sense, is the ultimate conservative, fighting an establishment that has turned its back on its founding principles, whether that of the United States' founding fathers in 1776 or the proclamation of equality in

France in 1789. It cannot be assumed, then, that material abundance was the cause of youth revolt. And if not abundance, then socio-economic causes as a whole are called into question, and we turn again to psychology. Max Scheler's concept of *ressentiment*, the anger and bitterness which accumulate in response to oppression, provides one model.[97] The oppression experienced in the Sixties, though, was of the soul. As Jerry Rubin, founder of the Yippies, or Yippees, wrote in March 1968:

> The yippee are the children of the middle class, children who refuse to grow up. A yippee is a stoned idealist, moved by a vision of a future utopia. He is a romantic. It is not fear which moves the yippee, It is faith and hope ... He is concerned with creating a clear alternative, an underground. He is involved in a cultural revolution. He is seducing the 10 year olds with happenings, community, youth power, media, music, legends, marijuana, action, myth, excitement and a new style.[98]

The United States, Rubin concluded, is a big prison. This rather gives the lie to the assumption that revolutionary and millenarian movements result from economic crisis and political oppression. Rubin's prison was one of the spirit and its bars and locks consisted of the comfortable prosperity and democratic freedoms of middle-class America, which he regarded as a trap for the soul; and the soul, according to Fukuyama's reading of Plato, yearns to be free.[99] It longs to escape the prison of material life, ignorance and blind conformity.[100] Worst of all, Plato said, we are willing participants in our own imprisonment.[101] And as Lebel said, one had to abolish slavery in one's mind.[102] Hippyism, like so many previous millenarian eruptions, sought an ecstatic liberation from Plato's spiritual prison. It was a deeply religious movement.

The major triggers of youth revolt were psychological: the rejection of both compulsive consumption and the 'passive spectatorship' by which fewer and fewer people engage with creative activity and more and more become members of the audience produced an exaggerated reaction summed up as 'expressiveness for its own sake'.[103] Young people were not oppressed in any material or political sense. Quite the opposite. However, they *felt* oppressed because they were unable to express their true, inner selves. Anyone, it was thought, had a right to develop their own creativity – that is, their own inner talents. At its extreme, notions of inner creativity were deeply embedded in the traditions of modern art; the popular notion that one should always 'do one's own thing', no matter what that thing was or what the consequences were.[104] The audience should reassert its right to participate in the performance. For Jung, who did so much to legitimize such attitudes, the urge towards self-realization was 'a law of nature and thus of invincible power', its ultimate purpose being not some form of soul salvation but the creation of consciousness.[105] Cynically, we might consider hippy millenarianism to be a 'compensatory fantasy', as Norman Cohn called it, in which sin and oppression, in this case the sins of materialistic United States and the oppression of conventional expectations, will succumb to the final victory of righteousness and freedom in personal and political relationships.[106]

The paradox whereby improving living standards can provoke discontent was noticed way back in 1846, two years before the great revolutionary year 1848: 'It would almost appear ... that the more civilised a society becomes, the more apt are visionary notions to spring up and flourish, just as we find hysterics and nervous vapours to prevail among fine ladies, while their robust maids are exempt from anything of the kind.'[107] But such dissatisfaction led less to despair and more to a thirst for renewal. It resulted in what Timothy Leary later referred to as 'a full-blown religious renaissance of the young.'[108] And this renaissance, being countercultural, was defined by an opposition to everything it found in the American dream of the Fifties: it distrusted the modernist theory of progress as the ascent to a technological, materially abundant future, valued the natural over the artificial and elevated the ancient, pre-modern and non-western over the modern and the western, and rejected all restraints on the rights of the individual.[109]

The counterculture's extreme individualism was the culmination of two strands in Enlightenment, if we can use that word; first its deep hostility to the organized religion of the west and second its conviction that it represented the highpoint of progress. And if it was intolerant, then this only takes us into the territory occupied by the Jacobins. Even among the nineteenth-century Romantics, it has been argued, the most pious tended to be become the most politically reactionary; for the rest, the Romantic project was to abstract from religion its essential 'feeling' and contemptuously leave behind its 'traditional formulations'.[110]

Paradoxically, the suburban United States of the 1950s also presented itself in utopian terms. New houses with fridges, air conditioning and central heating occupied by white, heterosexual nuclear families and new roads to take men in fast cars to white-collar jobs; such material wealth added up to a realized utopia for those who had survived the depression or escaped inner-city deprivation. Yet, to so many of the children who grew up in this paradise, it became a prison. The tension, then, was between the alienated desire of the young to express themselves, transcending the identities imposed on them by the post-war consensus, and a world in which they could only become who they were permitted to be. The utopianism both of the New Left and the hippies collided with the utopianism of 1950s American suburbia. However, negativity came with its own problems. Stuart Hall highlighted what he saw as the fragmentation inherent in modernity: 'The multiplication of new points of antagonism which is ... characteristic of our emerging "post-industrial" societies.'[111] For Hall, the utopia of post-war suburbanism was itself a manifestation of a culture in crisis. In turn it produced social fragmentation; many of the young launched themselves into a rhetorical and style battle with their elders, and the young competed with each other in fragmented countercultures. Being united in what you are against does not bring unity as to what is proposed to take its place. Opposition to mainstream culture was therefore necessarily disorganized and chaotic.[112] The problem was that the suburban, Fifties utopia was realizable, but the countercultural alternative, as had become clear by late 1967, was not.

Given that so much that contributed to the 1960s counterculture – traditions of protest, the search for social and political alternatives, artistic experimentation, anti-materialism and the quest for inner truth – was already present in the 1950s, the question is what made the Sixties special? George McKay, writing in 1998 about the radical protest culture of the 1990s, pointed out that there was a lot of material that said, as he put it, 'we are new, we are different, we are great, cheeky, active', but surprisingly little which asked 'Are we? Is this new?'[113]

It was a single external factor, the Vietnam War, which provided the unifying presence that radicals of all kinds could oppose, especially in the United States, whose number of combat troops leapt from 23,300 to 184,000 in the critical year from 1964 to 1965.[114] There was a close coincidence in time with two other unrelated developments, the Beatles arrival in the United States in 1964 and the serious beginning of the promotion of LSD in 1965. Aside from minor dissatisfaction over the details of college life, and engagement in the Civil Rights movement in the early years of the decade, the political discontent of the affluent white young was directed solely in opposition to US involvement in the Vietnam War. The beginning of troop reductions in 1970, leading to the Paris Peace accords in 1973, removed the one issue on which all youthful rebels find common cause, and the mythical Sixties entered its decline. The war was an external factor: young men were sent to the other side of the world to kill and die in a civil war which became a surrogate for Cold War rivalry. Such was the unifying power of anti-war sentiment across all counter and taste cultures that the peak period of Sixties enthusiasm coincides with the beginning of US combat operations in Vietnam and the serious troop reductions in 1972.[115] If we can allow ourselves a little counterfactual speculation, we can ask whether, without Vietnam, the disparate political, artistic, fashion and lifestyle changes of the 1960s would ever have been imagined as a single youth rebellion, as one unified, transformational counterculture.

The three Sixties taste cultures did not exist within hermetically sealed borders, and the vast majority of young people who engaged with any of them were able to move between the three without being significantly aware of the distinctions.[116] It was perfectly possible to be fashion conscious, to believe in inner transformation and to participate in protest culture at one and the same time. In some circles in the 1960s the word 'Revolution', like 'Progress', became an irresistible mantra. Just as supporters of urban development argued that nobody could stand in the way of progress, so disaffected youth accepted without question that revolution was automatically desirable. Both were metaphysical positions. One might even be a militant protester and a devout believer in the inner revolution, as was Abbie Hoffman, the founder of the Yippies, who played his part in embedding the vague and undefined notion of revolution as a good thing in his 1968 book, *Revolution for the Hell of It*.[117] At its least puritanical, the New Left merged smoothly with the inspirational and decadent aspects of hippy-ism: 'The left', Justin Vaisse wrote, then 'reached out beyond itself, inspired by the cultural upheaval and rejection of the stultifying conformity' of the 1950s, of both rock and roll and the Beats, 'the liberation of the individual, exaltation of creativity, the search for ecstasy, and rejection of the work ethic and cult of success'.[118]

However, profound differences remained and the collision between competing countercultural factions is most obvious in the implicit disagreement as to whether revolution must begin with inner transformation or with a direct challenge to the institutions of political and economic power. In 1968, for example, the photographer and journalist John Hopkins, who was prominent in the artistic and psychedelic wing of the London underground, bitterly attacked Tariq Ali, who was prominent in the New Left, for undermining demonstrations against the Vietnam War by promoting pointless confrontation.[119] Ali and the British New Left retained far stronger ties in orthodox Marxism than did their more individualistic American colleagues and Ali himself dismissed the Port Huron statement contemptuously as hardly revolutionary, even if he did approve of its declaration of war on the American Dream.[120] From its inception, hippy culture itself also incorporated fundamental tensions. Emmet Grogan, who was prominent amongst the San Francisco Diggers, took serious issue with Timothy Leary's mantra, 'Turn on, tune in, drop out', from the title of his 1965 book, and which he notably proclaimed at the Be-in, by arguing that it was fine to turn on, but emphatically not to drop out.[121] Like many people, Grogan blamed Timothy Leary for irresponsibly encouraging the young to think they could live without work, so promoting many of the problems of drug abuse and homelessness experienced by young drop-outs. Leary was actually derided by many older counterculturalists, and the artist Charles Perry, recalling his appearance at the 1967 Be-in, described him as a 'middle-aged creep'.[122] Perry's scepticism, in spite of his evident enjoyment of the event, was partly based on the observation that the Be-in was, to some extent, designed to heal childish resentment between the politicos of Berkeley and the apolitical hippies of Haight-Ashbury as to who was getting the most media attention: the participants' chant of 'we are all one' was necessary precisely because they weren't one. The same gulf between 'spaced-out hippies' and 'politicos' erupt again when the Chicago underground newspaper *Seed* advised 'gentle people' to stay away from the demonstrations at the Democratic Party convention.[123]

Grogan also identified a gulf between two philosophies within psychedelic culture: Jerry Rubin's confrontational, radical politics on the one hand and an ideology of love and peace on the other. Both, unlike the New Left, were sustained by drugs, but Rubin's activism was a world away from the belief that love by itself would usher in a new world. If we equate psychedelic culture and hippy culture, then the latter could no longer be seen as exclusively peaceful. Neither was hippyism necessarily opposed to violence. Abby Hoffman, who dreamt of burning Chicago before the 1968 Democratic convention, advocated gun use in the pursuit of the hippy dream.[124] Even Emmet Grogan's admiration for activism extended to the 'Mad Bomber' who bombed New York in the 1930s. Grogan was not concerned with what the bomber did; it was that he did something that mattered; Grogan himself boasted of being arrested for 'smashing a cop on the nose'.[125]

Rubin's own analysis identified an evolution in protest culture through three distinct forms in which the New Left created the teach-in; the hippy created the Be-in; and the yippee created the do-in or live-in.[126] The Diggers' strongest critique was reserved for the commodification of the underground. They despised such 'hip capitalists' as the boutique owners of Haight-Ashbury for whom there was no contradiction between making a profit and working for a better, gentler future. They denounced the hippies as nothing more than consumers and condemned hippy culture as a gimmick to sell products at a profit.[127] In 1967, Grogan said of the 'hip merchants' that 'they created the myth of the utopia; now they aren't going to do anything about it'.[128] He blamed them for fabricating the summer of love and attracting 200,000 teenagers to what was fundamentally a commercial exercise – utopia as a marketing ploy, contributing further to the social disaster promoted by Leary's irresponsibility.

Gerard Winstanley, who founded the original English Diggers in the 1640s, had believed devoutly that, since it was now 6,000 years since the Garden of Eden, the Day of the Lord was at hand, and that in the 'Fulness of Time', the whole world would be incorporated into the promised Kingdom of the Lord Christ. Winstanley looked back to a primeval paradise of rustic bliss and equality:

> In the beginning of time the great creator, Reason, made the earth to be a common treasury, to preserve beasts, birds, fishes and man, the lord that was to govern this creation...Not one word was spoken in the beginning that one branch of mankind should rule over another.[129]

The San Francisco Digger paradise was similarly one of service and devotion to the cause of history and restoration of a natural utopia, a far step from lazy, intoxicated, hedonism. Leary's utopia, by contrast, was one in which men can love without work and money, but they can have all the sex they want, as long as they take LSD and recite oriental mantras at the same time. Leary provoked derision, following his *Playboy* interview in 1966, in which he claimed that LSD could cure homosexuality, which he clearly regarded as a disease.[130] His statement that he had several hundred orgasms in one LSD trip is obviously nonsense but makes total sense if we imagine the psychedelic experience as eternal. At any rate it contributed to the idea that he was a ridiculous figure. Leary was widely regarded with suspicion and, according to his critics, he regarded himself as a prophet, a crime in a culture which was supposed to have no leaders.[131] Some denounced his psychedelic revolution as equally useless as those of anarchists, Marxists, pacifists and humanists.[132] Such sectarianism is the stuff of which revolutionary schisms are made, and the Diggers' denunciation of hippy culture prompted Abbie Hoffman to dissociate himself from the Diggers and, in 1968, found the Yippies in order to reinforce an uncompromising and unified confrontation with 'straight' society.[133] This tension between the two social groups, the 'ordinary hippies' with their decadence, and the Diggers, with their high-minded ideals, was characterized vividly as an internal struggle between 'an amorphous, shifting, and sometimes contentious amalgam of ex-political radicals, psychedelic mystics, Gandhians and Brechtian avant-garde thespians' possessed of 'ideological brio, articulateness, good works and flair for the dramatic event'.[134]

The Diggers positioned themselves exactly within the tradition of radical separatist utopianism which had flourished throughout the nineteenth century. Those who joined the culture of free sex and drugs, though, and followed the simple Crowleyite view that one should do whatever one wanted, were living like animals, in Platonic terms; their attempt to build a Heavenly City of self-indulgence was therefore automatically doomed. It collapsed when it encountered human frailty.

Utopianism and dystopianism merged seamlessly in the psychedelic imagination. The creative output of the English yippie Mick Farren was typical. His vision of a future of society in a state of terminal collapse ravaged by nomadic bikers was published in 1974 but was in line with the ominous, transgressive style he adopted when he originally founded his rock group the Social Deviants in 1967. Any extract of the dialogue in Farren's book makes the dystopian case: one character, Anna says 'Iggy's gonna get bored with us sooner or later. Unless he wastes us for fun first', to which her friend replies: 'He's sure weird. I thought he was gonna kill me a coupla times last night.'[135]

The counterculture's dark underbelly was embodied most vividly by the motorcycle gang, the Hells Angels, to whom attitudes were distinctly ambivalent. Comparing the Angels' casual violence to his own writing, Ken Kesey said without a shred of disapproval, 'we're in the same business: you break people's bones. I break people's heads'.[136] Not everyone agreed, and the Angels were likened by Ginsberg to Nazi Brown Shirts when, in October 1965, they attacked the first anti-war demonstration in Berkeley. Yet, convinced of the redemptive power of their psychedelic vision and in order to preempt a repeat at a demonstration planned in November, Ginsberg, Kesey and Cassady arranged a meeting at the house of the Angels' president, Sonny Barger. All except Ginsberg, who was regularly having bad trips, took LSD, and it was Ginsberg who brought the two sides together by chanting Indian mantras; one by one the Angels, as well as the Pranksters and others, joined in.[137] The plan was successful and the Angels vowed not to attack any more anti-war demonstrations, although they saved face by asserting that their reason was to avoid sullying themselves by touching the dirty protesters. Shortly afterwards Ginsberg took Barger and some of the Angels to occupy front row seats when Bob Dylan performed in San Francisco, after which it became fashionable in hippy culture to flirt with the Angels, seeing them as romantic outlaws. Ginsberg's aims were noble. He believed in the redemptive power of love, expressed through LSD and Indian mantras, to heal the Angels' violent instincts, although in the long run he failed. While the regular police were called pigs, somehow the Angels were considered acceptable. The relatively benign British Angels provided 'security' at the Rolling Stones' free concert in Hyde Park in London in July 1969, a policy which came tragically unstuck a few months later when their entirely more brutal American colleagues provided the same job at the Stones' performance at Altamont in October of the same year and murdered Meredith Hunter.

Not everyone agreed that the Angels violent culture was acceptable. Mick Farren, reviewing Hunter S. Thompson's book on the Angels in 1967, expressed the discomfort many felt at countercultural flirtation with them.[138] Jeff Nuttal, a hero to performance artists in Britain, so not exactly a conservative, vented his contempt for those who admired them:

> Eulogised by the poets Ginsberg, Kesey and McClure, the Angels, under their president Sonny Barger, terrorised Californian society by their arrogant mindless brutality, the extravagant splendour of their filthy array, and their custom of multiple rape.[139]

There was absolutely no condemnation of violence per se. The issue was, who perpetrated it? After all, Aleister Crowley had declared that everyone had the right to kill anyone who restricted their own rights, a statement reproduced without comment in the English underground newspaper, *International Times*, in January 1968.[140] From the mindless violence of the Hells Angels, idealized as a countercultural security force, to the dystopian biker novels of Mick Farren, Abbie Hoffman's flirtation with guns and to the general acceptance that psychedelic experiences could be grotesque and terrifying, darkness and pain were an integral part of the Sixties' experience.[141] Rock music was pervaded with images of absolute licence. The following description of a performance by the rock group the Doors, named in honour of Huxley's *Doors of Perception*, is typical:

> The Doors. Their style is early cunnilingual with overtones of the Massacre of the Innocents. An electrified sex slaughter. A musical blood bath ... The Doors scream into the darkened auditorium what all of us in the underground are whispering more softly in our hearts: we want the world and we want it ... NOW.[142]

The interplay of contradictory instincts, and the nuanced relationship between life-affirming optimism and nihilistic pessimism, was contextualized within notions of the encounter with the pale and fevered romantic poet, described by Robert Stone in his memoir:

> Sometimes we confused self-destructiveness with virtue and talent, obliteration with ecstasy, heedlessness with courage. Worshipping the doctrines of Hemingway as we did, we wanted constant grace under constant pressure, and stoicism before a disillusionment that never went stale. We wanted to die well every single day, to be a cool guy and a good-looking corpse.[143]

The Who's anthemic song 'My Generation', released in December 1965, contained the totemic declaration 'I hope I die before I get old', which could be read either as a desire to die, or a wish to remain young forever. Its nihilism was exuberant, reflecting the playful violence of the group's theatrical instrument smashing. The association of LSD and marijuana with an ideology purely of peace and love was propagated by Leary but never reflected the reality of hippy and psychedelic culture. Allen Ginsberg's poem 'Howl', which Roszak described as 'a founding document of the counterculture', documents one of his own terrifying psychedelic experiences.[144] Ginsberg emphasized the darkness of the psychedelic experience: 'I ... got high on peyote and saw an image of the robot skullface of Moloch in the upper stories of a big hotel glaring into my window ... I wandered down Powell Street muttering "Moloch Moloch" all night & wrote *Howl II* nearly intact in cafeteria at foot of Drake Hotel, deep in hellish vale.'[145] The poem begins with lines which emphasize the inseparability of the light and the dark: 'I saw the best minds of my generation destroyed by madness, starving hysterical naked ... Angel headed hipsters burning for the ancient heavenly connection to the starry dynamo in the machinery of night.'[146] Describing another terrifying drug-induced experience in Peru in 1960, Ginsberg wrote, graphically, 'the whole fucking cosmos broke loose around me ... I felt faced by Death.'[147]

Aside from the Vietnam War, the main feature of the Sixties that distinguishes it from previous excitable decades was one which provoked intense inner change; LSD, the most powerful mind-altering substance ever known. From the early 1960s to the early 1970s, the optimism that surfaced around 1960–1963 was translated into a brief and extraordinary wave of hope that, if only enough people took the drug, the psychedelic doors of perception would be opened to a world of peace, happiness and gratification. To take a pill which is little bigger than a pin head or a single drop of liquid on a piece of blotting paper but which has the power to provoke a visionary experience of such intensity, accompanied by vivid hallucinations lasting anywhere up to twelve hours, as a result of which what formerly seemed real – the material world – dissolves, is as profound an experience as anyone can imagine. What has until now been accepted as normal is replaced by a universe in which the imaginary and the psychic themselves become real. LSD has been described as a 'deconditioning agent', which at a stroke removes the conditioning of regular society and opens the user up to wonder, splendour and mystery of the universe.[148] The cosmos becomes an entity in itself, time and space all one. As Tom Wolfe reported:

> And Kesey – *Where does it go? I don't think man has ever been there. We're under cosmic control and have been for a long long time, and each time it builds, it's bigger, and it's stronger. And then you find out… about Cosmo, and you discover that he's running the show…*[149]

'The *kairos!*', Wolfe exclaimed, echoing Augustine, adding, 'we creatively brought the past, the future and the fictitious into the present moment'.[150] In Platonic terms the shadows of Becoming may be replaced by the truth of Being. The experience has the capacity to change anyone, whatever their background. This is why the starting point of hippy ideology was the vision of a world beyond this world.[151] Time is cut, in Žižek's phrase, and eternity is glimpsed: in the language of nineteenth-century esotericism, psychedelic drugs allow the user to penetrate the veil which conceals the truth. And the LSD evangelists, too, thought that shortly, everyone was destined to 'turn on', as part of an inevitable historical process. Beyond its intensity and capacity to provoke inner change, though, there is nothing essential in the psychedelic experience, and one person's heaven can be another's hell. Attempts to define an elite comprised of initiates who had undergone the LSD experience were sabotaged by the experience's very uneven quality.[152] Hippy utopianism merged seamlessly with Blakeian dystopian hell. There are as many examples of 'dark' hippyism as there are of light, and both were relished at the time: which was hardly surprising as the user of LSD could hallucinate demons as easily as angels and the appallingly grotesque as much as the sublimely beautiful. Huxley's premonition forecast the paradox which saw the rise in disease, theft and the frequent 'panicky incoherence of the LSD trip' which afflicted the Haight-Ashbury heart of hippie culture even as the summer of love became a world-wide media story.[153] Beginning in 1965, the UCLA medical centre began to see a rise in the number of psychiatric victims of psychedelic use.[154] In the same year there was a casual acceptance that people who were dosed with LSD at the Pranksters' Acid Tests might freak out and have 'a bad time for a few days'.[155] Amongst users, the lack of compassion for those who suffered was absolute. The dangers represented by the plea to avoid the 'bad acid' famous in the film of Woodstock were institutionalized in the presence of 'bad trip' tents at some festivals, to which sufferers could be taken, hopefully to be 'talked down'. By 1969, and the Woodstock Festival, the 'Freak Out' tent was an established part of the psychedelic repertoire.[156] Advice on how to deal with such often-terrifying experiences was published from at least 1967 onwards in underground papers such as the *East Village Other*.

Leary himself observed that, under the drug's influence, the urban New York scene produced very different effects to those at his rural home in Milbrook.[157] He coined the phrase 'set and setting' in order to make the point that the quality of the experience depends on the user's emotional condition and environment. He therefore set out to create his religious renaissance, taking youthful optimism and recasting it as ecstasy, framing the psychedelic experience within his chosen religious format, Tibetan Buddhism.[158] Contextualized by the writings of Aldous Huxley and Leary, the trappings of eastern wisdom and an extreme form of American individualism, the belief that LSD could transform the world gripped some of the counterculture's leaders, and they set out to achieve this new world as soon as possible. Beginning in November 1965 Ken Kesey's Merry Pranksters organized twenty-four events, which they called 'Acid Tests', at which 10,000 people were introduced to the drug.[159] Leary optimistically estimated that, encouraged by his organization, the League of Spiritual Discovery, between four and five million Americans would take the drug in 1966.[160] He believed that LSD liberated one's inner divine, but that if one ceased taking it the knowledge would vanish. His intolerance of those who didn't share his vision was absolute. Only regular users belonged in his new world and he expressed contempt for both non-users and lapsed users.[161] No back-sliding was to be permitted and apostasy was forbidden. There were even proposals to administer LSD to unwilling participants, an example of hippy fascism, designed to save those who didn't know they needed saving.[162] The community of LSD takers tended to see themselves as an elite, a caste apart, separated from people they dismissively referred to as 'straights'.[163]

In this sense, LSD takers mimicked the secrecy of charismatic groups. They were not literally secretive, far from it, but they possessed a secret. George Melly pointed out that, to publicize one's use of LSD was a means of maintaining one's position as one of the elite in the hierarchy of fashion, music and style.[164] Yet, what they publicised was their possession of secret knowledge. In George Simmel's words, 'the secret gives one a position of exception … everything mysterious is also important and essential'.[165] Secrecy, Michael Maffesoli argued, is a 'paroxysmal form of the aloofness' of the countercultural tribes, one which encourages marginalization as a means of resisting centralized power.[166] And, as David Hume had written of earlier representatives of 'Enthusiasm', 'The fanatic consecrates himself and bestows on his own person a sacred character, much superior to what forms and ceremonious institutions can confer on any other'.[167]

Timothy Leary was undoubtedly the most high-profile of the psychedelic evangelists. Although he was treading in Huxley's footsteps, he was more responsible than anyone for the sacralization of the LSD experience.[168] The psychedelic revolution would have happened without him, but whereas Aldous Huxley emphasized the utility of psychedelics in the quest for inner knowledge, Leary became convinced that their use would inevitably result in a complete transformation of society as a whole. There is a line of transmission from Swedenborg, Gurdjieff, Ouspensky and Krishnamurti though Huxley to Leary, in which the new world comes about entirely as a consequence of transformation in each individual, independent of historical patterns. Little or no attention is paid to the predetermined timing of history. Leary himself appears to have believed that prediction was actually impossible. In the 1990s, over thirty years after his first LSD experiments, he wrote, 'Until now, human beings have been neurologically unable to conceive of the future'.[169] Utopia, in the sense of perfect existence, was now available in the form of a tiny pill, or a single drop of liquid, hence the Beatles' injunction in the LSD-inspired song 'Tomorrow Never Knows', to give one's self up to the transcendence of the current moment. The prophecy of a coming age was rendered irrelevant, for it had already arrived. There is more than a hint of the Swedenborgian tradition in Leary. The entire millenarian struggle was aborted and the revolution consisted entirely in the consumption of a drug, and entry into the next phase of history was individual. It might eventually be collective, once enough people had joined, but in the meantime some people were in it and others were not. Leary's partner, Richard Alpert, looked back on the early 1960s and recalled 'We did have a higher vision of how we were trying to live life', but when his interviewer asked 'Did you still feel as if you were on the edge of a wave of utopia ... a transformation of society?', he agreed but moved the conversation swiftly on.[170]

Leary had set out on his spiritual quest in August 1960, having experienced a life-changing Damascene moment under the influence of psilocybin mushrooms.[171] He immersed himself in the existing, very small network of psychedelic enthusiasts and read Huxley for the first time in October 1960, just over a week before meeting him.[172] By 1961 he was mixing with the Beats in Paris, experiencing a world totally removed from his former life as a New England academic.[173] Leary was an inveterate networker who pursued all useful contacts in his evangelical dream and, after his initial encounter with Huxley, he drew everyone he could into his sphere. Alan Watts, who later became the decade's major populariser of Zen Buddhism, passed by in 1961, writing up his experiences in *The Joyous Cosmology* in 1962, and the psychiatrist R. D. Laing, famous for his redefinition of schizophrenia in *The Divided Self*, took LSD with Leary in the winter of 1963–1964.[174]

Leary followed Huxley in converting the LSD-inspired perception of the experiential unity of all things into a belief in the unity of all essential religious experience and his language mirrored Alice Bailey's because they shared a common lineage rather than because he was familiar with her teachings. The western strand of thought which occurs in Leary's writings was the Christian apocalyptic which would have surrounded him in American culture. Leary recorded one spiritual epiphany after an LSD trip in Mexico in June 1962: 'I was in heaven', he recorded, 'Illumination ... A sudden thought. Now that this breakthrough of consciousness had occurred, a new level of harmony and love was available. I must bring my family and friends to this new universe', and, in language directly borrowed from the New Testament, 'the new revelation demands a new body'.[175] 'Just as there is only one heaven', he continued, 'so too there is only one earth ... The earth in its devotion carries all things, good and evil, without exception'.[176] Yet, he retained a strong devotion to his materialist training and believed that just all religious phenomena could be reducible to biochemical terms, which is precisely why LSD's disruption of brain chemistry was so useful.[177]

Only later, in the 1970s, did Leary begin to identify himself in messianic terms as Crowley's heir.[178] Crowley's influence, though, was present from the beginning of psychedelic culture, along with esoteric currents coming from Bailey, Jung and other earlier twentieth-century prophets.[179] Crowley's 1922 autobiography, *Diary of a Drug Fiend*, chimed perfectly with the mood of the times and legitimized the use of psychedelics and narcotics within a framework which could be generally seen as spiritual, definitely with the acquisition of higher – or deeper – knowledge, and within the idea of human evolution into a higher state: 'We're in an intermediate state', Crowley wrote enigmatically, 'between the stupor of the peasant and – something that is not yet properly developed'.[180]

The connection between psychedelic culture and the Crowleyite and theosophical prophetic tradition was made via the Beats, in particular through John Cooke and Harry Smith. Cooke, who was born in 1920, knew L. Ron Hubbard, encountered the Sufis, assisted the Indian guru Meher Baba and studied Blavatsky, Bailey and Gurdjieff; in 1945, at the precocious age of 25, his story, 'Black Magic Question Mark', was published in the *American Theosophist*.[181] Harry Smith was born into a theosophical background in 1923 and achieved distinction as a collector of American folk music. His life reads like a record of the artistic-magical culture from the 1940s to 1980s. He became a prominent member of Crowley's OTO and moved to Berkeley in 1945 where his encyclopaedic knowledge of American music meant that he became a legend amongst the Bay Area musical community. He was also a noted experimental film maker and influenced Kenneth Anger.[182] Both Cooke and Smith converted their magical interests into performance. Cooke inspired what was to be one of the great Sixties' iconic events for a 'Gathering of the Tribes': the 'Human Be-in' in Golden Gate Park in January 1967, a happier version of Robespierre's festival of the supreme being. It was the perfect celebration of the hippy as noble savage, living in Montaignesque bliss. Seven months later, in October, Smith contributed to the 'Levitation of the Pentagon', one of the year's focal anti-war protests, attended by around 100,000 demonstrators.

Cooke, being disabled, remained at his home in Mexico in the early 1960s; but in 1966, aware of the emerging counterculture in San Francisco, he dispatched his spiritual protégé Michael Bowen to the city. Bowen was born in 1937, like Smith into a theosophical background, and had mixed with prominent Crowleyites in Los Angeles, including Kenneth Anger. Bowen met Cooke in mid-1958 and, after the advent of LSD and around the time as the early experiments at Leary's base at Millbrook, Bowen became one of Cooke's 'Psychedelic Rangers', a revolutionary vanguard established in order to promote the drug as a transformational religious sacrament. For Cook and Bowen the Be-in was supposed to be a vehicle for ushering in the Aquarian Age, 'a spiritual occasion of otherworldly dimensions that would raise the vibration of the entire planet'.[183] With iconography and costumes drawn from Asian and Native American sources, filtered through surrealism and Dada, the participants listened to Ginsburg and his fellow Beat, Gary Snyder, chanting Buddhist mantras. The reviewer for the underground newspaper *The San Francisco Oracle* declared:

> Now in this twentieth of recent centuries a generation, considered by many to be the reincarnation of the American Indian, has been born out of the ashes of World War Two, rising like a Phoenix, in celebration of the slightly psychedelic zeit-geist of this brand-new Aquarian Age.[184]

The reviewer quoted the Be-in's 'Master of Ceremonies', echoing Blavatsky and Jung: 'Brothers, the spirit of the New Messiah may not be coming to us, but from us'.[185] Later, looking back, Bowen referred specifically to Huxley's perennialism and Crowley's statement from the Book of the Law that people are like stars. He spoke about:

> The mystery of human equality, as well as unique star-like qualities and talents that are intrinsic within us all. This perennial truth has been with human civilisation since time immemorial. However on that magical day in San Francisco, this truth became clear and observable to everyone as the large gathering at the Human Be-In simultaneously realized and felt as One. A mystical experience of unity was effectively achieved.[186]

The ritual structure for the levitation of the Pentagon was mapped out by Harry Smith. From his experience in the OTO, Smith prescribed a consecration of the four cardinal directions – north, south, east and west – using the symbols of the four alchemical elements – fire, air, earth and water – and recommended the presence of a cow painted with mythic symbols in order to invoke the Egyptian goddess Hathor.[187] At a crucial moment the performance poet and writer Ed Sanders recited his 'exorgasm' text, proclaiming the unity of all male deities are one, and paraphrasing Dupuis, Higgins and Massey.

> In the name of the amulets of touching, seeing, groping, hearing and loving, we call upon the powers of the cosmos to protect our ceremonies in the name of Zeus, in the name of Anubis, god of the dead … in the name of Dionysus, Zagreus, Jesus, Yahweh, the unnamable, the quintessent finality of the Zoroastrian fire, in the name of Hermes, in the name of the Beak of Sok, in the name of scarab, in the name of the Tyrone Power Pound Cake Society in the Sky, in the name of Rah, Osiris, Horus, Nepta, Isis, in the name of the flowing living universe … we call upon the spirit to raise the Pentagon from its destiny and preserve it.[188]

The Pentagon didn't lift off, although some said they saw it rise a few inches into the air and others said it didn't really matter whether it rose or not. The point was the performance. In the following year, the Aquarian Age was to be commodified and broadcast to a much wider public via the musical *Hair*: 'This is the dawning of the Age of Aquarius.'[189]

In the UK the *International Times* – usually abbreviated to *IT* – was the medium by which Aquarian and New Age ideas entered psychedelic culture. The key figure was John Michel, a writer who was placed firmly within the Romantic New Age lineage and who was primarily responsible for feeding esoteric ideas into the counterculture from around 1966 to his death in 2009. In 1961, Michel was running a 'book-cum-records' shop in Powis Square with the 'poet, writer and junkie author' Alex Trocchi.[190] In 1966 Michel became one of the assorted group of key activists who wrote for *IT*, the first underground newspaper, which became his vehicle for introducing a range of ideas which were to become central to its iconography. Michel brought Jung's Aquarian Age theories directly into psychedelic culture in January 1967, in particular the belief that the world is in a state of crisis, that a new age is beginning, and that UFOs are the portent of this.[191] He followed this in October of the same year by introducing Theosophy, Crowley and Jung as part of a further discussion of UFOs as signs of a historical transformation.[192] The month after Michel's first article appeared, the *International Times* carried a second feature on the New Age. This reported on the portentously named 'Commission for Research into the Creative Faculties of Man', which had been set up in London in 1961 in order to assist with preparations for the Aquarian Age. Optimism and hope shone through: 'The New Age means to rise again, to be reborn ... A New Ager is someone in a position of absolute knowledge, possessing singleness of purpose and practicing a form of absolutism.'[193] Crowley himself became the focus of correspondence in the *International Times* in October 1967, followed in January 1968 by an article by his biographer, Kenneth Grant reporting the beginning of the New Aeon in 1904.[194] In his preface to the 1972 reprint of his 1969 book *The View over Atlantis* Michel paraphrased Jung and prophesied that:

> Despite the warnings of astrologers and students of sacred history, many find themselves unprepared for the changes that inevitably occur as the spring point enters Aquarius.[195]

Michel was one of the contributors to the 1971 Glastonbury Fayre, perhaps the UK's most iconic free festival. The 1987 review of all the Glastonbury festivals to date made the Fayre's political cosmology overt: 'many of the 12,000 who were there enjoyed the experience and felt it to be a turning point in their own lives. They saw it as a vision of what the Age of Aquarius could achieve with less emphasis on material possessions and more on caring and sharing.'[196] And so the Sixties moved seamlessly into the Seventies.

Yet, the fiction of the end of the Sixties is an enduring one. It was in 1974 that George Melly composed his obituary for the Sixties lamenting the end of a decade of hedonism: the party was over.[197] Utopia had been glimpsed, and lost, and the faithful had let the Millennium slip through their hands. With the benefit of hindsight many Sixties veterans looked back and identified their own weaknesses. Robert Stone, a deep insider in the counterculture, reflected on what he saw as the end of the Sixties dream as the inevitable consequence of the dialectical contradictions within the counterculture, mainly the extent to which its lack of realism undermined its ability to achieve goals, together with the fundamental conflict between its life-affirming optimism on the one hand and its pessimistic nihilism on the other:

> Our expectations were too high, our demands excessive, things were harder than we expected ... How absurd, because nothing is free, and we had to learn that at last ... We learned what we had to, and we did what we could. In some ways the world profited and will continue to profit by what we succeeded in doing. We were the chief victims of our own mistakes. Measuring ourselves against the masters of the present, we regret nothing except our failure to prevail.[198]

For some, the violence at the Altamont free festival in December 1969 marked the end of the mythical Sixties, providing a supposedly dystopian counter to the same year's utopia at Woodstock.[199] In his 2007 introduction to the 1960s classic, *The*

Psychedelic Experience, Daniel Pinchbeck, who was to succeed Timothy Leary as the counterculture's principal psychedelic evangelist, thought that 'the brief flowering of the psychedelic era ... ended abruptly when Woodstock gave way to Altamont ... and sensitive Beatles lyrics inspired the homicidal rages of Charles Manson's family.'[200] In this popularly accepted Manichean narrative, a period characterized by peace and light crashed into one characterized by darkness and violence. By 1969, or 1970 at the latest, a new Fall had taken place, a fresh expulsion from paradise. But what such narratives really represent is a sense of loss by some of the Sixties leading figures and a nostalgia from those, like Pinchbeck, who was born in 1966, were too young to experience the excitement which they could only read about. Timothy Leary, for his part, looked back with disdain at aspects of psychedelic culture, including his own dalliance with India:

> The drug culture of the 1960s wandered around, 'spaced out' and 'high', but with no place to go. They were too early for interstellar migration. Into this neural vacuum rushed the karma dealers, Jesus salesmen and spiritualists providing occult terms and otherworldly explanations for the new transcendental states.[201]

It is difficult to take Leary seriously. He had encouraged an overtly mystical approach to drug use from 1960 and continued to do so until his death. Yet his view that somehow the psychedelic revolution went wrong is typical. In many ways the Sixties were a repetition of a constant pattern of revolt and the search for alternatives. An awareness of precedents for the decade was already evident at the time, including the Europe-wide upheavals of 1848, or the 1920s, in which the fun and decadence of the jazz-age vied with enthusiasm for communism, very much as fashion and politics competed for attention in the 1960s: the revolutionary year 1968 then becomes a repetition of the revolutionary year 1848.[202] Actually, narratives of decline began in late 1967. The 'Death of Hippy' ritual in San Francisco was one symptom. In December 1967, reporting on the London underground, Peter Fryer reported that 'what amazed us in the spring of 1967 is already beginning to do no more than charm, and what charms must eventually pall'.[203] Fryer's problem was two-fold: he objected to both the underground's eclecticism and its commercialization. What had been a moment of purity nine months earlier had already been lost. And here lies the utopian's dilemma – that hopes for purity are always bound to be dashed because the world is imperfect.

One feature of the Sixties is supposed to have been the war between the generations. It is true that most rebels and drop-outs were young. But the idea that the younger generation was invented in the 1960s is another fiction. Back in 1928 F. Scott Fitzgerald, a member of the 'Lost Generation', who grew up during the First World War and its aftermath, had considered the matter and concluded:

> By a generation, I mean that reaction against the fathers which seems to occur about three times in a century. It is distinguished by a set of ideas, inherited in moderated form from the madmen and outlaws of the generation before. If it is a real generation it has its own leaders and spokesmen, and it draws into its orbit those born just before it and just after, whose ideas are less clear-cut and defiant.[204]

The idea that any cultural period can have a fixed beginning or end is likewise a fiction, and the Sixties had neither a defined beginning nor an end. The rhetorical, or mythical, Sixties, constituted a mindset, or series of mindsets, which became the focus of huge public attention during the decade, and are not quite the same as the 1960s as a historical period. All the various and competing states of mind that combined in the Sixties shared a hope that the world was suddenly entering a phase which was much better, in many respects, than any previous period in human history. As Bloch argued, such feelings are the psychological underpinning of utopian mentalities. The Sixties, rather than the 1960s, was an eruption of self-conscious utopianism, not unlike the 'Fin-de-Siècle', albeit in the middle of a century rather than the end. The Sixties were a classic example of improvisational millenarianism, updated to a context in which nothing mattered apart from personal expression, liberation and salvation.[205] The immediacy of the moment is much more important than the future prophecy: the kingdom of God happens now, not in years to come. The spirit of such movements is anti-dogmatic, averse to hierarchies and antinomian, dismissive of law and inclined to unconventional behaviour.[206]

The counterculture neither began nor ended in the 1960s. It consisted of different ideas and practices which passed seamlessly from the 1940s to the 1980s, in a thread connected by artists, performers, radical thinkers, hipsters, Beats and hippies. Californian esotericism moved seamlessly from Max Heindel's Rosicrucian Foundation and the foundation of the Theosophical Society's colony at Krotona in 1912 through both Krishnamurti and the OTO to psychedelic culture's adoption of esoteric and magical mentalities. Across the English-speaking world, the millenarian utopianism which carried the early English colonists connected the 1660s to the 1960s in an unbroken lineage. It was an Awakening.

Counterculture and Utopia after the Sixties

In the popular imagination the utopian Sixties came to an end sometime just before, or several years after, the close of the calendrical 1960s – usually sometime between 1969 and 1974, its hopes of a better world dashed. The belief in the end of the Sixties, though, is an enduring fiction. Simply, it is based in a kind of linear history in which movements rise and fall in a simple sequence, a position which ignores the fact that, as the 1960s became the 1970s there was no consciousness of a change in mood. Far from it: in 1971 Anthony Esler concluded that 'The Youth Revolution is not fading away. It is, in fact, a growing force in history'.[1] The historical 1960s and mythical Sixties simply do not coincide. For example, John D'Emilio, writing about gay activism, said that, if he was asked to remember the 1960s, he was more likely to think of events from the 1970s.[2] The idea of an ending to the Sixties actually obscures substantial elements of continuity. In 1996, for example, almost thirty years after the 'Summer of Love', Michael Maffesoli saw no change in the continuing vitality at work in what he defined as the 'avoidance lifestyles' which we might see as characteristic of countercultural mentalities.[3]

If there was a change in what Žižek called the 'gist' of a decade, it took place after 1970.[4] Altamont and the Manson murders certainly had nothing to do with it, for both were completely in line with the flirtation with nihilist violence which were an uncomfortable feature of Sixties culture. They challenged only one small part of the Sixties, the gentle, fey, naïve, culture of peace and love but chimed all too easily with Abbie Hoffman's flirtation with guns, Jim Morrison's self-indulgent, confrontational hedonism and Crowley's claim that an essential human right was the right to kill those who impinged on one's own rights.

The Sixties counterculture did not disappear. The optimistic Learyesque assumption that the new world would begin if only enough people took enough LSD and stopped working for a living largely faded, but the desire to build an alternative to the perceived evils of bourgeois, capitalist society did not. What really happened in the early 1970s was the end of the single overarching, unifying, countercultural factor, US involvement in the Vietnam War: by 1972, there were serious reductions in US troop levels in Vietnam and in 1973 the Paris Peace accords brought the US involvement in the war to an end.[5] The direct result was the winding down of the protest movement. There was no longer a single rallying cry, no more a single thing to be against. In addition, many of the more immediate grievances of university students had been resolved. Economic pressures were prompted by the OPEC oil embargo of 1973 and the resulting financial crisis, and compounded in the UK by the miners' strikes of 1973 and 1974 and the resulting power cuts and three-day week. Rising unemployment destroyed the illusion of endless wealth which had underpinned the happy-go-lucky drop-out mentality. The belief that the new era could be wished into existence during an LSD trip took a blow, but the belief in building alternatives remained as strong.

Academic announcements of a change in *zeitgeist* and the end of the Sixties began to appear in 1976, along with the proposition that 'the' counterculture, conceived mistakenly as a single entity, had fractured into different 'post-movement groups':

> Whereas freaks had found meaning in maintaining a position of defiance and opposition to the 'plastic world', post-movement groups find meaning in escape from the complexities and incongruities of the material world (or the world of the mind) into a more transcendent simplified view of the cosmos independent of material reality.[6]

According to some accounts, the young in the United States had switched from a rejection of conventional western values to an acceptance of them and had abandoned the individualistic 'expressivism' which had been a core quality of the hippy utopia.[7] The wider evidence suggests this is far from the case, if we consider the continuing vibrancy of the musical and art worlds in the 1970s. However, the narrative is a persistent one. The story tells how youthful rebels, once constituting a revolutionary counterculture or 'adversary culture' had become, by the 1970s, a new establishment consisting of media workers, college professors and others in the 'knowledge industry who, together, constituted a 'university-government-media complex'.[8] In this scenario, the revolution had been betrayed by the revolutionaries, and the utopian dreamers had woken from their reverie. All of which means simply that some hippies had grown up and some dropouts had dropped back in. The obvious failing in this scenario is that it doesn't account for those who didn't drop back in nor does it consider the difference between those whose hippy commitment was deep – such as former Diggers – on the one hand and so-called casual, weekend hippies on the other.[9] Neither does it allow for the rejuvenation of oppositional youth culture with new recruits.

In this questionable narrative, the transition from the Sixties consists of a crisis in which hopeful activism is replaced by confused and passive introversion, a retreat from engagement with the world and the here and now to an obsession with the self and the other world. To further confuse the issue there is an alternative theory which proposes the opposite, in which it was the Sixties that was self-obsessed and the Seventies that replaced the pointless narcissism of psychedelic culture with a more realistic concern with concrete political activity. Both versions of events pose a crisis in the utopian project, but both are mistaken in their dramatic oversimplification. The idea of clearly defined post-Sixties movements is itself suspect. For example, the first 'Earth Day' may have been held in 1970, but ecological and environmental concerns can be traced continuously back to the nineteenth century, to the Romantics and earlier.[10] Rachel Carson's seminal book, *Silent Spring*, which was central to the raising of environmental consciousness, was published in 1962, before the peak of Sixties enthusiasm, not after. The same is true of Second Wave Feminism. Betty Friedan's bestseller, *The Feminine Mystique*, was published in 1963, and in 1966 Friedan became the first president of the National Organisation of Women. Only the Gay Liberation movement was galvanized at the end of the Sixties, following the Stonewall riot in New York in June 1969. Even if some of the objects of discontent changed, protest culture continued from the 1960s to the 1970s without a break.[11]

For Roszak, the counterculture matured away from casual drug use and sexual indulgence into a genuine search for workable alternatives. In contrast to Leary and Pinchbeck's psychedelic pessimism, he wrote 'How far we have come since the callow days of LSD and Tolkien's hobbits', and considering the decade from 1965 to 1975 he mused: 'the taste for psychedelic delights has reached out to salvage a hundred occult and mystic disciplines, both traditional and experimental; the fairy tale reveries have assimilated (often with marvellous indiscrimination) all the myth and lore of the world.'[12] And so the idea gestates that New Ageism is a product of the Sixties, in spite of its much earlier vibrant existence. The belief that the New Age movement originated in the counterculture of the 1960s became accepted wisdom in the academic literature in 1991, when J. Gordon Melton, Jerome Clarke and Aidan Kelly set its launch date, with remarkable precision, as 1971.[13] The idea then proliferated through the literature. Antoine Faivre wrote of the 'New Age, a diverse movement that appeared the 1970s in California' qualifying himself partly by adding, 'originating in part with Alice Bailey'.[14] The idea spread and Harvey then quoted Faivre.[15] And in 2007 Martin Ramstedt wrote unequivocally that 'the beginnings of the New Age movement were definitely counter-cultural'.[16]

The story being told here is of a mass rejection of the unstructured culture of psychedelic drug use by a structured pursuit of psychological growth or spiritual salvation. There is plenty of evidence, although little research, to support the claim that the ranks of spiritual and esoteric groups were swelled by former – and ongoing – users of psychedelic drugs. But such people were not creating something new. They were entering a network of groups and organizations which was already around a century old. One could perhaps say that that the New Age movement 'piggy backed' on the counterculture.[17] But it had also played a part in creating it. The Sixties had already absorbed substantial input from New Age culture – from Leary's theosophically inspired use of the *Tibetan Book of the Dead* to Crowley's New Aeon and Jung's Aquarian Age.

What happened in the transition from the mythical Sixties to the mythical Seventies was the end of the illusion that there was a single counterculture, one youth revolution to which all tribes and taste cultures subscribed. The excitable commentary to the documentary of the Rolling Stones concert in Hyde Park in July 1969 had portrayed the audience as a single, peaceful 'gathering of the clans', following the 'gathering of the tribes' at the 1967 Be-in, all the different countercultural tribes – mods, rockers and hippies – finally coming together in one life-changing event.[18] Mick Jagger gently squashed that suggestion by comparing the event in bucolic English terms to a village fete.

The belief that LSD and rock music could change the world collapsed when it became clear that the psychedelic experience did not necessarily make people spiritually aware, while many rock musicians had no interest in anything other than playing rock music.[19] They had no ideals beyond the Crowleyesque freedom to do as they wished. The symbols of Sixties revolution lost their power: a prime example was the conversion of long hair on men from a symbol of rejection of all things American to one which celebrated the honest values of the frontier, a development encouraged by the emergence of so-called 'southern rock' in the United States, with bands such as Lynyrd Skynyrd. For many, delirious optimism was replaced by pragmatic realism, but not much else changed. The surviving Beats – Ginsburg and Burroughs amongst them – continued to occupy a distinguished and influential role.[20] Neither should we accept the sneer that the supposed post-countercultural survivals of the 1970s were degenerate forms of their pure Sixties originals, compromises which sucked the life out of something which had been noble, characterized by 'compromise, degeneracy or hypocrisy'.[21] This is the construction of the Sixties as a Golden Age, an exercise in nostalgia, a tale of paradise lost, preserved only in the memories of those who were there.

The idea of a post-countercultural phase of history is contained within a much wider general tendency in the 1970s to identify the present as coming after something else, to which it was supposedly completely different. The 1970s could be defined less in their own terms than by what they followed. For example, in 1976, Daniel Bell, the influential neoconservative, argued that history had entered a third phase. In the first, he claimed, reality had been located in nature; in the second, it was technological; and in the third, which had now been entered, it was social.[22] The world, or the United States, at least, he thought, was now to be defined not by what one made but by whom one was, a remarkably prescient forecast in view of the rise of social media, forty years later. It is also somewhat in line with Marx's statement that 'the standpoint of the old materialism is *"civil"* society; the standpoint of the new is *human* society, or socialised humanity'.[23] Marx in turn was paraphrasing Hegel, for whom the final state was social.[24] In 1987, ten years after Bell, Boris Frankel looked back and wondered whether the previous twenty years, since 1967, could be seen as a kind of repetition of the first few decades of the nineteenth century, particularly between the 1820s and 1840s. Back then, industrialization had transformed life in much of Western Europe and led to the development of utopian socialism, including Marxism.[25] Frankel thought that the increasing problems experienced by heavy industry in the west and the presumed crisis in modernity in the 1970s and 1980s seemed to reverse the experience of the 1820s to 1840s: in the first phase, the west had industrialized and in the second, it deindustrialized. Regardless of whether there was a kind of strange mirroring of one phase of history by another, there was a widespread view that western history had entered a new phase and an obsession with naming eras according to what they came after, novelty now consisting only in decline. The new period might be 'post-bourgeois', 'post-economic' or 'post-industrial'.[26] And then there is the ubiquitous 'postmodern' which caught on as an almost universal academic label of a certain kind of worldview, eschewing whatever might be called modern. And in to this general soup of 'post' periods we may consign the idea of post-Sixties movements. The practice of naming eras as if they were self-contained distinct, uniform periods became a habit, if a misleading one, so much so that in 2003, Ken Jowitt referred to the 'proliferation of prefixes' by intellectuals and journalists to describe the 1990s.[27] Others eschewed the idea of 'post' periods. In 1976 Theodore Roszak used the term 'Aquarian Frontier' as a metaphor for the transition which he now saw as underpinning the counterculture.[28] In 1980, Marilyn Ferguson attracted much greater attention to Aquarianism as a metaphor for New Age culture in *The Aquarian Conspiracy*.[29]

Throughout all these post-Sixties historical periods, New Age culture remained as resolutely consistent and optimistic as it had ever been, and enjoyed a public vogue not seen since the 1930s. New Age material was disseminated via events which by the late 1970s were known as 'New Age festivals' or 'Psychic Fayres', of which the one of the earliest was the 'Celestial Synapse' held in San Francisco in 1969.[30] The largest, most commercial and enduring of such events, the London-based Festival of Mind, Body, Spirit, was first held in 1977 and attracted a wide and largely non-countercultural public by tapping into a much deeper interest in spiritualism and the occult which posed alternatives to mainstream science and the church but had never sought an overthrow of society. The Festival became a global franchise; a New York version was held in 1979 and the London festival was still being held in 2015.[31] Once they had found a settled form, such events included stalls set up to sell wares, spread information and recruit members to a variety of esoteric groups espousing all sorts of wisdom and activities perceived to have been rejected by the scientific and religious mainstream. The eclectic mix included UFO religions, transcendental meditators, vegetarians, circle dancers, depth and growth psychologists, Buddhists, Hare Krishna monks, tarot readers, clairvoyants, spiritualists and environmentalists; and those present were motivated by a combination of a proselytizing mission and the need to earn a living. Only a few groups, such as the Aetherius Society and Benjamin Crème, had any explicit interest in the coming New or Aquarian Ages. Crème himself was a follower of Alice Bailey and former vice-president of the Aetherius Society who claimed to have made contact with extra-terrestrial beings in 1959 and began to teach in London in 1975.[32] He attracted huge media attention, and a great deal of derision, when he announced that the Aquarian Age would be inaugurated on 21 June 1982 with the arrival of the Lord Maitreya, the cosmic Christ. Most participants at the Mind-Body-Spirit festivals, though, had little interest in an imminent historical transition to a new world, even if they subscribed in general to the idea that spirituality, however vaguely defined, was a good thing and was increasing. Crème was a favourite amongst journalists at the time but was a minor figure in the esoteric underground as a whole.

It was on the basis of such events and the accompanying literature that Christian evangelicals such as Constance Cumbey constructed their lists of what constituted New Age activities, in order to better alert the faithful to the danger confronting them.[33] The scientific sceptics soon followed and Martin Gardner randomly included everything he classed as pseudo-science as New Age, from ESP to perpetual motion machines.[34] What now passes for wider New Age culture is therefore partly an academic adaptation of an evangelical construct created on the basis of an eclectic commercial event. In addition, the concept of the New Age as a recent, post-Sixties phenomenon has encouraged the view that it is ephemeral and hence easily dispensed with. Having pronounced the end of the Sixties, historians could now pronounce the New Age over. William Irwin declared the New Age 'dead'; Gordon Melton introduced the 'post New-Age', announcing that 'the New Age Movement has passed into history'; and Massimo Introvigne introduced the 'Next Age'.[35] All are influential, but all fail to recognize the

New Age movement's long history. If the notion of the counterculture as a unique, self-enclosed chronological zone collapses, then so does the fallacious argument that New Age culture emerged from its ruins.

The declaration that the New Age was over came from insiders as well as academics, largely because it was felt that the culture was being taken over by commerce.[36] The reaction against commercialization in the 1970s and 1980s, extending to a rejection of the term New Age itself, replicated the Digger rejection of the commodification of hippyism from 1967 onwards. For example, William Bloom, who was deeply influenced by Alice Bailey, rejected the term New Age in reaction against its apparent take over by the media, epitomized by the involvement of the Hollywood star Shirley MacLaine. However, there was nothing in Blavatskyanism or the teachings of Alice Bailey or Rudolf Steiner which said that one couldn't be in business. The anti-commercial critics might accuse MacLaine of promoting money above the spiritual message, but the counter-argument was that commerce was necessary to spread the message.

There were a number of enthusiastic New Age evangelists in the 1970s, all of whom were deeply influenced by Alice Bailey. The first was David Spangler. In 1980 Spangler announced unequivocally that: 'Now humanity is undergoing another vast evolutionary change which is symbolised both factually and allegorically by the concept of a new age, the age of Aquarius.'[37] From a background in childhood clairvoyance, Spangler discovered the New Age through reading Bailey in 1959, settled at the New Age community at Findhorn in Scotland and, after around 1970, became the most prolific author in the field.[38] Findhorn itself was one of the places that Taves was thinking of when he argued that the new age networks of the 1950s were 'transformed into a more activist form' by 1960s utopian communities.[39] Spangler himself was part of a cultural milieu entirely separate to hippyish Aquarianism. He was in San Francisco in 1968, but his route into the New Age community was via its esoteric Christianity rather than LSD.[40] It was Spangler's books, *Festivals in the New Age*, published in 1975, and *Revelation: the birth of a new age*, which appeared in 1977, which brought the term New Age into a wider usage, efforts which were reinforced by his colleague and collaborator Sir George Trevelyan (1906–1966), who contributed the foreword to *Revelation*.[41]

George Trevelyan was likewise a Baileyite and was to be influential through the lectures he organized though the Wrekin Trust, which he set up in 1971, and his own writing, beginning in 1975. He paraphrased Fox, Curtiss and the other New Age teachers from the pre-war period, offering a message of hope:

> Change could come rapidly because if human consciousness blended with the higher consciousness, light and power could sweep through human lives and bring about a veritable new society, a New Age. Many are convinced that this is coming, and that great changes are already afoot, but man is doing such damage to the whole structure of the planet that the very living being of Earth may react against him...for the redemption of man, nature and the earth. We have got to do our part in invoking and calling down the forces of light, but we may feel the assurance that the Cosmic Christ...'The Revealer of the Word', is already overlighting mankind and working in human hearts and thinking.[42]

The third of the major Alice Bailey evangelists in the 1970s was the California-based Dane Rudhyar (1895–1985), who had been one of the Arcane School's early students, back in the 1930s. Unlike Spangler, Rudhyar had engaged with the San Francisco hippy scene in the 1960s, but like Spangler and Trevelyan, he was a devout esoteric Christian.[43] Rudhyar began his writing career in 1930 and published a series of books on New and Aquarian Age millenarianism from 1969.[44] He paraphrased Blavatsky's *The Secret Doctrine*, dealt with questions such as the dating of the Aquarian Age, and argued that the coming leap in human evolution provided a possible solution to the potentially catastrophic apocalyptic threats of the late twentieth century:

> The basic question today is indeed whether or not the social, psychological and biological or telluric processes and modes of human response which we have known in our limited experience of the past may not be made obsolete and superseded by basically new developments. We can perhaps expect a totally new 'mutation' of mankind or a basic transformation of society.[45]

Or as Spangler put it: 'Now humanity is undergoing another vast evolutionary change which is symbolised both factually and allegorically by the concept of a new age, the age of Aquarius.'[46] Gerald Heard's 'leptoid man' was alive and well. There was nothing new in any of this work. Neither Spangler nor Trevelyan nor Rudhyar made any original contribution to New Age discourse. But this was not their intention. Their goal was to bring work first disseminated in the 1910s to a new audience, and in this they were successful. Rudhyar's books probably sold less than the others, but he was highly regarded and taken seriously by other teachers. New Age activism in the Popperian sense is based primarily around individual preparation for the New Age through education and spiritual development. The production of books and magazines; attendance at workshops; and private meditation all constitute a form of action even if of a different kind to direct confrontations with the police. Such activity could be characterized as 'avoidance', in that it avoids confrontation while still constituting a form of mass resistance.[47]

There is a certain amount of academic discussion as to whether the New Age movement constitutes a movement in an organized, card-carrying sense, which of course it doesn't. The clearest answer to the problem is Michael York's suggestion that it is an 'emergent network', a description which suggests a fluid coalition of individuals, schools and societies which are in a state of constant formation, innovation and, sometimes, collapse.[48] William Bloom's description settles the matter: 'The New Age is neither a movement nor a religion set apart from others. It is not something one can choose or not to join … It is a mass movement in which humanity is reasserting its right to explore spirituality in total freedom'.[49] Similarly, the concept of the power of collective enterprise pervades Spangler's work and the very sense of being part of a movement is important to him.[50]

Most critical discussion of New Age culture confuses the prophetic tradition in the predictive sense from a non-prophetic one. The early twentieth-century distinction between Bailey, Steiner and Jung, for whom inner development was necessary in order to prepare for a future age, and Gurdjieff and Ouspensky, for whom inner development is an end in itself, facilitating human evolution in the here and now only, continues.

In the wider sense, New Age became a synonym for much of what could otherwise be bracketed under other rubrics such as 'New Religious Movement' or 'Alternative Spirituality'. A case in point is provided by some of the therapeutic activities and organizations described as belonging to the 'Human Potential Movement', all of which shared a concern with individual freedom, self-awareness or 'psychological growth'. For example, Erhard Seminar Training, or EST, which was very much in vogue in the late 1970s, is often described as 'New Age'.[51] EST was based in the organization of large events, with up to a thousand individuals, who were engineered into experiencing an often ecstatic revelation of personal meaning. But Erhard had no interest in preparation for a coming, collective spiritual age, and he never described EST as New Age. Instead he operated within the anti-prophetic, individualist tradition laid out by Gurdjieff and Ouspensky: all that mattered was the self or, rather, the Self. When Erhard's work was described as New Age, participants might react with bewilderment. A monk who attended a workshop in the 1990s had this to say: 'Some critics say our workshop is "New Age." We Trappist monks say we're the New Age. The New Age came when Jesus Christ was born; he added, 'It's tragic the way the American press works, accenting the negative and eliminating the positive.'[52]

The construction of the New Age as a cultural category owes a considerable debt to the Christian critiques which appeared in the 1980s. Earlier evangelical Protestants appear to have ignored the New Age's esoteric Christianity from the 1910s through the 1920s and 1930s. However, media interest in the 1970s attracted evangelical attention and concern that the moral laxity of the 1960s mixed with eastern teachings and Hinduism combined to produce a synthesis that was truly satanic.[53] New Age teachers were condemned as the false prophets who were due to appear before the End Times and who were warned about in Matthew 7.15. One form of millenarianism clashed with another, each claiming the same scriptural heritage in the Book of Revelation. It was precisely because the New Age adopted Christ as its central prophet that the struggle was so bitter.[54] The evangelicals believed that the New Age movement was part of a deliberate demonic conspiracy which was intended to inaugurate the rule of the Antichrist; it was a fully fledged religion related to Nazism, and a warning of the approach of the Last Days. New Agers, Constance Cumbey announced in 1983, were planning

> religious war, forced redistribution of the world's resources, Luciferic initiations, mass planetary initiations, theology for the New World Religion [sic], disarmament campaign [sic], and elimination or selling away of obstinate religious orthodoxies … the last stages of the New Age scheme to take the world for Lucifer.[55]

Supposedly a secret cabal of New Agers had launched an attempt in 1975 to take over the world, timed to coincide with the centenary of the foundation of the Theosophical Society.[56] According to the typical view contained on the anti-New Age website 'Planned Parenthood: Military Arm of the New Age Movement', this metaphysical coup d'état was carefully planned:

> Bailey developed the networks and the doctrine under the direction of the 'masters' while keeping a low profile: the secret doctrines about the New Age 'Christ' and

about 'Hierarchy' should be unveiled only in 1975, a century after the beginning of the Theosophical Society.[57]

The turf war between competing millenarianisms extends beyond rival Christian factions, though. New Age culture arouses particular anger amongst Marxists. The attitude was expressed most clearly by Slavoj Žižek, who recognized that New Age thought existed as part of a wider family of Christian apocalyptic, without recognizing that his own contempt for both was driven by his own vision of a perfect future.

One of the most deplorable aspects of the postmodern era and its so-called 'thought' is the return of the religious dimension in all its guises: from Christian and other fundamentalisms, through the multitude of New Age spiritualisms, up to the emerging religious sensitivity within deconstructionalism itself (so-called 'post-secular' thought). How is a Marxist, by definition a 'fighting materialist' (Lenin), to counter this massive onslaught of obscurantism.[58]

Žižek was not alone in his view of New Age as false ideology. There was also a challenge to New Age cosmology from the paganizing tendencies which also became evident in the 1970s. The New Age tendency to assert the existence of universal truths to which all people were subject jarred with assertions of individual autonomy which were central to radical, goddess feminism.[59] One critique of New Age culture, then, was based in the magical world of eco-protesters, and anti-globalization activists, from the 1980s onwards. Another, similar argument against the existence of universal laws originates in modern occultish magic. For example, the Crowley-influenced performance artist Genesis P-Orridge declared that in a universe with no boundaries in space or time, there is nothing for a deity to do, nothing to create or destroy, and so all deities must be human inventions; '"soul" is the brand name for the brain', he added, borrowing from Leary's scientizing and the anti-prophetic tradition which he inhabited.[60] And from a feminist perspective, Monica Sjoo, one of the most influential theorists of the emerging goddess religion, denounced New Agers for their other-worldly absolutism, finding it impossible to accept spiritual remedies for her terminally ill son.[61]

If one branch of hippy culture provided converts for the New Age, elsewhere in the counterculture, there was a pronounced challenge to one facet of hippyism: its docile, peace-and-love ideology. British punk, as it emerged quite suddenly in the summer of 1976 with the appearance of the Sex Pistols, was a paradoxical phenomenon. Stylistically it presented itself as a self-conscious and deliberate rupture with previous fashions in the UK, unlike punk in the United States (epitomized by bands such as the New York Dolls or Ramones), which emerged seamlessly from the Sixties. It completely rejected the Romantic naturalism of hippy fashion as well as the feminized garishness of early seventies glam rock. It played with symbolic paradox, combining Nazi imagery – the swastika – with behaviour that would have shocked the Nazis. It reified the artificial, the grotesque and sadomasochistic and its overt nihilism was combined with what Jon Savage called 'raging emotions' concealed behind a 'blank sarcastic, hostile facade'.[62] Socio-economically it was a response to economic crisis of 1973–1975, as well as the loss of the musicians who had once fulfilled a role as countercultural heroes; chief offenders were the Rolling Stones who moved in a few years from demonic revolutionaries and countercultural heroes, the status they held when they performed at Hyde Park in 1969, to a corporate brand.

To participants in the punk revolution as well as to defenders of hippy quietism who were the target of its rhetoric, punk itself was experienced as a complete break with the past. The notion that to change the world 'All You Need is Love', to quote the Beatles, was rejected as having been a naive failure. As Žižek would have said, the gist of the decade had completely changed.[63] The rhetoric of the Sex Pistols, whose music caused a nationwide shock, created the mood: with song titles such as 'Anarchy in the UK', 'Pretty Vacant' and their cover of the American Iggy Pop's 'No Fun', along with constant references to unfeeling pointlessness. The dystopian prophecy of a violent future was replaced by the rhetorical claim that there was no future: dystopia was here and now. Punk culture was not millenarian. It couldn't be, for it had no vision of the future.

However, with the passage of time, continuities emerge between punk and those dystopian and confrontational aspects of hippy culture, represented in music by Mick Farren and in politics by protest as performance. The paradox that was embodied in Abbie Hoffman's advocacy of violence in the pursuit of peace is a familiar one in utopian thought. And it was central to the vision of Vivienne Westwood and Malcolm McLaren, who created the Sex Pistols and invented British punk style in what has been described as a 'sixties art-school, hippie kind of way. All that Revolution, anti-materialism, Yippie'.[64] Westwood and McLaren, it has been said, 'simultaneously used and abused sixties libertarianism', encouraged both free and easy attitudes to sex as well as disgust, and adopted a revolutionary stance while flirting with far-right imagery.[65] They fabricated an image of the Sixties in which it was solely represented by peace and love culture, editing out its confrontational and violent features. Westwood and McLaren shared the Diggers' disdain for the hypocrisy of the hippy capitalists who made a profit from spirituality, but mainly they espoused a yippie contempt for hippy passivity; they rejected what they saw as the yippies' protest politics but followed their love of theatre. They were the Seventies' heirs to Jerry Rubin and Abbie Hoffman and when the Sex Pistols ranted about hippies, they were following Emmet Grogan and the Diggers. Punk found an instant and enthusiastic audience in 1976 and appealed to a generation of teenagers for whom the countercultural heroes of the Sixties had lost their allure. But through Westwood and McLaren, punk's roots were in the unfettered hedonism of such Sixties bands as the Doors and the Velvet Underground, as well as a lineage of aggressive music originating in 1966 to 1967 with Iggy Pop and the MC5 in 1967, and Mick Farren's Social Deviants in the UK.

However, hippy culture didn't stop when punk arrived. Rather it continued via a community based around the steadily growing festival movement, while punk occupied the media's need for a transgressive threat to ordered society.[66] Hippy culture was no longer dangerous. It was no longer news, no longer a media event. Punk, on the other hand, deliberately set out to provide copy for journalists eager to shock their readers. According to George McKay, it revitalized radical youth culture by continuing a particular quality it shared with the hippies: 'an oppositional impulse ... an idealism or rhetoric of idealism (and a) language of utopian desire'.[67] Speaking of the mid-1990s McKay added: 'Utopian desire doesn't go away – it may even be stronger than ever today ... the utopian project of the sixties is still with us – in fact (it) never really went away'.[68]

In both the United States and the UK, there was a clear continuity of 1960s hippy culture into the 1970s, populated by bands, events, gatherings and styles for which the primary reference was 1966–1968, the peak years of cultural revolution. In the United States, a key focus for the continuation of an egalitarian, performative, joyful hippy ethos was the Grateful Dead, who retained the ideals which led to them being potent symbols of the Haight-Ashbury scene in 1966–1967 and remained the most popular touring band in the United States through to the 1980s.[69] Meanwhile a post-1960s successor to the 1967 Be-in was the Burning Man Festival, founded in San Francisco in 1986 and subsequently relocated to Nevada, where it remains a huge annual event. Burning Man explicitly locates itself in the positive principles of hippy culture: it is inclusive, turning no-one away, combines individuality with community, and advocates artistic self-expression and radical participation in democracy.[70] In the UK, where the cultural trajectory was slightly different, connections were also made through music and free festivals. Bands such as Hawkwind and the Social Deviants spin-off, the Pink Fairies, who had always espoused an aggressively anti-commercial ethos, moved easily between hippy and punk environments.

The key to punk ideology was its belief in total cultural revolt, inherited from the Beats, and there was, it has been observed, a 'lot of Burroughs in punk'.[71] The cut-up style of punk fanzines, using letters cut from newspapers and magazines to make whole words is a clear homage to Burroughs. The project, exactly as it had been in the Sixties, was to dissolve the boundaries between art and everyday life and to confront every taboo head on, rather than look for alternatives.[72] But in mood, Punk was closer to the Allen Ginsberg of 'Howl' than of the Human Be-in in Golden Gate Park. It followed Blake's insistence that one should experience Hell while ignoring his belief that this was so that one might better know Heaven. Its dark death obsessions positioned it securely in the lineage of Romantic artists and its insistence that anyone could form a punk band or produce art placed it in the expressive individualism of the Sixties. And neither should we imagine that nihilism was the beginning and end of the Punk worldview. Punk could be colourful, exuberant. That it was transgressive didn't mean that it could not be joyful: in spite of the song, punks could have fun; they were, as Bloch foresaw, struggling to be themselves.

Like Diggers and yippie culture, Punk was based around the idea that protest should be active and creative, positively focusing on building alternatives and taking direct action rather than handing out leaflets at factory gates.[73] The means of cultural production should be open to anyone so, for example, punk bands might make their own records and their fans created their own fanzines, independent of media chains. Punk expressiveness was manifested through what has been termed Do-it-Yourself, or DiY, culture, described as a 'youth-centred and direct cluster of interests and practices around green radicalism, direct action politics, new musical sounds and experiences'.[74] Further, according to George McKay, DiY culture was characterized by 'a combination of inspiring action, narcissism, youthful arrogance, principle, idealism, indulgence, creativity, plagiarism, as well as the rejection and embracing alike of technological innovation' and 'a project of newness'.[75] Yet, if one didn't know better, what is presented as a description of the 1970s could equally be a picture of the 1960s or 1890s. Exactly as in the 1960s, there was a movement against 'the totality of bourgeois social relations', underpinned by 'visions' and 'myths', some inspired by drugs and others not.[76] Additionally, punk's transgressive instincts and opposition to mainstream society also, following the rebels of the 1960s, appealed heavily to the white and the middle class notwithstanding substantial working-class elements.[77] Punks placed themselves entirely outside the mainstream, affecting a working classness, whatever their individual backgrounds, while concealing even that identity behind their nihilist persona. As all notions of identity were challenged, so were any claims to a place in history: all was declared pointless. Yet DiY culture is optimistic, in that there is an essential hope that drives the protesters: they have to believe their actions will make a difference, otherwise they would not bother. DiY optimism also exists as a rebuke to the nostalgic idea that the 1960s represented a unique period of optimism which disappeared in the 1970s and has never been recovered. Diversity is central and positive. Michael Maffesoli wrote that the complexity of social existence was that

> its strength resides precisely in the fact that each of its acts is at once an expression of a certain alienation and of a certain resistance. It is a mixture of the ordinary and the exceptional, the morose and the exciting, the effervescent and the relaxing.[78]

Once competing styles are put to one side, the movement from Beat to hippy to punk becomes one of continuity rather than radical breaks, with similarities as pronounced as differences. Even the tension between artistic purity and political idealism on the one hand and compromise and commercialization on the other was faithfully reproduced from the 1960s to 1970s, from hippy to punk.[79]

Millenarian, countercultural and utopian protest culture is always DiY for one simple reason: it has to be. We might consider organized Theosophy as a DiY movement; from 1875 onwards the Theosophists built their own organizations, networks, literature and ideologies. And as Theosophy spawned New Age culture so it, too, is DiY. In millenarian terms, DiY is of the 'improvisational' kind in which rules are flexible and made up from day-to-day. The emergence of punk in 1976, brought obvious and substantial aesthetic difference in fashion, style and rhetoric, but the sense of challenging mainstream and established norms and institutions provides insistent evidence of continuity.

> The crucial importance of the Youth Revolution of our times lies not in its alleged uniqueness, but in that very continuity with history which the Movement itself – and most of its critics – have so vehemently denied. Practically everything our insurrectionary youth have tried – from New-Left militance to hippie-style withdrawal from society, from the campus revolt to the commune movement – has been tried before.[80]

The relationship between punk and the Sixties is best understood through Gans' five types of youth culture.[81] We may analyse these as follows. First was the 'original' hippy culture which, by 1974, had lost its utopianism and degenerated into a 'drug-and-music' culture. Second we can identify a communal culture, which was attempting to create new models of family and community, often in a pastoral environment. Third, there was an anti-capitalist political culture, usually radically socialist or anarchist and sometimes, but not always, in favour of violence. Fourth was a neo-Dadaist culture which believed in the creation of new social, political and cultural forms as a means of criticizing the existing order rather than necessarily expecting them to succeed. Lastly there was the religious culture typified by such groups as the Hare Krishna movement and the hippy-Christian 'Jesus Freaks' and which became identified with New Age culture. Only the first of Gans' taste cultures declined as the Sixties faded, and all the others continued undisturbed. UK punk culture held on to features of the Sixties in other significant ways. It was militantly egalitarian (all were welcome and anyone could play a musical instrument); it drew heavily on radical art-school traditions of surrealism and performance; it was heavily expressive, encouraging everyone to act as they pleased, obviously within the framework provided by an assertive and confrontational manner; it formed alliances with the radical anti-racist and anti-capitalist left, notably in the brief 'Rock Against Racism' organization, which was a front for the Trotskyite Socialist Workers Party.

The punk reaction to hippy culture is best seen as a reform movement, borne of irritation at hippyism's alleged political impotence. But punk found an overlap with 1960s utopianism within a few years, one which was epitomized by so-called 'New Traveller' movement, popularly known as 'New Age Travellers', a name apparently originating with the 'New Age Gypsy Fair of 1980'.[82] The travellers embodied the anarchic, drug-taking, golden-age romantic and bitter rejection of bourgeois values that had previously been found in the yippies. They found their collective power in the so-called Peace Convoy, in which they travelled from festival to festival, until it was broken up by the police in June 1985, en route to celebrate the summer solstice at Stonehenge. The travellers' disorganized drug-enhanced love of music, and perceived threat to the normal run of domestic society, deliberately echoed gypsy culture and travelling fairground folk, and inherited the recent traditions of hippy free festivals.

A direct continuity linking the Sixties to the Seventies was evident in the institution and ideology of the free festival, the 'utopia of joy' according to contemporaneous and anonymous leaflet. The festival constituted 'a pivotal moment, when the possibility of a kind of change, or something different, was glimpsed, when energy, a good time and some sort of community became woven together.[83] Cultures of resistance produce their own zones in which they are able to define themselves against the majority culture, so free festivals became countercultural zones from which majority culture was excluded. The first small free events were held from 1966 onwards. The centrality of free festivals to the counterculture was a major feature of the mid-1970s onwards. The point about free festivals is that they weren't just free to enter, but one could live there free. The 1971 Glastonbury Fayre set the model with free food provided by the English Diggers, who modelled themselves on the San Francisco Diggers, and even free drugs – marijuana was dispensed from an ice-cream van and LSD thrown in bags from the stage. While the New Age ideologues of the early twentieth century had envisaged neither free drugs nor 'free' sex, they had most certainly maintained the notion of a communist utopia with no money and no private property. Both the Glastonbury Fayre's timing (the summer solstice) and location (at the heart of the 'Glastonbury Zodiac') were seen by the organizers as profoundly significant and as the basis of an overt political purpose. Andrew Kerr, one of the organizers, was quoted as saying that 'the energy could create a new fertility in the land of this part of the world. It must sound cranky', he laughed. 'We are going to tap the universe'.[84] In this respect the festival was judged a success. The conclusion was that

> We didn't have a religious experience, but in a strange way we found some sort of enlightenment. We…got stoned, fell down, drank a lot of cider, failed to find God, but discovered a confirmation that if our culture is left to itself it can survive. We are able to live in harmony with each other. The (festival) gave a glimpse of alternative ways in which people could live their lives outside the present death culture.[85]

The first Windsor Free Festival in the following year, 1972, was central to the utopian experimentation of British DiY culture.[86] Along with the Stonehenge Free Festival, which ran in a continual series from 1974 (following the break-up of the Windsor festival by the police) to 1985, both festivals were a direct response to the absence of a successor to the 1971 Glastonbury Fayre and extended the idealistic, mystical, psychedelic and anti-materialistic wing of the 1960s counterculture in the UK. As the festivals proliferated from the mid-1970s onwards, the idea of travelling from one to another took hold – it was already present at least by 1971. By 1980 the New Age traveller phenomenon was based firmly in an individualistic commitment to personal autonomy and transitoriness and a 'spark of transgression', plus a deeply English romantic love of nature and rural living.[87] This was made explicit in the nostalgic and self-conscious identification of New Age Diggers of the 1990s to the radical, communist, Diggers of the English revolution of the 1640s.[88] So far this sounds rather unlike the futuristic, transcendental spiritualizing of Alice Bailey and Rudolf Steiner. Indeed, sections of the New Age travelling community were deeply devoted to nihilistic drug abuse and violence. McKay quotes one traveller as saying that some others were 'so nasty, not even I would talk to them'.[89] The central feature, again, was diversity. The prevailing opinions and lifestyles were as varied and diverse as in the Sixties, ranging from confrontation to passivity and spiritual growth to self-destruction. The question is, though, to what extent the raft of ideas and activities classified broadly as New Age were represented amongst the New Age travellers? Most evident was a broad adoption of the paganizing mysticism characteristic of psychedelic culture, accompanied by the use of psilocybin mushrooms as the vision-inducing drug of choice. McKay picked up on this association, adopting Christopher Partridge's word 'occulture' as a suitable description.[90]

Indeed traveller culture possessed its share of specialists in the activities associated with the New Age *sensu lato* – crystal healers, tarot readers, neo-shamans – in its romantic idealism. McKay identified a number of activities amongst the Dongas, a community within the New Age travellers, in the 1990s. He described 'the usual diverse New Age sources such as Celtic myth, stone circles, world music and drumming, equinox and solstice celebrations', contained within 'a millenarian perspective, much tinged by current New Age thought'.[91] He cited one informant who told him that 'Donga people feel that the awareness process is speeding up, a necessary response triggered by the fact that we are also moving towards ecological disaster and the extinction of our species at an alarming rate'.[92] Elsewhere, New Age language provided a narrative in support of environmental protest, as in the idea that road building might be resisted by the recently wakened 'Earth Dragon'.[93] The Donga's own 'wildly New Age' practices ranged from playing music to enhance the magical power of a stone circle on the one hand and their practical role in the anti-road protests on the other. The Dongas themselves were aware of claims that their opposition to 'progress' in the form of road building exposed them to allegations of being reactionary, a charge which could be countered by reference to the millennial narrative – that they too are serving the dictates of history. As Popperian activists, the approach of the millennial crisis required that the Donga intervene to save the planet and convert the threat of pre-millennial trauma to the promise of post-millennial bliss.

Aquarian Age ideas continued to penetrate the wider New Age and pagan literature largely through the writings of John Michel, who introduced the 1972 edition of his *The View over Atlantis* with a warning that the current shift into the Aquarian Age gave the book's content an added urgency. Quoting Jung and repeating his earlier warnings from 1967, Michel prophesied that:

> many find themselves unprepared for the changes that inevitably occur as the spring point enters Aquarius. Yet, as events move towards the pattern foreshadowed by prophecy, as portents, long awaited, stir the primeval spirits from the depths of mythology, the changeable and impermanent nature of the structure evolved during the preceding two thousand years, …becomes ever more apparent… Old secrets rise to the surface and dissolve into the consciousness of the human race to fertilise the seed of evolutionary growth.[94]

This was the book which triggered the modern 'earth mysteries' movement, with its sentimental attachment to a golden age when people and nature lived together in a supposed harmony, when it was first published in 1969. The pagan world also provided a means for disseminating news of the coming Aquarian Age. A core text on witchcraft in the 1980s by Marian Green, whose series of books on magic did much to spread popular paganism, considered the prospects of an improvement in the human condition, as the Piscean Age gives way to the Aquarian.[95] Later she wrote:

> A lot is happening, even in the political world … This is only the start of the many changes the next couple of hundred years will bring. We could be on the verge of a true Golden Age, for the Water Bearer (i.e. Aquarius) is the Grail Carrier who has found the vessel of rebirth and brought it into the world that its redeeming waters may be poured out for all in need.[96]

The influential Wiccan writers Janet and Stewart Farrar also drew on Jung. They regarded what they saw as the current 'reintegration of the Ego and the Unconscious, on a new and higher level' as the prelude to a 'new and unimaginable fruitful evolutionary phase; call it, if you will, the Aquarian Age'.[97] Another prominent Wiccan, Vivianne Crowley, identified the New Age and the Age of Aquarius, which she regarded as synonymous, as particularly favourable to the spread of Wicca, on the grounds that one of the Aquarian/New Age's manifestations is the awakening of the Goddess in human consciousness. Culturally it is the Age's pluralism which provides a sympathetic environment for Wicca; theologically it is its emphasis on the inner divinity which, being so sympathetic to Wiccan cosmology, will enable the new religion 'to serve the religious needs of many in the Aquarian Age'.[98] And so, the rise of Wicca is not just beneficial, it is also close to inevitable.

Other groups have seized on the Age of Aquarius in order to legitimate their political programmes. The Raelians, whose New Age religion is based in a close connection with extra-terrestrials, are a notable example. Rael, the prophetic leader, was born Claude Vorilhon in 1946 and founded the group after an 'encounter of the third kind' in 1973, followed by what he claims was a Swedenborg-style visit to the aliens' host planet. The Raelians believe that the Age of Aquarius commenced with Vorilhon's birth in 1946, and their prophecy of the future age's character accords perfectly with the prevailing literature, even if a little more decadent in tone: the Raelian Age of Aquarius will be a Sixties' style egalitarian, secular meritocracy and sexual paradise.[99] In December 2002 the Raelians gave a new twist to New Age prophecies of an imminent leap in human evolution by claiming to have created the first cloned human being.

There was clearly an existential crisis in hippy culture when punk nihilism arrived in 1976, which is precisely what McLaren, Westwood and the Sex Pistols intended. But psychedelic 'occulture' reasserted itself in the 1980s via a new medium: rave and trance culture.[100] The emergence of rave culture, based around the use of ecstasy, rather than LSD, bought a reassessment and revival of hippy sentiment, liberated from the oppressive punk rhetoric of the 1970s. Even the phrase 'summer of love' was revived and applied to the sudden arrival of rave and dance culture into a wider public awareness in 1988. Ecstasy is very different drug to LSD, sparking a surge of physical energy and emotional joy and without the profound hallucinations which make LSD so other-worldly and potentially so dangerous. Rave produced a moral panic as great as any in the Sixties and the marriage between free festivals and travelling Raves resulted in a clamp down represented by sections in the 1994 Criminal Justice and Public Order Act which prohibited the playing of repetitive dance music in certain circumstances. In the late 1980s local farmers in mid-Wales set up 'Hippy Watch', with road blocks and helicopters employed in order to obstruct likely rave organizers.

According to Fraser Clark, the rave scene, with its liberated mores, represented an intellectual, cultural and spiritual leap forward: 'What Rave did in Britain was to transform the New Age from an essentially bourgeois lifestyle into a national movement towards shamanic group mind and away from purely personal liberation.'[101] Whether there was a shift from the personal to the collective is doubtful and, in any case, impossible to demonstrate. What's important is that New Age culture in its widest sense – its concern with spiritual growth and exploring consciousness – reasserted its connection with a revived psychedelic culture. 'Easternization' persisted in rave culture, as evident in the Goan trance scene in the 1990s, when the beaches of the

Indian state became the venue for ecstasy-driven gatherings of seekers and dancers. But trance culture's emphasis on dance as an ecstatic event led the way back to a form of westernism, especially a powerful and seductive blend of paganism and shamanism.[102]

And from rave culture, the path also led straight to two other psychedelic evangelists, Terence McKenna and José Argüelles, who formulated an entirely new millenarian time fetish; they forecast that the New Age would begin when the 'long count' of the Maya calendar, which had begun in 3114 BCE, came to an end on 21 December 2012. The so-called '2012 Phenomenon', or 'Maya Prophecy Movement', appropriated and adapted all the revolutionary, egalitarian and spiritual claims of the Aquarian Age.[103]

Both McKenna and Argüelles were part of the Sixties Californian Awakening. Mckenna was born in 1946 and enrolled in the University of California at Berkeley in 1965, where he became deeply involved in student radicalism.[104] He entered that overlapping world of revolutionary protest and occultish magic which characterized the Californian counterculture, developing a fascination for shamanism, eastern teachings and psychedelics. After he graduated in 1968, he joined the hippy-trail to India, in search of that seductive combination of readily available hashish and spiritual truth that the country offered to refugees from the spiritual wilderness of 'straight' American society. From the early 1970s McKenna established himself as a psychedelic guru on a par with Leary. As Leary became a fugitive from the US legal system and his constituency in the culture of Californian flower power ran out of energy, McKenna took over Leary's mantle. McKenna is far less known than Leary because the psychedelic revolution was no longer news, but he was equally prolific. Like Leary, he believed that the key to global salvation lay in the use of hallucinatory drugs or entheogens, as they came to be called. Through a series of books from the early 1970s, he pioneered the exploration of naturally occurring substances such as ayahuasca, the more familiar name for yagé, which, when publicized by William Burroughs, had launched the modern psychedelic movement.

McKenna embarked on his life's work in 1971 when, exactly twenty years after Burroughs' trip to Mexico; he visited the Amazon basin with his brother Dennis and a party of other travellers, in search of organic hallucinogens. McKenna described his experiences in his most important book, *True Hallucinations*. His worldview was very much the same as Leary's in that he was a scientizer for whom the *I Ching* and quantum mechanics were capable of providing equal and compatible evidence of the true nature of reality. But, unlike Leary, he was very conscious of the tradition within which he operated. For a start, he understood his debt to the 1950s, deliberately using, for example, the word 'beatific', as an obvious tribute to Kerouac. He had discovered Jung's *Psychology and Alchemy* when he was fourteen and adapted Jung's concept of alchemy as being concerned with the totality of psychological, spiritual and material transformation, and of UFOs as signs of millennial transformation. Combining the two, and borrowing from Carlos Castaneda's influential portrayal of hallucinogenic plants as containing living spirits, McKenna incorporated the notion of nature as transformative into his belief that natural hallucinogens were alien intelligences which could transport human beings to a higher level of existence.[105] Culturally, this is perhaps McKenna's most important contribution. It dovetailed with what Partridge termed 'eco-enchantment', referring to eco-pagan ideas of the earth as a living being.[106]

If Sixties psychedelic culture had lost its political focus with the end of the Vietnam War in the mid-1970s, it found it again with the environmental crisis in the 1980s. Once again the counterculture had something to struggle against, this time the despoliation of the world by global capitalism and technology. Initially, though, McKenna was concerned by the disenchanted condition of the modern world and its loss of soul. In his journal for 23 February 1971 McKenna wrote:

> We are losing distance with the most profound event
> a planetary ecology can encounter:
> The emergence of life
> From the dark chrysalis of matter.[107]

McKenna deliberately positioned himself within a tradition of millenarian prophecy. He was familiar with Christian apocalyptic writings and believed that planetary movements and key dates in the calendar dates possessed profound significance. 'To see through the eyes of history', he wrote, 'is to see one's place in the spiral scheme and to know and anticipate when the transition to new epochs will occur'.[108] But his preferred apocalyptic text was the *I Ching*. By 1975 he had used the Chinese oracle to formulate a cyclical theory of world history in which he concluded that the winter solstice, 21 December – the day of the 'rebirth of the saviour' as he called it – possessed profound significance.[109] He arrived at what he called the 'zero time' or 'zero date' of 21 December 2012, as the fulcrum of history and 'to my amazement', he later declared, he discovered that this same day marked the end of the Maya calendar.[110] McKenna's description of the zero point was somewhat abstruse. Paraphrasing Plato's description in the *Timaeus* of time as the 'moving image of eternity', he wrote:

> The zero point is … the point at which the ingression into novelty and the degree of interconnectedness of the separate elements that comprise the concrescence will be such that the ontological nature of time itself will be transformed. History will end, and the transcendental object that has been drawing being into ever deeper reflections of itself since the first moments of the existence of the universe will finally be completely concrescent in the three-dimensional space-time continuum. The moving image of eternity will have discovered itself to be Eternity.[111]

And so McKenna took the idea of the end of the Maya calendar, matched it against his moment of supreme transformation, the zero-point, and gave it a constituency in the trance, rave and psychedelic communities of the 1980s. For the first time since the 1960s, young people could take drugs and imagine they were on the cusp of a wonderful new world. The end of the Maya calendar was to become the new emblem, the time-fetish of New Age millenarianism and, for a while, a highly effective one.

Once McKenna had laid the way, the Maya Prophecy movement was to be largely the brainchild of one man, José Argüelles.[112] Argüelles was himself was an artist, performer and art historian who was based for much of his career in California, a decision which he had taken deliberately in order to be close to the countercultural epicentre in San Francisco.[113] Argüelles was one of the generation who caught the tail end of jazz and Beat culture in the late 1950s and came of age in the psychedelic awakening of the mid-1960s. His first experience of LSD in 1965 confirmed what he saw as the truth of his previous mystical inclinations and laid the foundations for what he later understood as his own messianic role. He was lecturing at the University of California, Davis, in Sacramento, during the high point of radical hippy culture in the late 1960s and was deeply influenced by it.[114] His millennial vision was eclectic and syncretic and he was deeply attracted to the Romantics as well as to notions of art and performance as initiatory. From Aldous Huxley, he borrowed the notion of a universal perennial philosophy and the idea that psychedelics opened the doors of perception, a phrase he used in one of his artworks. From Jung, he adopted the concept of synchronicity, together with the argument that the appearance of UFOs was a sign of a major shift in global history. Ouspensky exposed Argüelles to concepts of the evolution of humanity to higher stages of consciousness while Alice Bailey, who he discovered in 1967, contributed the certainty that the inevitability of such developments was assured by astronomical patterns. After participating in the Levitation of the Pentagon in 1967, he borrowed his language from Bailey when he described the authorities' repressive response as a violent reaction as a response to 'an attempted act of seventh ray ceremonial magic to dispel hatred with love'.[115] His engagement with New Age ideology and Aquarian Age historiography deepened in 1969, when he read two important theosophical works: Alice Bailey's *Education in the New Age* and Dane Rudhyar's *The Pulse of Life*. He contacted Rudhyar, who immediately saw that Argüelles was already implementing his vision of the New Age and introduced him to Blavatsky's teachings, deepening his understanding of the current crisis in history and the coming transformation of the world.[116] The two men became close friends and in 1971 Argüelles moved into Rudhyar's home, where he became totally immersed in the theosophical vision of the coming rise in global consciousness. Rudhyar, in turn, spent the late summer of 1971 as a guest of José Argüelles and his wife Miriam, in Palo Alto.[117] Argüelles adopted unquestioningly the fear that humanity was in a state of unparalleled millennial crisis as a precursor to the beginning of the New Age but reframed it within the environmental crisis; for by 1970, environmental degradation was seen as an equal threat to military conflict. In April 1972, he helped organize the first Whole Earth Festival on the campus at Berkeley. Afterwards he wrote a summary of his conclusions for the future of education, which he titled (deliberately evoking the Human Be-in of five years earlier) 'The Believe-in, an Aquarian Age Ritual'.[118]

Throughout the 1970s Argüelles, like McKenna, became increasingly convinced that Maya civilization had been the most technologically sophisticated ever to exist, and that it was connected with inter-Galactic intelligences; this belief that the Maya were the carriers of an ancient, lost, superior knowledge has since been characterized as 'Mayanism'.[119] It provides an authenticity by performing one of the key rhetorical manoeuvres of New Age – and much other religious – thought: it appeals to tradition.[120] Yet the descriptions of the supposed true nature of Maya civilization are couched very much in the style of the *Star Wars* films (the first film in the franchise was released in 1976); in the eighth century, Argüelles claimed, 'a crack Mayan galactic engineering team...placed (the Earth) in attunement with resonant transmitter receivers in far-flung space points of the galaxy.[121] And now he, prophesied:

> Like the Maya who preceded us, we shall understand that the path to the stars is through the senses and the proper utilisation of our mind as the auto-regulatory control factor will help facilitate the passage to different levels or dimensions of being.[122]

And as one of his followers phrased it:

> [T]he meaning of December 21, 2012, has everything to do with shifting time-frequencies. This transition is anticipated as the transformation of the present material-industrial order of the planet into a full renewal of the human mind, where telepathy is universal.[123]

'The Earth will be illumined', Argüelles wrote, and 'In that moment of understanding, we shall be collectively projected into an evolutionary domain that is presently inconceivable.'[124] The scriptural reference, which he did not give, is to Corinthians 15.50–2 which in the King James version reads:

> Now I say this, brethren, that flesh and blood cannot inherit the kingdom of God; nor does the perishable inherit the imperishable.
> Behold, I tell you a mystery; we will not all sleep, but we will all be changed, in a moment, in the twinkling of an eye, at the last trumpet; for the trumpet will sound, and the dead will be raised imperishable, and we will be changed...

In some recent translations the word 'changed' is translated as the more New Age friendly 'transformed'. Christian moralizing was never far below the surface, the Maya Prophecy movement being accurately described as a call 'for us to contemplate-our-wicked-ways before it is too late'.[125] Here it is Argüelles himself who reveals the mystery. His adaptation of such a core text of Christian millenarianism to his own version is entirely consistent with the flexible interpretative traditions characteristic of American fundamentalism.[126] As Susan Harding observed, while modern fundamentalist readings of scripture presume a literalist revelation of the truth, in actuality the 'Bible is read within a complex, multidimensional, shifting field of...folk narrative practices'.[127] Argüelles then introduced folk narrative themes from New Age and psychedelic culture to produce his own variant on contemporary Christian millenarianism.

Argüelles articulated his ecotopian, eco-apocalyptic, philosophy in 1987 in *The Mayan Factor*. In language adopted from left-leaning environmentalism he angrily denounced what he called the 'Faustian development of global industrialisation' which has led to an 'unnecessary military economy and the production of wasteful and even toxic consumer goods'.[128] Argüelles was very aware of the tradition within which he was working, explicitly challenging Marxism, which he regarded as a parallel, if mistaken, feature of the apocalyptic imagination.[129] His vision was deeply Manichaean and he couched the environmental crisis within the struggle of opposing forces. He believed that global industrialization represented 'a turning away from the light – our guiding inner "soul-light" – in order to pursue the short-term profit'. He added, 'In truth this turning away is a surrender to the force of darkness, called by the ancient Mexicans, Tezcatlipoca, the Dark Lord of Time'.[130] All lost golden ages from which humanity has been alienated – or alienated itself – are equivalent. One version of Britain – 'Arthur's ancient Albion' – had been desecrated by coal mining and the industrial revolution.[131] Once capitalism, consumerism and industrialization have been rejected, he believed, the former golden age will be restored. Argüelles' counterculturalism did not require a rejection of technology and science per se, only of what he saw as its destructive, materialistic varieties. But his Manichaean perspective is clear: the world is engaged in a final struggle of good and evil. We can detect the influence of Tom Paine and William Blake when he speaks of the 'summons to Jerusalem' as

> essentially a post-Einsteinian vision, a realm of consciousness in which man has passed into another dimension of being. Jerusalem – the biblical City of Peace – is the very notion of liberty, or liberation from the condition of restrictive sense desire bound by ... the sleep of matter.[132]

Science fiction was also an inspiration. From Arthur C. Clarke and Stanley Kubrick, Argüelles conjured a picture of a galactic utopia: 'Blake's vision', he wrote, 'is beyond *2001*, far beyond the dreams of technocrats. It is a vision of the true space age, in which even astronomical space has become totally enfolded in the mind of man'.[133] This is not simple solipsism though, for the mind and the material universe are not separate, but embedded in each other. If Argüelles' first aim in the book was to demonstrate the universal relevance of the visionary experience, as expressed through art and artists – Raymond Williams' 'exiles' – his second was to establish a universal basis for different traditions of world ages from all cultures, in order to demonstrate the truth of their predictions.[134] He was fully engaged with central currents of western thought in some ways, keen to locate himself within what he saw as the apocalyptic transcendence of the Beats and psychedelic culture – Huxley, Ginsberg and Leary.[135]

Yet after 1975, Arguelles seems to have carefully avoided any mention of the central time fetishes of western esotericism, the New Age or the Aquarian Age. It's as if he was extending Jung's dislike of the teachings of the Theosophical Society and its offshoots into a wariness of the Theosophists' two key time fetishes: he was Americanizing, and so renewing, the discourse of New Age millenarianism. Americanizing ideas were not new. Aquarian Age dreams had already been merged with imagined pre-Columbian histories in the teachings of the French Grande Fraternité Universelle, which originated in 1947, and was active in Latin America.[136]

A pronounced distaste for the New Age emblem later became evident in the work of some other 2012 evangelists.[137] The schismatic tendencies of Marxist millenarians come to mind. It has, for example, been argued that only the Maya calendar allows for a true understanding of the wave pattern of history, where western astronomy can only portray history as random, chaotic events.[138] And so the Maya Prophecy Movement paradoxically came to define itself partly by opposition to that form of esoteric millenarianism from which, through Rudhyar's influence on Argüelles, it had emerged.

Pinchbeck thought that when an ordinary New Ager looked to the sky for salvation, it was shallow and empty of content, but that when a devotee of the Maya calendar performed the same act, it was full of meaning and possessed the power to save the Earth.[139] In Marxist terms, Daniel Pinchbeck saw New Age as false consciousness, but Maya prophecies as true consciousness. Conventional New Agers were recast as mainstream culture against whom the countercultural Mayanists could compete. The French revolutionaries' institution of a new calendar, like that of the Khmer Rouge in Cambodia, is then replicated in the belief that one way of measuring time yields truths which another conceals.

McKenna and Argüelles finally met in 1985. Argüelles was particularly impressed that McKenna had discussed the significance of 21 December 2012 while under the influence of ayahuasca; an apparent coincidence which only confirmed his suspicions of the date's significance. Argüelles was aware of the discussions of utopias as automatically unrealizable, by virtue of being utopian, to which his answer was that his version was inevitable.[140] It was therefore, by definition, bound to come into existence. As a result of their encounter Argüelles became aware of his higher purpose: to organize a worldwide movement to facilitate the transition from one age of history to another. The result was the Harmonic Convergence on 16–17 August 1987, the event which brought the 2012 prophecies to a wider media attention.[141] At particular moments, at special places all over the world (such as Glastonbury Tor in England), the faithful gathered to meditate. The belief was that a mass ritual event held simultaneously across the globe would avert the violent disorder threatened by the approach of the change of world ages. The use of group meditations in order to enhance world peace was an established practice, familiar to Argüelles from Alice Bailey's Lucis Trust. However, Argüelles' talent for publicity created a brief media frenzy. In Argüelles' own account, 'everybody from Shirley MacLaine and Johnny Carson, to nameless thousands in small town in the USA and the world, from Leningrad in the USSR to sunny Rio de Janeiro – got swept up in the act'.[142] The Convergence's success, he reasoned, was because all the participants 'had been zapped by ... the call and the tickle of the *Zu-vu-ya* ... the Mayan term for the big memory circuit ... the interdimensional thread' which links the individual to the collective and the past to the future.[143]

The rejection of the Aquarian Age emblem, tainted as it was by association with what were considered to be shallow New Age ideas, has not affected the wider apocalyptic culture, in which the Maya Calendar and the western zodiac allow different perspectives on the same event.[144] The year 2012 is then the new metanarrative within which all previous millenarian hopes are contained, from all cultures, from the Maori to the Maya and the Chinese, and from India to the Jewish and Christian.[145] Argüelles, like Pinchbeck, encouraged the connection, announcing his new era as the 'New Kingdom' and the 'Kingdom of Heaven on Earth'.[146] From the number of the saved in Revelation, he stated that the number of participants – 'sun-dancers' – in the Harmonic Convergence should number 144,000.[147] The boundary between Christian and New Age millenarianism is porous and ideas easily feed from one to the other, in spite of rhetorical distinctions. Daniel Pinchbeck, one of the prominent 2012 writers, actually contextualized the 2012 prophecies within a shared current of spiritual questing and a search for salvation which included Christian Fundamentalism and hope for the Rapture.[148] Even some evangelical Christians could find support in the 2012 prophecies for the coming Rapture.[149] The two millenarian narratives then found enhanced authenticity in mutual support rather than rivalry.

The complex interweaving of American and European, Maya and western cosmologies in Mayanism is a vivid example of transculturation, the mixing of cultures on an equal footing or, as Fernando Ortiz put it, the 'highly varied phenomena that ... come about ... as a result of ... extremely complex transmutations of culture.'[150] American anthropologists, users of psychedelic drugs and white middle-class individuals who are alienated from what they regard as the deficiencies of their own culture, combine with Christian evangelicals and theosophical New Agers, as well as with Mexicans themselves, to create a new language for millenarianism – one which engages with Nietzschean ideas of leaps in consciousness; Jungian theories of UFOs as bringers of meaning; and fictional accounts of galactic quests.

Argüelles' utopia envisioned an end to all human freedom in the sense of the freedom to be different. Humans could only be free because they are all the same. There would be no individual creativity, only creativity sanctioned by the Solar Being. Such totalizing New Ageism had been pioneered elsewhere, as by Heaven's Gate, but its closest parallel is with the Stoic-oriented Leninist belief that freedom lies in freely choosing what one has to do. And, as Jerry Rubin had said: 'A yippee is anyone who wants to be.'[151]

Science fiction was evident in Argüelles' vision of the anti-democratic, totalitarian political structure to be spontaneously recognized after 2012. Ra, the Egyptian sun god, who he addressed as the 'supreme solar lord' and the 'Great Solar Being', was to preside over the whole world as undisputed master and was to be worshipped in the solar temples that would be located at the heart of each community. Ra's instructions would then be disseminated via bodies such as the Council of Solar-Planetary Affairs, who would control the economy, education and the flow of information and monitor all activity. Argüelles borrowed his model from Leninist democratic centralism, and just as orders descended down the organizational hierarchy from Ra, so individuals would come together in networks that could then send emissaries to the governing councils. There would be no need for any discussion, though, as all would agree that the system was perfect.

Argüelles' spiritual eco-utopia was the very epitome of the nightmare envisioned by Isaiah Berlin. It was the consummation of the incipient totalitarianism identified by the neoconservatives in the opening stages of the Sixties student rebellion. In the very detail with which Argüelles elaborated the psychedelic version of the New Age dream, he had unwittingly exposed the paradox in all utopias: in order to establish perfection forever, time and space have to be frozen at the moment of emancipation.[152] Nobody can refuse to be free. His system was based on one single law governing all things to which all people must be subservient and in submitting to it they become free.[153] Argüelles himself was sensitive enough to the traditions within which he was working to anticipate allegations that his utopia would be undemocratic.[154] His answer was that the democratic value of the individual, as he put it, would not be lost but that the nature of the new galactic system would render old notions of democracy redundant – as redundant as they would be in the Christian scheme which his so closely resembled and with which he was very familiar from his childhood.

Argüelles was completely honest about the source of his information: it was the 'voices' inside his head, which he described as his own higher self, a disembodied Maya shaman, or both.[155] In 1992, instructed by his voices, he assumed his full messianic persona as the voice of Pakal, the seventh-century king of the Maya city-state of Palenque.[156] It is difficult to know how seriously to take Argüelles. His constant references to science fiction classics, such as *2001: A Space Odyssey* or the 1950s sci-fi series *The Twilight Zone*, suggest a pranksterish joke.[157] After all, in *Revolution for the Hell of It*, Abbie Hoffman had argued that revolution was myth and that myth, in turn, had to have 'a high element of risk, drama, excitement and bullshit'.[158] Or, as Tom Wolfe had put it, recollecting his LSD experiments with the Pranksters in 1964,

> My happiness...arose from the freedom to experience everything imaginable simultaneously, to exchange outward and inward easily, to move Time and Space about like scenes in a theatre...we creatively brought the past, present, the future and the fictitious into the present moment.[159]

Argüelles' utopia is similar in its crazy quality to that already satirized by Huxley in *Brave New World*. He inhabited that realm familiar to psychedelic culture in which one can be a total believer and yet recognize that the entire world is absurd, a huge cosmic game. To the user of hallucinogenic drugs, schooled in Jungian ides of the outer world as a projection of the inner, there is no inconsistency to be found in mixing the factional and the factual. The millenarian is shielded from disappointment by the very knowledge that utopian dreams are ridiculous, although no less genuine for that: surrealism and Dada meet the apocalypse. Yet Argüelles was outstandingly successful, and the Maya Prophecy Movement has generated hundreds of books and thousands of websites, all devoted to the idea of a dramatic leap in consciousness, a rise in spirituality and contacts with superior galactic intelligence to help humanity solve the environmental threat and enter a new era.

Meanwhile public interest was generated by media claims that the end of the world was due, fears promoted by a blockbuster Hollywood film, Roland Emmerich's *2012*, and acres of newsprint as December 2012 approached.[160] The flow of publicity increased, boosted by a substantial presence on the World Wide Web, which had not existed in 1987. The global context at the time was one of general crisis, following the inauguration of the 'war on terror' in 2001, the US invasion of Iraq in 2003 and the predicted total breakdown of the biosphere – and human society – as a result of global warming. In Daniel Pinchbeck's view, only the Maya Calendar provided the apocalyptic focus necessary to save the planet, whereas the Christian and New Age alternatives were completely inadequate to the task.[161] In spite of its science fiction-inspired fantasies of extra-terrestrial salvation, Mayanism emerges as profoundly this-worldly. Like socialism, its utopia is on the Earth. And like Marx, Pinchbeck regarded capitalism as a 'religion of destruction', whose final end was to be a necessary prerequisite for the dawn of the new world.[162] Inspired by Jung, Pinchbeck thought that the transition to the new world may well be 'a psychic event...like a collective dream coming to life', but its material manifestation is no less real.[163] Material renewal is dependent on the spiritual awakening. Once the soul has risen from its sleep, matters in the world will arrange themselves according to a higher metaphysic of time.

The Maya calendar prophecies attracted a certain amount of anger amongst some astronomers and sceptics, who have devoted attention to refuting the phenomenon's apocalyptic claims.[164] However, the critics, like the media, focused exclusively on the supposed prediction of the end of the world, a catastrophe that would be caused by possible comet collision or perhaps by 'pole shifts' as the Earth's axis goes through a violent readjustment or both.[165] The media propagation of end-of-the-world scenarios did indeed apparently result in some apocalyptic predictions for example, among American survivalists. However, '2012' as a media event had virtually nothing to do with the predictions of leading ideologues and the beliefs of their followers, all of whom were vigorous opponents of the notion of a violent apocalypse.[166] While public and media attention focused exclusively on pre-millenarian prophecies of a violent cataclysm, the majority of active apologists for the notion that the end of the Maya calendar possessed a millenarian significance advocated a post-millennial peaceful transition. Even the prolific apocalyptic writer Zecharia Sitchin, whose millennial tract *End of Days* was unintentionally responsible for the idea that an extra-terrestrial people who he called the Annunaki would return in their spaceships from the planet Nibiru on 21 December 2012, resisted any precise forecast of violent disaster in 2012.[167] A message posted posthumously on Sitchin's website in July 2011 by his niece Janet Sitchin carried the following unambiguous statement: 'neither cataclysmic events on December 21, 2012 nor Nibiru come into play as a concern in 2012'.[168] Catastrophism was a minority position. Instead the faithful were being called to build the new world. The millennial paradox surfaces again: the coming age is inevitable but requires humanity to actively encourage it.

Calls for participatory engagement in order to encourage the coming historical shift are widespread within the Maya prophecy movement. Carl Calleman, for example, calls for a 'massive participation' in a public programme which encourages the 'shift to consciousness of the ninth wave', in order to take advantage of 'the last chance that human beings will have to truly align themselves with the cosmic plan' and which will require involvement in social media, funding initiatives and mass events.[169] One of the most popular websites was 13Moon, which summed up the nature of the transformation to the 'New World Age':

> December 21, 2012 is a clear marker of the transition of World Ages. This synchronization is inviting all of humanity to open to imagining, envisioning and actualizing the possibilities of gradual, positive transformation of our human culture in harmony with the Earth. As we *internally align* with this grand shifting of cycles we can contribute our personal inspiration and commitment to being part of this collective transformation ... humanity must confront our severe disconnection from Nature, and re-establish our harmonious interconnection with all of life that we may awaken our human potential and align with the next evolutionary stage that Earth is entering into.[170]

The activist imperative is prevalent elsewhere on 2012 Prophecy websites, promoting opportunities for personal and collective spiritual transformation. The 'Birth2012' website advertised the following:

- Join us for Activation Week and you can
- Discover your unique contribution to the global path
- Renew your hope for our world
- Learn all the exciting initiatives that are coming together
- Receive practical training on creating hubs, events and grassroots activities
- Become part of a worldwide positive change movement
- Receive potent wisdom from dozens of our world's most beloved teachers.[171]

As in almost all previous New Age activism, no attention was paid to the mainstream political process – to the normal institutions of political power. Why should it, given that as the magical hour approached, they would all cease to exist? Meditation was the substitute for conventional political engagement. The 13Moon website advertised a meditation in order to encourage peace and healing of the oceans at the 2012 autumnal equinox, the last before the transition was due.

> In honor of the Equinox – all day Friday Sept 21 and Sat 22 around the globe synchronizations for peace are taking place – some at the exact moment of Equinox (PDT Sept 22 7:49A.M.), others all day, some at Sunset and Sunrise – including The International Day of Peace, The Solar Wave, Earth Dance, Didjeridoo Meditations, Meditations for Healing the Ocean, ETC. SPREAD THE WORD! BLESSINGS, Eden Skywalker.

Even the traumas that followed the Arab Spring were to be resolved:

> The new cycle will be full of light and of new possibilities. Imagine what the situation would be on our planet if the show was run by enlightened beings whose first priority was the welfare and evolution of all life forms, instead of being run by the greedy, war-mongering, Assad-esque leaders we have today.[172]

The outstanding issue, politically, is how we understand Argüelles' totalitarianism. John Gray sees anti-modernism, the nostalgic attempt to recreate societies supposedly obliterated by modernism, as an automatic failure which ends in fundamentalisms such as Nazism.[173] One cannot revive a lost past, he insists, and the attempt to do so is doomed to fail. The attempt to restore Maya civilization to its full glory as the coming global civilization therefore cannot work. In any case we know now that the detail of Argüelles' political forecasts for 2012 never came to pass. Whether or not Gray is right that anti-modernism is necessarily autocratic, or even whether the 2012 Prophecies are anti-modern, the question of whether one can revive the past is central to golden-age utopianism. The past cannot be restored if one subscribes to the forward motion of time's arrow; yet persistent currents of classical thought in the modern west maintain notions that time moves in waves or cycles. As Gurdjieff had said, 'all life flows in waves'.[174] Nietzsche would have understood.

The story of the counterculture, or countercultures, after the 1960s is one of interlocking strands of thought and action which came to public attention at different times. A rhetorical reaction against a caricatured flower-power hippyish Sixties by the yippyish punk explosion of 1976 obscures more general evidence of continuity which eventually brought the descendants of the two together in 1980s rave culture. This, in turn, provided fertile ground for the LSD and ayahuasca-inspired Maya prophecy movement.

The 2012 phenomena was explicitly countercultural in the sense that it specifically preached the complete and imminent end of all current culture. It was thoroughly rooted in Christian millenarianism, its direct inspiration being the New Age movement of the nineteenth and twentieth centuries. Yet it represents the cumulative, improvisational element in the millenarian tradition. It drew on Jung's work on UFOs from 1959, Aldous Huxley's and Timothy Leary's belief that psychedelic drugs revealed transcendent wisdom, and science fiction, such as *2001: A Space Odyssey*. Its culture of expectation framed itself within the recent traditions of environmental protest, presenting its struggle not as one of spiritual growth but ecological salvation. Its vision of a new world was utopian and its challenge to capitalism and the state were countercultural. It was deeply rooted in tradition; yet, in its detail, it was new.

Remaking the World: Neoconservatism and the Global Utopia

Two of Plato's ideas are particularly persistent. One is his Idealism; the belief that soul, psyche and consciousness underpin existence, rather than matter. The other is that history possesses direction, pattern and purpose. Both were fundamental to western esotericism, especially from the Renaissance onwards. And both were also transmitted to the modern world by the nineteenth-century Idealists, particularly Hegel. In particular, they proved especially influential in one important modern political ideology, American neoconservatism. This emerged in the 1960s from an alliance of political liberals and conservatives who were appalled at what they saw as the mindless violence and totalitarian tendencies of the New Left and anti-war protesters, compounded by the self-indulgent morality of hippy culture.[1] The wider context was, as Steven Lukes put it, the development of 'a new proactive and utopian "neo-liberal" right whose increasingly hegemonic ideology gripped the world in the latter part of the century with the ascendancy of Ronald Reagan and Margaret Thatcher'.[2]

There has been much discussion concerning the differences and similarities between neoliberalism and neoconservatism, and the argument is really inconclusive. Some emphasize neoliberalism as a doctrine of economic deregulation and neoconservatism as dependent on an aggressive foreign policy.[3] Others regard the two as identical.[4] But, whatever the conclusion, it is clear that neither is a self-contained category. It is safest to say that the neoconservatives share a neoliberal devotion to economic freedom. Neoliberalism retained previous right-wing attachments such as patriotism and a devotion to law and order, but was distinguished from the mainstream conservatism of the twentieth century by its transformation into a radical movement, challenging economic regulation and turning free markets into a mechanism for social improvement.[5] The neoliberals followed devoutly Adam Smith's prescription of economic liberty as a prescription for human perfectibility.

Neoconservatism, meanwhile, is based on a set of principles and consists, in practice, like all other movements, of a coalition, or network, of competing individuals and policy positions.[6] It no more exists as a coherent, single movement than does the New Age movement; its ideology is difficult to pin down and it is based on no single current of thought. Justin Vaïsse described 'discontinuity, heterogeneity and contradiction' as 'integral' to neoconservatism, adding that the word 'is constantly in danger of losing any precise meaning'.[7] Francis Fukuyama, the most important neoconservative historical theorist, prefers to define the abstract ideas at the heart of neoconservatism as 'mindsets or world views rather than principled positions'.[8] Neoconservatism is, like the Enlightenment, neo-liberalism and the New Age, a broad-gauge generalization which may emerge in a variety of sometimes inconsistent policy details and which has multiple points of origin. Stuart Hall bracketed the various features of the new right of Reagan and Thatcher together as what he called New Times, and deliberately made an explicit connection with New Age.[9]

The free market is central to the neoliberal dream of human progress and equality. However, neoconservatism was galvanized by political concerns, particular by shock at the emergence of the counterculture. The liberal-conservative reaction against the rhetorical Sixties began almost as the decade began. The philosopher Daniel Bell denounced the New Left in 1962, almost at its inception, and around the same time as the Port Huron Statement: 'For among the "new Left", there is an alarming readiness to create a tabula rasa, to accept the word "Revolution" as an absolution for outrages, to justify the suppression of civil rights and opposition'.[10] To some liberal academics in America, the protesters' willingness to ransack university offices rather than engage in debate brought uncomfortable reminders of Stalinist Russia and Nazi Germany. When such liberals looked at the countercultural utopia they saw less a wonderful Rousseau-esque return to a state of nature than a descent to Hobbesian brutishness.

The neoconservatives saw the United States entering a battle for its very survival in the 1960s: Michael Lind, a prominent independent-minded conservative, used a military analogy, describing neoconservatives as engaging in a 'culture war'.[11] In this narrative the rebels of the 1960s had become, by the 1970s, a new establishment, a 'university-government-media complex' who were threatening the freedoms on which American identity was founded.[12] The neoconservatives resembled the eighteenth-century *philosophes*, a network of intellectuals brought together in opposition to a political mainstream which it perceived as having lost its way and abandoned its principles. Like the Jacobites in the 1700s, they became a new counterculture, bitterly opposing what they saw as a dominant culture in Washington, one which was intent on pursuing state-sponsored, social-engineering solutions to domestic problems. They objected to a foreign policy dominated firstly by détente with the communist world, and secondly by the subordination of US interests to supranational organizations such as the United Nations. Both the domestic and foreign policies of the 1970s were seen as exhbiting signs of weakness.

Neoconservatism's origins lie in two formative struggles, the first being the progressive alienation of former Marxist Jewish intellectuals from the brutal realities of communism, the second being that against the counterculture and emerging liberal establishment of the 1960s.[13] Typical of the disillusioned Stalinists was Eugene Lyons, a Jewish immigrant, born in 1898, who had arrived in New York at the age of nine. Appalled by the injustice and poverty he witnessed, he became a communist, was employed by TASS, the Soviet news agency, and worked as a journalist in Moscow from 1928 to 1934.[14] He later rejected what he realized was a brutal, totalitarian system and published his denunciation of it in his 1937 work, *Assignment in Utopia*. To Lyons, and others who shared his view, Marxism was no longer a preferable alternative to

Nazism. Both were, instead, varieties of utopian totalitarianism, their similarities greater than their differences.

Even though most of this early Jewish-communist network had abandoned Marxism by the Second World War (or at least by the 1950s), they retained a familiarity with such features as love of socio-economic statistics, the central role of the intellectual and the notion of 'correct doctrine' (as opposed to false ideology).[15] They also retained a devotion to the view that history must follow a broadly predetermined, teleological path towards a certain outcome. The paradox of Neoconservative historical theory was its complete rejection of Marxist millenarianism, allied to its acceptance of a different version, in which history ended with capitalism rather than communism.[16] When the 1960s witnessed an upsurge in fashionable Trotskyism, tinged with a fondness for Stalinist iconography (the predilection for posters of Che Guevara and Ho Chi Minh comes to mind), the ex-communists were horrified at the naivety of Tom Hayden and the SDS, the other youthful sympathizers for communism, and the liberals who supported them.

The struggle between the neoconservatives and the liberals was framed within the competition between two of the Enlightenment's intellectual heirs, individualism on the one hand, and the pursuit of social justice through government regulation, on the other. In the neoconservative's own view, they aimed to restore a genuine lost liberalism based on individual freedom, while the conventional liberalism of the 1960s, had sacrificed freedom on the altar of state-sponsored social engineering of the kind promoted by Presidents Roosevelt and Johnson.[17] So successful was the neoconservative denunciation of liberalism as inimical to true human values that it remains a key feature of American political discourse.

The neoconservatives had no direct roots in Christian millenarianism, even though some of their number formed marriages of convenience with the Christian Right in order to gain power. However, while texts such as the Book of Revelation may not figure in neoconservative thinking, the cumulative impact of the many utopian exercises associated with successive evangelical Awakenings did provide important background. The legacy of hundreds of small experiments in utopian living since the eighteenth century underpinned a conviction that the history of the United States itself provided evidence of 'the working of the hand of God in time as He willed the United States to be not only a "city on a hill" but also the "light of the world"'.[18] Meanwhile, the conservative philosopher Leo Strauss claimed that Anglo-American democracy was the one true universal regime.[19] The nation's political and economic systems are seen to be both divinely ordained and at the progressive, cutting edge of the forward march of time. During the twentieth century, as its own wealth rose in relation to the decline of its European rivals, the United States came to identify itself as the vehicle for the 'Utopia of global capitalism'.[20] In John Gray's critical summary,

> The contemporary American faith that it is a universal nation implies that all humans are born American, and become anything else by accident – or error. According to this faith American values are, or will soon be, shared by all humankind … The United States has built the illusions and superstitions of the Enlightenment into its view of itself.[21]

America's idea of itself as a messianic state is not unique idea, and it is shared by, amongst other countries, Britain, France and Germany. Russia and China also share traditions which place themselves at the centre of the world. At the beginning of the twentieth century, British imperialists had also regarded their empire as the final phase of history.[22]

American Sixties counterculturalism and neoconservatism pose as opposites, but like evangelical Christianity and New Ageism, they are fighting over the same turf, in this case the origins of American utopianism in the pure ideals of the open frontier, the domestic paradise of the small town and the heroic qualities of the rugged individualist. New Left and neoconservatives shared a sense that the founding fathers' respect for the individual had been abandoned.[23] Both hippy culture and neoconservatism were driven by a keen advocacy of individual rights and a profound hostility to the authority of state. The neoconservatives may have been reacting against what they saw as the totalitarianism of countercultural youth, but a major component of youthful rebellion was itself rejection of those same Liberal statist and Marxist regimes which the Neoconservatives loathed. The difference was that for the neoconservative libertarians, personal behaviour should be controlled and conservative, whereas for hippy libertarians it should be unrestrained and spontaneous. And aside from the continuing interest of some on the American New Left in collective state solutions, it is difficult to see any fundamental neoconservative principles which disagree with those set out in the SDS's Port Huron Statement of 1962. Both were deeply moral, rejected materialist consumerism and greed, were suspicious of the state and advocated freedom for the individual based on reason.[24] The neoconservatives' prime objection was to the behaviour of the student protestors, chiefly their illiberal refusal to compromise. So close was the anti-statist individualism of the radical counterculturalists and that of the neoconservatives, that there was actually an attempt by the conservative Libertarian politician Murray N. Rothbard to bring the two together, forging an alliance against Washington.[25] Rothbard failed but his identification of shared qualities between the New Left and the neoconservatives was correct.

The neoconservatives identified themselves as brining a decisive break with a recent dominated by the rise of totalitarian Marxism abroad and liberal statism at home. Central to this narrative was the belief that the mistakes of the past must be undone for the future to be built, for the lost golden age of American innocence and liberty to be restored.

In the 1950s, the idea that the world, or at least the west, had reached the end of a long phase of struggle between rival ideologies stirred up endless debates.[26] The general proposition was that politics had entered a phase in which there was a broad consensus over the nature of the socio-economic system which had reached its final state in the triumph of capitalism (even if the geopolitical struggle between the capitalist west and the communist east was still unresolved) and, at most, could be subject to minor reforms. Marxism, the twentieth century's most potent millenarian movement, was seen as fatally discredited and the millennium, as we might put it, had been realized in the United States.

The notion that a final point in political development was approaching was evident in the title of Daniel Bell's 1962 book, *The End of Ideology*. However, endings must be followed by new beginnings and Bell's book, published, coincidentally, in the same year as the Port Huron Statement, and remarkably similar in tone, was an apocalyptic call to revive the American utopia:

> The end of ideology is not – should not be the end of utopia well. If anything, one can begin anew the discussion of utopia only by being aware of the trap of ideology... There is now, more than ever, some need for utopia, in the sense that men need – as they have always needed – some vision of the potential, some manner of using passion with intelligence. Yet the ladder to the City of Heaven can no longer be a 'faith ladder', but an empirical one.

Actually, such optimism is always tinged with a despair which lies at the heart of the entire neoconservative worldview: the belief that western culture has reached a point of near-terminal decline and that the attempt to recover the lost golden age may be doomed. One of the key texts of neoconservative pessimism was Daniel Bell's seminal article 'Unstable America', published in *Encounter* in 1970.[27] Bell's apocalyptic, doom-laden tone now sounds somewhat naive: in spite of the facts and figures he used to promote his case, Bell's list of problems were no more than the standard list of problems found in golden age and millenarian narratives for millennia. In his narrative the golden age was the 1950s, when the United States was 'mobilized' by the single purpose of anti-communism.[28] Social fragmentation, rising crime, racial tensions, the failure of liberalism and a crisis in political legitimacy, had compounded the pressures of the Vietnam War. All were symptoms of an unprecedented crisis, but Bell could offer no solution other than an appeal in his closing sentence for 'intelligent leadership'.[29]

The notion of unprecedented moral collapse across all sectors of American society became a persistent theme from the 1970s to the 2000s. As Gertrude Himmelfarb put it in 1995, 'civil society has been infected by the same virus that has contaminated the entire culture: irresponsibility, incivility, a lack of self-discipline and self-control'.[30] Her apocalyptic diagnosis for this 'grievous moral disorder' was plain: 'moral pathology requires strenuous moral purgatives and restoratives'.[31] Domestically, neoconservatism is engaged in a moral crusade, promoting a cultural revolution intended to restore a nostalgic vision of a society in which universal order prevailed; that is, the fantasy of wholesome, small-town life and the all-American family. This may mean small government, but not necessarily so; strictly, it is neo-liberalism which shares the Marxist insistence on the withering of the state.[32]

The neoconservatives' foreign policy, established in a defence plan written by Donald Wolfowitz in the closing days of the Bush senior administration in 1992, has been described as a 'curious combination of optimism and pessimism (in which) the United States was endowed by Providence with the power to make the world better if only it would take the risks of leadership – if only it were sufficiently "forward-leaning"'.[33] Civilization is hanging by a thread and if destiny is to do its work, it requires human help. The various prescriptions by which the neoconservatives thought that the American utopia could be restored were summarized by Michael Lind, who came to be very critical of what he saw as the intellectual flaws in the movement's philosophy. He summarized neoconservative domestic strategy as creating a coalition between religious Protestants,

Catholics and Jews in order to resist secularism.[34] Each of these groups had its own deep-seated millenarian traditions. But it was the southern Baptists' belief in the imminence of the *parousia* that came to be a particularly effective driver of neoconservative foreign policy, particularly its unqualified support for the far-right anti-Palestinian wing of Israeli politics from 2002.[35] All Jews, it was thought, had to return to the Holy Land before the Messiah could return.[36] Opposition to Palestinian rights, insistence that Jerusalem must be Israel's capital and the subversion of the peace process and two-state solution then become divine obligations on the pain of eternal damnation. Such events as the Republican-dominated Congress's invitation to Israeli prime minister Benjamin Netanyahu in 2015 to give a speech which directly undercut the Obama administration's attempt to reach a deal with Tehran on Iran's nuclear programme are then contextualized within the millenarianism of the Christian Right.[37] For the evangelicals, if the deal with Iran was done and Israel was threatened, God's plan would be disrupted.

This brings us to the enigma of the second Gulf War of 2003. The first question is why was it so important to the neoconservatives that Iraq should be invaded? One answer, following Bell's analysis, was to restore the mobilized society of the 1950s; mobilized in the sense that the whole country was supposedly mobilized against a foreign enemy. As Peter Steinfels wrote, originally in 1979, 23 years before the war, neoconservative international relations theory was based on the following formula: 'A precarious international order requires a stable, unified society at home; renewed emphasis on the Communist threat and on the Third World's rejection of liberal values is needed to generate the requisite national allegiance and discipline'.[38] One reason for the domestic chaos of the 1960s, it was thought, was that young people had abandoned the previous consensus that communism represented a universal threat. Freed from this external pressure, there was an immediate moral decline. Simply put, domestic cohesion requires the existence of clearly defined foreign enemies and, if none exist, they must be manufactured.

The goal was not in doubt but the strategy was. This all changed in 1989 when, enthused by the collapse of the communist regimes in Eastern Europe, Francis Fukuyama published his famous claim that Hegel was right, and the final stage of history, defined as the end of ideological struggle, was evident in the inevitable triumph of American-style liberal democracy and capitalism. Borrowing from Bell, he titled his book *The End of History and the Last Man*. The book was a publishing sensation in 1991 and prompted a whole spate of 'end of' books, all postulating an end to some aspect of human activity or knowledge. The book was widely ridiculed by historians for its obvious millenarian agenda but it galvanized the neoconservatives by giving them a historical mission. While Fukuyama devoted considerable attention to philosophical nuances, his core claim was unambiguous. Liberal democracy, he proclaimed, being uniquely free from internal defects, irrationalities and contradictions, represented 'the end point of mankind's ideological evolution...the final form of human government...(and) the end of history'.[39]

Fukuyama later moderated the extreme historicist position he adopted in 1989. In 1999, on the tenth anniversary of the publication of *The End of History*, he maintained that he had been correct in his assertion that 'history is directional and progressive, and that it culminates in the modern liberal state'; he only added that science and technology introduced an additional variable factor that could speed history up or slow it down.[40] This was the essence of Lenin's argument in 1902, when he attacked social democrats for being diverted into reformism and instead argued for the creation of a revolutionary vanguard in order to promote revolution, rather than wait for.[41]

Even then, though, the paradoxes inherent in the utopian-millenarian worldview intruded. On the one hand, Fukuyama argued that 'there can be no end of science' and therefore no end to history but, on the other, that when bio-technology finally allowed science to manipulate humanity, achieving what decades of social engineering had failed to accomplish, 'we shall then finally have definitely finished human history, because we shall have abolished human beings as such. And then a new, post-human history will begin'.[42] Fukuyama provided the neoconservatives with a culture of expectation which spanned the whole world. Yet it was a culture which failed to take into account the variety of systems which replaced communism, including the continuation in power of the old elites in Romania and Bulgaria. Neither did it take heed of reactions, when disappointment set in, such as nostalgia for the old Soviet days or right wing nationalism.[43]

Fukuyama found support for his prophecy of the end of history in his analysis of the 1989 revolutions in Eastern Europe. Like Bloch, Fukuyama drew on Hegel. The driver of Fukuyama's millenarian narrative was psychological and focused on the needs of the *thymos*, the part of the Platonic soul which craves recognition as a basis of self-esteem.[44] The need to feel special, to be recognized as special, to be more than one is, is one of the psychological drivers of utopianism as a private, rather than collective, experience. Fukuyama referred neither to Bloch's view of the basis of utopianism as the need to be one's self, nor to Scheler's concept of *ressentiment*, but he could have done; the oppressed of Eastern Europe were devalued and bullied, and became resentful and rebellious. The engine of history is psychological and, as dictatorships deny the universal need for recognition, Fukuyama argued, they are bound to collapse sooner or later, while democracies, which encourage it, are equally bound to succeed. The 'Last Man' in the title of Fukuyama's book is therefore the 'victorious slave', the individual who has cast off oppression and is therefore able to realize his or her potential.[45] Fukuyama's last man directly parallels other ideal individuals in the Platonic, Idealist, tradition, including the Nietzschean *übermensch*, the Theosophical 'Seed Man', Jung's 'modern man', the spiritually aware person whose task is to assist in the inauguration of the New Age, and the individuated beneficiary of Jungian analytical psychology. The truly thymotic man rejects comfortable materialism and must continue to strive for self-realization.[46] As Hegel realized, the 'peace and prosperity' of the last age was not enough, for these conditions would breed complacency and decay.[47] The parallels with Sixties hippyish individualism are not just close; they are exact. The youthful Sixties rebel rejected the comfortable materialism of the suburban life in order to live on the street in Haight-Ashbury, or hurl petrol bombs in Paris. But the rebel, in a sense, is the ultimate conservative, fighting an establishment which has turned its back on its founding principles, whether of the founding fathers of 1776 in the United States, or the proclamation of equality in France in 1789.

Fukuyama identified four threads in the neoconservative mindset, of which the crucial one for foreign policy was a belief that 'US power can be used for moral purposes'.[48] This is entirely different to the geopolitical world view advocated by such previous theorists as Henry Kissinger, in which foreign policy is simply an amoral matter of great power rivalry. It was on this basis that Kissinger, for example, engineered Richard Nixon's visit to America's mortal enemy, communist China. The neoconservatives rejected such realism, particularly resenting the pragmatism which had left Saddam Hussein in power in Iraq following the first Gulf War of 1990. Throughout the 1990s, the Neoconservatives developed a foreign policy based on the need for certain practical steps in order to manifest their moral vision. These included pre-emption of likely attacks against the United States and encouraging regime change in hostile states. It was recognized that the world was now unipolar and the United States was the only superpower, a situation seen as good for the entire world as the metaphysics of 'American exceptionalism' automatically meant that Washington's global domination was defined as 'benevolent hegemony'.[49]

Fukuyama resembled his fellow neoconservatives in his balance of pessimism and optimism. The consequence of two world wars and the horrors of Nazism and Communism, he wrote, was that 'We in the West have become thoroughly pessimistic with regard to the possibility of overall progress in democratic institutions'.[50] And then, he announced, 'good news has come', the cause for optimism being the progressive collapse of the world's dictatorships under the weight of their own inadequacies.[51] In the wake of 1989, neoconservative foreign policy analysis was one in which the abolition of all the previous political and economic structures of the state made perfect sense: into the vacuum would inevitably flow the benefits of American exceptionalism.[52] The vehicle for the neoconservative mission to remake the world in the image of America was the 'Project for the New American Century', founded in 1997. The Project's vision statement, written by its chairman, William Kristol, the husband of Gertrude Himmelfarb, articulated the practical applications of Fukuyama's historicism. The Project, he wrote, was 'dedicated to a few fundamental propositions: that American leadership is good both for America and for the world; and that such leadership requires military strength, diplomatic energy and commitment to moral principle', and intends to 'strive to rally support for a vigorous and principled policy of American international involvement...'.[53] From the outset, the Project campaigned actively for an invasion of Iraq. For example, a memorandum of 7 January 1999 stated clearly that 'Now that the dust has settled from the 70-hour aerial attack on Iraq, it has become clear that the only solution for the threat Iraq poses is to remove Saddam'.[54] At first, the neoconservatives lacked a pretext for war, having no equivalent of the Gulf of Tonkin incident in 1964, an alleged attack by the North Vietnamese navy on US warships, which enabled Lyndon Johnson to send ground troops to Vietnam. All this changed after 9/11 – the al-Qaeda attacks on the World Trade Center Twin Towers and the Pentagon on 11 September 2001. The attacks galvanized American policy in a number of ways, of which the ascendancy of the foreign-interventionists was the most obvious, resulting in the invasions of Afghanistan and Iraq.[55] Encouraged by the Christian Right, there was also a heightened sense of other apocalyptic conditions, such as a heightened sense of the Muslim world's threat to Israel.[56]

The Bush White House developed a foreign policy based on three core principles. One was military dominance, which is to be expected. The other two were pre-emption and regime change, both of which represented radical breaks with previous American policy. Both were based in the assumption, derived from Hegel and Condorcet, via Fukuyama, that, as the whole world was destined to become like America, political 'transformation' could be achieved by converting a 'transition to democracy' envisaged in Fukuyama's passive model to its 'imposition'.[57] That is, the pace of history could be speeded up. Just as Fukuyama's reliance on Hegel revealed a shared legacy with New Ageism, so it also reinforced the neoconservatives' Marxist legacy. One of the key differences between different varieties of Marxism is whether one must allow history to take its course on the one hand or, on the other, whether it can be speeded along. The problem was originally framed by Condorcet. Being a Newtonian, he believed that history had to take its own course, in its own time. However, he also distinguished countries where the inevitable process of adopting the civilized values of America and France would occur naturally, on the one hand, and those, more resistant to progress, where it would have to be forced, on the other.[58] In Newton's view, only God, acting via Providence, could interfere in the operation of the universe.[59]

Later, Marxism split between the social democrats, who believed in incremental, gradual change, and the revolutionaries, who thought the pace of history could be forced, as Lenin had outlined in 1902 in one of his most important tracts, 'What is to be Done'. In 1917 Lenin was distinguished from many of his fellows by his belief that Russia, which was hardly ready for a transition to the dictatorship of the proletariat, might still be pushed into revolution. The notion of forced regime change as formulated by the neoconservatives then becomes Leninist.[60] The guiding ideology behind neoconservative foreign policy may then be described as what Jowitt called 'Marx-Fukuyama'.[61] The Bush White House, following *The End of History*'s view that the rest of the world would inevitably become more like the west, but without the nuances and subtleties in Fukuyama's discussion, subscribed to the idea (like Lenin) that the process could be speeded up. In Jowitt's summary, 'History, the Bush administration has concluded, needs deliberate organisation, leadership, and direction'.[62] Neoconservative foreign policy was messianic in its belief that it could transform the world and inaugurate the final phase of history, rather than passively waiting for it to occur.[63] The connection between American messianism and Marxism is also made by John Gray, on the grounds that both are products of Enlightenment modernism.[64] Both share the belief that, while war is a developmental phase in human history, historic sources of human conflict can be transcended, and that traditional diplomacy, which sought to control conflict without any idea that it could be eradicated, is redundant. The model was dramatically simplified by Thomas Friedman in 1999, who argued that not only *would* the whole world become American, but that it *wanted* to be American. Friedman was a huge fan of Fukuyama, although he doubted the finality implied by the title, *The End of History*. Nonetheless, he popularized the view that Americanism represented history's end game: 'Culturally speaking', he wrote, 'globalization has tended to involve the spread of Americanization – from Big Macs to iMacs to Micky Mouse'.[65]

The consequences for practical policy focused on Iraq. Prior to 9/11, the passive version of 'Marx-Fukuyama' prevailed, in which history could take its own course in its own time, and deterrence of Saddam Hussein was sufficient. Following 9/11, the mood changed, 'Marx-Fukuyama' became the driver of foreign policy and it was decided that history should be forced along and the pace of Americanization encouraged. Fukuyama objected to this on the grounds that it was a fundamental break with what he saw as the Hegelian principle that history should be allowed to proceed at its own pace. He argued that the new policy was bound to lead to disaster, but his objections were ignored. American policy was now based on the premise that, because East Germany and Poland had become democratic in 1989, after dictatorship was overthrown, Iraq would also necessarily become democratic after dictatorship was overthrown. The formula was simple, and completely ignored all local cultural, historical, social, ethnic and religious distinctions. There was an explicit rejection of any regard for regional variations in favour of an idealistic universalism and the unshakeable law of history. It was hoped that the overthrow of Saddam Hussein would release a blockage in the flow of history across the whole Middle East and result in a domino effect in which democracy would spread in turn to Iran, Syria, Jordan, Egypt, Saudi Arabia and the whole of the Arab world. Indeed, in November 2003, after the invasion of Iraq, George W. Bush gave the first of series of speeches in which he announced a few 'forward strategy' intended to promote democracy in the middle east as the only sure guarantor of peace.[66] The decision to invade Iraq was therefore a moral one, regardless of such practical questions as the existence or not of weapons of mass destruction, which provided the pretext.[67] This is not to say that there were no geopolitical concerns. The outcome was indeed to be of benefit to hard American power – the beginning of the creation of 'a ring of American bases', which would enable 'the US writ … to run everywhere'.[68] Yet this was a noble goal for what was good for America, as the Project for the New American Century proclaimed, was necessarily good for everyone.

An additional and still controversial question is why there was so little, if any, planning for the aftermath of the invasion, and here one possible answer lies in the neoconservatives' optimistic culture of expectation, in which it was thought that if the old system was torn down, the new one would automatically arise. The fiasco of the post-war occupation of Iraq has been well documented: there was no thought given to administering the country after Saddam was overthrown and when administrators were hired they often had neither experience nor interest.[69] There was actually a brief interval between the US occupation of Baghdad on 9 April and 11 May 2003, when the lead administrator, Jay Garner, was working with elements of the previous regime to restore independence as soon as possible. However, there was an apparent policy shift in Washington, and the neoconservatives succeeded in replacing Garner with Paul Bremer, who replaced pragmatism with ideology. Bremer set about disbanding the organs of state, the Baath Party and the army, and instituted a policy of privatization, 'the switch from value-destroying public enterprises to value-creating private ones', which would then, he hoped, provide a foundation for a free, democratic system.[70] Bremer's confidence was drawn from the collapse of communism in Eastern Europe, and he implemented the bold leadership required by the neoconservative foreign policy analysis, one in which the abolition of all the previous political and economic structures of the state made perfect sense: into the vacuum would inevitably flow the benefits of American exceptionalism.[71] Prior to the invasion, the neoconservatives' optimism had known no bounds: "After Baghdad, Beijing" ran one boast. They saw especially in the Middle East a web of corrupt dictators, whose people would, if given the chance, embrace a Jeffersonian view of democracy. Iraq was top of the list.[72] The invasion of Iraq was a war of liberation and, as such, historical necessity therefore removed the need for planning: the law of progress would take care of the aftermath, just as it had in Eastern Europe. Michael Codner put it delicately in his review; in spite of the experience gained in the former Yugoslavia, 'As subsequent events showed, British planning did not take into account the range of likely outcomes following invasion and regime change … This might be seen as the behaviour of a liberating army rather than an occupying force.'[73] It was Fukuyama who identified the core problem: what was seen as good for the United States was seen as automatically good for the world and faith in the outcome was, according to Fukuyama, responsible for the United States' lack of preparation:

> By invading Iraq, the Bush administration saw itself not as acting out of narrow self-interest but as providing a global public good. The administration's belief in its own good motives explains much of its failure to anticipate the highly negative international reaction to the war.[74]

Fukuyama had developed his own doubts about the wisdom of invading Iraq prior to the war, and finally repudiated his connections with the neoconservatives in 2004, when it became clear that the invasion had been a spectacular failure.[75] The neoconservatives, in his view, had repudiated their own principles, entering into the social engineering they hated on a nationwide scale on the other side of the world.[76] Those in favour of invasion had assumed that local conditions were irrelevant in the face of universal prescriptions. They thought that, because the overthrow of dictatorship in Eastern Europe had resulted in democracy, the same consequence must follow in the Arab world. Fukuyama stuck to his Hegelian principles but argued that the flow of time varied with cultural conditions. Not all people were ready to enter the final phase of history at the same time so what applied to Eastern Europe in 1989 did not apply to Iraq in 2003. Neoconservatism, in the Bush White House, had become an ideology which pursued Ideal solutions irrespective of the evidence. It took the idea of the Heavenly City at face value, ignoring the reality of human frailty.

No longer concerned with pragmatic solutions to immediate problems, neoconservative had become an over-arching millennial means of bringing history to an end. It vested all its hopes in Plato's pure Being and forgot that we live in the flawed world of Becoming. Utopia is impossible and the noble aspirations of 'regime-change' therefore destined to fail. Neither is it possible to wish utopia into existence by tearing something down and waiting for history to do the rest. Contemplating the disaster of Iraq in 2014, Christopher Meyer, former British Ambassador to Washington, later wrote, in an article calling for the return to a foreign policy of national interest rather than abstract principle, that having deposed Saddam, 'we were, in effect, telling the Iraqi people to please start the business of nation-building all over again … '.[77] There is more than a whiff of the Jacobins' revolutionary calendar or the Khmer Rouge's Year Zero, in the idea that history could be reset. For the neoconservatives, to lead the world to freedom was a bold dream. Jowitt commented that the belief that American-style democracy could be established in Iraq and the Middle East possessed 'all the unreality of Don Quixote'.[78] It was also no more realistic than the Yippies' attempt to levitate the Pentagon.

Conclusion: Making the Future

The belief that history has a direction and a purpose is remarkably persistent. This should not be surprising, for human beings spend much of their lives searching for meaning. Some say that we cannot function effectively without a sense of purpose, so it would therefore be astonishing if we did not identify purpose in history. This belief in collective purpose is the foundation of two ways of engaging with history that pervade western culture. The first is that a millennium is coming, a point of liberation, salvation and release embodied in a new period of history, a new world or mode of existence. The millennium is preordained and will happen whether we want it to or not, and yet it is an obligation the faithful that they play a part in hastening its arrival; it is a participatory experience on a grand scale. The second is that we can ourselves create utopias: perfect societies which will, being shorn of all previous social and political flaws, require no further change. In both, history will come to an end. In some versions of millenarianism the creation of a utopia is a necessary part of the process, a means of managing the upheaval that coincides with a change of historical ages. And in others, the end of history is not a final end, just the prelude to another new beginning and future ending. All such ideas also tend to be countercultural. They identify a dominant culture to which they then pose a deliberate alternative and the logic of the millenarian mentality confers a sense of absolute, unshakeable faith in the believer's eventual success. The twentieth century was a heyday of such beliefs. The communist east subscribed to the belief that it was forging the final phase of history, on the way to the logical conclusion of Karl Marx's law of history. The capitalist west was equally sure of its destiny as the final point of the law of progress.

Two other forms of millenarianism flourish in more discrete areas of western culture. The first is Christian belief in Christ's imminent return in order to launch a final battle with evil and inaugurate God's eternal kingdom. For centuries a force for revolutionary turmoil, its political influence is now largely confined to the Christian Right in the United States. The second is the conviction that a new spiritual age is about to begin. This shares a lineage with Christianity, but also owes a debt to Platonic concepts that history moves forward according to patterns and cycles. Although the Platonic system is eternal and each ending precedes another beginning, in perpetuity, in normal circumstances the focus of attention is always on the immediate crisis, and the current transitional moment. The Platonic scheme is esoteric, meaning that it emphasizes inner change as the engine of historical change, the principle being that when enough people have realized their inner potential (whether spiritually or psychologically), the New Age will begin. True to the paradox that runs through millenarian mentalities, the coming of the future Age is inevitable, but human action is necessary in order to guarantee its inevitability. The purpose of human engagement in history is not just to enable the transition from one age to another to take place, but to manage it. To complicate matters, the prophecy of the coming New Age is now associated with a wider culture, also known as New Age, which consists of a collection of activities and ideas which can be ancient or modern, western or not. These activities all share one common feature: that consciousness is more important than matter and that ideas shape the world on a deep level by directly affecting the environment. Many who engage in such practices have no interest whatsoever in a coming historical transformation. However, believers in the coming historical shift, though small in number, are influential on account of their motivation and commitment. What matters to them is that sufficient people become psychologically self-aware and spiritually evolved in order to guarantee a smooth transition to the coming era. According to this scenario, war, plague and environmental catastrophe can all be averted if enough individuals have achieved a higher state of consciousness. And so action and activism are vital if the coming trauma is to be averted. New Age culture is evidence of utopia's programmatic nature, the importance of working out a clear strategy for managing the transition. The paradox of time intervenes: the future is fated but can be managed.

Within this general New Age culture there are different attitudes to time and history, depending on the relationship with the key emblem, or time-fetish, which signifies the transitional moment, usually the beginning of the Age of Aquarius or, from the 1980s onwards, the end of the Maya calendar. This moment may be conceived of as primarily historical and collective or as individual. In the latter case, the key moment is the personal entry to the age. In some teachings the personal is highlighted to such an extent that the historical becomes irrelevant. All that matters is personal enlightenment. Prophecy of the future then becomes irrelevant, although individual teachers may still be classed as prophets in that they claim to reveal higher truth. Their discourses, though, tend to be stridently anti-predictive. The future is of no concern and all that matters is an enthusiasm for enlightenment in the here and now and a belief that any individual can enter the new era at any time, regardless of historical conditions.

Utopianism and millenarianism are both inspired by hope, generating a culture of expectation. Their optimism that a better world is possible, or that it is actually about to arrive, runs directly counter to pessimistic and cynical currents which preach a gospel of despair and hopelessness, and encourages people work not just for violent revolution, but peaceful social reform. The two currents are not self-contained, and the boundary between utopian paradise and dystopian hell is fluid, while millenarians may have cause to fear the approaching apocalypse. Utopianism, dystopianism and millenarianism are all psychological conditions, consisting of a matrix of interlocking mentalities dominated by the past and the future. Nostalgia for a lost golden age is pivotal, as is the longing for its return. The immediate past is often rejected in favour of a culture of novelty and newness, frequently driven by belief in progress: that as time passes the world must inexorably become a better place. Sometimes utopian communities aim to be pluralist and democratic, but often, whether by accident or design, they are totalitarian. The belief that history is on our side all too easily results in the belief that other people stand in the way of history. They become a problem to be dealt with, whether by denying their rights, re-educating them, or subjecting them to revolutionary terror. The ethical problem millenarian and utopian thinking is impossible to resolve, for there is no logical, ethical position. If the emphasis is on the need to serve people then the result may be humane. But if there is an emphasis on history as the determinant of human welfare, then individuals often cease to matter.

New Age culture is often said to be irrational and belong to those strands of thought in eighteenth- and early nineteenth-century European culture – the 'Counter Enlightenment' and 'Romanticism' – which supposedly rejected the forward march of civilization in the form of the 'Age of Reason' and the 'Enlightenment'. This comfortable assumption was challenged in the 1990s.[1] Looked at closely, New Age culture possessed qualities supposedly central to the Enlightenment, in particular its opposition to established religion and its frequent appeal to reason. The place of the New Age in western culture is therefore a matter of dispute: does it belong to Romanticism or to the Enlightenment? It can easily be both, especially if they share certain qualities, such as a reverence for nature. And from the eighteenth-century *philosophes* in particular, the New Age has borrowed a devotion to the principle of free inquiry in defiance of traditional authorities, whether church, state or, now, what is seen as an overly conservative and dogmatic scientific establishment.

The academic study of New Age ideas tends to be confined to the study of religions, where much good work has been done. However, New Age beliefs are ignored in other areas where we might expect to find mention of them, and we find little or no reference to them in cultural studies or the history of ideas. Yet, to borrow Wittgenstein's theory of family resemblances, it is clear that they form part of a larger family of millenarianism and utopianisms. They include the eruptions of hope which manifested in the United States in 1776, France in 1789 and Russia in 1917. They are similar to religious awakenings and are related to ideas of destiny which are also found in British and American imperialism. We can apply the same terms to New Age prophecy as we do to other, related phenomena. The prediction of the imminent New Age embodies a culture of expectation, with its adherents practicing avoidance lifestyles and engaging in mass resistance to religious and scientific norms. It depends on expressivism, the belief that the highest calling is to be true to one's self. It deploys the memory of lost golden ages to the revolutionary cause. And its hope for an end to the selfish brutalities of capitalism and the bureaucratic state preserve revolutionary aspirations which have been all but lost since the sudden demise of Marxism. Indeed, such ideas now flourish only on the left of the Green movement, where ideas that have been nurtured by the New Age movement provide a religious context. Chief of these is the Gaia hypothesis which, in its New Age form, treats the earth as a living being. As a form of millenarianism, New Age is progressive, cumulative and improvisational, aiming for a peaceful transition to the millennium, assisted by the inevitable process of spiritual evolution, building on past traditions, such as Christianity, while adding new forms appropriate to the late twentieth century, such as science fiction. And it shares its metaphysics of time as an engine of destiny with the wider family of millenarian beliefs.

It is often said that the New Age movement of the 1970s and onwards was a product of the counterculture of the 1960s. As we have seen, the New Age movement was evident in the nineteenth century and contributed to the Sixties, as much as it benefited from them. The problem of the Sixties therefore assumes substantial significance in the history of New Age thought. Millenarian and utopian ideas were in evidence, but at its heart the Sixties were characterized by hope, which Ernst Bloch identified as the universal psychological origin of all utopianism. The Sixties therefore provide an ideal case study of the collective excitement which leads some people to live, and announce that a New Age is beginning. There was never a single counterculture in the 1960s. There were instead many rival taste cultures: ideas, fashions, networks, ideologies which adopted competing or overlapping styles – all united by hope, newness and a challenge to social or political norms, sentiments which extended into the 1970s and beyond.

Such phenomena find their place within the history of ideas. In the 1940s R.G. Collingwood, in despair at the grand historical theories of Oswald Spengler and Arnold Toynbee, let alone of Karl Marx, wrote that

> We have so far gone back to the medieval view of history that we think of nations and civilisations as rising and falling in obedience to a law that has little to do with the purpose of human beings that compose them. This brings us into somewhat close contact with the Medieval historians'.[2]

Bruno Latour was more sanguine, pointing out that the idea that modern westerners are somehow more advanced than their distant ancestors is an error.[3] New Age is part of what Latour called the anthropological matrix, the complex pattern of belief and practice which connects westerners to their prehistoric ancestors. This continuity may be masked by the superficial gloss of technological change, but it is not substantially affected by it. It is in the nature of future ages that they never arrive. We are permanently stuck, Godot-like, in an eternal waiting room. It's not the arrival that matters, as they say, but the journey. The believer inhabits a perpetual transitional moment, in which utopia and the expectation of the millennium provide a method for living, exploring the self and managing global politics.

Notes

Chapter 1

1 Lucien Lévi-Bruhl, *How Natives Think*, trans. Lillian A. Clare (London: George Allen & Unwin, 1926), 69. Also see Richard Evans, *In Defence of History* (London: Granta Books, 1997), 155.

2 Hayden White, *Metahistory: The Historical Imagination in Nineteenth Century Europe* (Baltimore and London: The Johns Hopkins University Press, 1973).

3 Francis Fukuyama, *The End of History and the Last Man* (London: Penguin, 1991), xiii.

4 W.H. Auden, 'Spain 1937', lines 35–6, in *W.H. Auden Poems Selected by John Fuller*, ed. John Fuller (London: Faber and Faber, 2000), 24.

5 James Rado, Gerome Ragni, and Galt MacDermot, 'Aquarius', 1968, http://www.metrolyrics.com/aquarius-lyrics-5th-dimension.html.

6 Fred Davis, 'Why All of Us May Be Hippies Someday', *Trans-Action* 5, no. 2 (1967): 15.

7 Ludwig Wittgenstein, *The Blue and Brown Books, Preliminary Studies for 'Philosophical Investigations'* (Oxford: Blackwell, 1958), 17. See also Ludwig Wittgenstein, *Philosophical Investigations*, trans. G.E.M Anscombe, P.M.S Hacker and Joachim Schulte (Oxford: Wiley-Blackwell, 2009), 54, 55.

8 Charles Webster, *From Paracelsus to Newton: Magic and the Making of Modern Science* (Cambridge: Cambridge University Press, 1982).

9 Raymond Williams, *The Long Revolution* (London: Hogarth Press, 1992), xii.

10 Richard Landes, *Heaven on Earth: The Varieties of the Millennial Experience* (Oxford: Oxford University Press, 2011); David S. Katz and Richard H. Popkin, *Messianic Revolution: Radical Religious Politics to the End of the Second Millennium* (London: Penguin, 1999), 222.

11 Amy Johnson Frykholm, *Rapture Culture: Left Behind in Evangelical America* (Oxford: Oxford University Press, 2004).

12 Landes, *Heaven on Earth*, 421–66; See also, for example, Graeme Wood, 'What ISIS Really Wants', *The Atlantic Monthly* (March 2015), http://www.theatlantic.com/features/archive/2015/02/what-isis-really-wants/384980/, accessed 23 February 2015, and the reply in Murtaza Hussein, 'The Atlantic Ignores Muslim Intellectuals, Defines "True Islam" As ISIS', *The Intercept*, https://firstlook.org/theintercept/2015/02/20/atlantic-defines-real-islam-says-isis/, accessed 23 February 2015.

13 Moojan Momen, *An Introduction to Shi'i Islam: the History and Doctrines of Twelver Shi'ism* (Oxford: George Ronald, 1987).

14 See for example Wouter J. Hanegraaff, *New Age Religion and Western Culture* (Leiden and New York: E.J. Brill, 1996), 96, 98–103; Stuart Sutcliffe, *Children of the New Age: A History of Spiritual Practices* (London: Routledge, 2003), 9, 11, 17.

15 Alfred North Whitehead, *Process and Reality* (London: Free Press, 1979), 39.

16 Kocku von Stuckrad, *Western Esotericism: A Brief History of Secret Knowledge* (London: Equinox, 2005), 9.

17   Hans Jonas, *The Gnostic Religion: The Message of the Alien God and the Beginnings of Christianity*, 2nd ed. (Boston: Beacon Press, 1963).

18   Dylan Burns, 'An Unlikely Love Affair: Plato, the Netherlands, and Life after Westotericism', in *Hermes in the Academy: Ten Years' Study of Western Esotericism at the University of Amsterdam*, eds.Wouter J. Hanegraaff and Joyce Pijnenburg (Amsterdam: Amsterdam University Press, 2009), 107–9.

19   Karl Marx and Friedrich Engels, *The Communist Manifesto*, trans. Gareth Stedman Jones (London: Penguin Books, 1967), 241.

20   Benjamin E. Zeller, *Heaven's Gate: America's UFO Religion* (New York: New York University Press, 2014).

21   J. MiltonYinger, 'Contraculture and Subculture', *American Sociological Review* 25, no. 5 (1960): 627.

22   Theodore Roszak, *The Making of a Counter Culture: Reflections on the Technocratic Society and Its Youthful Opposition* (Garden City, NY: Anchor Books, 1969), xi.

23   Wittgenstein, *Blue and Brown Books*, 17.

24   Murray N. Rothbard, 'Life in the Old Right', *Chronicles* (August 1994): 15.

25   Stuart Hall, 'The Meaning of New Times', in *New Times: The Changing Face of Politics in the 1990s*, eds. Stuart Hall and Martin Jacques (London: Verso, 1990), 116–7.

26   Nigella Lawson, 'Astrology and the Need to Believe: Why Are We Going to New Age cranks for Old-style Cures?', *Times*, 13 November 1996, 17.

27   Derek Draper, 'I Used to Live a Shallow Life', *Times*, 21 February 2001, 3.

28   Ken Goffman, and Dan Joy, *Counter Culture Through the Ages: from Abraham to Acid House* (New York: Villard Books, 2005), 326.

29   George McKay, *Senseless Acts of Beauty; Cultures and Resistance since the Sixties* (London, and New York: Verso, 1996), 51.

30   George McKay, ed., *DiY Culture; Party and Protest in Nineties Britain* (London and New York: Verso, 1998), 43.

31   Waldemar Januszczak, 'The Cosmic Occultist Who Made It Hip to Be Square', *Sunday Times*, 'Culture', 7 February 2010, 14.

32   Jason Mankey, 'Paganism & the New Age', *Raising the Horns*, 1 September 2014, http://www.patheos.com/blogs/panmankey/2014/09/paganism-the-new-age/, accessed 9 April 2015.

33   National Secular Society, 'Jonathan Meades', http://www.secularism.org.uk/jonathanmeades.html, accessed 6 August 2014.

34   Michel Foucault, *History of Madness* (London: Routledge, 2006).

35   Lennard Davis, *Enforcing Normalcy: Disability, Deafness and the Body* (London: Verso, 1995), 50, 73.

36   Nigel Fountain, *Underground: The London Alternative Press, 1966–74* (London: Routledge, Chapman and Hall, 1988), 53–4.

37   Steven Altman, 'Path of the Quetzalcoatl: Sacred Pilgrimage to Mexico', *Caduceus* 89 (2014): 9.

38   Stephen Nation, 'Feminine on the Rise', *Caduceus* 89 (2014): 4.

39   Arthur Martin, 'Swampy's New Life', *Daily Mail*, 13 September 2013, http://www.dailymail.co.uk/news/article-2420429/Swampys-new-life-Former-eco-warrior-40-lives-yurt-children-job.html.

40   Herbert J. Gans, *Popular Culture and High Culture: An Analysis and Evaluation of Taste*, revised edition (New York: Basic Books, 1999), 68, 87.

41   Karl Marx, 'Theses on Feuerbach', in *On Historical Materialism*, eds. Karl Marx, Frederick Engels, and V.I. Lenin, compiled T. Borodulina (Moscow: Progress Publishers, 1972), VIII.

42   Antonio Gramsci, *Selections from the Prison Notebooks*, eds. Quintin Hoare and
     Geoffrey Nowell Smith (London: Lawrence and Wishart, 1971), 12–13, 416–7.
43   Theodor Adorno, Else Frenkel-Brunswick, Daniel J. Levinson, and R. Nevitt Sanford,
     The Authoritarian Personality, abridged edition (1950; New York and London: W. W.
     Norton and Company, 1982).
44   Roszak, *The Making of a Counter Culture*, 139.
45   Wouter J. Hanegraaff, *Esotericism and the Academy: Rejected Knowledge in Western
     Culture* (Cambridge: Cambridge University Press, 2012).
46   Marx and Engels, *The Communist Manifesto*, 241.
47   Karl Marx, 'A Contribution to the Critique of Hegel's Philosophy of Right',
     Introduction, *Deutsch-Französische Jahrbücher*, 7 and 10 February 1844, https://www.
     marxists.org/archive/marx/works/1843/critique-hpr/intro.htm.
48   Dominic Strinati, *An Introduction to Theories of Popular Culture* (London: Routledge,
     1995) 64.
49   David Halberstam, *The Fifties* (New York: Random House, 1993), ix–x.
50   Stuart Hall, 'Cultural Studies: Two Paradigms', *Media, Culture and Society* 2, no. 1
     (1980): 57–72; Gordon Lynch, *Understanding Theology and Popular Culture* (Oxford:
     Blackwell, 2005), 3.
51   Norman Cohn, *The Pursuit of the Millennium: Revolutionary Millenarians and
     Mystical Anarchists of the Middle Ages* (London: Paladin, 1970), 108–9.
52   John Gray, *Black Mass: Apocalyptic Religion and the Death of Utopia* (London:
     Penguin, 2007), 2.
53   Krishan Kumar, *Utopianism* (Milton Keynes: Open University Press, 1991), 94.
54   Ruth Levitas, *Utopia as Method: The Imaginary Reconstitution of Society* (London:
     Palgrave MacMillan, 2013), 67–72.
55   Nicholas Campion, *The Great Year: Astrology, Millenarianism, and History in the
     Western Tradition* (London: Penguin, 1994).
56   Anonymous, 'Sociology Must Steer Our Society Towards a Utopia', *Network:
     Magazine of the Sociological Association* 117 (Summer 2014): 17.
57   Malcolm Bradbury, *The History Man* (London: Penguin, 1975), 106.
58   Anthony Giddens, 'Neopogressivism: A New Agenda for Social Democracy', in *The
     Progressive Manifesto*, ed. Anthony Giddens (Cambridge: Polity Press, 2003), 29;
     see also 3.
59   Patrick Wintour, 'Green Party's Flagship Economic Policy Would Hit Poorest
     Hardest, Say Experts', *The Guardian*, 27 January 2015, http://www.theguardian.com/
     politics/2015/jan/27/green-party-citizens-income-policy-hits-poor, accessed 28
     January 2015.
60   'Syriza's Dead End', *The Times*, 27 April 2015, 29.
61   Ruth Levitas, 'The Imaginary Reconstitution of Society, or Why Sociologists and
     Others Should Take Utopia More Seriously' (Inaugural Lecture, University of Bristol,
     24 October 2005), 16.
62   Michael D. Gordin, Helen Tilley, and Gyan Prakesh, 'Introduction: Utopia and
     Dystopia Beyond Space and Time', in *Utopia/Dystopia: Conditions of Historical
     Possibility*, eds. Michael D. Gordin, Helen Tilley, and Gyan Prakash (Princeton:
     Princeton University Press, 2010), 9.
63   Steven Lukes, 'The Grand Dichotomy of the Twentieth Century', in *The Cambridge
     History of Twentieth Century Political Thought*, eds. Terence Ball and Richard Bellamy
     (Cambridge: Cambridge University Press, 2003), 602–26.
64   Paul Heelas et al., *The Spiritual Revolution: Why Religion Is Giving Way to Spirituality*
     (Oxford: Blackwell, 2005).

65 Evans, *In Defence of History*, 291.
66 Paul Heelas, *The New Age Movement: The Celebration of the Self and the Sacralization of Modernity* (Cambridge, MA: Blackwell, 1996), 23, 34, 138.
67 Terry Eagleton, *Ideology: An Introduction* (London: Verso, 1991), 2.
68 Roy Porter, *Enlightenment: Britain and the Creation of the Modern World* (London: Penguin, 2000), 3.

Chapter 2

1   Max Scheler, *Ressentiment*, trans. William H. Holdheim (New York: Noonday, 1973).
2   Ruth Levitas, *The Concept of Utopia* (Hemel Hempstead: Allen Lane, 1990); Kumar, *Utopianism*.
3   Barbara Bender and Margaret Winer, *Contested Landscapes: Movement, Exile and Place* (Oxford: Berg, 2001).
4   Thomas More, *Utopia* (London: Penguin, 1965), Book 1, 67.
5   Peter Thompson, 'Religion, Utopia and the Metaphysics of Contingency', in *The Privatization of Hope: Ernst Bloch and the Future of Utopia, SIC 8*, vol. 8, eds. Peter Thompson and Slavoj Žižek (London: Duke University Press, 2013), 82.
6   Herbert Marcuse, *Five Lectures: Psychoanalysis, Politics, and Utopia* (Harmondsworth: Penguin, 1970), 63.
7   Hebrews 11.16.
8   Plato, *Laws*, 2 vols., trans. R.G. Bury (Cambridge, MA and London: Harvard University Press, 1934), book V, V.738B, 745B–C, VI.759B–C.
9   Plato, *Republic*, 2 vols., trans. Paul Shorey (Cambridge, MA and London: Harvard University Press, 1935), 592A–B.
10 Plato, *Timaeus*, trans. R.G.Bury (Cambridge, MA and London: Harvard University Press, 1931), 28A–30D.
11 Ibid., 36E–37A.
12 Libellus I. 25 in Walter Scott, trans. *Hermetica: The Ancient Greek and Latin Writings Which Contain Religious or Philosophic Teachings Ascribed to Hermes Trismegistus*, vol. 1 (Boulder, CO: Shambala, 1982), 129. Libellus I.25, in Scott, *Hermetica*.
13 Revelation 7.4, 14.1.
14 Stanley B. Frost, *Old Testament Apocalyptic* (London: Routledge and Kegan Paul, 1952), 32.
15 Plato, *Timaeus*, 29C.
16 Kelsey Wood, *Žižek: A Reader's Guide* (Oxford: Wiley-Blackwell, 2012), 155.
17 Jerry Vardaman and Edwin N. Yamauchi, *Chronos, Kairos, Christos: Nativity and Chronological Studies Presented to Jack Finegan* (Winona Lake, IN: Eisenbrauns, 1989).
18 Daniel Bell, *The End of Ideology: On the Exhaustion of Political Ideas in the Fifties* (New York: The Free Press, 1962), 297.
19 Helmer Ringgren, 'Akkadian Apocalypses', in *Apocalypticism in the Mediterranean World and the Near East: Proceedings of the International Colloquium on Apocalypticism, Uppsala, August 12–17*, ed. David Hellholm (Tübingen: J.C.B. Mohr, 1989), 379–86; Paul Hanson, *The Dawn of Apocalyptic: The Historical and Sociological Roots of Jewish Apocalyptic Eschatology* (1975; Philadelphia, PA: Fortress Press, 1983); D. S. Russell, *The Method and Message of Jewish Apocalyptic* (Philadelphia, PA: The

Westminster Press, 1964); and, Norman Cohn, *Cosmos, Chaos and the World to Come: The Ancient Roots of Apocalyptic Faith* (New Haven, CT and London: Yale University Press, 1993). John R. Hall, *Apocalypse Observed: Religious Movements and Violence in North America, Europe, and Japan* (London and New York: Routledge, 2000).

20 Bryan R. Wilson, *Magic and the Millennium* (New York: Harper and Row, 1973); Thomas Robbins and Susan J. Palmer, *Millennium, Messiahs and Mayhem: Contemporary Apocalyptic Movements* (London: Routledge, 1997); Hall, *Apocalypse*; and Jon R. Stone, *Expecting Armageddon: Essential Readings in Failed Prophecy* (London: Routledge, 2000).

21 Slavoj Žižek, *The Fragile Absolute* (New York: Verso, 2000), 89.

22 Ninian Smart, *The Phenomenon of Religion* (London: MacMillan, 1973), 93.

23 Caítríona Ní Dhúil, 'Engendering the Future: Bloch's Utopian Philosophy in Dialogue with Gender Theory', in *The Privatization of Hope: Ernst Bloch and the Future of Utopia, SIC 8*, vol. 8, eds. Peter Thompson and Slavoj Žižek (London: Duke University Press, 2013), 156.

24 Hillel Schwartz, *The French Prophets: The History of a Millenarian Group in Eighteenth-Century England* (Berkeley and Los Angeles: University of California Press, 1980), 5.

25 Leon Festinger, Henry W. Riecken, and Stanley Schachter, *When Prophecy Fails* (1956; New York: Harper and Row, 1964). See the discussion in Robbins and Palmer, *Millennium*; Hall, *Apocalypse*; and Stone, *Expecting Armageddon*.

26 J.C. Davis, 'Thomas More's Utopia: Sources, Legacy and Intepretation', in *The Cambridge Companion to Utopian Literature*, ed. Gregory Claeys (Cambridge: Cambridge University Press, 2010), 28.

27 Ruth Levitas, 'The Imaginary Reconstitution of Society', 2.

28 W.H. Auden, 'Atlantis', lines 1–5, in *W. H. Auden Poems Selected by John Fuller*, ed. John Fuller (London: Faber and Faber, 2000), 42.

29 Isaiah Berlin, 'The Pursuit of the Ideal', in *The Crooked Timber of Humanity: Chapters in the History of Ideas*, 1–19 (1959; New York: Random House, 1991), 4–5.

30 Bloch, *The Principle of Hope*, 3 vols., trans. Neville Plaice, Stephen Plaice, and Paul Knight, revised edition (Cambridge, MA: MIT Press, 1986). See also Frank E. Manuel, *Shapes of Philosophical History* (London: Allen and Unwin, 1965); and Frank E. Manuel and Fritzie P. Manuel, *Utopian Thought in the Western World* (Oxford: Basil Blackwell, 1979).

31 Landes, *Heaven on Earth*; Damian Thompson, *The End of Time: Faith and Fear in the Shadow of the Millennium* (London: Sinclair-Stevenson, 1996); Katz, and Popkin, *Messianic Revolution*.

32 For Cohn's summary, to which I have added, see Cohn, *Millennium*, 13.

33 Virgil, *Georgics*, 2 vols., trans. H.R. Fairclough (Cambridge, MA: Harvard University Press, 1916), 4.4–10.

34 Revelation 20.1–7; Augustine, *City of God*, trans. Henry Bettenson (Harmondsworth, Middlesex: Penguin, 1972), xx.7.

35 Luke 21.10–11.

36 Revelation 21.1–2.

37 Matthew 12.32.

38 See for example, J. Bradley Chance, *Jerusalem, the Temple, and the New Age in Luke-Acts* (Georgia: Mercer University Press, 1988).

39   Mark 9.1, 13.30.

40   Fred Davis, 'Why All of Us May Be Hippies Someday', 15, 17.

41   Ibid., 15.

42   Lukacher, *Time* Fetishes, x–xi.

43   Hesiod, *Works and Days*, trans. Dorothea Wender (London: Penguin, 1973), 180–6.

44   Samuel Kramer, 'Man's Golden Age: A Sumerian Parallel to Genesis XI.1', *Journal of the American Oriental Society* LXIII (1943): 191–4.

45   Hesiod, *Works and Days*, 121–9.

46   See the discussion in Svetlana Boym, *The Future of Nostalgia* (New York: Basic Books, 2001), 3.

47   Steen F. Larsen, 'Remembering without Experiencing: Memory for Reported Events', in *Remembering Reconsidered: Ecological and Traditional Approaches to the Study of Memory*, eds. Ulric Neisser and Eugene Winograd (New York: Cambridge University Press, 1988), 326–55.

48   Umberto Eco, 'Travels in Hyperreality', chap. 1 and 'The Return of the Middle Ages: Dreaming of the Middle Ages', chap. 2, in *Faith in Fakes: Travels in Hyperreality* (London: Minerva, 1995), 1–58, 61–85; Jean Baudrillard, *Simulacra and Simulations* (Chicago: University of Michigan Press, 1994).

49   Timothy Morton, *Hyperobjects: Philosophy and Ecology After the End of the World* (Minneapolis: University of Minnesota Press, 2013).

50   Henri Desroche, *The Sociology of Hope*, trans. Carol Martin-Sperry (London: Routledge & Kegan Paul, 1979), 93; Catherine Wessinger, 'Millennialism with and without the Mayhem', in *Millennium, Messiahs and Mayhem: Contemporary Apocalyptic Movements*, eds. Thomas Robbins and Susan J. Palmer (London: Routledge, 1999), 47.

51   Marjorie Reeves, *The Influence of Prophecy in the Later Middle Ages: A Study of Joachismism* (Oxford: Oxford University Press, 1969); Marjorie Reeves, *Joachim of Fiore and the Prophetic Future* (London: SPCK, 1976); see also Hanegraaff, *New Age Religion*.

52   Matthew 16.28; Mark 9.1; Luke 9.27.

53   Isaiah 13.10. See also Isaiah 61.19–20; Jeremiah 4.23; Habakkuk 3.3–6.

54   Plato, *Timaeus*, 39D.

55   Mircea Eliade, *The Myth of the Eternal Return or, Cosmos and History* (Princeton, NJ: Princeton University Press, 1954).

56   E.S. Kennedy and David Pingree, *The Astrological History of Masha'Allah* (Cambridge, MA: Harvard University Press, 1971); David Pingree, *The Thousands of Abu Ma'shar* (London: Warburg Institute, 1968).

57   Keith Thomas, *Religion and the Decline of Magic* (Harmondsworth: Peregrine Books, 1971), 386–7.

58   See also Matthew 13.29–36 and Luke 21.25–33.

59   I Thessalonians 5.2; Revelation 16.15.

60   Marx and Engels, *The Communist Manifesto*, 233.

61   Matthew 5.27–8; Anthony Low, *Aspects of Subjectivity: Society and Individuality from the Middle Ages to Shakespeare and Milton* (Pittsburgh, PA: Duquesne University Press, 2003), 26; Michel Foucault, 'Technologies of the Self', in *Technologies of the Self: A Seminar with Michel Foucault*, eds. L.H. Martin, H. Gutman, and P.H. Hinton (Amherst: University of Massachusetts Press, 1988), 17.

62   Augustine, *City of God*, XI.21.

63 Bloch, *The Principle of Hope*, 1: 9.
64 Matthew 6.34.
65 Karl Popper, *The Open Society and Its Enemies*, 2 vols. (1945; London and New York: Routledge, 1986 revised edition), I: 210, 244.
66 Karl Popper, *The Poverty of Historicism* (London: Routledge, 1957), 8.
67 Marx, 'Feuerbach', III, XI.
68 Momen, *Shi'i Islam*, 236.
69 Régis Debray, *Revolution in the Revolution?*, trans. Bobbye Ortiz (Harmondsworth: Penguin 1967), 39.
70 A.A. Long, *Stoic Studies* (Cambridge: Cambridge University Press, 1996), 164–5.
71 Diogenes Laertius, 'Zeno', in *Lives of Eminent Philosophers*, trans. R.D. Hicks (London: William Heinemann, 1925), VII.149.
72 Ibid., VII.122.
73 Bloch, *The Principle of Hope*, 3: 927; see also Vincent Geoghegan, *Marxism and Utopianism* (London: Methuen, 1987), 3.
74 Ernest Bloch, *The Spirit of Utopia*, trans. Anthony A. Nassar (Stanford, CA: Stanford University Press, 2000), 1.
75 Bloch, *The Principle of Hope*, 3: 927.
76 V.I. Lenin, 'The Theory of Knowledge of Dialectical Materialism and of Empirio-Criticism'. III, chap. 3.6 'Freedom and Necessity', https://www.marxists.org/archive/lenin/works/1908/mec/; James Klagge, 'Marx's Reams of Freedom and Necessity', *The Canadian Journal of Philosophy* 16, no. 4 (December 1986): 769–72.
77 Frederic Jameson, *Archaeologies of the Future: The Desire Called Utopia and Other Science Fictions* (London: Verso, 2005), 168.
78 Levitas, *The Concept of Utopia*, 83.
79 Vladimir Ilyich Lenin, 'What Is to Be Done?', in *Essential Works of Lenin* (no place: bn publishing, 2015), 115, 120, 137.
80 Frederic Jameson, 'Utopia as Method, or the Uses of the Future', in *Utopia/Dystopia: Conditions of Historical Possibility*, eds. Michael D. Gordin, Helen Tilley, and Gyan Prakash (Princeton, NJ: Princeton University Press, 2010), 23.
81 Timothy Harvie, *Jürgen Moltmann's Ethics of Hope: Eschatological Possibilities for Moral Action* (Furnham: Ashgate, 2009).
82 Catherine L. Albanese, *A Republic of Mind and Spirit: A Cultural History of American Metaphysical Religion* (New Haven, CT: Yale University Press, 2007); Edward Royle, *Robert Owen and the Commencement of the Millennium* (Manchester: Manchester University Press, 1998).
83 Matthew Avery Sutton, *American Apocalypse: A History of Modern Evangelicalism* (Cambridge, MA: Harvard University Press, 2014).
84 Ruth Levitas, 'The Imaginary Reconstitution of Society', 4.
85 Gregory Claeys, *Searching for Utopia: The History of an Idea* (London: Thames and Hudson, 2011), 28–57.
86 Umberto Eco, *The Book of Legendary Lands* (London: Thames and Hudson, 2013).
87 Henri Corbin, 'Mundus Imaginalis, the Imaginary and the Imaginal', *Spring* 15 (1972): 1.
88 Ibid., 1.
89 Gordin, Tilley, and Prakesh, 'Introduction: Utopia and Dystopia Beyond Space and Time', 9–10.
90 Levitas, *The Concept of Utopia*, 181–2.

91   Schwartz, *The French Prophets*, 6.

92   Desroche, *Sociology*, 99.

93   C.G. Jung, 'Psychology and Literature', in *The Spirit in Man. Art and Literature, Collected Works*, vol. 15, trans. R.F.C. Hull (London: Routledge and Kegan Paul, 1971), para 152.

94   Michael Barkun, *A Culture of Conspiracy: Apocalyptic Visions in Contemporary America* (Berkeley: University of California Press, 2003), 18–21.

95   Bloch, *The Principle of Hope*, 3: 1374–5.

96   Cohn, *Millennium*, 108–9; See also Bell, *The End of Ideology*, 297.

97   Žižek, *The Fragile Absolute*, xxix.

98   John Baillie, *The Belief in Progress* (London, Glasgow, Toronto: Oxford University Press, 1951), 64–5.

99   Isaiah Berlin, *The Crooked Timber of Humanity: Chapters in the History of Ideas* (1959; New York: Random House, 1991), 1.

100 Levitas, *Utopia as Method*.

101 Cohn, *Millennium*, 223.

102 As is clear from the literary selection in John Carey, ed., *The Faber Book of Utopias* (London: Faber and Faber, 1999).

103 Berlin, *The Crooked Timber*, 15.

104 Ibid.

105 George W. Bush, *State of the Union Address*, 29 January 2002, http://www.usa-presidents.info/union/gwbush-2.html, accessed 23 April 2015.

106 Krishan Kumar, 'Utopia and Anti-Utopia in the Twentieth Century', in *Utopia: The Search for the Ideal in the Western World*, eds. Roland Schaer, Gregory Claeys, and Lyman Tower Sargent (New York: New York Public Library/Oxford University Press, 2000), 251–67.

107 Gregory Claeys, 'The Origins of Dystopia: Wells, Huxley and Orwell', in *The Cambridge Companion to Utopian Literature*, ed. Gregory Claeys (Cambridge: Cambridge University Press, 2010), 107.

108 Thomas Malthus, *An Essay on the Principle of Population* (Harmondsworth: Penguin, 1970), 67, 69.

109 Thomas Carlyle, 'Signs of the Times', in *The Spirit of the Age: Victorian Essays*, ed. Gertrude Himmelfarb (Yale: Yale University Press, 2007), 41, 43, 49.

110 Arthur Herman, *The Idea of Decline in Western History* (New York and London: The Free Press, 1997).

111 Quoted in Krishan Kumar, *Prophecy and Progress: The Sociology of Industrial and Post-Industrial Society* (Harmondworth: Penguin, 1996), 79.

112 Gertrude Himmelfarb, 'This Will Hurt', in *This Will Hurt: The Restoration of Virtue and Civic Order, The Social Affairs Unit*, ed. Digby C. Anderson (London: The Social Affairs Units, 1995), x.

113 Malthus, *An Essay on the Principle of Population*, 68.

114 'Letter to Lorenzo de' Medici', in Niccolo Machiavelli, *The Prince*, trans. George Bull (Harmondsworth: Penguin, 1961), 30.

115 R. Buckminster Fuller, *Utopia or Oblivion: The Prospects for Humanity* (Harmondsworth: Penguin, 1972), 335.

116 Jeremy Bentham, 'From an Introduction to the Principles of Morals and Legislation', in J.S. Mill and Jeremy Bentham, *Utilitarianism and Other Essays*, ed. Alan Ryan (London: Penguin, 1987), 65.

117   Frank Kermode, *The Sense of an Ending: Studies in the Theory of Fiction with a New Epilogue* (1966; Oxford: Oxford University Press, 2000), 98–9.

118   Michel de Montaigne, 'Of Cannibals', chap. 31, in *The Complete Essays*, trans. M.A.Screech (London: Penguin Classics, 1993), 233.

119   William Shakespeare, *The Tempest*, Act 2, Scene 1, lines 173–4, see also lines 153–62, 165–70; see also Charlotte Scott, *Shakespeare's Nature: From Cultivation to Culture* (Oxford: Oxford University Press, 2014), 197–202.

120   John Dryden, *Almanzor and Almahide: Or, the Conquest of Granada by the Spaniards. A Tragedy* (London, 1673), 7.

121   Jean-Jacques Rousseau, *The Social Contract*, trans. Maurice Cranston (London: Penguin, 2006), I.1.

122   Jean-Jacques Rousseau, *Emile*, trans. Barbara Foxley (London: J.M.Dent and Sons, 1974), 5.

123   Jean-Jacques Rousseau, *A Discourse on Inequality*, trans. Maurice Cranston (London: Penguin, 1984), 57.

124   Rousseau, *The Social Contract*, 35.

125   Thomas Hobbes, *Leviathan, or the Matter, Form, and Power of a CommonWealth Ecclesiastical and Civil*, ed. C.B. MacPherson (Harmondsworth: Penguin, 1968), Chap. XIII, 186.

126   Rousseau, *Emile*, 164.

127   Jean-Jacques Rousseau, *The Confessions*, trans. J.M. Cohen (Harmondsworth: Penguin, 1953), 311.

128   David Pinder, *Visions of the City* (Edinburgh: Edinburgh University Press, 2005), 108.

129   Thomas Paine, 'The Rights of Man', in *The Thomas Paine Reader*, eds. Michael Foot and Isaac Kramnick (London: Penguin, 1987, 2003), 217.

130   John Stuart Mill, 'On Liberty', in *On Liberty* and *The Subjection of Women* (London: Penguin, 2006), 7.

131   Stephen Coleman and Paddy O'Sullivan, eds., *William Morris and News from Nowhere: A Vision for Our Time* (Bideford: Green Books, 2000), 28.

132   William Morris, *News from Nowhere and Other Writings* (London: Penguin, 2004), 116.

133   Oscar Wilde, 'The Soul of Man Under Socialism', in *De Profundis and Other Writings*, ed. Hesketh Pearson (Harmondsworth: Penguin, 1973), 27.

134   H.G. Wells, *A Modern Utopia* (London: J.M.Dent, 1994), 105.

135   Ibid., 20.

136   Ibid., 21.

137   Samuel Butler, *Erewhon*, 2nd edition (1901; New York: Dover Publications, 2002), 118–50.

138   Ernest Callenbach, *Ecotopia* (Berkeley, CA: Banyan Tree Books, 2004), 31.

139   Ibid., 30.

140   Marius de Geus, *Ecological Utopias: Envisioning the Sustainable Society* (Utrecht: International Books, 1999), 62–7.

141   Transition Network, https://www.transitionnetwork.org/, accessed 25 October 2014.

142   Vincent Geoghegan, 'An Anti-Humanist Utopia?', in *The Privatization of Hope: Ernst Bloch and the Future of Utopia*, *SIC 8*, vol. 8, eds. Peter Thompson and Slavoj Žižek (London: Duke University Press, 2013), 50–1.

143   See the discussion in John Gray, *Endgames: Questions in Late Modern Political Thought* (Cambridge: Polity, 1997), 70–1.

144 Rainer E. Zimmermann, 'Transforming Utopian into Metopian Systems: Bloch's Principle of Hope Revisited', in *The Privatization of Hope: Ernst Bloch and the Future of Utopia, SIC 8*, vol. 8, eds. Peter Thompson and Slavoj Žižek (London: Duke University Press, 2013), 246–68; and Kumar, 'Utopia and Anti-Utopia', 264.

145 Erik Davis, *Techgnosis: Myth, Magic, and Mysticism in the Age of Information* (Berkeley, CA: North Atylantic Books, 2015); Margaret Wertheim, *The Pearly Gates of Cyberspace: A History of Space from Dante to the Internet* (New York: W.W. Norton & Company, 1999).

146 Elizabeth Nelson, *The British Counter Culture, 1966-73: A Study of the Underground Press* (New York: St. Martin's Press, 1989), ix, 45.

147 Anonymous, 'Massage to the Underground', *IT*, 15–28 December 1967, 2; Jack Kerouac, *On the Road* (New York: Signet Books, 1958), 46.

148 Joseph Berke, 'Counter Culture: The Creation of an Alternative Society', *IT*, 13–31 December 1968, 20–1; Joseph Berke, ed., *Counter Culture: The Creation of an Alternative Society* (London: Peter Owen, 1969).

149 Terry Eagleton, *The Idea of Culture* (Oxford: Blackwell, 2000), 1.

150 Clifford Geertz, 'Religion as a Cultural System', in *Anthropological Approaches to the Study of Religion*, ed. Michael P. Banton (New York: Frederick A. Praeger Press, 1966), 3.

151 Yinger, 'Contraculture and Subculture', 628.

152 Dick Hebdidge, *Subculture: The Meaning of Style* (London: Routledge, 1979), esp. 5–19.

153 Yinger, 'Contraculture and Subculture', 625–35. See the discussion in Nelson, *The British Counter Culture*, 1–8; Milton M. Gordon, 'The Concept of the Sub-Culture and Its Application' [1947], in *The Subcultures Reader*, eds. Ken Gelder and Sarah Thornton (London: Routledge, 1997), 40–3.

154 Yinger, 'Contraculture and Subculture', 627–8.

155 J. Milton Yinger, *Counter Cultures: The Promise and Peril of a World Turned Upside Down* (New York: The Free Press, 1984).

156 McKay, *Senseless Acts of Beauty*, 7, 52.

157 Lionel Trilling, *Beyond Culture: Essays in Literature and Learning* (San Diego, CA: Harcourt, 1978). See also Peter Steinfels, *The Neoconservatives: The Origins of a Movement* (New York: Simon and Schuster, 2013), 59.

158 Michael Maffesoli, *The Time of the Tribes: The Decline of Individualism in Mass Society*, trans. Don Smith (London: Sage, 1996), 92.

159 James L. Spates, 'Counterculture and Dominant Culture Values: A Cross-National Analysis of the Underground Press and Dominant Culture Magazines', *American Sociological Review* 41, no. 5 (October 1976): 868.

160 Murray G.H. Pittock, *Inventing and Resisting Britain; Cultural Identities in Britain and Ireland, 1685-1789* (New York: St. Martin's Press, 1997), 98–127.

161 Timothy Leary, foreword to *Counterculture Through the Ages: From Abraham to Acid House*, by Ken Goffman and Dan Joy (New York: Villard Books, 2005), x.

162 Eagleton, *Ideology: An Introduction*, 35.

163 Leary, foreword to *Counterculture Through the Ages*, ix.

164 Goffman and Joy, *Counterculture Through the Ages*, 33.

165 Michael Barkun, *Disaster and the Millennium* (Syracuse, NY: Yale University Press, 1986), 37.

166 Albanese, *A Republic of Mind and Spirit*, 121.

167 Michael York, *The Emerging Network: A Sociology of the New Age and Neo-Pagan Movements* (London: Rowman and Littlefield, 1995); Heelas, *The New Age Movement*; Hanegraaff, *New Age Religion*.

168 The *Library Journal*, quoted on *Helen Weaver: Writer, Translator, Astrologer*, http://www.helenweaver.com/, accessed 26 May 2014. Also see Helen Weaver, *The Awakener: A Memoir of Kerouac and the Fifties* (San Francisco, CA: City Lights, 2009).

169 Nicholas Campion, *Astrology and Popular Religion in the Modern West: Prophecy, Cosmology and the New Age Movement* (Abingdon: Ashgate, 2012), 29–39.

170 Hanegraaff, *New Age Religion*, 96–103.

171 James R. Lewis and J. Gordon Melton, eds., *Perspectives on the New Age* (New York: State University of New York Press, 1992); York, *The Emerging Network*; Hanegraaff, *New Age Religion*; Heelas, *The New Age Movement*; Sutcliffe, *Children of the New Age*; and Daren Kemp, *New Age: A Guide: Alternative Spiritualities from Aquarian Conspiracy to Next Age* (Edinburgh: Edinburgh University Press, 2004).

172 Campion, *Prophecy*, 78.

173 For evangelical Christian commentators see Elliot Miller, *A Crash Course in the New Age Movement* (Eastbourne: Monarch Publications, 1990), 27; and for academic commentators see Grace Davie, *Religion in Britain Since 1945: Believing without Belonging* (Oxford: Wiley-Blackwell, 1994), 83; Hanegraaff, *New Age Religion*, 98–103; and Sutcliffe, *Children of the New Age,9*, 11–17.

174 Peter Thompson, 'Religion, Utopia and the Metaphysics of Contingency', 101.

175 Olav Hammer, *Claiming Knowledge: Strategies of Epistemology from Theosophy to the New Age* (Leiden: Brill, 2001), 330–453.

176 Hanegraaff, *New Age Religion*, 96–103; see also Lewis and Melton, *Perspectives*, x; and Stuart Sutcliffe, 'Between Apocalypse and Self-Realisation: "Nature" as an Index of New Age Spirituality', in *Nature Religion Today: Paganism in the Modern World*, eds. Joanne Pearson, Richard H. Roberts, and Geoffrey Samuel (Edinburgh: Edinburgh University Press,1998), 43, n1.

177 York, *The Emerging Network*, 39.

178 Ibid., 49; Sutcliffe, *Children of the New Age*, 9–11; Steven J. Sutcliffe, 'New Age, World Religions and Elementary Forms', in *New Age Spirituality: Rethinking Religion*, eds. Steven J. Sutcliffe and Ingvild Saelid Gilhus (Durham: Acumen, 2013), 17–35.

179 Hanegraaff, *New Age Religion*, 2.

180 William Bloom, *The New Age: An Anthology of Essential Writings* (London: Rider, 1991), xvi.

181 York, *The Emerging Network*, 39.

182 Hanegraaff, *New Age Religion*, 409, 521.

183 Joscelyn Godwin, *The Theosophical Enlightenment* (New York: State University of New York Press, 1994), xi.

184 William Braden, *The Age of Aquarius: Technology and the Cultural Revolution* (London: Eyre and Spottiswoode, 1971), 17.

185 Miller, *A Crash Course*, 4; also see 20.

186 Paul Heelas, *The New Age Movement*, 28.

187 Marcuse, *Five Lectures*, 62–82. But see also Isaiah Berlin, 'The Decline of Utopian Ideas in the West', *Crooked Timber*, 21–50.

188 Kumar, 'Utopia and Anti-Utopia', 265, 266.

189 John Gray, *Black Mass: Apocalyptic Religion and the Death of Utopia* (London: Penguin, 2007), 3.

190 Claeys, 'The Origins of Dystopia', 108.

191 Popper, *Historicism*, 9.

192 Wilde, 'The Soul of Man Under Socialism', 34.
193 Gabriel García Márquez, *Strange Pilgrims*, trans. Edith Grossman (London: Penguin, 2013), xiii.

Chapter 3

1   Arthur O. Lovejoy, *The Great Chain of Being* (Cambridge, MA and London: Harvard University Press, 1936).
2   Rousseau, *Social Contract*, I.7.
3   Ernst Cassirer, *The Philosophy of the Enlightenment* (1951; Princeton: Princeton University Press, 1979), 9.
4   Max Weber, *From Max Weber: Essays in Sociology*, eds. H.H. Garth and C. Mills Wright (London: Kegan Paul, Trench, Trubner & Co., 1947), 139.
5   Graeme Garrard, *Rousseau's Counter-Enlightenment: A Republican Critique of the Philosophes* (Albany: State University of New York Press, 2003), 17.
6   Cassirer, *The Philosophy of the Enlightenment*, 9.
7   Simon Schaffer, 'Newtonianism', in *Companion to the History of Modern Science*, eds. R.C. Olby, G.N. Cantor, J.R.R. Christie, and M.J.S Hodge (London and New York: Routledge, 1996), 610–26. See also Michael Hoskin, 'Newton and Newtonianism' in *The Cambridge Concise History of Astronomy*, ed. Michael Hoskin (Cambridge: Cambridge University Press, 1999), 130–67.
8   Nicholas Campion, 'Astronomy and Political Theory', in *The Role of Astronomy in Society and Culture*, eds. David Valls-Gabaud and Alec Boksenberg (Cambridge: Cambridge University Press, 2011), 599.
9   Carl Becker, *The Declaration of Independence: A Study in the History of Political Ideas* (New York: Vintage, 1958), 59–60.
10 Thomas Paine, *The Age of Reason* (Mineola, NY: Dover Publications, 2003), 191–2; Paine, 'The Rights of Man', 207.
11 Paine, 'The Rights of Man', 217.
12 Thomas Paine, *Common Sense* (London: Penguin, 1986), 66.
13 Alexander Pope, 'Epitaphs. Intended for Sir Isaac Newton, in Westminster-Abbey, 1730', in *The Complete Poetical Works of Alexander Pope*, ed. Henry W. Boynton (Boston and New York: Houghton, Mifflin and Company, 1903).
14 John Theophilus Desaguliers, *The Newtonian System of the World, the Best Model of Government: An Allegorical Poem*, II.17–18, cited in Porter, *Enlightenment*, 137.
15 Denis O'Brien, *Empedocles' Cosmic Cycle: A Reconstruction from the Fragments and Secondary Sources* (Cambridge: Cambridge University Press, 1969).
16 Voltaire, *Letters Concerning the English Nation* (London, 1726), XII:65.
17 Sydney Pollard, *The Idea of Progress: History and Society* (Harmondsworth: Penguin, 1971), 98.
18 Auguste Comte, *System of Positive Polity, or Treatise on Sociology, Instituting the Religion of Humanity*, 4 vols., trans. John Henry Bridges (Paris, 1851–4; London: Longmans, 1875), I: 399–400.
19 Bryan Ball, *A Great Expectation: Eschatological Thought in English Protestantism to 1660* (Leiden: Brill, 1975); Christopher Hill, *The World Turned Upside Down: Radical Ideas During the English Revolution* (London: Penguin, 1978).
20 Schwartz, *The French Prophets*, 229.

21 Isaac Newton, *The Chronology of Ancient Kingdoms Amended* (London, 1728, facsimile edition; London, 1988), 25.

22 Voltaire, *Letters Concerning the English Nation*, XVII: 120–2.

23 Hoskin, 'Newton and Newtonianism', 143–4.

24 Libellus I.6, in Scott, *Hermetica*, 117.

25 Libellus I.18, in Ibid., 125.

26 Nicolaus Copernicus, *On the Revolutions of the Heavenly Spheres*, trans. Charles Glenn Wallis (Amherst, NY: Prometheus Books, 1995), I.10, 24–5.

27 James Schmidt, 'Inventing the Enlightenment: Anti-Jacobins, British Hegelians, and the Oxford English Dictionary', *Journal of the History of Ideas* 64, no. 3 (July 2003): 427.

28 Charles Webster, *From Paracelsus to Newton: Magic and the Making of Modern Science* (Cambridge: Cambridge University Press, 1982).

29 Newton, Isaac, 'Tabula Smaragdina, Hemetic Trismegistri Philosophorum Patris', in Keynes MS 28, in The Chymistry of Isaac Newton, King's College Library, Cambridge University, lines 1–4, http://webapp1.dlib.indiana.edu/newton/mss/dipl/ALCH00017

30 Everard, John, 'The Eleventh Book, Of the Common Mind to Tat', lines 3–4 in *The Corpus Hermeticum*; The Divine Pymander in XVII books, London, 1650, lines 3–4.

31 John I.5.

32 Ibid. 8.12.

33 Anthony Ashley Copper, 3rd Earl of Shaftsbury, to Jean Le Clere (1706), cited in Porter, *Enlightenment*, 3.

34 Anne-Robert-Jacques Turgot, 'A Philosophical Review of the Successive Advances of the Human Mind', in *Turgot on Progress, Sociology and Economics*, ed. Ronald L. Meek (Cambridge: Cambridge University Press, 1991), 53.

35 Turgot, 'A Philosophical Review', 57.

36 Ibid., 59.

37 Ibid., 56.

38 Carl Becker, *The Heavenly City of the Enlightenment Philosophers* (Storrs Lectures) (New Haven and London: Yale University Press, 1932), 62–3.

39 John Locke, *An Essay Concerning Human Understanding* (London: Penguin, 1997), 59.

40 Schmidt, 'Inventing the Enlightenment', 428.

41 For recent discussions see, for example, Jamie Stern-Weiner, 'What Are Enlightenment Values'?, New Left Project, 20 July 2011, http://www.newleftproject. org/index.php/site/article_comments/what_are_enlightenment_values, accessed 11 January 2015; Matthew Taylor, 'Enlightenment values and the politics of transformation', *Transformation*, 19 August 2013, https://www.opendemocracy. net/transformation/matthew-taylor/enlightenment-values-and-politics-of-transformation, accessed 11 January 2015.

42 See James Schmidt, 'What Enlightenment Project?', *Political Theory* 28, no. 6 (2000): 734–57; Christian Delacampagne, 'The Enlightenment Project: A Reply to Schmidt', *Political Theory* 29, no. 1 (2001): 80–5.

43 Stern-Weiner, 'What Are Enlightenment Values'?

44 Anthony Pagden, *The Enlightenment: And Why It Still Matters* (Oxford: Oxford University Press, 2013), vii–xiv.

45 Pagden, *The Enlightenment*, viii.

46 Cassirer, *The Philosophy of the Enlightenment*, 9.

47 Schaffer, 'Newtonianism', 610–26.

48 See the discussion in Pagden, *The Enlightenment*, 1–18; Graeme Garrard, *Counter-Enlightenments from the Eighteenth Century to the Present* (London: Routledge, 2006), 5–11.

49 Cited in Pagden, *The Enlightenment*, 6.

50 See Ibid.,1–18.

51 Darrin M. McMahon, *Enemies of the Enlightenment: The French Counter-Enlightenment and the Making of Modernity* (Oxford: Oxford University Press, 2001), 11–12, 90–6.

52 For de Maistre, see Joseph de Maistre, *Considerations on France*, trans. Richard A. Lebrun (Cambridge: Cambridge University Press, 1999), 29.

53 Richard A. Lebrun, *Joseph de Maistre: an Intellectual Militant* (Quebec: McGill University Press, 1988).

54 Isaiah Berlin, 'The Pursuit of the Ideal', 5.

55 Garrard, *Counter-Enlightenments*, 80–94.

56 John Gray, *Enlightenment's Wake: Politics and Culture at the Close of the Modern Age* (London and New York: Routledge, 1995), 230–1.

57 Garrard, *Counter-Enlightenments*, 2.

58 Garrard, *Rousseau's Counter-Enlightenment*.

59 Richard Wolin, *The Seduction of Unreason: The Intellectual Romance with Fascism: from Nietzsche to Postmodernism* (Princeton: Princeton University Press, 2006).

60 See the discussion in Hanegraaff, *New Age Religion*, especially 411–3.

61 Garrard, *Counter-Enlightenments*.

62 Jonathan I. Israel, *Radical Enlightenment: Philosophy and the Making of Modernity, 1650-1750* (Oxford: Oxford University Press, 2001), 521.

63 McMahon, *Enemies of the Enlightenment*.

64 Dan Edelstein, *The Enlightenment: A Genealogy* (Chicago: Chicago University Press, 2010), 7–28; Pagden, *The Enlightenment*, 7.

65 Voltaire, 'The Negro' in *Philosophical Letters, The Works of Voltaire. A Contemporary Version*, 21 vols., trans. William E. Fleming (New York: E.R. DuMont, 1901). Kindle Edition, http://oll.libertyfund.org/titles/voltaire-the-works-of-voltaire-vol-xix-philosophical-letters.

66 Delacampagne, 'The Enlightenment Project', 80.

67 See for example, William Herbrechtsmeier, 'Buddhism and the Definition of Religion: One More Time', *Journal for the Scientific Study of Religion*, 32, no. 1 (1993): 1–18; J. Milton Yinger, 'A Structural Examination of Religion', *Journal for the Scientific Study of Religion*, 8 (1969): 88–99.

68 Geertz, 'Religion as a Cultural System', 63.

69 Paine, *The Age of Reason*, 179, 190–1.

70 Rousseau, *A Discourse on Inequality*, 158.

71 Immanuel Kant, 'An Answer to the Question: What Is Enlightenment? (1784)', in *What Is Enlightenment?: Eighteenth-Century Answers and Twentieth-Century Questions*, ed. James Schmidt (Berkeley: University of California, 1996), 58.

72 Immanuel Kant, *Critique of Practical Reason*, Great Books of the Western World 42 (London: Encyclopaedia Britannica, 1952), 360–1.

73 Porter, *Enlightenment*, 3.

74 David Allen Harvey, *Beyond Enlightenment: Occultism and Politics in Modern France* (DeKalb: Northern Illinois University Press, 2005), 9.

75 Berlin, *The Crooked Timber*, 42.

76 Cited in John Barber, *The Road to Eden: Studies in Christianity and Culture* (Palo Alto, CA: Academic Press, 2008), 363.

77 Edward Lucie-Smith, *Symbolist Art* (London: Thames and Hudson, 1972), 23.

78 Lucie-Smith, *Symbolist Art*, 23.

79   Berlin, *The Crooked Timber,* 43.

80   Ibid.

81   Hanegraaff, *New Age Religion,* 415.

82   Jonathan Israel, *Revolutionary Ideas: An Intellectual History of the French Revolution from the Rights of Man to Robespierre* (Princeton: Princeton University Press, 2014), 77.

83   Pagden, *The Enlightenment,* 2; see also Israel, *Revolutionary Ideas,* 77.

84   Adam Smith, *The Wealth of Nations* (no place: Shine Classics, 2014), 187.

85   J.B. Bury, *The Idea of Progress: An Inquiry into Its Growth and Origin* (London: Macmillan, 1932), 206–20.

86   Antoine-Nicolas de Condorcet, *Sketch for a Historical Picture of the Progress of the Human Mind,* trans. June Barraclough (New York: Noon Day Press, 1955), 173.

87   Condorcet, 173.

88   Alexis de Tocqueville, *Democracy in America* (London: Penguin, 2003), 54–5.

89   Isaiah Berlin, *Against the Current: Essays in the History of Ideas* (London: Pimlico, 1979), 15; see also 5.

90   Kumar, *Prophecy and Progress,* 153.

91   Mill, 'On Liberty', 54.

92   Peter J. Bowler, *The Invention of Progress, The Victorians and the Past* (Oxford: Basil Blackwell, 1989), vii, 2.

93   Johann Fichte, 'Idea of Universal History in Characteristics of the Present Age', 'The Origins and Limits of History', in *Works,* vol. 2, trans. William Smith (London, 1844), 4.

94   Glenn Alexander Magee, *Hegel and the Hermetic Tradition* (Ithaca: Cornell University Press, 2001), 3.

95   G.W.F. Hegel, *The Philosophy of History,* trans. J. Sibree (New York: Dover Publications, 1956), 442.

96   Hegel, *Philosophy of History,* especially 79–81, 103–4, 412; G.W.F. Hegel, *The Philosophy of Right,* trans. T.M. Knox (London and Oxford: Clarendon Press, 1952), especially 220–3.

97   Hegel, *Philosophy of Right,* 358.

98   Hegel, *Philosophy of History,* 103, 412.

99   Eric Dale, *Hegel, the End of History and the Future* (Cambridge: Cambridge University Press, 2014), 3.

100 Rolf Gruner, *Philosophies of History: A Critical Essay* (Aldershot: Gower,1985), 57; Popper, *The Open Society,* 2: 38–9, 42.

101 Karl Marx and Frederick Engels, 'The German Ideology', in *On Historical Materialism,* eds. Karl Marx, Frederick Engels, and V.I. Lenin, compiled T. Borodulina (Moscow: Progress Publishers, 1972), 14–17; Frederick Engels, 'Socialism: Utopian and Scientific', in *On Historical Materialism,* eds. Karl Marx, Frederick Engels, and V.I. Lenin, compiled T. Borodulina (Moscow: Progress Publishers, 1972), 179–80.

102 John Gage, 'JMW Turner, and Solar Myth', in *The Sun Is God: Painting, Literature and Mythology in the Nineteenth Century,* ed. J.B. Bullen (Oxford: Oxford University Press, 1989), 39.

103 A.M. Jones, ed., *The Works of Sir William Jones: With the Life of the Author by Lord Teignmouth* (London, 1807), 3: 385–6, cited in Gage, 'Turner', 42.

104 Max Müller, 'Solar Myths', *The Nineteenth Century* (1885): 900–22.

105 Nicholas Campion, 'The Age of Aquarius: A Modern Constellation Myth', in *Astronomy and Cultural Diversity, Proceedings of the 1999 Oxford VI Conference on*

Archaeoastronomy and Astronomy in Culture, eds. César Esteban and Juan Antonio Belmonte (Tenerife Oranismo Autonomo de Museos del Cablido de Tenerife, 2000), 277–82.

106 Godwin, *Theosophical Enlightenment*, 337.

107 Ibid., 27.

108 For a summary of Dupuis' theories and significance see Godwin, *Theosophical Enlightenment*, 27–44.

109 Voltaire, *Lettres sur l'Atlantide*, cited in John Baillie, *The Belief in Progress* (London: Oxford University Press,1950), 15; H.P. Blavatsky, *The Secret Doctrine*, 2 vols. (Los Angeles: The Theosophy Company, 1982, facsimile of 1888 edition), 2: 742.

110 See the discussion in Eric Sharpe, *Comparative Religion: A History* (London: Duckworth, 1975), 1–6; Rodney Stark, 'Atheism, Faith, and the Social Scientific Study of Religion', *Journal of Contemporary Religion* 14, no. 1 (1999): 41–62.

111 J.F.C. Harrison, *The Second Coming: Popular Millenarianism, 1780–1850* (Brunswick: Rutgers University Press, 1979).

112 Israel, *Revolutionary Idea,* 484; For de-Christianization also see Nigel Aston, *Religion and Revolution in France, 1780–1804* (Washington, DC: Catholic University of America Press, 2000), 259–76.

113 Nicholas Campion, Patrick Curry, and Jacques Halbronn, *La Vie Astrologique Il Y A Cent Ans* (Paris: Edition Guy Trédaniel, 1992), 89.

114 Matthew Shaw, *Time and the French Revolution: The Republican Year, 1789 – Year XIV* (Woodbridge: Boydell and Brewer, 2011).

115 Mona Ozouf, *Festivals of the French Revolution*, trans. Alan Sheridan (Cambridge, MA: Harvard University Press, 1988).

116 Landes, *Heaven on Earth*, especially, 253–282.

117 William Wordsworth, 'French Revolution', in *Poetical Works*, 3: 1805, William Knight (London: MacMillan, 1896), l: 4–5, http://www.gutenberg.org/files/12383/12383-h/Wordsworth3b.html

118 Cited in Landes, *Heaven on Earth*, 257–8.

119 Malthus, *An Essay on the Principle of Population*, 67.

120 Becker, *The Heavenly City,* 122.

121 Gregory Claeys, ed., *Utopias of the British Enlightenment* (Cambridge: Cambridge University Press, 1994), xxvi.

Chapter 4

1 Albanese, *A Republic of Mind and Spirit*, 121.

2 Godwin, *Theosophical Enlightenment*.

3 Claeys, *Utopias of the British Enlightenment*, xviii.

4 Bell, *The End of Ideology*, 95.

5 Robert S. Ellwood, *Religious and Spiritual Groups in Modern America* (Englewood Cliffs, NJ: Garland, 1973), 64, 66; see also Michael W. Stanley, 'The Relevance of Emanuel Swedenborg's Theological Concepts for the New Age as It Is Envisioned Today', in *Emanuel Swedenborg: A Continuing Vision*, ed. Robert Larson (New York: Swedenborg Foundation, 1988); Heelas, *The New Age Movement*, 17.

6 See Clarke Garrett, 'Swedenborg and the Mystical Enlightenment in Late Eighteenth Century England', *Journal of the History of Ideas* 45, no. 1 (1984): 69; for

Swedenborg's teachings see Emanuel Swedenborg, *The Apocalypse Revealed Wherein Are Disclosed the Arcana Foretold Which Have Hitherto Remained Concealed,* English translation of the Latin Edition of 1766 (no date), The Swedenborg Digital Library, http://www.swedenborgdigitallibrary.org/contets/AR.html, accessed 20 June 2009.

7   Emanuel Swedenborg, *The Last Judgment and Babylon Destroyed: All the Predictions in the Book of Revelation Are at This Day Fulfilled from Things Heard and Seen, 1758* (West Chester, PA: Swedenborg Foundation, 2009), 44–5.

8   Emanuel Swedenborg, 'Arcana Caelestia', 1285, cited in *Emanuel Swedenborg,* ed. Michael Stanley (Berkeley, CA: North Atlantic Books, 2003), 131.

9   Garrett, 'Swedenborg', 68.

10   David Spangler, 'Revelation – Birth of a New Age', in *The New Age: An Anthology of Essential Writings,* ed. William Bloom (London: Rider, 1991), 29; see also Peter Lemesurier, *This New Age Business: The Story of the Ancient and Continuing Quest to Bring Down Heaven on Earth* (Forres: Findhorn Press, 1990), 232.

11   Garrett, 'Swedenborg', 67.

12   Joseph Priestley, *Letters to Members of the New Jerusalem Church, Formed by Baron Swedenborg* (Birmingham, 1791), 6.

13   For the demise of the New Church see Garrett, 'Swedenborg', 81.

14   Immanuel Kant, 'Dreams of a Spirit Seer', in *Kant on Swedenborg: Dreams of a Spirit Seer and Other Writings,* ed. Gregory R. Johnson (Westchester, PA: Swedenborg Foundation, 2002), 42–57; Immanuel Kant, *Dreams of a Spirit-Seer,* trans. Emanuel F. Goerwitz (1900; Bristol: Theommes Press, 1992).

15   H. P. Blavatsky, *Isis Unveiled* (1877; Pasadena, CA: Theosophical University Press, 1976), I.73, II.471.

16   Ibid., I:308.

17   Constantin-François Volney, *The Ruins, or a Survey of the Revolutions of Empires* (London, 1795), Chap. XIII; see also Chaps. V and XV.

18   Godwin, *Theosophical Enlightenment,* 35.

19   William Blake, 'Annotations to Swedenborg's the Wisdom of Angels Concerning Divine providence, c. 1790, Milton', in *Complete Writings,* ed. Geoffrey Keynes (Oxford: Oxford University Press, 1971), 131.

20   William Blake, 'Milton', in *Complete Writings with Variant Readings,* ed. Geoffrey Keynes (Oxford: Oxford University Press, 1971), Preface, line 9, 480. See also Hanegraaff, *New Age Religion,* 95 n.6.

21   William Blake, 'Jerusalem', in *Complete Writings with Variant Readings,* ed. Geoffrey Keynes (Oxford: Oxford University Press, 1971), Preface, plate 4, lines 6–7; plate 5, lines 2–4; 18–20, 622–3.

22   David V. Erdman, 'Blake's Early Swedenborgianism: A Twentieth-Century Legend', *Comparative Literature* 5, no. 3 (Summer 1953): 253–5.

23   I. P. Couliano, *Out of This World: Otherworldly Journeys from Gilgamesh to Albert Einstein* (Boston, MA: Shambhala, 1991).

24   William Blake, *The Marriage of Heaven and Hell* (London, 1790; Cambridge: The Blake Archive Fitzwilliam Museum, 2008), plate 1, http://www.blakearchive.org/exist/blake/archive/work.xq?workid=mhh.

25   James M. Morris and Andrea L. Kross, *Historical Dictionary of Utopianism* (Lanham, MD: Scarecrow Press, 2004), xxx.

26   Ruth H. Bloch, *Visionary Republic: Millennial Themes in American Thought, 1756–1800* (Cambridge: Cambridge University Press, 1985).

27 Thomas S. Kidd, *The Great Awakening: The Roots of Evangelical Christianity in Colonial America* (New Haven, CT: Yale University Press, 2007).

28 Barry Hankins, *The Second Great Awakening and the Transcendentalists* (Westport, CT: Greenwood Press, 2004).

29 I Thessalonians 5.

30 John Greenleaf Whittier, *The Supernaturalism of New England* (Norman: University of Oklahoma Press, 1969), 30.

31 Ruth Alden Doan, *The Miller Heresy, Millennialism, and American Culture* (Philadelphia, PA: Temple University Press, 1987).

32 Whittier, *The Supernaturalism of New England*, 31–2.

33 Ibid., 31.

34 Philip Hoare, *England's Lost Eden: Adventures in a Victorian Utopia* (London: Harper Collins, 2005), 101–94.

35 Christopher H. Partridge, *The Re-Enchantment of the West, Volume II Alternative Spiritualities, Sacralization, Popular Culture, and Occulture* (London: T&T Clark Ltd., 2005), 279–92.

36 Arthur Versluis, *Wisdom's Children: A Christian Esoteric Tradition* (New York: State University of New York Press, 1999).

37 Hankins, *The Second Great Awakening*, 24–40.

38 Ralph Waldo Emerson, *Ralph Waldo Emerson*, ed. Richard Poirier (Oxford: Oxford University Press, 1990), 101–2. See also Paula Blanchard, *Margaret Fuller: From Transcendentalism to Revolution* (Reading, MA: Addison-Wesley Publishing Company, 1987).

39 Ralph Waldo Emerson, 'Nature', in *Nature and Selected Essays* (London: Penguin, 1982), 35.

40 Ibid., 37.

41 Diogenes Laertius, 'Zeno', VII.142.

42 Horatio W. Dresser, *A History of the New Thought Movement* (Nu Vision, 2008), 8.

43 Anthony Esler, *Bombs, Beards and Barricades: 150 Years of Youth in Revolt* (New York: Stein and Day, 1971), 456.

44 Dresser, *A History of the New Thought Movement*.

45 Mary Baker Eddy, *Science and Health with Key to the Scriptures* (Boston, MA: The First Church of Christ, Scientist, revised edition, 1875), 465, 493.

46 Albanese, *A Republic of Mind and Spirit*, 322–4.

47 Warren Felt Evans, *The New Age and the Messenger* (1864; Memphis, TN: General Books, 2012); Heelas, *The New Age Movement*, 17.

48 Evans, *The New Age*, 25.

49 Ibid., 19.

50 Robert Chambers, *Vestiges of the Natural History of Creation and Other Evolutionary Writings* (1844; Chicago, IL: University of Chicago Press, 1994).

51 James A. Secord, *Victorian Sensation: The Extraordinary Publication, Reception, and Secret Authorship of Vestiges of the Natural History of Creation* (Chicago, IL: University of Chicago Press, 2000), 13, 329.

52 Ibid., 13, 329.

53 Cited by Godwin, *Theosophical Enlightenment*, 32.

54 Samson Arnold Mackey, *Mythological Astronomy of the Ancients Demonstrated* (Norwich, 1822). See the discussion of Mackey's theories and politics in Godwin, *The Theosophical Enlightenment*, 68–76.

55 Robert Taylor, *The Devil's Pulpit: Or Astro-Theological Sermons* (London: Richard Carlile, 1831), 28–9. See also Robert Taylor, *The Diegesis; Being a Discovery of the Origin, Evidences, and Early History of Christianity* (London: Richard Carlile, 1829).

56 Taylor, *The Devil's Pulpit*, 31.

57 For Higgins' claim that he was a Christian, see G. Higgins, *Anacalypsis, an Attempt to Draw Aside the Veil of the Saitic Isis; or an Inquiry into the Origins of Languages, Nations and Religions*, 2 vols. (London: Res, Orme, Brown, Green and Longman, 1836), II: 449.

58 Higgins, *Anacalypsis*, I: 268, 638, II: 445; see also Heelas, *The New Age Movement*, 17.

59 Ibid., II: 144.

60 Ibid., I: 634, 637.

61 See Bruce H. Campbell, *Ancient Wisdom Revived: A History of the Theosophical Movement* (Berkeley: University of California Press, 1980).

62 G. A. Farthing, *Theosophy: The Truth Revealed* (London: The Theosophical Publishing House, 2000), 31–3. Catherine Tumber, *American Feminism and the Birth of New Age Spirituality: Searching for the Higher Self, 1875–1915* (Oxford: Rowman and Littlefield, 2002), 19.

63 Blavatsky, *Isis*; Blavatsky, *The Secret Doctrine*.

64 Theodor Adorno, *The Stars Down to Earth* (London: Routledge, 1994), 119.

65 Robert S. Ellwood, 'The American Theosophical Synthesis', in *The Occult in America: New Historical Perspectives*, eds. Howard Kerr and Charles Crow (Urbana: University of Illinois Press, 1983), 111.

66 Claude Lévi-Strauss, *The Savage Mind* (Chicago, IL: University of Chicago Press, 1966), 17.

67 For Blavatsky on the solar origin of male deities see *Isis* I:48, 270 and *The Secret Doctrine*, I: xliii; and on the Platonic Great Year see *The Secret Doctrine* II: 784. For Blavatsky on Volney see *Isis* I: 24, 268, 347, II: 142, 288, 456; on Bailey see *Isis* I: 171 and *The Secret Doctrine*, II: 265; and on Dupuis see *Isis* I: 24 and *The Secret Doctrine* I: 652 and II: 32.

68 Blavatsky, *The Secret Doctrine*, I: 641.

69 Blavatsky, *Isis*, II. 455–6.

70 Friedrich Nietzsche, 'Eternal Recurrence', in *A Nietzsche Reader*, selected and translated by R.J. Hollingdale (Harmondsworth: Penguin, 1977), 252–3.

71 Berlin, *Crooked Timber*, 3.

72 Blavatsky, *The Secret Doctrine*, II: 353.

73 Gerald Massey, *The Hebrew and Other Creations* (London: Williams and Norgate, 1887), 25.

74 Gerald Massey, *The Natural Genesis*, 4 vols. (London: Williams and Norgate, 1883), II: 337; see also Massey, *Creations*, 7.

75 Massey, *Creations*, 8.

76 Godwin, *Theosophical Enlightenment*, 333, 338, 340, 344.

77 Cited in Ibid., 358.

Chapter 5

1 Holbrook Jackson, *The Eighteen Nineties* (1913; Harmondsworth: Penguin, 1939), especially 15–29.

2 Mikuláš Teich and Roy Porter, 'Introduction' in *Fin de siècle and Its legacy*, eds. Roy Porter and Mikuláš Teich (Cambridge: Cambridge University Press, 1990), 1.

3 Jackson, *The Eighteen Nineties*, 27.

4 Miriam Akhtar and Steve Humphries, *Far Out: The Dawning of New Age Britain* (Bristol: Sansom and Company, 1999).

5 Dresser, *A History of the New Thought Movement*, 7.

6 Akhtar and Humphries, *Far Out*.

7 Virginia Nicholson, *Among the Bohemians: Experiments in Living 1900–1939* (London: Penguin, 2003), 174.

8 Eric Hobsbawm, *Fractured Times: Culture and Society on the Twentieth Century* (London: Little, Brown, 2013), 187.

9 W. B. Yeats, *A Vision* (1937; London: MacMillan, 1981).

10 W. B. Yeats, 'The Second Coming', http://www.potw.org/archive/potw351.html, accessed 21 November 2014.

11 John Symonds, *The Great Beast: The Life and Magic of Aleister Crowley* (St Albans: Mayflower Books, 1973); see also Marco Pasi, *Aleister Crowley and the Temptation of Politics* (Durham: Acumen, 2014); Tobias Churton, *Aleister Crowley: The Biography* (London: Watkins, 2011).

12 Gary Valentine Lachman, *Turn Off Your Mind: The Mystic Sixties and the Dark Side of the Age of Aquarius* (London: Macmillan, 2001); Kenneth Grant, Preface to *The Confessions of Aleister Crowley: An Autobiography*, by Aleister Crowley, eds. John Symonds and Kenneth Grant (1979; London: Penguin, 1989), 9.

13 Aleister Crowley, *The Book of the Law: Liber Al Vel Legis* (San Francisco, CA: Red Wheel/Weiser, 2011), 13.

14 Ibid., 13; Aleister Crowley, *The Book of Oz* (Liber LXXVII), http://hermetic.com/crowley/libers/lib77.html, accessed 4 December 2014.

15 Peter-Robert Koenig, 'Ordo Templi Orientis Phenomenon Birth of a New American O.T.O.: History of the Solar Lodge of the O.T.O. Charles Manson and the Occult', 2011, http://www.parareligion.ch/sunrise/manson.htm, accessed 5 February 2015.

16 Crowley, *The Book of the Law*, 15–17; Henrik Bogdan, 'Envisioning the Birth of a New Aeon: Dispensationalism and Millenarianism in the Thelemic Tradition', in *Aleister Crowley and Western Esotericism*, eds. Henrik Bogdan and Martin P. Starr (Oxford: Oxford University Press, 2012), 89–106.

17 Heelas, *The New Age Movement*, 18, 23.

18 Adam Curtis, 'The Century of the Self', 2002, http://www.imdb.com/title/tt0432232/.

19 J. F. C. Fuller, *The Star in the West: A Critical Essay Upon the Works of Aleister Crowley* (London: Walter Scott Publishing, 1907), 212.

20 Symonds, *The Great Beast*, 292.

21 Aldo Pellegrini, 'Xul Solar', in *Xul Solar*, ed. Mario H. Gradowczyk (Buenos Aires: Pan Klub Foundation/Xul Solar Museum, 1990), 25–50.

22 Churton, *Aleister Crowley*, 285.

23 P. D. Ouspensky, *In Search of the Miraculous: Fragments of an Unknown Teaching* (1949; London: Harvest, 1991), 312–14; James Moore, *Gurdjieff: The Anatomy of a Myth* (Shaftsbury: Dorset, 1999), 74.

24 'Saturday 29 July 1922', in *Gurdjieff's Early Talks 1914–1931*, by G. I. Gurdjieff (Book Studio, 2014), 148.

25 P. D. Ouspensky, *A Record of Meetings* (London: Arkana, 1992), 481; P. D. Ouspensky, *A New Model of the Universe* (1931; London: Arkana, 1984), 119, 414–513.

26 Ouspensky, *A New Model of the Universe*, 121.

27 Ibid., 121, 510–11.

28 'The Conscious Feeling of One's Real Self', in *Gurdjieff's Early Talks 1914–1931*, by G. I. Gurdjieff (Book Studio, 2014), 99.

29 Philip Mairet, *A.R. Orage: A Memoir* (London: J. M. Dent & Sons, 1936), 16–18, 87–105; Paul Selver, *Orage and the New Age Circle: Reminiscences and Reflections* (London: George Allen and Unwin Ltd., 1959), 73.

30 Ian Matthews, 'A.R. Orage and the Politics of the New Age' (PhD Thesis, London: University of London, 2003), 5; Selver, *Orage*, 33–45.

31 Wallace Martin, *The New Age Under Orage: Chapters in English Cultural History* (Manchester: Manchester University Press, 1967), 4–8.

32 Aleister Crowley, *The Confessions of Aleister Crowley*, eds. John Symonds and Kenneth Grant (1979; London: Penguin, 1989), 544.

33 See Matthews, 'A.R. Orage', 5.

34 Quoted in Selver, *Orage*, 87.

35 A.R. Orage, *Consciousness: Animal, Human, & Superman* (1907; New York: Samuel Weiser, 1974), 60, 68, 83; Adam Thomas Trexler, 'Modernist Poetics and "New Age" Political Philosophy' (PhD thesis, London: University of London, 2006), 18–19.

36 Jackson cited in Selver, *Orage*, 87.

37 Gerald Heard, *The Five Ages of Man: The Psychology of Human History* (New York: The Julian Press, 1963).

38 Nietzsche, *A Nietzsche Reader*, 232–48.

39 Lenin, 'What Is to Be Done', 115.

40 E. A. Wodehouse, 'The Order of the Star in the East: Its Outer and Inner Work', from the *Adyar Bulletin* (September 1911), http://www.katinkahesselink.net/his/stareas1. html, accessed 7 December 2014.

41 Rudolf Steiner, *An Autobiography* (New York: Steiner Books, 1980); Geoffrey Ahern, *Sun at Midnight: The Rudolf Steiner Movement and the Western Esoteric Tradition* (Wellingborough: Aquarian Press, 1984).

42 J. Krishnamurti, *Total Freedom: The Essential Krishnamurti* (New York: Harper Collins, 1996), 5.

43 Ibid., 33; also see 82–3.

44 Ibid., 80.

45 Anonymous, 'Donald Curtis (1915–1997). Prolific Science of Mind Speaker and Writer', http://cornerstone.wwwhubs.com/Donald_Curtis.html, accessed 4 November 2014; for Dowling's work see Levi Dowling, *The Aquarian Gospel of Jesus the Christ* (1907; Chadwell Heath: L.N. Fowler, 1980).

46 Jess Stearn, *Edgar Cayce on the Millennium* (New York: Warner Books, 1998), 143–4, 168; see also John Willner, *The Perfect Horoscope* (New York: Paraview Press, 2001), 93–119.

47 C. G. Jung, *Psychology of the Unconscious* (New York: Moffat, Yard and Company, 1917), 226–7 and 523, n. 60. https://archive.org/stream/ psychologyuncon00junggoog#page/n0/mode/2up, accessed 20 October 2014.

48 Rudolf Steiner, *The Spiritual Beings in the Heavenly Bodies and in the Kingdoms of Nature* (1951; Vancouver: Steiner Book Centre, 1981).

49 John Oliphant, *Brother Twelve: The Incredible Story of Canada's False Prophet and His Doomed Cult of Gold, Sex and Black Magic* (Toronto: McClelland and Stewart, 1991).

50 Alice A. Bailey, *The Unfinished Autobiography* (New York and London: Lucis Publishing Company, 1951), 193.

51   Deniz Ertan, *Dane Rudhyar, His Music, Thought and Art* (New York: University of Rochester Press, 2009).

52   Dane Rudhyar, *New Mansions for New Men* (New York: Lucis Publishing Company. 1938), xiii.

53   Michael R. Meyer, 'Rudhyar: Friend, Exemplar and Sage', http://www.khaldea.com/articles/dr_fes.shtml, accessed 16 August 2014.

54   Thomas Sugrue, *The Story of Edgar Cayce* (1943; Virginia Beach, VA: A.R.E. Press, 1973), 205–6.

55   C. G. Jung, 'Flying Saucers: A Modern Myth of Things Seen in the Skies', in *Civilisation in Transition, Collected Works*, vol. 10 (London: Routledge and Kegan Paul, 1964), 589.

56   Rudolf Steiner, *World History in the Light of Anthroposophy* (1950; London: Rudolf Steiner Press, 1977), 150.

57   Bailey, *The Unfinished Autobiography*, 191.

58   Alice A. Bailey, 'Seed Groups in the New Age', 1937, in *The Externalisation of the Hierarchy*, ed. Alice A. Bailey (New York: Lucis Publishing Company 1957), 35.

59   Julius R. Bennet, *The Riddle of the Aquarian Age* (London: London Astrological Research Society, 1925), 7.

60   Rudolf Steiner, *The Reappearance of Christ in the Etheric* (Spring Valley, NY: Anthroposophic Press, 1983), 15.

61   Cheiro, *Cheiro's World Predictions: The Fate of Europe, the Future of the USA, the Coming War of Nations, the Restoration of the Jews* (Albuquerque, NM: Sun Publishing Company, 1981), 178–9, 184.

62   Alice A. Bailey, 'The Subjective Basis of the New World Religion', in *The Externalisation of the Hierarchy*, ed. Alice A. Bailey (New York: Lucis Publishing Company, 1957), 502; Dowling, *The Aquarian Gospel*, 12; Emmet Fox, *The Zodiac and the Bible: The End of the World* (1933; Marina del Ray, CA: DeVorss and Company, 1961), 11, 16–17, 19, 35; Steiner, *The Reappearance of Christ*, 15–16, 17–18, 19–20, 39; Sugrue, *The Story of Edgar Cayce*, 205–6.

63   Max Heindel, *The Message of the Stars* (1919; Oceanside, CA: The Rosicrucian Fellowship, 1976), 27–8.

64   Harriette Augusta Curtiss and Frank Homer Curtiss, *The Message of Aquaria* (London: L.N. Fowler & Co., 1927), viii; also see Cheiro, *World Predictions*, 170, 174.

65   C. G. Jung, 'The Sign of the Fishes', in *Aion, Collected Works*, vol. 9, part 2, trans. R. F. C. Hull (London: Routledge and Kegan Paul, 1959), 87.

66   Curtiss and Curtiss, *The Message of Aquaria*, 31.

67   Quoted in Stearn, *Edgard Cayce on the Millennium*, 145.

68   Jung, 'The Sign of the Fishes', 87.

69   C. G. Jung, 'Definitions', in *Psychological Types, The Collected Works*, vol. 6, trans. R. F. C. Hull (London: Routledge and Kegan Paul, 1971), 757.

70   Fox, *The Zodiac and the Bible*, 21, 39.

71   Alice A. Bailey, *The Reappearance of the Christ* (London and New York: Lucis Publishing Companies, 2012), 126–7; Cheiro, *World Predictions*, 178–9, 184; Cyril Fagan, 'Interpretation of the Zodiac of Constellations', *Spica* 1, no. 1 (October 1951): 24.

72   William Morris, 'How Matters Are Managed', chap. XIV, in *News from Nowhere and Other Writings* (London: Penguin, 2004), 131–135.

73   John Moore, *Aleister Crowley: A Modern Master* (Oxford: Mandrake, 2009), 143.

74   Fox, *The Zodiac and the Bible*, 22–5.

75   Paul Le Cour, *L'Ère du Verseau* (Paris: Les Editions de L'Omnium Littéraire, 1962), 15–16.

76   Antoine Faivre, *Access to Western Esotericism* (Albany: State University of New York Press, 1994), 104.

77   Symonds, *The Great Beast*, 446, 451.

78   Hans Thomas Hakl, *Eranos: An Alternative Intellectual History of the Twentieth Century*, trans. Christopher McIntosh (Montreal and Kingston: McGill-Queens University Press, 2013); Symonds, *The Great Beast*, 446, 451.

79   Hakl, *Eranos: An Alternative Intellectual History of the Twentieth Century*, 28–31.

80   C. G. Jung, Preface to *Aion, Collected Works*, vol. 9, part 2, trans. R. F. C Hull (London: Routledge and Kegan Paul, 1959), x; C. G. Jung, 'Wotan', in *Civilisation in Transition, Collected Works*, vol. 10 (London: Routledge and Kegan Paul, 1964), 179–193.

81   C. G. Jung, 'Archetypes of the Collective Unconscious', in *The Archetypes and the Collective Unconscious, Collected Works*, vol. 9, part 1, trans. R. F. C. Hull (London: Routledge and Kegan Paul 1968), 14.

82   C. G. Jung, 'The Spiritual Problem of Modern Man', in *Civilisation in Transition, Collected Works*, vol. 10, trans. R. F. C. Hull (London: Routledge and Kegan Paul, 1964), 74–94.

83   Stephen Polcari, 'Contexts, Influences, References', in *Jackson Pollock et Le Chamanisme*, eds. Mickie Klein, Stephen Polcari, Marc Restellini, and William Rubin (Paris: Pinacothèque de Paris, 2008), 12; Leonard Emmerling, *Pollock* (Koln: Edition Taschen, 1999), 94.

84   C. G. Jung, *Letters 1906–1950*, eds. Gerhard Adler et al. (Princeton, NJ: Bollingen, 1992), 1:479; Edward F. Edinger, *The Aion Lectures: Exploring the Self in C. G. Jung's Aion* (Toronto: Inner City Books, 1996), 11–13.

85   Jung, 'The Sign of the Fishes', 72–94.

86   Jung, 'Flying Saucers', 589.

87   George King, *Become a Builder of the New Age*, Kindle ed. (1964; Hollywood, CA: The Aetherius Society, 2014). See also George King, *Contacts with the Gods from Space: Pathway to the New Age* (Hollywood CA: Aetherius Society), 1996.

88   C. G. Jung, 'Foreword', in *The I Ching or Book of Changes*, ed. Richard Wilhelm, 3rd ed. (1951; London: Routledge and Kegan Paul, 1968), xxi–xxxix.

89   See Jeffrey J. Kripal, *Esalen: America and the Religion of No Religion* (Chicago, IL: University of Chicago Press, 2008).

90   John Carter, *Sex and Rockets: The Occult World of Jack Parsons* (Port Townsend WA: Feral House, 2004); Martin P. Starr, *The Unknown God: W.T. Smith and the Thelemites* (Bolingbrook, IL: The Teitan Press, 2003).

91   Russell Miller, *Bare Faced Messiah: The True Story of L. Ron Hubbard* (London: Sphere Books, 1988), 146–68.

92   J. W. Parsons, *Freedom Is a Two-Edged Sword* (Tempe, AZ: New Falcon Publications, 1989), 49.

93   Bill Landis, *Anger: An Unauthorised Biography of Kenneth Anger* (New York: Harper Collins, 1996), 33–4, 164–8; Alice L. Hutchison, *Kenneth Anger: A Demonic Visionary* (London: Black Dog Publishing, 2004).

94   Gregory Stephenson, *The Daybreak Boys: Essays on the Literature of the Beat Generation* (Carbondale: Southern Illinois University Press, 2009), 6.

95   Ibid., 6.

96   Ibid., 5.

97   Ibid., 2.

98   Ibid., 4.

99   Jack Kerouac, 'The Origins of the Beat Generation', *Playboy,* June 1969, 42.

100 Ibid., 42.

101 Cited in Richard Candida Smith, *Utopia and Dissent: Art, and Poetry, and Politics in California* (Berkeley: University of California Press, 1995), 146.

102 Allen Ginsberg, 'Notes for Howl and Other Poems', in *The New American Poetry 1945-1960*, ed. Donald M. Allen (Berkeley and Los Angeles: University of California Press, 1999), 415; Roszak, *The Making of a Counter Culture*, 67, 127.

103 Jack Kerouac, *On the Road* (New York: Signet Books, 1957), 46.

104 Daniel A. Foss, *Freak Culture: Lifestyle and Politics* (New York: E. P. Dutton & Co., 1972), 48.

105 John Clellon Holmes, 'This Is the Beat Generation', *The New York Times Magazine,* 16 November 1952, 10, http://www.litkicks.com/Texts/ThisIsBeatGen.html, accessed 15 October 2014.

106 Robert A. Nisbet, *The Quest for Community* (New York: New York University Press, 1953), 3; also see 7.

107 William S. Burroughs, 'The Fall of Art', in *The Adding Machine*, ed. William S. Burroughs (New York: Grove Press, 2013), 75.

108 Allen Ginsberg to Jack Kerouac, ca. 29 June 1949, in *Jack Kerouac and Allen Ginsberg: The Letters*, eds. Bill Morgan and David Stanford (New York: Penguin, 2011), 93.

109 Holmes, 'This Is the Beat Generation', 10.

110 Stephenson, *The Daybreak Boys*, 6.

111 William Fowler, 'Beats and Beatniks, from New York to London and Beyond', in *The Party's Over* (London: BFI, 2010), 15, 18.

112 Matthew Levi Stevens, *The Magical Universe of William S. Burroughs* (Oxford: Mandrake, 2014), 42–9.

113 Tim Cumming, 'Destination Further: William Burroughs' South American Adventure', http://timcumming.wordpress.com/, accessed 17 October 2014.

114 William S. Burroughs, *Junky* (London: Penguin, 2008), 128.

115 William S. Burroughs and Allen Ginsberg, *The Yage Letters* (London: Penguin, 1979), 70.

116 Ibid., 70; William S. Burroughs, 'The Name Is Burroughs', in Burroughs, *The Adding Machine*, 12–13; Stevens, *The Magical Universe*, 40–9.

117 Robert Palmer, 'Brion Gysin 1916-1986', in *The Process*, ed. Brion Gysin (New York: The Overlook Press, 1987), xv.

118 Robert A. Sobieszek, *Ports of Entry: William S. Burroughs and the Arts* (Los Angeles County Museum of Art: Thames and Hudson, 1996), 26; Burroughs, 'The Fall of Art', 76.

119 Brion Gysin and Terry Wilson, *Here to Go: Planet R-101. Brion Gysin Interviewed by Terry Wilson* (San Francisco, CA: Berry Tomas, S. X. Summerville, 1982), vii.

120 Burroughs, *The Adding Machine*, 60, 75, 124.

121 Barry Miles, *Call me Burroughs: A Life* (New York: Twelve, 2013), 1–5.

122 Burroughs, *The Adding Machine*, 12.

123 James Grauerholz, Introduction to Burroughs, *The Adding Machine*, vii–xxiii, ix.

124 'Civilian Defence' in Burroughs, *The Adding Machine*, cited in Stevens, *The Magical Universe*, 106.

125 Cited in Stevens, *The Magical Universe*, 106.

126 Burroughs and Ginsberg, *The Yage Letters*, 50.

127 Jack Kerouac interviewed by Alfred Aronowitz for 'The Year of Zen', *Escapade* (October 1960), cited in Barry Miles, *Jack Kerouac: King of the Beats* (London: Virgin, 2010), 231.

128 Weaver, *The Awakener*, 194–5.

129 Allen Ginsberg to Jack Kerouac, ca. 18 June 1954, in *Jack Kerouac and Allen Ginsberg: the Letters*, eds. Bill Morgan and David Stanford (New York: Penguin, 2011), 221.

130 Allen Ginsberg to Jack Kerouac, 5 September 1954, in *Jack Kerouac and Allen Ginsberg: the Letters*, eds. Bill Morgan and David Stanford (New York: Penguin, 2011), 243.

131 Weaver, *The Awakener*, 196.

132 Miles, *Jack Kerouac*, 232–3.

133 Jack Kerouac to Allen Ginsberg, ca. March 1954, in *Jack Kerouac and Allen Ginsberg: The Letters*, eds. Bill Morgan and David Stanford (New York: Penguin, 2011), 212.

134 Allen Ginsberg to Jack Kerouac, 18 January 1954, in *Jack Kerouac and Allen Ginsberg: The Letters*, eds. Bill Morgan and David Stanford (New York: Penguin, 2011), 206.

135 Allen Ginsberg to Jack Kerouac, 18 June 1949, in *Jack Kerouac and Allen Ginsberg: The Letters*, eds. Bill Morgan and David Stanford (New York: Penguin, 2011), 221.

136 Ibid., 221.

137 Burroughs and Ginsberg, *The Yage Letters*, 66.

138 Ibid., 64.

139 Jack Kerouac to Allen Ginsberg, ca. late May 1954, in *Jack Kerouac and Allen Ginsberg: The Letters*, eds. Bill Morgan and David Stanford (New York: Penguin, 2011), 218–19.

140 Roland Vernon, *Star in the East: Krishnamurti, the Invention of a Messiah* (London: Constable, 2000), 205.

141 Huston Smith, Introduction to *The Divine Within, Selected Writings on Enlightenment*, ed. Aldous Huxley (New York: Harper Perennial, 2003), 1.

142 Nicholas Berdiaeff (1874–1948) cited in *Brave New World*, ed. Aldous Huxley (Braunschweig: Diesterweg, 2013), 22.

143 Aldous Huxley, *Ends and Means* (New York: Harper and Brothers, 1937), 5.

144 Aldous Huxley, *The Perennial Philosophy* (1954; New York: Harper Perennial, 2004), 184.

145 Aldous Huxley, *The Doors of Perception and Heaven and Hell* (1954; London: Vintage Books 2004), 7–8.

146 Ibid., 27.

147 Wood, *Žižek: A Reader's Guide*, 155.

148 Huxley, *The Doors of Perception*, 46, also see 49, 67, 89.

149 Ibid., 26–7.

150 Ibid., 75.

151 Ibid., 46, also see 48–9.

152 Ibid., 46, see also 63.

153 Aldous Huxley, 'Action and Contemplation', in Huxley, *The Divine Within*, 191.

154 Smith, 'Introduction', in Huxley, *The Divine Within*, 2.

155 Timothy Leary, 'To Aldous Huxley', 3 March 1961, http://www.leary.ru/english/letters/?n=04, accessed 14 November 2014; also see Sybille Bedford, *Aldous Huxley: A Biography* (London: Pan MacMillan, 1993), 664.

156 Bedford, *Aldous Huxley*, 717.

157 Ibid., 718; for Huxley's influence see Partridge, *The Re-Enchantment of the West*, 92–4.

158 Timothy Leary, 'To Arthur Koestler', n.d., http://www.leary.ru/english/letters/?n=00, accessed 14 July 2014.

159 Ibid.

160 Timothy Leary, 'How to Change Behaviour', presentation at the International Congress of Applied Psychology, Copenhagen, August 1961, in *Timothy Leary: The Harvard Years*, edited by James Penner (Rochester, VT: Park Street Press, 2014), 20–37.

Chapter 6

1 *Sex, Drugs and Rock 'N' Roll: The Sixties' Revealed*, UK Channel 5 TV series, http://www.channel5.com/shows/sex-drugs-and-rock-n-roll-the-60s-revealed/episodes/episode-1-381, accessed 10 October 2014; http://yesterday.uktv.co.uk/shows/Sixties/watch-online/, accessed 10 October 2014.

2 David Eisenhower, 'Grandfather Leaves the White House', in *The Sixties: The Decade Remembered Now, by the People Who Lived It Then*, ed. Lynda Rosen Obst (New York: Random House/Rolling Stone, 1977), 21.

3 Philip Larkin, 'Annus Mirabilis', in *High Windows*, ed. Philip Larkin (London: Faber and Faber, 1979), 34.

4 Roszak, *The Making of a Counter Culture*, 63.

5 José Argüelles, *The Transformative Vision: Reflections on the Nature and History of Human Expression* (Berkeley, CA: Shambhala, 1975), 270.

6 Aristotle, *Poetics*, trans. Stephen Halliwell (Cambridge, MA: Harvard University Press, 1999), 1459a, 16–21.

7 Robert Hewison, *Too Much: Art and Society in the Sixties, 1960–75* (New York: Oxford University Press, 1987), 76.

8 Brian Harrison, *Seeking a Role: The United Kingdom 1950–70 (The New Oxford History of England)* (Oxford: Clarendon Press, 2011), 472.

9 See for example, Hobsbawm, *Fractured*, 107; and Jonathon Green, *Days in the Life: Voices from the English Underground 1961–1971* (London: Heinemann, 1988), vii.

10 'THE NEW SOCIETY: Who's Winning the Battle of the Generations?' *Observer* Colour Supplement, 3 December 1967, 7.

11 J. Gordon Melton, Jerome Clarke, and Aidan A. Kelly, *New Age Almanac* (London and New York, 1991), xi–xvi, 1.

12 Daniel A. Foss and Ralph W. Larkin, 'From "The Gates of Eden" to "Day of the Locust": An Analysis of the Dissident Youth Movement of the 1960s and Its Heirs in the Early 1970s – The Post-movement Groups', *Theory and Society* 3, no. 1 (Spring 1976): 45–64. See also Maffesoli, *The Time of the Tribes*, 92.

13 Williams, *The Long Revolution*, xii.

14 Davis, 'Why All of Us May Be Hippies Someday', 10–12.

15 C. G. Jung, *Modern Man in Search of a Soul* (London: Routledge, 2001).

16 Irving Kristol, 'What's Bugging the Students?', in *The Neoconservative Persuasion: Selected Essays, 1942–2009*, ed. Gertrude Himmelfarb (New York: Basic Books, 2011), 117.

17 Lenin, 'What Is to Be Done', 80; see also 115, 120, 137, 174.

18 Slavoj Žižek, *Living in the End Times* (London: Verso, 2011), vii. Slavoj Žižek, *The Year of Living Dangerously* (London: Verso, 2012), 63–75.

19 Timothy Leary, *High Priest* (Berkeley, CA: Ronin Publishing, 1995), 133.

20 Michael Bloomfield, 'Dylan Goes Electric', in *The Sixties: The Decade Remembered Now, by the People Who Lived It Then*, ed. Lynda Rosen Obst (New York: Random House/Rolling Stone, 1977), 151.

21 Tom Wolfe, *The Electric Kool-Aid Acid Test* (London: Black Swan, 1989), 115.

22 Halberstam, *The Fifties*, x.

23 Anthony Sampson, *Anatomy of Britain* (London: Hodder and Stoughton, 1962), xiii.

24 Nisbet, *The Quest for Community*, 3, 7.

25 Guy Hamilton, 'Guy Hamilton Recalls Making the Party's Over', in *The Party's Over* (London: BFI, 2010), 7.

26 Horace Love quoted in Green, *Days in the Life*, 45.

27 Alan Bennett, 'The Festival of Britain', published in the 'Interior Worlds' supplement (December 2000) to *World of Interiors*, cited in Harrison, *Seeking a Role*, xv.

28 Eisenhower, 'Grandfather Leaves the White House', 21.

29 Michael Lind, *The Next American Nation: The New Nationalism and the Fourth American Revolution* (New York: The Free Press, 1995), 11, 34.

30 Allen Ginsberg, 'Coming to Terms with the Hells Angels', in *The Sixties: The Decade Remembered Now, by the People Who Lived It Then*, ed. Lynda Rosen Obst (New York: Random House/Rolling Stone, 1977), 160.

31 John Peel quoted in Green, *Days in the Life*, 128–9.

32 Robert Stone, *Prime Green: Remembering the Sixties* (New York: Harper Perennial, 2007), 239.

33 Locke, *An Essay Concerning Human Understanding*, 615–16.

34 Bloch, *The Principle of Hope*, 1:45.

35 George Melly, writing in the *Observer*, 1 September 1974, cited in Dominic Sandbrook, *State of Emergency, the Way We Were: Britain 1970–1974* (London: Penguin, 2011), 178.

36 Anonymous, 'Love, Leary, LSD', *Los Angeles Free Press*, 13 January 1967, in *The Hippie Papers: Notes from the Underground Press*, ed. Jerry Hopkins (New York: Signet Books, 1968), 87.

37 Jim Haynes quoted in Green, *Days in the Life*, 129; see also 126.

38 Richard Neville, *Playpower* (London: Jonathan Cape, 1970).

39 Green, *Days in the Life*, 45.

40 Lewis Yablonsky, *The Hippie Trip* (New York: Pegasus, 1968), 159.

41 For taste cultures see Gans, *Popular Culture*, 94, 96. Gans identified five cultures; I focus on three.

42 Tom Hayden, 'Writing the Port Huron Statement', in *The Sixties: The Decade Remembered Now, by the People Who Lived It Then*, ed. Lynda Rosen Obst (New York: Random House/Rolling Stone, 1977), 71.

43 'Port Huron Statement of the Students for a Democratic Society' Courtesy Office of Sen. Tom Hayden, http://www.h-net.org/~hst306/documents/huron.html. See also Hayden, 'Writing the Port Huron Statement', 70–1.

44 Heelas, *The New Age Movement*, 18, 23.

45 Jack Levin and James L. Spates, 'Hippie Values: An Analysis of the Underground Press', *Youth and Society* 2 (1970): 59–73.

46 Yablonsky, *The Hippie Trip*, 143–4.

47 George Melly, *Revolt into Style: The Pop Arts* (London: Faber and Faber, 1970), 118.

48 Barkun, *Disaster and the Millennium*, 117–18.
49 Mark Donnelly, *Sixties Britain* (Harlow: Pearson Education Ltd., 2005), 116–30.
50 Weber, *Essays in Sociology*, 139.
51 Nisbet, *The Quest for Community*, 3; see also 7.
52 Bloch, *The Principle of Hope*, 3: 1376.
53 Levin and Spates, 'Hippie Values', 63.
54 Ibid., 63.
55 Allen Ginsberg, 'Demonstration or Spectacle as Example, As Communication, or How to Make a March/Spectacle', *Berkeley Barb*, 19 November 1965, in *The Portable Sixties Reader*, ed. Ann Charles (London: Penguin, 2002), pp. 208–12.
56 Yablonsky, *The Hippie Trip*, 143–4.
57 Warren Hinckle, 'Ramparts', *Oz* 3 (1967): 4–5.
58 Melly, *Style*, 121, 123.
59 Spates, 'Counter Culture and Dominant Culture Values', 870.
60 Melly, *Style*, 120.
61 Jay Stevens, *Storming Heaven: LSD and the American Dream* (New York: Harper and Row, 1987), 301; Yablonsky, *The Hippie Trip*, 340–66.
62 Hinckle, 'Ramparts', 8.
63 Davis, 'Why All of Us May Be Hippies Someday', 18.
64 Hinckle, 'Ramparts', 8.
65 Burroughs, 'The Fall of Art', 77.
66 Margaret Thatcher, Interview for *Woman's Own* ('no such thing as society'), 23 September 1987, Margaret Thatcher Foundation, http://www.margaretthatcher.org/document/106689.
67 Hayden, 'Writing the Port Huron Statement', 71.
68 Hinckle, 'Ramparts', 5. Brook Farm was a Transcendentalist community in the 1840s. See Richard Francis, 'The Ideology of Brook Farm', in *Studies in the American Renaissance* (Boston, MA: Twayne, 1978), 1–48. Edith Roelker Curtis, *A Season in Utopia: The Story of Brook Farm* (New York: Thomas Nelson and Sons, 1961).
69 *Easy Rider*, http://www.imdb.com/title/tt0064276/.
70 Joni Mitchell, 'Woodstock Lyrics', *Lyricsfreak*, http://www.lyricsfreak.com/j/joni+mitchell/woodstock_20075381.html, accessed 18 April 2015.
71 Spates, 'Counterculture and Dominant Culture Values', 876; Levin and Spates, 'Hippie Values', 68.
72 Jean-Jacques Lebel, 'Notes on Political Street Theatre, Parts: 1968, 1969', cited in Claire Bishop, *Artificial Hells: Participatory Art and the Politics of Spectatorship* (London: Verso, 2012), 102.
73 Ginsberg, 'Coming to Terms with the Hells Angels', 161.
74 Ibid., 161.
75 Ginsberg, 'Notes for Howl and Other Poems', 417; Roszak, *The Making of a Counter Culture*, 125.
76 Abbie Hoffman, *Revolution for the Hell of It* (1968; New York: Avalon Publishing, 2005), 102–3.
77 Claire Bishop, *Artificial Hells: Participatory Art and the Politics of Spectatorship* (London: Verso, 2012), 77–104.
78 Alexander Bloom, ed., *Long Time Gone: Sixties America Then and Now* (Oxford: Oxford University Press, 2001).
79 Peter Fryer, 'Inside the Underground', *Observer*, colour magazine, 3 December 1967, 13; 'Mister Tambourine Mind', http://www.artgallery.nsw.gov.au/collection/works/DA17.1970/, accessed 4 March 2015.

80 Barbara Hulanicki, *From A to BIBA: The Autobiography of Barbara Hulanicki* (London: V&A Publications, 2008).

81 Cilla Black in 'Tribes', episode 1 of *Oh You Pretty Things: The Story of Music and Fashion*, BBC4, 20 September 2014.

82 Melly, *Style*, 1.

83 'Great Britain: You Can Walk Across It on the Grass', *Time*, Friday, 15 April 1966, http://content.time.com/time/magazine/article/0,9171,835349,00.html; http://www.tranceaddict.com/forums/showthread.php?threadid=464372&referrerid=2#.U4WhwvldW2o.

84 Maffesoli, *The Time of the Tribes*.

85 Hewison, *Too Much*, 77.

86 Lauren Langman, 'Dionysus – Child of Tomorrow: Notes on Post-industrial Youth', *Youth and Society* 3, part 1 (1971–1972): 82.

87 Bloch, *The Principle of Hope*, 3: 927.

88 See Hebdidge, *Subculture*, esp. 113–27.

89 Diana Vreeland, 'Chatting About Style' in *The Sixties: The Decade Remembered Now, by the People Who Lived It Then*, ed. Lynda Rosen Obst (New York: Random House/Rolling Stone, 1977), 146.

90 Gans, *Popular Culture*, 94, 96, 122–6.

91 Grauerholz, 'Introduction', ix.

92 Daniel Bell, 'Unstable America: Transitory & Permanent Factors in a National Crisis', *Encounter*, 34 (June 1970): 17–18.

93 Fukuyama, *The End of History*, 330.

94 Ibid., 331, 335.

95 Ibid., 329.

96 Williams, *The Long Revolution*, 88–91.

97 Scheler, *Ressentiment*.

98 Jerry Rubin, 'Yippees Are Coming, Coming, Coming to Chicago', *Oz* 11 (1968): 9.

99 Fukuyama, *The End of History*, 163; also see 223–34, 300–12.

100 Plato, *Republic*, X, 517B, 611 D, 612 A; Plato, *Phaedrus*, trans. H.N. Fowler (Cambridge, MA and London: Harvard University Press, 1914), 247 BC.

101 Plato, *Phaedo*, trans. H.N. Fowler (Cambridge, MA and London: Harvard University Press, 1914), 82E–83A.

102 Lebel, 'Notes on Political Street Theatre, Parts: 1968, 1969', 102.

103 Davis, 'Why All of Us May Be Hippies Someday', 13, 14.

104 Spates, 'Counterculture and Dominant Culture Values', 870.

105 Carl Jung, 'The Psychology of the Child Archetype', in *The Archetypes and the Collective Unconscious*, Collected Works vol. 9, pt 1, trans. R.F.C. Hull (1959; New York: Princeton University Press, 1969), 289.

106 Cohn, *Millennium*, 27.

107 'The Delusions of the Day', *Torch* (10 January 1846), 21–3 (21), cited in Secord, *Victorian Sensation*, 13.

108 Leary, *High Priest*, 133.

109 Nelson, *The British Counter Culture*, 9; Roszak, *The Making of a Counter Culture*, xi–xii, 1, 16, 74–5.

110 Roszak, *The Making of a Counter Culture*, 139.

111 Stuart Hall, 'Thatcher's Lessons', *Marxism Today*, March 1988, 27; also see Levitas, *Utopia as Method*, 197.

112 Bell, 'Unstable America', 17.

113 McKay, *DiY Culture*, 2.

114   Neville, *Playpower*; Barbara G. Myerhoff, 'The Revolution as a Trip: Symbol and
        Paradox', *Annals of the American Academy of Political and Social Science, Students
        Protest* 395 (May 1971), 107; Bell, 'Unstable America', 18, 23; Steinfels, *The
        Neoconservatives*, 46; Gans, *Popular Culture*, 124; and 'Vietnam War: Allied Troop
        Levels 1960–73', http://www.americanwarlibrary.com/vietnam/vwatl.htm, accessed
        24 May 2014.
115   Spates, 'Counterculture and Dominant Culture Values', 868–9, 880–1.
116   Green, *Days in the Life*, x.
117   Abbie Hoffman, *Revolution for the Hell of It* (New York: Dial, 1968).
118   Justin Vaïsse, *Neoconservatism: The Biography of a Movement*, trans. Arthur
        Goldhammer (Harvard: Harvard University Press, 2011), 41.
119   John Hopkins, 'An Open Letter to Mr Tariq Ali', *IT* no. 29 (19 April–2 May
        1968): 11.
120   Tariq Ali, *Street Fighting Years: An Autobiography of the Sixties* (London: Verso,
        1995), 186.
121   Hinckle, 'Ramparts', 8.
122   Charles Perry, 'The Gathering of the Tribes', in *The Sixties: The Decade Remembered
        Now, by the People Who Lived It Then*, ed. Lynda Rosen Obst (New York: Random
        House/Rolling Stone, 1977), 190.
123   Abe Peck, 'The Other Convention in Chicago', in *The Sixties: The Decade
        Remembered Now, by the People Who Lived It Then*, ed. Lynda Rosen Obst (New
        York: Random House/Rolling Stone, 1977), 260.
124   Abbie Hoffman, *Steal This Book* (Cambridge, MA: De Capo Press, 1996), 215.
125   Hinckle, 'Ramparts', 9.
126   Rubin, 'Yippees Are Coming, Coming, Coming to Chicago', 10.
127   For tensions between capitalism and anti-capitalism in hippy culture see Thomas
        Frank, *The Conquest of Cool: Business Culture, Counter Culture, and the Rise of Hip
        Consumerism* (Chicago, IL: University of Chicago Press, 1997), 1–3.
128   Hinckle, 'Ramparts', 8; see also Emmett Grogan, *Ringolevio: A life Played for Keeps*
        (St. Alban: Granada Books, 1974), 278, 289; Joseph Heath and Andrew Potter, *The
        Rebel Sell: How the Counter Culture became Consumer Culture* (Chichester: Capstone
        Publishing, 2006); Barry Miles, *Hippie* (New York: Sterling, 2004), 106.
129   George H. Sabine, *The Works of Gerrard Winstanley* (Ithaca, NY: Cornell University
        Press, 1941), 251. See also Timothy Kenyon, *Utopian Communism and Political
        Thought in Early Modern England* (London: Pinter, 1989), 121–224.
130   Hinckle, 'Ramparts', 7.
131   Ibid., 7.
132   Anonymous, 'An Address to Politicians', *Oz* 3 (1967): 13–14.
133   Jonah Raskin, *For The Hell of It: The Life and Times of Abbie Hoffman* (Berkeley and
        London: University of California Press, 1988), 128–9.
134   Davis, 'Why All of Us May Be Hippies Someday', 10, 17.
135   Mick Farren, *The Texts of Festival* (London: Granada Publishing, 1973), 164.
136   Hinckle, 'Ramparts', 6.
137   Ginsberg. 'Coming to Terms with the Hells Angels,' 160–2.
138   Mick Farren, 'Angels and Violence', *International Times*, 17–30 November 1967: 13.
139   Jeff Nuttall, *Bomb Culture* (London: Paladin, 1979), 35.
140   Kenneth Grant, 'The Golden Dawn', *International Times*, 14–29 January 1968, 12.
141   Ginsberg, 'Coming to Terms with the Hells Angels', 160–2; Farren, *The Texts
        of Festival*, 164; Hoffman, *Steal This Book*, 215; Wavy Gravy, 'Hog Farming at

Woodstock', in *The Sixties: The Decade Remembered Now, by the People Who Lived It Then*, ed. Lynda Rosen Obst (New York: Random House/Rolling Stone, 1977), 274; Martin A. Lee and Bruce Shlain, *Acid Dreams: The Complete Social History of LSD: The CIA, the Sixties, and Beyond* (New York: Grove Press, 1992), 110.

142 The Seattle underground newspaper *Helix*, July 1967, cited by Roszak, *The Making of a Counter Culture*, 75. See also Huxley, *The Doors of Perception*, especially 88–9.

143 Robert Stone, *Prime Green: Remembering the Sixties* (New York: Harper Perennial, 2007), 239.

144 Roszak, *The Making of a Counter Culture*, 67.

145 Ginsberg, 'Notes for Howl and Other Poems', 416.

146 Allen Ginsberg, 'Howl, Parts I and II', lines 1–6, in *The New American Poetry 1945–1960*, ed. Donald M. Allen (Berkeley and Los Angeles: University of California Press, 1999), 182.

147 Burroughs and Ginsberg, *The Yage Letters*, 60.

148 Stevens, *Storming Heaven*, 300.

149 Kesey, *Acid Test*, 115, cited in Wolfe.

150 Wolfe, *Acid Test*, 131.

151 Sherri Cavan, *Hippies of the Haight* (St Louis: New Critics Press, 1972), 61–5.

152 Melly, *Style*, 122.

153 Davis, 'Why All of Us May Be Hippies Someday', 10, 17–18.

154 Yablonsky, *The Hippie Trip*, 251.

155 Hinckle, 'Ramparts', 7.

156 Wavy Gravy, 'Hog Farming at Woodstock', 274. See also Lee and Shlain, *Acid Dreams*, 110.

157 Timothy Leary, *Flashbacks: An Autobiography* (Los Angeles, CA: Jeremy B. Tarcher, 1990), 109–10.

158 Ibid., 45–50; Timothy Leary, *The Politics of Ecstasy* (Oakland, CA: Ronin Publishing, 1998).

159 Hinckle, 'Ramparts', 7.

160 *International Times* 2, 16–27 October 1966, 6.

161 Timothy Leary, 'You Are a God: Act Like One', *International Times*, 2–15 February 1968, 11.

162 Miles, *Hippie*, 121.

163 Cavan, *Hippies of the Haight*, 62.

164 Melly, *Style*, 121.

165 Georg Simmel, *The Sociology of Georg Simmel*, trans. and ed. Kurt H. Wolff (Glencoe, IL: The Free Press, 1950), 336, cited in Kenneth Jowitt, *New World Disorder: The Leninist Extinction* (Berkeley: University of California Press, 1992), 135.

166 Maffesoli, *The Time of the Tribes*, 92.

167 David Hume, 'Of Enthusiasm and Superstition', in David Hume, *Selected Essays* (Oxford: Oxford University Press, 1998), 39.

168 Partridge, *The Re-Enchantment of the West*, 81–134.

169 Timothy Leary, *Musings on Human Metamorphoses* (Oakland, CA: Ronin Publishing, 2003), 60.

170 Ram Dass and Ralph Metzner with Gary Bravo, *Birth of a Psychedelic Culture: Conversations About Leary, the Harvard Experiments, Millbrook and the Sixties* (Santa Fe: Synergetic Press, 2010).

171 Leary, *High Priest*, 324.

172 Ibid., 65.

173 Burroughs, *The Adding Machine*, 15.

174 Robert Greenfield, *Timothy Leary: A Biography* (New York: Harcourt, 2006), 154–5, 213–4.

175 Leary, *High Priest*, 328, 324.

176 Ibid., 336.

177 Timothy Leary, *Turn On, Tune In, Drop Out* (Oakland, CA: Ronan Publishing, 1999).

178 John Higgs, 'The High Priest and the Great Beast', *Sub Rosa* 4 (March 2006): 15–23; 'Timothy Leary e Aleister Crowley', extract from interview on PBS 'Late Night America', 1980, http://www.youtube.com/watch?v=DaVeGZE6VU8. See also Leary, *Flashbacks*, 199.

179 Spates, 'Counterculture and Dominant Culture Values', 871; Levin and Spates, 'Hippie Values', 63; Lachman, *Turn Off Your Mind*.

180 Aleister Crowley, *Diary of a Drug Fiend* (1922; York Beach: Samuel Weiser, 1970), 7.

181 John Starr Cooke, 'Black Magic Question Mark', *American Theosophist* 33, no. 8 (August 1945), http://www.royalmaze.com/john-starr-cooke/black-magic-question-mark/, accessed 1 September 2014. See also Gysin and Wilson, *Here to Go*, 125; Lee and Shlain, *Acid Dreams*, 157–9; Anonymous, 'Introduction: Prophecy of the Royal Maze', http://www.royalmaze.com/john-starr-cooke/introduction-prophecy-of-the-royal-maze/, accessed 1 September 2014; John Cooke and Rosalind Sharp, 'The World of One', http://www.royalmaze.com/the-word-of-one/, accessed 1 September 2014.

182 See Ed Sanders' biographical essay in Harry Smith, ed., *Anthology of American Folk Music*, vol. 4, Revenant RVM 211 (2000), 4–5, 24, 29; 'Harry Smith (1923–1991)', http://www.harrysmitharchives.com/1_bio/index.html, accessed 11 October 2014; Landis, *Anger*, 34–5; Barry Miles, *In the Seventies: Adventures in the Counter Culture* (London: Profile Books, 2011), 165–6.

183 Lee and Shlain, *Acid Dreams*, 159.

184 Steve Levine, 'The First American Mehla', *The San Francisco Oracle*, January 1967, in *The Hippie Papers: Notes from the Underground Press*, ed. Jerry Hopkins (New York: Signet Books, 1968), 20–1.

185 Ibid., 20–1.

186 Michael Bowen, 'My Odyssey', http://www.royalmaze.com/my-odyssey-the-first-human-be-in/chapter-one-part-2/, accessed 1 September 2014.

187 Ed Sanders' biographical essay in Smith, *Anthology of American Folk Music*, 24.

188 Nadine Bloch, 'The Day They Levitated the Pentagon', *Waging Nonviolence*, 21 October 2012, http://wagingnonviolence.org/feature/the-day-they-levitated-the-pentagon/, accessed 1 September 2014.

189 James Rado, Gerome Ragni and Galt MacDermot, 'Aquarius', 1968, line 4.

190 Fountain, *Underground*, 8.

191 John Michell, 'Flying Saucers as a Portent of the Revelation Which Will Attend the Opening of the Aquarian Age', *International Times*, 30 January–12 February 1967, 7; John Michell, *The Flying Saucer Vision* (New York: Ace Books, 1967), 13–16; John Michell, *The View over Atlantis*, revised edition (London: Garnstone Press, 1972); foreword.

192 John Michell, 'Centres & Lines of the Latent Power in Britain', *International Times*, 5–20 October 1967, 5.

193 Peter Stansill, 'Psyching in the New Age', *IT*, 27 February–12 March 1967, 12.

194 Grant, 'The Golden Dawn', 11–12.

195 Michell, *The View over Atlantis*, foreword.
196 Lynne and Anne Howes, *The Glastonbury Festivals* (Glastonbury: Gothic Image Publications, 1987), 21.
197 George Melly, writing in the *Observer*, 1 September 1974, cited in Sandbrook, *State of Emergency*, 178.
198 Stone, *Prime Green*, 239.
199 McKay, *Senseless Acts of Beauty*, 14.
200 Daniel Pinchbeck, 'Introduction', in *The Psychedelic Experience*, eds. Timothy Leary, Ralph Metzner, and Richard Alpert (1964; London: Penguin, 2008).
201 Leary, *Musings*, 61.
202 Esler, *Bombs, Beards and Barricades*, 249.
203 Fryer, 'Inside the Underground', 17.
204 F. Scott Fitzgerald, 'My Generation', *Esquire* (October 1928), cited in Stephenson, *The Daybreak Boys*, 4.
205 Partridge, *The Re-Enchantment of the West*, 318.
206 Barkun, *Disaster and the Millennium*, 20–1.

Chapter 7

1 Esler, *Bombs, Beards and Barricades*, 303; McKay, *Senseless Acts of Beauty*, 3, also see 4–6.
2 John D'Emilio, 'Placing Gay in the Sixties', in Bloom, *Long Time Gone*, 210.
3 Maffesoli, *The Time of the Tribes*, 92.
4 Wood, *Žižek: A Reader's Guide*, Chapter 12.
5 Spates, 'Counterculture and Dominant Culture Values', 868–9, 880–1.
6 Foss, and Larkin, 'From "The Gates of Eden" to "Day of the Locust"', 46.
7 Spates, 'Counterculture and Dominant Culture Values', 876; Levin, and Spates, 'Hippie Values', 68.
8 Steinfels, *The Neoconservatives*, 60.
9 Yablonsky, *The Hippie Trip*, 36. The figure was repeated uncritically in Terry Anderson. *The Movement and the Sixties: Protest in America from Greensboro to Wounded Knee* (Oxford: Oxford University Press, 1995), 241, who converted Yablonsky's 'several hundred thousand' to 300,000.
10 Terence Ball, 'Green Political Theory', in *The Cambridge History of Twentieth Century Political Thought*, eds. Terence Ball and Richard Bellamy (Cambridge: Cambridge University Press, 2003), 534.
11 Simon Hall, 'Protest Movements in the 1970s: The Long 1960s', *Journal of Contemporary History* 43, no. 4 (2008): 655–72.
12 Theodore Roszak, *Unfinished Animal: The Aquarian Frontier and the Evolution of Consciousness* (London: Faber and Faber, 1976), 35; see also Douglas R. Groothuis, *Unmasking the New Age: Is There A New Religious Movement Trying to Transform Society?* (Downer's Grove, IL: Intervarsity Press, 1986), 51.
13 Melton, Clarke, and Kelly, *New Age Almanac*, xi–xvi, 1.
14 Faivre, *Access to Western Esotericism*, 105.
15 Harvey, *Beyond Enlightenment*, 23.
16 Martin Ramstedt, 'New Age and Business' in 'The New Age Movement and Western Esotericism' in *Handbook of New Age*, eds. Daren Kemp and James R. Lewis (Leiden and Boston: Brill, 2007), 187; also see 186.

17 David Spangler, 'The New Age: The Movement Toward the Divine' in *New Age Spirituality: An Assessment*, ed. Duncan Sheldon Ferguson (Louisville: Westminster/ John Knox Press, 1993), 86; see also David Spangler, *A Pilgrim in Aquarius* (Forres: Findhorn Press, 1996), 55.

18 The Rolling Stones, *The Stones in the Park*, directed by Leslie Woodhead and Jo Durden-Smith (London: Granada Media, 2001), DVD.

19 Michael J. Kramer, *The Republic of Rock: Music and Citizenship in the Sixties Counterculture* (Oxford: Oxford University Press), 2013.

20 Miles, *In the Seventies*.

21 Maffesoli, *The Time of the Tribes*, 92.

22 Daniel Bell, *The Coming of Post-Industrial Society* (Harmondsworth: Penguin, 1976), 488.

23 Marx, 'Theses on Feuerbach', X.

24 Hegel, *Philosophy of History*, 107.

25 Boris Frankel, *The Post-Industrial Utopians* (Cambridge: Polity Press, 1987), 1.

26 Kumar, *Prophecy and Progress*, 193–4.

27 Kenneth Jowitt, 'Rage, Hubris and Regime Change: The Urge to Speed History Along', *Policy Review* 118 (April–May 2003): 33.

28 Roszak, *Unfinished Animal*, 30–1.

29 Marilyn Ferguson, *The Aquarian Conspiracy: Personal and Social Transformations in the 1980s* (London: Paladin Books, 1982).

30 Roszak, *Unfinished Animal*, 34.

31 London Wellbeing Festival, http://www.mindbodyspirit.co.uk/events/london-festival-2015, accessed 19 May 2014.

32 Benjamin Crème, *The Reappearance of the Christ and the Masters of Wisdom* (London: Tara Press, 1980).

33 Constance E. Cumbey, *The Hidden Dangers of the Rainbow: The New Age Movement and Our Coming Age of Barbarism* (Shreveport, LA: Huntingdon House, 1983).

34 Martin Gardner, *The New Age: Notes of a Fringe Watcher* (Buffalo, NY: Prometheus Books, 1988).

35 William Irwin Thompson, 'Sixteen Years of the New Age', in *Reimagination of the World: A Critique of the New Age, Science, and Popular Culture: The Chinnok Summer Conferences of David Spangler and William Irwin Thompson, July 1988 and 1989*, eds. David Spangler and William Irwin (Santa Fe: Thompson Bear & Company, 1991), 17; J. Gordon Melton, 'The Future of the New Age Movement', in *New Religions and New Religiosity*, eds. Eileen Barker and Margot Warburg (Aarhus: Aarhus University Press, 2001), 142–3, 147; Massimo Introvigne, 'After the New Age: Is There a Next Age?', in *New Age Religion and Globalization*, ed. Mikael Rothstein (Aarhus: Aarhus University Press, 2001), 61–2.

36 Lemesurier, *This New Age Business*, 185; Spangler, *A Pilgrim in Aquarius*, 55.

37 David Spangler, *Explorations: Emerging Aspects of the New Culture* (Forres: Findhorn Publications, 1980), 78; see also Spangler, *A Pilgrim in Aquarius*, 247.

38 See in particular David Spangler, *Festivals in the New Age* (Forres: Findhorn Publications, 1975); David Spangler, *Revelation: The Birth of a New Age* (Forres: Findhorn Publications, 1976).

39 Annand Michael Kinsella Taves, 'Hiding in Plain Sight: The Organisational Forms of "Unorganised Religion"', in *New Age Spirituality: Rethinking Religion*, eds. Steven J. Sutcliffe and Ingvild Saelid Gilhus (Durham: Acumen, 2013), 84.

40 David Spangler, *Apprenticed to Spirit: The Education of a Soul* (New York: Penguin, 2011), 178.

41 Spangler, *Revelation*, 27–30.

42 George Trevelyan, 'Spiritual Awakening in Our Time', lecture given at the Royal Commonwealth Society, November 1972, http://www.wrekintrust.org/downloads/sir_george_spiritual_awakening.pdf.

43 Dane Rudhyar, *Fire Out of the Stone: A Reinterpretation of the Basic Images of the Christian Tradition* (The Hague: Servire, 1963).

44 Dane Rudhyar, *Astrological Timing: The Transition to the New Age* (San Francisco, New York and London: Harper and Row, 1969); Dane Rudhyar, *Occult Preparations for a New Age* (Madras and London: Theosophical Publishing House, 1975); Dane Rudhyar, *The Planetarisation of Consciousness* (1970; New York: Aurora Press, 1977).

45 Dane Rudhyar, *An Astrological Mandala: The Cycle of Transformation and Its 360 Symbolic Phases* (1972; New York: Vintage Books, 1974), 31.

46 Spangler, *Explorations*, 78.

47 McKay, *DiY Culture*, 9; Maffesoli, *The Time of the Tribes*, 92–3.

48 York, *The Emerging Network*.

49 Bloom, *The New Age: An Anthology of Essential Writings*, xiii, xv–xvi.

50 Spangler, 'The New Age', 101.

51 John Ankerberg, and John Weldon, *Encyclopaedia of New Age Beliefs* (Eugene, OR: Harvest House, 1996), especially 259–304.

52 Dan Wakefield, 'Erhard's Life After Est', *Common Boundary*, published March/April 1994, http://www.wernererhard.com/boundary.html, accessed 6 January 2015.

53 Randall N. Baer, *Inside the New Age Nightmare* (Lafayette: Huntington House, 1989), 1, 37, 164; see also Walter Martin, *The New Age Cult* (Minneapolis: Bethany House Publishers, 1989), 8; Miller, *A Crash Course*, 15, 23–4; Michael Cole et al., *What Is the New Age?* (London: Hodder and Stoughton, 1990), 9–11; John P. Newport,*The New Age Movement and the Biblical Worldview: Conflict and Dialogue* (Grand Rapids: William B. Eerdmans, 1998), 8, 163.

54 Phillip C. Lucas, 'The New Age Movement and the Pentecostal/Charismatic Revival: Distinct Yet Parallel Phases of a Fourth Great Awakening', in *Perspectives on the New Age*, eds. James R. Lewis and J. Gordon Melton (New York: State University of New York Press, 1992), 204, 210. Also for New Age Christianity see Duncan S. Ferguson, *New Age Spirituality: An Assessment* (Louisville: Westminster/John Knox Press, 1993); Donald Curtis, *New Age Understanding* (Unity Village, Missouri: Unity Books, 1973), 204; Daren Kemp, *The Christaquarians: A Sociology of Christians in the New Age* (PhD thesis, King's College, London, 2003).

55 Cumbey, *The Hidden Dangers*, 52.

56 See for example, Barry Chamish, 'Amazing and Accurate Expose of the New Age by a Secular Jew', http://www.jesus-is-lord.com/newage.htm, accessed 20 June 2009; Steve Johnson, 'The New Age Movement', http://www.drstevej.com/newage.pdf, accessed 20 June 2009.

57 Anonymous, 'Planned Parenthood: Military Arm of the New Age Movement', http://www.trdd.org/EUGBR_5E.HTM, accessed 20 June 2009.

58 Žižek, *The Fragile Absolute*, 1.

59 Starhawk, *The Spiral Dance* (New York: Harper and Row, 1979); Monica Sjöö, *New Age and Armageddon: The Goddess or the Gurus? Towards a Feminist Vision of the Future* (London: The Women's Press, 1990).

60   Genesis Breyer P-Orridge, 'General Order Master', in *Ultraculture Journal*, One (2007; revised edition, 2014), 12, 15.

61   Sjöö, *New Age and Armageddon*.

62   Jon Savage, *England's Dreaming: Sex Pistols and Punk Rock* (London: Faber and Faber, 1991), xiii.

63   Wood, *Žižek: A Reader's Guide*, Chapter 12.

64   Robin Scott quoted in Savage, *England's Dreaming*, 39.

65   Savage, *England's Dreaming*, 189.

66   See Partridge, *The Re-Enchantment of the West*, 105.

67   McKay, *Senseless Acts of Beauty*, 5.

68   Ibid., 6.

69   Dennis McNally, *A Long Strange Trip: The Inside Story of the Grateful Dead and the Making of Modern America* (London: Corgi, 2003).

70   Burning Man, http://burningman.org/culture/philosophical-center/10-principles/, accessed 21 April 2015.

71   Savage, *England's Dreaming*, 440. See also Fowler, 'Beats and beatniks', 19.

72   Ibid., 421.

73   McKay, *DiY Culture*.

74   McKay, *DiY Culture*, 2.

75   Ibid., 2, 45.

76   Foss and Larkin, 'From "The Gates of Eden" to "Day of the Locust"', 360.

77   Stephen Duncombe, *Notes from Underground: Zines and the Politics of Alternative Culture* (London: Verso, 1997), 12; Hebdidge, *Subculture*, 121.

78   Maffesoli, *The Time of the Tribes*, 52.

79   Duncombe, *Notes from Underground*, 190; Hebdidge, *Subculture*, 121.

80   Esler, *Bombs, Beards and Barricades*, 7–8.

81   Gans, *Popular Culture*, 94, 96, 122–6.

82   Don Aitken, 'Twenty Years of Festivals', *Festival Eye*, Summer 1990, 19, cited in MacKay, *Senseless Acts of Beauty*, 45.

83   Ibid., 8–9.

84   Unsourced press preview quoted in commemorative festival programme.

85   Ibid.

86   McKay, *Senseless Acts of Beauty*, 8–9.

87   Ibid., 9, 46–7, 51.

88   Ibid., 134, 7.

89   Ibid., 52; also see 66–7.

90   Ibid., 52. See also Pat Kane, 'In Thrall to New Age Thrills', *Guardian*, section 2, 4 January 1995, 13.

91   McKay, *Senseless Acts of Beauty*, 139.

92   Ibid.

93   Ibid., 144.

94   Michell, *The View over Atlantis*, foreword.

95   Marian Green, *Magic for the Aquarian Age: A Contemporary Textbook of Practical Magical Techniques* (Wellingborough: Aquarian Press, 1983), 32–3.

96   Green, *Magic*, 211–12.

97   Janet Farrar and Stewart Farrar, *The Witches Way: Principles, Rituals and Beliefs of Modern Witchcraft* (London: Robert Hale, 1984), 159–60.

98　Vivianne Crowley, *Wicca: The Old Religion in the New Age* (Wellingborough: Aquarian Press, 1989), 49, 162, 242, 255.

99　George D. Chryssides, 'Is God a Space Alien? The Cosmology of the Raëlian Church', *Culture and Cosmos* 4, no. 1 (Spring/Summer, 2000), 36–53; Landes, *Heaven*, 408–7.

100　Partridge, *The Re-Enchantment of the West*, 103.

101　Fraser Clark, 'The Final Word on Drugs', in *Psychedelia Britannica: Hallucinogenic drugs in Britain*, ed. Antonio Melechi (London: Turnaround, 1997), 199, 202.

102　Partridge, *The Re-Enchantment of the West*, 110–1.

103　Nicholas Campion, 'The 2012 Mayan Calendar Prophecies in the Context of the Western Millenarian Tradition', in *Archaeoastronomy and Ethnoastronomy: Building Bridges between Cultures*, Proceedings of International Astronomy Union Symposium 278, ed. Clive Ruggles (Cambridge: Cambridge University Press, 2011), 249–54; Nicholas Campion, 'The 2012 Phenomenon in Context: Millenarianism, New Age and Cultural Astronomy', in *Ancient Cosmologies and Modern Prophets*, eds. Ivan Šprac and Peter Pehani (Lubljana: Anthropological Notebooks year XIX, supplement, 2013), 15–31.

104　For this and other details of McKenna's life in the 1960s, see Terence McKenna, *True Hallucinations: Being an Account of the Author's Extraordinary Adventures in the Devil's Paradise* (London: Rider, 1994), 5, 19–20.

105　Carlos Castaneda, *The Teachings of Don Juan: A Yaqui Way of Knowledge* (Oakland: University of California Press, 1968).

106　Partridge, *The Re-Enchantment of the West*, 42–81.

107　McKenna, *True Hallucinations*, 41.

108　Ibid., 198.

109　Ibid., 174, also see 26, 116, 149, 175, 199–202; Terence McKenna, *The Archaic Revival* (New York: Harper Collins, 1991), 110; Terence McKenna, and Dennis McKenna, *The Invisible Landscape: Mind, Hallucinogens, and the I Ching* (New York: Harper Collins, 1993), 135–80.

110　McKenna, *True Hallucinations*, 200; McKenna, *The Archaic Revival*, 110.

111　McKenna, *The Archaic Revival*, 113; Plato, *Timaeus*, 37 D-E.

112　Robert K. Sitler, 'The 2012 Phenomenon: New Uses for an Ancient Maya Calendar', in *2012: Decoding the Countercultural Apocalypse*, ed. Joseph Gelfer (Sheffield: Equinox, 2011), 10.

113　For the details of Argüelles' life see Stephanie South, *2012: Biography of a Time Traveller: the Journey of José Argüelles* (Franklin Lakes: New Page Books, 2009).

114　South, *2012: Biography of a Time Traveller*, 112–16.

115　Ibid., 1–101; also see Argüelles, *The Transformative Vision*, 273–4.

116　South, *2012: Biography of a Time Traveller*, 133–6.

117　Michael R. Meyer, 'Rudhyar: Friend, Exemplar and Sage', http://www.khaldea.com/articles/dr_fes.shtml, accessed 16 August 2014.

118　South, *2012: Biography of a Time Traveller*, 117.

119　John Hoopes, 'Mayanism Comes of (New) Age', in *2012: Decoding the Countercultural Apocalypse*, ed. Joseph Gelfer (Sheffield: Equinox, 2011), 38–59; also see John Major Jenkins, *The 2012 Story: The Myths, Fallacies, and Truth Behind the Most Intriguing Date in History* (New York: Penguin, 2009), 224–30.

120　Hammer, *Claiming Knowledge*, 85–200.

121　José Argüelles, *Surfers of the Zuvuya: Tales of Interdimensional Travel* (Rochester, VT: Bear and Company, 1989), 36.

122 José Argüelles, *The Mayan Factor: Path Beyond Technology* (Santa Fe: Bear and Company, 1987), 190.

123 South, *2012: Biography of a Time Traveller*, 34.

124 Argüelles, *The Mayan Factor*, 195–6.

125 Mark Van Stone, 'Maya Prophecies: 2012 and the Problematic Nature of Truth', in *2012: Decoding the Countercultural Apocalypse*, ed. Joseph Gelfer (Sheffield: Equinox, 2011), 23.

126 Frykholm, *Rapture Culture*, 117.

127 Susan Harding, *The Book of Jerry Falwell: Fundamentalist Language and Politics* (Princeton, NJ: Princeton University Press, 2000), 28.

128 Argüelles, *The Mayan Factor*, 178, 190.

129 Argüelles, *The Transformative Vision*, 137.

130 Argüelles, *The Mayan Factor*, 178; also see 190.

131 Ibid., 179.

132 Argüelles, *The Transformative Vision*, 89.

133 Ibid., 91; also see 272.

134 Ibid., 136–7, 231, 297–311.

135 Ibid., 270–2.

136 Faivre, *Access to Western Esotericism*, 104.

137 Daniel Pinchbeck, *2012: The Year of the Mayan Prophecy* (New York: Penguin, 2006), 11; Daniel Pinchbeck, *2012: The Return of Quetzalcoatl* (New York: Penguin, 2007), 109.

138 Carl Johan Calleman, *The Mayan Calendar and the Transformation of Consciousness* (Rochester, VT: Bear and Company, 2004), 50.

139 Pinchbeck, *2012: The Year of the Mayan Prophecy*, 5–11; Pinchbeck, *2012: The Return of Quetzalcoatl*, 1–2.

140 Argüelles, *The Mayan Factor*, 196.

141 Ibid., 41.

142 Argüelles, *Surfers of the Zuvuya*, 15.

143 Ibid.

144 Alexandra Bruce, *2012: Science or Superstition* (New York: The Disinformation Company, 2009).

145 Geoff Stray, *Beyond 2012: Catastrophe or Ecstasy: A Complete Guide to End-of-Time Predictions* (Lewis: East Sussex, 2006).

146 Argüelles, *The Mayan Factor*, 189, 192.

147 South, *2012: Biography of a Time Traveller*, 226–8; Revelation 7.4 and 14.3.

148 Pinchbeck, *2012: The Year of the Mayan Prophecy*, 4–5; Pinchbeck, *2012: The Return of Quetzalcoatl*, 108–9.

149 Mark Hitchcock, *2012: The Bible and the End of the World* (Eugene OR: Harvest House, 2009), 24, 125.

150 Fernando Ortiz, *Cuban Counterpoint: Tobacco and Sugar*, trans. Harriet de Onis (Durham: Duke University Press, 1995), 98.

151 Rubin, 'Yippees Are Coming', 9.

152 Pinder, *Visions of the City*, 109.

153 José Argüelles, *Earth Ascending: An Illustrated Treatise on the Law Governing Whole Systems* (1984; Rochester, VT: Bear and Co, 1996).

154 Argüelles, *The Mayan Factor*, 192, 196.

155 Argüelles, *Surfers of the Zuvuya*, 17, 19.

156 Jenkins, *The 2012 Story*, 86.

157 Argüelles, *Surfers of the Zuvuya*, 43.

158   Cited in Raskin, *Hoffman*, 129.

159   Wolfe, *Acid Test*, 131.

160   Hoopes, 'Mayanism Comes of (New) Age', 30; Pete Lentini, 'The 2012 Milieu?
      Hybridity, Diversity and Stigmatised Knowledge', in *2012: Decoding the
      Countercultural Apocalypse*, ed. Joseph Gelfer (Sheffield: Equinox, 2011), 70.

161   Pinchbeck, *2012: The Year of the Mayan Prophecy*, 5–11; Pinchbeck, *2012:
      The Return of Quetzalcoatl*, 1–2.

162   Daniel Pinchbeck, *Breaking Open the Head: A Psychedelic Journey into the Heart of
      Contemporary Shamanism* (London: Harper Collins, 2004), 100–1.

163   Pinchbeck, *2012: The Year of the Mayan Prophecy*, 10.

164   Phil Plait, '2012: The Year Nothing Will Happen', *Discover*, 19 May 2008, http://
      blogs.discovermagazine.com/badastronomy/2008/05/19/2012-the-year-nothing-
      will-happen/, accessed 1 September 2012.

165   See, for example, Patrick Geryl, *How to Survive 2012: Tactics and Survival Places for
      the Coming Pole Shift* (Kempton, IL: Adventures Unlimited Press, 2007).

166   Calleman, *The Mayan Calendar*; Barbara Hand Clow, *Catastrophobia: The Truth
      Behind Earth Changes* (Rochester: Bear and Company, 2001); Barbara Hand Clow,
      and Gerry Clow, *Alchemy of Nine Dimensions: The 2011/2012 Prophecies and Nine
      Dimensions of Consciousness* (Charlottesville, VA: Hampton Roads Publishing
      Company, 2010); Jenkins, *The 2012 Story*; John Major Jenkins, 'Approaching 2012:
      Modern Misconceptions versus Reconstructing Ancient Maya Perspectives', in *2012:
      Decoding the Countercultural Apocalypse*, ed. Joseph Gelfer (Sheffield: Equinox,
      2011), 163–81.

167   Zecharia Sitchin, *The End of Days* (New York: William Morrow, 2009).

168   The Official Website of Zechariah Sitchin, http://www.sitchin.com/, accessed 20
      September 2012.

169   Calleman, *The Mayan Calendar*, 105.

170   '13moon', http://www.13moon.com/prophecy%20page.htm, accessed 20 September
      2012.

171   'Birth2012', http://birth2012activation.com/, accessed 20 September 2012.

172   'The End of the World', *Cuzco Inti*, 26 September 2012, http://www.cuscointi.
      com/2012/09/the-end-of-the-world-2012/, accessed 20 October 2012.

173   Gray, *Enlightenment's Wake*, 231.

174   'Saturday, 29 July 1922', in G.I. Gurdjieff, *Gurdjieff's Early Talks 1914–1931* (Book
      Studio, 2014), 148.

Chapter 8

1   Noel O'Sullivan, 'Conservatism', in *The Cambridge History of Twentieth Century
      Political Thought*, eds. Terence Ball and Richard Bellamy (Cambridge: Cambridge
      University Press, 2003), 160.

2   Steven Lukes, 'The grand dichotomy of the twentieth century', in *The Cambridge
      History of Twentieth Century Political Thought*, eds. Terence Ball and Richard Bellamy
      (Cambridge: Cambridge University Press, 2003), 623.

3   See, for example, James Kielkopf, 'What Are the Differences and Similarities between
      Neoliberalism and Neoconservatism?', http://www.quora.com/What-are-the-
      differences-and-similarities-between-neoliberalism-and-neoconservatism, accessed
      22 April 2015.

4   Thomas H. Naylor, 'Neoliberalism: Neoconservatism without a Smirk', *The Second Vermont Republic*, 22 March 2010, http://vermontrepublic.org/neoliberalism-neoconservatism-without-a-smirk/, accessed 22 April 2015.

5   Patricia Ventura, *Neoliberal Culture: Living with American Liberalism* (Farnham: Ashgate, 2012).

6   Francis Fukuyama, *After the Neocons: America at the Crossroads* (London: Profile Books, 2007), 12–13. See also Jean-François Drolet, *American Neoconservatism: The Politics and Culture of a Reactionary Idealism* (London: Hurst and Company, 2011), 53–89; Paul Edward Gottfried, *Leo Strauss and the Conservative Movement in America* (Cambridge: Cambridge University Press, 2012).

7   Vaïsse, *Neoconservatism: The Biography of a Movement*, 7–8.

8   Fukuyama, *After the Neocons*, 5.

9   Hall, *New Times*, 116–7.

10 Bell, *The End of Ideology*, 405. See also Steinfels, *The Neoconservatives*, 47; Spates, 'Counterculture and Dominant Culture Values', 869.

11 Michael Lind, *Made in Texas: George W. Bush and the Southern Takeover of American Politics* (New York: Basic Books, 2003), 115.

12 Steinfels, *The Neoconservatives*, 60.

13 George Nash, 'Forgotten Godfathers: Premature Jewish Conservatives and the Rise of *National Review*', *American Jewish History* 87 no. 2 (1999): 123–57; Rothbard, 'Life in the Old Right', 15–19; Lind, *Made in Texas*, 116–17; Murray Friedman, *The Neoconservative Revolution: Jewish Intellectuals and the Shaping of Public Policy* (Cambridge: Cambridge University Press, 2005), 51, 57; Fukuyama, *After the Neocons*, 18.

14 Nash, 'Forgotten Godfathers', 132.

15 Steinfels, *The Neoconservatives*, 29.

16 Francis Fukuyama, 'The end of history? Well, certainly the end of humans', *Independent*, Review section, 16 June 1999, 4.

17 Drolet, *American Neoconservatism*, 3–5.

18 Morris and Kross, *Historical Dictionary of Utopianism*, xxx.

19 Grant N. Havers, *Leo Strauss and Anglo-American Democracy: A Conservative Critique* (DeKalb, IL: Northern Illinois University Press, 2013).

20 John Gray, *False Dawn: The Delusions of Global Capitalism* (London: Granta, 1998), 100.

21 Gray, *False Dawn*, 132.

22 J.A. Cramb, *The Origins and Destiny of Imperial Britain and Nineteenth Century Europe* (London:Macmillan, 1915).

23 Irving Segal, 'A Teacher's Letter to Young People', in *The Hippie Papers: Notes from the Underground Press*, ed. Jerry Hopkins (New York: Signet Books, 1968), 14.

24 'Port Huron Statement of the Students for a Democratic Society'.

25 Rothbard, 'Life in the Old Right', 15–19; Justin Raimondo, *An Enemy of the State: The Life of Murray N. Rothbard* (Amherst, MA: Prometheus Books, 2000); Nash, 'Forgotten Godfathers', 141.

26 Steinfels, *The Neoconservatives*, 41.

27 Bell, 'Unstable America', 11–26.

28 Ibid., 13.

29 Ibid., 26.

30 Himmelfarb, 'This Will Hurt', x.

31 Gertrude Himmelfarb, Preface to *This Will Hurt: The Restoration of Virtue and Civic Order*, ed. Digby Anderson (New York: The Social Affairs Unit, 1995), x.

32 Gray, *Black Mass*, 95.

33 John Kampfner, *Blair's Wars* (London: The Free Press, 2004), 24.

34 Lind, *Made in Texas*, 115; Steinfels, *The Neoconservatives*, xx.

35 Lind, *Made in Texas*, 137.

36 David S. Katz and Richard H. Popkin, *Messianic Revolution: Radical Religious Politics to the End of the Second Millennium* (London: Penguin, 1999), 222.

37 Washington Post Staff, 'The complete transcript of Netanyahu's address to Congress', *The Washington Post*, 3 March 2015, http://www.washingtonpost.com/blogs/post-politics/wp/2015/03/03/full-text-netanyahus-address-to-congress/, accessed 25 April 2015.

38 Steinfels, *The Neoconservatives*, 71.

39 Fukuyama, 'The end of history?'

40 Ibid., 4.

41 Lenin, 'What Is to Be Done?', 137.

42 Fukuyama, 'The End of History?, 4.

43 Žižek, *End Times*, vii–viii.

44 Fukuyama, *The End of History*, 163; also see 223–34, 300–12.

45 Ibid., 300–1.

46 Ibid., 328.

47 Ibid., 329.

48 Fukuyama, *After the Neocons*, 4, 48–9.

49 Ibid., 3.

50 Fukuyama, *The End of History*, xiii.

51 Ibid., xiii.

52 Fukuyama, *After the Neocons*, 3, 95–113.

53 The Project for the New American Century, archived copy from 9 June 2013, https://web.archive.org/web/20130609154959/http://www.newamericancentury.org/, accessed 24 July 2014.

54 Mark Lagon, 'Memorandum to Opinion Leaders', The Project for the New American Century, 7 January, 1999, https://web.archive.org/web/20130609165624/http://www.newamericancentury.org/iraqjan0799.htm, accessed 24 July 2014.

55 Fukuyama, *After the Neocons*, 1–2.

56 Ibid., x, 70–1.

57 Kenneth Jowitt, 'Rage, Hubris and Regime Change: The Urge to Speed History Along'. *Policy Review* 118 (April–May 2003): 34–8. http://www.hoover.org/research/rage-hubris-and-regime-change, accessed 1 October 2014.

58 Condorcet, *Sketch for a Historical Picture*, 175.

59 Hoskin, 'Newton and Newtonianism', 143–4.

60 Kenneth, Jowitt, *New World Disorder: The Leninist Extinction*. Berkeley: University of California Press, 1992, 88.

61 Jowitt, 'Rage, Hubris and Regime Change', 38.

62 Ibid., online version. http://www.hoover.org/research/rage-hubris-and-regime-change, accessed 5 January 2015.

63 Alan Frachon and Daniel Vernet, *L'Amérique messianique: Les guerres de néo-conservateurs* (Paris: Seuil, 2004).

64 Gray, *Enlightenment's Wake*, 230–1.

65   Thomas Friedman, *The Lexus and the Olive Tree* (New York: Farrar, Strauss and Giroux, 1999), 9; also see xxi.

66   'Bush demands Mid-East democracy', *BBC News* 6 November 2003, http://news.bbc.co.uk/1/hi/world/middle_east/3248119.stm, accessed 25 April 2015

67   Fukuyama, *After the Neocons*, 2, n. 1.

68   Kampfner, *Blair's Wars*, 25.

69   Peter W. Galbraith, *The End of Iraq: How American Incompetence Created a War without End* (London: Simon and Schuster, 2007), 127.

70   L. Paul Bremer III, 'Operation Iraqi Prosperity', *Wall Street Journal*, 20 June 2003, http://online.wsj.com/news/articles/SB105606663932885100, accessed 14 October 2014; see also Fukuyama, *After the Neocons*, 8.

71   Fukuyama, *After the Neocons*, 95–113.

72   Kampfner, *Blair's Wars*, 25.

73   Michael Codner, 'The Two Towers, 2001–13', in *Wars in Peace: British Military Operations since 1991*, ed. Adrian L. Johnson (London: Royal United Services Institute, 2014), 61–2.

74   Fukuyama, *After the Neocons*, 95.

75   Ibid., viii–ix.

76   Ibid., 6.

77   Christopher Meyer, 'Our national interest demands the mother of all U-turns', *The Daily Telegraph*, 23 August 2014, 122.

78   Jowitt, 'Rage, Hubris and Regime Change', on line version http://www.hoover.org/research/rage-hubris-and-regime-change, accessed 5 January 2015.

Chapter 9

1   Hanegraaff, *New Age Religion*, 411–21.

2   R.G. Collingwood, *The Idea of History* (Oxford: Clarendon Press, 1946), 56.

3   Bruno Latour, *We Have Never Been Modern* (Cambridge, MA: Harvard University Press 2006), 107.

Bibliography

Documentaries

Curtis, Adam. *The Century of the Self*, 2002, http://www.imdb.com/title/tt0432232/.

Blogs

Mankey, Jason. 'Paganism & the New Age', *Raising the Horns* (1 September 2014). http://www.patheos.com/blogs/panmankey/2014/09/paganism-the-new-age/.

Web Sites

'13moon', http://www.13moon.com/prophecy%20page.htm.

Anonymous, 'Bush demands Mid-East democracy', BBC News 6 November 2003, http://news.bbc.co.uk/1/hi/world/middle_east/3248119.stm, accessed 25 April 2015.

Anonymous. 'Donald Curtis (1915–1997). Prolific Science of Mind Speaker and Writer', http://cornerstone.wwwhubs.com/Donald_Curtis.html.

Anonymous. 'Introduction: Prophecy of the Royal Maze', http://www.royalmaze.com/john-starr-cooke/introduction-prophecy-of-the-royal-maze/.

Anonymous. 'John Starr Cooke', http://www.royalmaze.com/john-starr-cooke/introduction-prophecy-of-the-royal-maze/.

Anonymous. 'Planned Parenthood: Military Arm of the New Age Movement', http://www.trdd.org/EUGBR_5E.HTM.

'Birth 2012', http://birth2012activation.com/.

Bowen, Michael. 'My Odyssey', http://www.royalmaze.com/my-odyssey-the-first-human-be-in/introduction-to-my-odyssey/.

Bush, George W. *State of the Union Address*, 29 January 2002, http://www.usa-presidents.info/union/gwbush-2.html.

Cooke, John Starr. 'Black Magic Question Mark'. *American Theosophist* 33, no. 8 (August 1945), http://www.royalmaze.com/john-starr-cooke/black-magic-question-mark/.

Cooke, John, and Rosalind Sharp. 'The World of One', http://www.royalmaze.com/the-word-of-one/.

Easy Rider, http://www.imdb.com/title/tt0064276/.

'The End of the World 2012'. *CuzcoInti*, 26 September 2012, http://www.cuscointi.com/2012/09/the-end-of-the-world-2012/.

'Harry Smith (1923–1991), http://www.harrysmitharchives.com/1_bio/index.html.

Helen Weaver: Writer, Translator, Astrologer. http://www.helenweaver.com/.

London Wellbeing Festival, http://www.mindbodyspirit.co.uk/events/london-festival-2015.

'Mister Tambourine Mind', http://www.artgallery.nsw.gov.au/collection/works/
DA17.1970/.
National Secular Society. 'Jonathan Meades', http://www.secularism.org.uk/
jonathanmeades.html.
The Official Website of Zechariah Sitchin, http://www.sitchin.com/.
Port Huron Statement of the Students for a Democratic Society', Courtesy Office of Sen.
Tom Hayden, http://www.h-net.org/~hst306/documents/huron.html.
The Project for the New American Century, archived copy from 9 June 2013, https://
web.archive.org/web/20130609154959/http://www.newamericancentury.org/.
Sex, Drugs and Rock 'N' Roll: The Sixties' Revealed, UK Channel 5 TV series, http://
www.channel5.com/shows/sex-drugs-and-rock-n-roll-the-60s-revealed/episodes/
episode-1-381, accessed 10 October 2014.
'The Sixties', UKTV – Yesterday, http://yesterday.uktv.co.uk/shows/Sixties/watch-online/,
accessed 10 October 2014.
'Timothy Leary e Aleister Crowley'.Extract from interview on PBS 'Late Night America',
1980, http://www.youtube.com/watch?v=DaVeGZE6VU8.
Transition Network. https://www.transitionnetwork.org/.
'Vietnam War: Allied Troop Levels 1960–73', http://www.americanwarlibrary.com/
vietnam/vwatl.htm.

Books and Articles

Adorno, Theodor. *The Stars Down to Earth*. London: Routledge, 1994.
Adorno, Theodor, Else Frenkel-Brunswick, Daniel J. Levinson, and R. Nevitt Sanford.
The Authoritarian Personality, abridged edition. 1950. New York and London: W.W.
Norton and Company, 1982.
Ahern, Geoffrey. *Sun at Midnight: The Rudolf Steiner Movement and the Western Esoteric
Tradition*. Wellingborough: Aquarian Press, 1984.
Akhtar, Miriam, and Steve Humphries. *Far Out: The Dawning of New Age Britain*. Bristol:
Sansom and Company, 1999.
Albanese, Catherine L. *A Republic of Mind and Spirit: A Cultural History of American
Metaphysical Religion*. New Haven, CT: Yale University Press, 2007.
Alcott, Louisa May. *A Perilous Play*. 1869, reprint Dido Press, n.d.
Ali, Tariq. *Street Fighting Years: An Autobiography of the Sixties*. London: Verso, 1995.
Altman, Steven. 'Path of the Quetzalcoatl: Sacred Pilgrimage to Mexico'. *Caduceus*
89(2014): 6–9.
Anderson, Terry. *The Movement and the Sixties: Protest in America from Greensboro to
Wounded Knee*. Oxford: Oxford, 1995.
Ankerberg, John, and John Weldon. *Encyclopaedia of New Age Beliefs*. Eugene, OR:
Harvest House, 1996.
Anonymous. 'An Address to Politicians'. *Oz* 3 (1967): 13–14.
Anonymous. 'Massage to the Underground'. *International Times*, 15–28 December 1967.
Anonymous. 'THE NEW SOCIETY: Who's winning the battle of the generations?'
Observer Colour Supplement, 3 December 1967, 7.
Anonymous. 'The Great Beast – 666 Revisited', *International Times*, 5–20 October
1967, 16.

Anonymous. 'Love, Leary, LSD'. *Los Angeles Free Press*, 13 January 1967. In *The Hippie Papers: Notes from the Underground Press*, edited by Jerry Hopkins, 82–7. New York: Signet Books, 1968.

Anonymous. 'Sociology Must Steer Our Society Towards a Utopia'. *Network: Magazine of the Sociological Association* 117 (Summer 2014): 17.

Anonymous, 'Syriza's Dead End', *The Times*, 27 April 2015, 29.

Argüelles, José. *The Transformative Vision: Reflections on the Nature and History of Human Expression*. Berkeley: Shambhala, 1975.

Argüelles, José. *The Mayan Factor: Path Beyond Technology*. Santa Fe: Bear and Company, 1987.

Argüelles, José. *Surfers of the Zuvuya: Tales of Interdimensional Travel*. Rochester, VT: Bear and Company, 1989.

Argüelles, José. *Earth Ascending: An illustrated Treatise on the Law Governing Whole Systems*. 1984. Rochester, VT: Bear and Co., 1996.

Aristotle. *Poetics*. Translated by Stephen Halliwell. Cambridge, MA: Harvard University Press, 1999.

Aston, Nigel. *Religion and Revolution in France, 1780–1804*. Washington, DC: Catholic University of America Press, 2000.

Auden, W.H. *W. H. Auden Poems Selected by John Fuller*. London: Faber and Faber, 2000.

Augustine. *City of God*. Translated by, Henry Bettenson. Harmondsworthand Middlesex: Penguin, 1972.

Baer, Randall N. *Inside the New Age Nightmare*. Lafayette: Huntington House, 1989.

Bailey, Alice A. *The Unfinished Autobiography*. New York and London: Lucis Publishing Company, 1951.

Bailey, Alice A. 'The Subjective Basis of the New World Religion'. In *The Externalisation of the Hierarchy*, edited by Alice A. Bailey, 502. New York: Lucis Publishing Company, 1957.

Bailey, Alice A. *The Reappearance of the Christ*. London and New York: Lucis Publishing Companies, 2012.

Baillie, John. *The Belief in Progress*. London, Glasgow, and Toronto: Oxford University Press, 1951.

Ball, Bryan. *A Great Expectation: Eschatological Thought in English Protestantism to 1660*. Leiden: Brill, 1975.

Ball, Terence. 'Green Political Theory'. In *The Cambridge History of Twentieth Century Thought*, edited by Terence Ball and Richard Bellamy, 534–50. Cambridge: Cambridge University Press, 2003.

Ball, Terence, and Richard Bellamy, eds. *The Cambridge History of Twentieth Century Thought*. Cambridge: Cambridge University Press, 2003.

Barber, John. *The Road to Eden: Studies in Christianity and Culture*, 363. Palo Alto, CA: Academic Press, 2008.

Barkun, Michael. *A Culture of Conspiracy: Apocalyptic Visions in Contemporary America*. Berkeley: University of California Press, 2003.

Barkun, Michael. *Disaster and the Millennium*. Syracuse: Yale University Press, 1986.

Baudrillard, Jean. *Simulacra and Simulations*. Chicago: University of Michigan Press, 1994.

Becker, Carl. *The Heavenly City of the Enlightenment Philosophers*. Storrs Lectures. New Haven and London: Yale University Press, 1932.

Becker, Carl. *The Declaration of Independence: A Study in the History of Political Ideas*. New York: Vintage, 1958.

Bedford, Sybille. *Aldous Huxley: A Biography*. London: Pan Macmillan, 1993.

Bell, Daniel. *The End of Ideology: On the Exhaustion of Political Ideas in the Fifties*. New York: The Free Press, 1962.

Bell, Daniel. 'Unstable America: Transitory & Permanent Factors in a National Crisis'. *Encounter* 34 (June 1970): 17–18.

Bell, Daniel. *The Coming of Post-Industrial Society*. Harmondsworth: Penguin, 1976.

Bender, Barbara, and Margaret Winer. *Contested Landscapes: Movement, Exile and Place*. Oxford: Berg, 2001.

Bennet, Julius R. *The Riddle of the Aquarian Age*. London: London Astrological Research Society, 1925.

Bennett, Alan. 'The Festival of Britain'. Published in the 'Interior Worlds' supplement (December 2000) to *World of Interiors*, cited in Harris, Brian. *Seeking a Role: The United Kingdom 1950–7 (The New Oxford History of England)*. Oxford Clarendon Press, 2011.

Bentham, Jeremy. 'From An Introduction to the Principles of Morals and Legislation'. In J.S. Mill and Jeremy Bentham, *Utilitarianism and Other Essays*, edited by Alan Ryan, 65–112. London: Penguin, 1987.

Berke, Joseph. 'Counter Culture: the creation of an alternative society'. *IT (International Times)*, 13–31 December 1968.

Berke, Joseph. *Counter Culture: the Creation of an Alternative Society*. London: Peter Owen, 1969.

Berlin, Isaiah. *Against the Current: Essays in the History of Ideas*. London: Pimlico, 1979.

Berlin, Isaiah. *The Crooked Timber of Humanity: Chapters in the History of Ideas*. New York: Random House, 1991.

Bishop, Claire. *Artificial Hells: Participatory Art and the Politics of Spectatorship*. London: Verso, 2012.

Blackmore, Susan. *The Meme Machine*. Oxford: Oxford University Press, 1999.

Blake, William. 'Annotations to Swedenborg's "The Wisdom of Angels Concerning Divine providence", c. 1790, Milton'. In *Complete Writings*, edited by Geoffrey Keynes. Oxford: Oxford University Press, 1971.

Blake, William. 'Jerusalem'. In *Complete Writings with Variant Readings*, edited by Geoffrey Keynes. Oxford: Oxford University Press, 1971.

Blake, William. 'Milton'. In *Complete Writings with Variant Readings*, edited by Geoffrey Keynes. Oxford: Oxford University Press, 1971.

Blake, William. *The Marriage of Heaven and Hell*. London, 1790. Cambridge: The Blake Archive Fitzwilliam Museum, 2008, http://www.blakearchive.org/exist/blake/archive/work.xq?workid=mhh.

Blanchard, Paula. *Margaret Fuller: From Transcendentalism to Revolution*. Reading, MA: Addison-Wesley Publishing Company, 1987.

Blavatsky, H.P. *Isis Unveiled*, 2 Vols. 1877. Pasadena: Theosophical University Press, 1976.

Blavatsky, H.P. *The Secret Doctrine*, Vols. 1 and 2, facsimile of the original edition of 1888. Los Angeles: The Theosophy Company, 1982.

Bloch, Ernst. *The Principle of Hope*, 3 Vols. Translated by Neville Plaice, Stephen Plaice, and Paul Knight, revised edition. Cambridge, MA: MIT Press, 1986.

Bloch, Ernst. *The Spirit of Utopia*. Translated by Anthony A. Nassar. Stanford: Stanford University Press, 2000.

Bloch, Nadine. 'The day they levitated the Pentagon'. *Waging Nonviolence* 21 (October 2012), http://wagingnonviolence.org/feature/the-day-they-levitated-the-pentagon/.

Bloch, Ruth H. *Visionary Republic: Millennial Themes in American Thought, 1756–1800*. Cambridge: Cambridge University Press, 1985.

Bloom, Alexander, ed. *Long Time Gone: Sixties America Then and Now*. Oxford: Oxford University Press, 2001.

Bloom, William, ed. *The New Age: An Anthology of Essential Writings*. London: Rider, 1991.

Bloomfield, Michael. 'Dylan Goes Electric'. In *The Sixties: The Decade Remembered Now, By the People Who Lived It Then*, edited by Lynda Rosen Obst, 150–2. New York: Random House/Rolling Stone, 1977.

Bogdan, Henrik. 'Envisioning the Birth of a New Aeon: Dispensationalism and Millenarianism in the Thelemic Tradition'. In *Aleister Crowley and Western Esotericism*, edited by Henrik Bogdan and Martin P. Starr, 89–106. Oxford: Oxford University Press, 2012.

Bogdan, Henrik, and Martin P. Starr, eds. *Aleister Crowley and Western Esotericism*. Oxford: Oxford University Press, 2012.

Bowler, Peter J. *The Invention of Progress, The Victorians and the Past*. Oxford: Basil Blackwell, 1989.

Boym, Svetlana. *The Future of Nostalgia*. New York: Basic Books, 2001.

Bradbury, Malcolm. *The History Man*. London: Penguin, 1975.

Braden, William. *The Age of Aquarius: Technology and the Cultural Revolution*. London: Eyre and Spottiswoode, 1971.

Bremer III, L. Paul. 'Operation Iraqi Prosperity'. *Wall Street Journal*, 20 June 2003, http://online.wsj.com/news/articles/SB105606663932885100.

Bruce, Alexandra. *2012: Science or Superstition*. New York: The Disinformation Company, 2009.

Burning Man, http://burningman.org/culture/philosophical-center/10-principles/.

Burns, Dylan. 'An Unlikely Love Affair: Plato, the Netherlands, and Life after Westotericism'. In *Hermes in the Academy: Ten Years' Study of Western Esotericism at the University of Amsterdam*, edited by Wouter J. Hanegraaff and Joyce Pijnenburg, 107–9. Amsterdam: Amsterdam University Press, 2009.

Burroughs, William S. *Junky*. London: Penguin, 2008.

Burroughs, William S. 'The Fall of Art'. In *The Adding Machine*. New York: Grove Press, 2013.

Burroughs, William S., and Allen Ginsberg. *The Yage Letters*. London: Penguin, 1979.

Bury, J.B. *The Idea of Progress: An Inquiry into Its Growth and Origin*. London: Macmillan, 1932.

Butler, Samuel. *Erewhon*, 2nd ed. 1901. New York: Dover Publications, 2002.

Calleman, Carl. *The Mayan Calendar and the Transformation of Consciousness*. Rochester, VT: Bear and Company, 2004.

Callenbach, Ernest. *Ecotopia*. Berkeley: Banyan Tree Books, 2004.

Campbell, Bruce H. *Ancient Wisdom Revived: A History of the Theosophical Movement*. Berkeley: University of California Press, 1980.

Campbell, Colin. *The Romantic Spirit and the Spirit of Modern Consumerism*. no place: Alcuin Academics, 2005.

Campion, Nicholas. *The Great Year: Astrology, Millenarianism, and History in the Western Tradition*. London: Penguin (Non-Classics), 1994.

Campion, Nicholas. 'The Age of Aquarius: a Modern Constellation Myth'. In *Astronomy and Cultural Diversity, Proceedings of the 1999 Oxford VI Conference on Archaeoastronomy and Astronomy in Culture*, edited by César Esteban and Juan Antonio Belmonte, 277–82. Tenerife Oranismo Autonomo de Museos del Cablido de Tenerife, 2000.

Campion, Nicholas. 'The Beginning of the Age of Aquarius'. *Correlation* 19, no. 1 (Summer 2000): 7–16.

Campion, Nicholas. 'From Stonehenge to Seattle: Eco-Protest, Archaeoastronomy and New Age Cosmology'. In *Proceedings of the INSAP III Conference, Memorie della Società Astronomica Italiana (Journal of the Italian Astronomical Society)* Special Number 1, edited by Salvatore Serio, 202–5. Roma: Istituti Editoriali E Poligrafici Internatazionali, 2002.

Campion, Nicholas. 'The 2012 Mayan Calendar Prophecies in the Context of the Western Millenarian Tradition'. In *Archaeoastronomy and Ethnoastronomy: Building Bridges Between Cultures*, Proceedings of International Astronomy Union Symposium 278, edited by Clive Ruggles, 249–54. Cambridge: Cambridge University Press, 2011.

Campion, Nicholas. 'Astronomy and Political Theory'. In *The Role of Astronomy in Society and Culture*, edited by David Valls-Gabaud and Alec Boksenberg, 595–602. Cambridge: Cambridge University Press, 2011.

Campion, Nicholas. *Astrology and Popular Religion in the Modern West: Prophecy, Cosmology and the New Age Movement*. Abingdon: Ashgate, 2012.

Campion, Nicholas. 'The 2012 Phenomenon in Context: Millenarianism, New Age and Cultural Astronomy'. In *Ancient Cosmologies and Modern Prophets*, edited by Ivan Šprac and Peter Pehani, 15–31. Lubljana: Anthropological Notebooks year XIX, supplement, 2013.

Campion, Nicholas, Patrick Curry, and Jacques Halbronn. *La Vie Astrologique Il Y A Cent Ans*. Paris: Edition Guy Trédaniel, 1992.

Carey, John, ed. *The Faber Book of Utopias*. London: Faber and Faber, 1999.

Carlyle, Thomas. 'Signs of the Times'. In *The Spirit of the Age: Victorian Essays*, edited by Gertrude Himmelfarb, 31–49. Yale: Yale University Press, 2007.

Carter, John. *Sex and Rockets: The Occult World of Jack Parsons*. Port Townsend, WA: Feral House, 2004.

Cassirer, Ernst. *The Philosophy of the Enlightenment*. 1951. Princeton: Princeton University Press, 1979.

Castaneda, Carlos. *The Teachings of Don Juan: a Yaqui Way of Knowledge*. Oakland: University of California Press, 1968.

Cavan, Sherri. *Hippies of the Haight*. St Louis: New Critics Press, 1972.

Chambers, Robert. *Vestiges of the Natural History of Creation and Other Evolutionary Writings*. 1884. Chicago: University of Chicago Press, 1994.

Chamish, Barry. 'Amazing and Accurate Expose of the New Age by a Secular Jew', http://www.jesus-is-lord.com/newage.htm.

Chance, J. Bradley. *Jerusalem, the Temple, and the New Age in Luke-Acts*. Georgia: Mercer University Press, 1988.

Cheiro. *Cheiro's World Predictions: The Fate of Europe, the Future of the USA, the Coming War of Nations, the Restoration of the Jews*. Albuquerque, NM: Sun Publishing Company, 1981.

Chryssides, George D. 'Is God a Space Alien? The Cosmology of the Raëlian Church'. *Culture and Cosmos* 4, no. 1 (Spring/Summer 2000), 36–53.

Churton, Tobias. *Aleister Crowley: The Biography*. London: Watkins Books, 2011.

Claeys, Gregory, ed. *Utopias of the British Enlightenment*. Cambridge: Cambridge University Press, 1994.

Claeys, Gregory. 'The Origins of Dystopia: Wells, Huxley and Orwell'. In *The Cambridge Companion to Utopian Literature*, edited by Gregory Claeys, 107–31. Cambridge: Cambridge University Press, 2010.

Claeys, Gregory. *Searching for Utopia: the History of an Idea*. London: Thames and Hudson, 2011.

Clark, Fraser. 'The Final Word on Drugs'. In *Psychedelia Britannica: Hallucinogenic Drugs in Britain*, edited by Antonio Melechi, 185–204. London: Turnaround, 1997.

Clow, Barbara Hand. *Catastrophobia: The Truth behind Earth Changes*. Rochester, VT: Bear and Company, 2001.

Clow, Barbara Hand with Gerry Clow. *Alchemy of Nine Dimensions: The 2011/2012 Prophecies and Nine Dimensions of Consciousness*. Charlottesville, VA: Hampton Roads Publishing Company, 2010.

Codner, Michael. 'The Two Towers, 2001–13'. In *Wars in Peace: British Military Operations since 1991*, edited by Adrian L. Johnson, 49–87. London: Royal United Services Institute, 2014.

Collingwood, R.G. *The Idea of History*. Oxford: Clarendon Press, 1946.

Cohn, Norman. *The Pursuit of the Millennium: Revolutionary Millenarians and Mystical Anarchists of the Middle Ages*. 1957. London: Paladin, 1970.

Cohn, Norman. *Cosmos, Chaos and the World to Come: The Ancient Roots of Apocalyptic Faith*. New Haven and London: Yale University Press, 1993.

Cole, Michael et al. *What Is the New Age?* London: Hodder and Stoughton, 1990.

Coleman, Stephen, and Paddy O'Sullivan, eds. *News from Nowhere: A Vision for Our Time*. Bideford: Green Books, 2000.

Collingwood, R.G. *The Idea of History*. Oxford: Clarendon Press, 1946.

Comte, Auguste. *System of Positive Polity: or, Treatise on Sociology, Instituting the Religion of Humanity*, 4 Vols. Translated by John Henry Bridges. Paris 1851–4. London: Longmans, 1875.

Copernicus, Nicolaus. *On the Revolutions of the Heavenly Spheres*. Translated by Charles Glenn Wallis. Amherst, NY: Prometheus Books, 1995.

Corbin, Henri. 'Mundus Imaginalis: The Imaginary and the Imaginal'. *Spring* 15 (1972): 1–19.

Couliano, I.P. *Out of This World: Otherworldy Journeys from Gilgamesh to Albert Einstein*. Boston: Shambhala, 1991.

Cramb, J.A. *The Origins and Destiny of Imperial Britain and Nineteenth Century Europe*. London: Macmillan, 1915.

Crème, Benjamin. *The Reappearance of the Christ and the Masters of Wisdom*. London: Tara Press, 1980.

Crowley, Aleister. *The Book of Oz* (Liber LXXVII), http://hermetic.com/crowley/libers/lib77.html.

Crowley, Aleister. *Diary of a Drug Fiend*. 1922. York Beach: Samuel Weiser, 1970.

Crowley, Aleister. *The Confessions of Aleister Crowley*. edited by John Symonds and Kenneth Grant. 1979. London, Penguin, 1989.

Crowley, Aleister. *The Book of the Law: Liber Al Vel Legis*. San Francisco, CA: Red Wheel/Weiser, 2011.

Crowley, Vivianne. *Wicca: the Old Religion in the New Age*, Wellingborough: Aquarian Press, 1989.

Cumbey, Constance E. *The Hidden Dangers of the Rainbow: The New Age Movement and Our Coming Age of Barbarism*. Shreveport, LA: Huntingdon House, 1983.

Cumming, Tim. 'Destination Further: William Burroughs' South American Adventure', http://timcumming.wordpress.com/.

Curtis, Donald. *New Age Understanding*. Unity Village, MO: Unity Books, 1973.

Curtis, Edith Roelker. *A Season in Utopia: The Story of Brook Farm*. New York: Thomas Nelson and Sons, 1961.

Curtiss, Harriette Augusta, and Frank Homer Curtiss. *The Message of Aquaria*. London: L.N. Fowler & Co., 1927.

Dale, Eric. *Hegel, the End of History and the Future*. Cambridge: Cambridge University Press, 2014.

Dass, Ram, and Ralph Metzner with Gary Bravo. *Birth of a Psychedelic Culture: Conversations about Leary, the Harvard Experiments, Millbrook and the Sixties*. Santa Fe: Synergetic Press, 2010.

Davie, Grace. *Religion in Britain since 1945: Believing Without belonging*. Oxford: Wiley-Blackwell, 1994.

Davis, Fred. 'Why all of us may be hippies someday'. *Trans-Action* 5, no. 2 (1967): 10–18.

Davis, Lennard. *Enforcing Normalcy: Disability, Deafness and the Body*. London: Verso, 1995.

Dawkins, Richard, *The Selfish Gene*, Oxford: Oxford University Press, 1989.

Davis, J.C. 'Thomas More's Utopia: Sources, Legacy and Interpretation'. In *The Cambridge Companion to Utopian Literature*, edited by Gregory Claeys, 28–50. Cambridge: Cambridge University Press, 2010.

Debray, Régis. *Revolution in the Revolution?* Translated by Bobbye Ortiz. Harmondsworth: Penguin, 1967.

De Condorcet, Antoine-Nicolas. *Sketch for a Historical Picture of the Progress of the Human Mind*. Translated by June Barraclough. New York: Noon Day Press, 1955.

De Geus, Marius. *Ecological Utopias: Envisioning the Sustainable Society*. Utrecht: International Books, 1999.

Delacampagne, Christian. 'The Enlightenment Project: A Reply to Schmidt'. *Political Theory* 29, no. 1 (February 2001): 80–5.

De Maistre, Joseph. *Considerations on France*. Translated by Richard A. Lebrun. Cambridge: Cambridge University Press, 1999.

D'Emilio, John. 'Placing Gay in the Sixties'. In *Long Time Gone: Sixties America Then and Now*, edited by Alexander Bloom, 210, 209–29. Oxford: Oxford University Press, 2001.

De Montaigne, Michel. 'Of Cannibals'. In *The Complete Essays*, translated and edited by M.A. Screech, 233. London: Penguin Classics, 1993.

Desaguliers, John Theophilus. *The Newtonian System of the World, the Best Model of Government: an Allegorical Poem*, II, 17–18. London: 1728.

Desroche, Henri. *The Sociology of Hope*. Translated by Carol Martin-Sperry. London: Routledge & Kegan Paul, 1979.

De Tocqueville, Alexis. *Democracy in America*, translated by Gerald E. Bevan. London: Penguin, 2003.

Dhúil, CaítríonaNí. 'Engendering the Future: Bloch's Utopian Philosophy in Dialogue with Gender Theory'. In *The Privatization of Hope: Ernst Bloch and the Future of Utopia*, SIC 8, vol. 8, edited by Peter Thompson and Slavoj Žižek, 144–63. London: Duke University Press, 2013.

Diogenes Laertius. 'Zeno'. In *Lives of Eminent Philosophers*. Translated by R.D. Hicks, vol. 2, 110–263. London: William Heinemann, 1925.

Dixon, Jeanne. *My Life and Prophecies*. New York: William Morrow and Company, 1969.

Doan, Ruth Alden. *The Miller Heresy, Millennialism, and American Culture*. Philadelphia, PA: Temple University Press, 1987.

Donnelly, Mark. *Sixties Britain*. Harlow: Pearson Education Ltd., 2005.

Dowling, Levi. *The Aquarian Gospel of Jesus the Christ*. 1907. Chadwell Heath: L.N. Fowler, 1980.

Draper, Derek. 'I used to live a shallow life'. *Times*, 21 February 2001, 3.

Dresser, Horatio W. *A History of the New Thought Movement*. 1919. Nu Vision, 2008.

Drolet, Jean-François. *American Neoconservatism: The Politics and Culture of a Reactionary Idealism*. London: Hurst and Company, 2011.

Dryden, John. *Almanzor and Almahide, or, the Conquest of Granada by the Spaniards. A Tragedy*. London, 1673.

Duncombe, Stephen. *Notes from Underground: Zines and the Politics of Alternative Culture*. London: Verso, 1997.

Eagleton, Terry. *Ideology: An Introduction*. London: Verso, 1991.

Eagleton, Terry. *The Idea of Culture*. Oxford: Blackwell, 2000.

Eco, Umberto. 'Travels in Hyperreality', chap. 1, and 'The Return of the Middle Ages: Dreaming of the Middle Ages', chap. 2. In *Faith in Fakes: Travels in Hyperreality*, edited by Umberto Eco, London: Minerva, 1995, 1–58, 61–85.

Eco, Umberto. *The Book of Legendary Lands*. London: Thames and Hudson, 2013.

Eddy, Mary Baker. *Science and Health with Key to the Scriptures*. Boston: The First Church of Christ, Scientist, revised edition, 1875.

Edelstein, Dan. *The Enlightenment: A Genealogy*. Chicago: Chicago University Press, 2010.

Edinger, Edward F. *The Aion Lectures: Exploring the Self in C.G. Jung's Aion*. Toronto: Inner City Books, 1996.

Eisenhower, David. 'Grandfather leaves the White House'. In *The Sixties: The Decade Remembered Now, by the People Who Lived It Then*, edited by Lynda Rosen Obst, 20–1. New York: Random House/Rolling Stone, 1977.

Eliade, Mircea. *The Myth of the Eternal Return or, Cosmos and History*. Princeton: Princeton University Press, 1954.

Ellwood, Robert S. *Religious and Spiritual Groups in Modern America*. New Jersey: Garland, 1973.

Ellwood, Robert S. 'The American Theosophical Synthesis'. In *The Occult in America: New Historical Perspectives*, edited by Howard Kerr and Charles Crow. Urbana: University of Illinois Press, 1983.

Elstob, Lynne, and Howes, Anne. *The Glastonbury Festivals*. Glastonbury: Gothic Image Publications, 1987.

Emerson, Ralph Waldo. 'Nature'. In *Nature and Selected Essays*. London: Penguin, 1982.

Emerson, Ralph Waldo. *Ralph Waldo Emerson*, edited by Richard Poirier. Oxford: Oxford University Press, 1990.

Emmerling, Leonard. *Pollock*. Koln: Taschen, 1999.

Engels, Frederick, 'Socialism: Utopian and Scientific'. In Karl Marx, Frederick Engels, and V.I. Lenin, *On Historical Materialism*, compiled T. Borodulina. Moscow: Progress Publishers, 1972, 179–98.

Erdman, David V. 'Blake's Early Swedenborgianism: A Twentieth-Century Legend', *Comparative Literature* 5, no. 3 (Summer, 1953): 247–57.

Ertan, Deniz, *Dane Rudhyar, His Music, Thought and Art*. New York: University of Rochester Press, 2009.

Esler, Anthony. *Bombs, Beards and Barricades: 150 Years of Youth in Revolt*. New York: Stein and Day, 1971.

Evans, Richard. *In Defence of History*. London: Granta Books, 1997.

Evans, Warren Felt. *The New Age and the Messenger*. 1874. Memphis: General Books, 2012.

Everard, John. 'The Eleventh Book, Of the Common Mind to Tat'. In *The Corpus Hermeticum; The Divine Pymander in XVII books*. London: 1650.

Fagan, Cyril. 'Interpretation of the Zodiac of Constellations'. *Spica* 1, no. 1 (Oct 1951): 20–4.

Faivre, Antoine. *Access to Western Esotericism*. Albany: State University of New York Press, 1994.

Farrar, Janet, and Stewart Farrar. *The Witches Way: Principles, Rituals and Beliefs of Modern Witchcraft*. London: Robert Hale, 1984.

Farren, Mick. 'Angels and Violence'. *International Times*, 17–30 November 1967: 13.

Farren, Mick. *The Texts of Festival*. London: Granada Publishing, 1973.

Farthing, G.A. *Theosophy: The Truth Revealed*. London: The Theosophical Publishing House, 2000.

Ferguson, Duncan Sheldon, ed. *New Age Spirituality: An Assessment*. Louisville: Westminster/John Knox Press, 1993.

Ferguson, Marilyn. *The Aquarian Conspiracy: Personal and Social Transformations in the 1980s*. London: Paladin Books, 1982.

Festinger, Leon, Henry W. Riecken, and Stanley Schachter, *When Prophecy Fails*. 1956. New York: Harper and Row, 1964

Fichte, Johann. 'Idea of Universal History in Characteristics of the Present Age', 'The Origins and Limits of History'. In *Works*, Vol. 2. Translated by William Smith. Edinburgh, 1844.

Fitzgerald, F. Scott. 'My Generation'. *Esquire* (October 1928), cited in Stephenson, *The daybreak boys*.

Foss, Daniel A. *Freak Culture: Lifestyle and Politics*. New York: E.P. Dutton & Co., 1972.

Foss, Daniel A., and Ralph W. Larkin. 'From "The Gates of Eden" to "Day of the Locust": An Analysis of the Dissident Youth Movement of the 1960s and Its Heirs in the Early 1970s – the Post-movement Groups'. *Theory and Society* 3, no. 1 (Spring 1976): 45–64.

Foucault, Michel. 'Technologies of the Self'. In *Technologies of the Self: A Seminar with Michel Foucault*. edited by L.H. Martin, H. Gutman, and P.H. Hinton, 16–49. Amherst: University of Massachusetts Press, 1988.

Foucault, Michel. *History of Madness*. London: Routledge, 2006.

Fountain, Nigel. *Underground: The London Alternative Press, 1966–74*. London: Routledge, Chapman and Hall, 1988.

Fowler, William. 'Beats and beatniks, from New York to London and Beyond'. In *The Party's Over*. London: BFI, 2010.

Fox, Emmet. *The Zodiac and the Bible: The End of the World*. 1933. Marina del Ray, CA: De Vorss and Company 1961.

Frachon, Alan, and Daniel Vernet. *L' Amérique messianique: Les guerres de néo-conservateurs*. Paris: Seuil, 2004.

Francis, Richard. 'The Ideology of Brook Farm'. In *Studies in the American Renaissance*, edited by Joel Myerson, 1–48. Boston: Twaynbe, 1978.

Frank, Thomas. *The Conquest of Cool: Business Culture, Counterculture, and the Rise of Hip Consumerism*. Chicago: University of Chicago Press, 1997.

Frankel, Boris. *The Post-Industrial Utopians*. Cambridge: Polity Press, 1987.

Friedman, Murray. *The Neoconservative Revolution: Jewish Intellectuals and the Shaping of Public Policy*. Cambridge: Cambridge University Press, 2005.

Friedman, Thomas. *The Lexus and the Olive Tree*. New York: Farrar, Strauss and Giroux, 1999.

Frost, Stanley B. *Old Testament Apocalyptic*. London: Routledge and Kegan Paul, 1952.

Fryer, Peter. 'Inside the Underground', *Observer*, colour magazine, 3 December 1967, 13–17.

Frykholm, Amy Johnson. *Rapture Culture: Left Behind in Evangelical America*. Oxford: Oxford University Press, 2004.

Fukuyama, Francis. 'The End of History?', *The National Interest* 16 (Summer 1989): 3–18.

Fukuyama, Francis. *The End of History and the Last Man*. London: Penguin, 1991.

Fukuyama, Francis. 'The end of history? Well, certainly the end of humans'. *Independent,* Review section, 16 June 1999, 4.

Fukuyama, Francis. *After the Neocons: America at the Crossroads*. London: Profile Books, 2007.

Fuller, J.F.C. *The Star in the West: A Critical Essay Upon the Works of Aleister Crowley*. London: Walter Scott Publishing, 1907.

Fuller, R. Buckminster. *Utopia or Oblivion: The Prospects for Humanity*. Harmondsworth, Penguin, 1972.

Gage, John. 'JMW Turner and Solar Myth'. In *The Sun Is God: Painting, Literature and Mythology in the Nineteenth Century*, edited by J.B. Bullen, 39. Oxford: Oxford University Press, 1989.

Galbraith, Peter W. *The End of Iraq: How American Incompetence Created a War Without End*. London: Simon and Schuster, 2007.

Gans, Herbert J. *Popular Culture and High Culture: An Analysis and Evaluation of Taste*, 1974. New York: Basic Books, 1999, revised edition.

Garin, Eugenio, *Astrology in the Renaissance: The Zodiac of Life*. London and Boston: Routledge, 1976.

Garrard, Graeme. *Rousseau's Counter-Enlightenment: A Republican Critique of the Philosophes*. Albany: State University of New York Press, 2003.

Garrard, Graeme. *Counter-Enlightenments from the Eighteenth Century to the Present*. London: Routledge, 2006.

Garrett, Clarke. 'Swedenborg and the Mystical Enlightenment in Late Eighteenth Century England'. *Journal of the History of Ideas* 45, no. 1 (1984): 69.

Geertz, Clifford. 'Religion as a Cultural System'. In *Anthropological Approaches to the Study of Religion*, edited by Michael P. Banton, 1–46. New York: Frederick A. Praeger Press, 1966.

Gelfer, Joseph, ed. *2012: Decoding the Countercultural Apocalypse*. Sheffield: Equinox, 2011.

Genesis Breyer P-Orridge. 'General Order Master'. *Ultraculture Journal, One* (2007; revised edition, 2014), 12–27.

Geoghegan, Vincent. *Marxism and Utopianism*. London: Methuen, 1987.

Geoghegan, Vincent. 'An Anti-humanist Utopia?' In *The Privatization of Hope: Ernst Bloch and the Future of Utopia*, edited by Peter Thompson and Slavoj Žižek, 37–60. London: Duke University Press, 2013.

Geryl, Patrick. *How to Survive 2012: Tactics and Survival Places for the Coming Pole Shift*. Kempton, IL: Adventures Unlimited Press, 2007.

Giddens, Anthony. 'Neoprogressivism: A New Agenda for Social Democracy'. In *The Progressive Manifesto*, edited by Anthony Giddens, Cambridge: Polity Press, 2003, 1–34.

Ginsberg, Allen. 'Coming to Terms with the Hells Angels'. In *The Sixties: The Decade Remembered Now, by the People Who Lived It Then*, edited by Lynda Rosen Obst, 160–2. New York: Random House/Rolling Stone, 1977.

Ginsberg, Allen. 'Howl, Parts I and II', lines 1–6. In *The New American Poetry 1945–1960*, edited by Donald M. Allen, 182. Berkeley and Los Angeles: University of California Press, 1999.

Ginsberg, Allen. 'Notes for Howl and Other Poems'. In *The New American Poetry 1945–1960*, edited by Donald M. Allen, 414–18. Berkeley and Los Angeles: University of California Press, 1999.

Ginsberg, Allen, 'Demonstration or Spectacle as Example, As Communication, or How to Make a March/Spectacle', *Berkeley Barb,* 19 November 1965, in *The Portable Sixties Reader*, edited by Ann Charles, 208–12. London: Penguin, 2002.

Godwin, Joscelyn. *The Theosophical Enlightenment*. New York: State University of New York Press, 1994.

Goffman, Ken, and Dan Joy. *Counter Culture through the Ages: From Abraham to Acid House*. New York: Villard Books, 2005.

Gordin, Michael D., Helen Tilley, and Gyan Prakesh, 'Introduction: Utopia and Dystopia Beyond Space and Time'. In *Utopia/Dystopia: Conditions of Historical Possibility*, edited by Michael D. Gordin, Helen Tilley, and Gyan Prakash. Princeton: Princeton University Press, 2010, 1–17.

Gordon, Milton M. 'The Concept of the Sub-Culture and Its Application'. 1947. In *The Subcultures Reader*, edited by Ken Gelder and Sarah Thornton, 40–3. London: Routledge, 1997.

Gottfried, Paul Edward. *Leo Strauss and the Conservative Movement in America*. Cambridge: Cambridge University Press, 2012.

Gramsci, Antonio. *Selections from the Prison Notebooks*, edited by Quintin Hoare and Geoffrey Nowell Smith. London: Lawrence and Wishart, 1971.

Grant, Kenneth. 'The Golden Dawn'. *International Times*, 14–29 January 1968, 11–12.

Grant, Kenneth. 'Preface to Crowley, Aleister'. In *The Confessions of Aleister Crowley*, edited by John Symonds and Kenneth Grant, 9–10. 1979. London, Penguin, 1989.

Grauerholz, James. 'Introduction'. In *The Adding Machine*, edited by William S. Burroughs, vii–xxiii. New York: Grove Press, 2013.

Gravy, Wavy. 'Hog Farming at Woodstock'. In *The Sixties: The Decade Remembered Now, by the People Who Lived It Then*, edited by Lynda Rosen Obst, 274–6. New York: Random House/Rolling Stone, 1977.

Gray, John. *Enlightenment's Wake: Politics and Culture at the Close of the Modern Age*. London: Routledge and New York, 1995.

Gray, John. *Endgames: Questions in Late Modern Political Thought*. Cambridge: Polity, 1997.

Gray, John. *False Dawn: The Delusions of Global Capitalism*. London: Granta, 1998.

Gray, John. *Black Mass: Apocalyptic Religion and the Death of Utopia*. London: Penguin, 2007.

'Great Britain: You Can Walk Across It on the Grass'. *Time*, 15 April 1966, http://content.time.com/time/magazine/article/0,9171,835349,00.html

Green, Jonathon. *Days in the Life: Voices from the English Underground 1961–1971*. London: Heinemann, 1988.

Green, Marian. *Magic for the Aquarian Age: A Contemporary Textbook of Practical Magical Techniques*, Wellingborough: Aquarian Press, 1983.

Greenfield, Robert. *Timothy Leary: A Biography*. New York: Harcourt, 2006.

Grogan, Emmett. *Ringolevio: A Life Played for Keeps*. St. Albans, Herts: Granada Books, 1974.

Groothuis, Douglas R. *Unmasking the New Age: Is There a New Religious Movement Trying to Transform Society?* Downer's Grove, IL: Intervarsity Press, 1986.

Gruner, Rolf. *Philosophies of History: A Critical Essay.*Aldershot: Gower1985.

Gurdjieff, G.I. *Gurdjieff's Early Talks 1914–1931*. Book Studio, 2014.

Gysin, Brion, and Terry Wilson. *Here to Go: Planet R-101. Brion Gysin interviewed by Terry Wilson*. San Francisco, CA: Berry Tomas, S.X. Summerville, 1982.

Hakl, Hans Thomas. *Eranos: An Alternative Intellectual History of the Twentieth Century*. Translated by Christopher McIntosh. Montreal and Kingston: McGill-Queens University Press, 2013.

Halberstam, David. *The Fifties*. New York: Random House, 1993.

Hall, John R. *Apocalypse Observed: Religious Movements and Violence in North America, Europe, and Japan*. London and New York: Routledge, 2000.

Hall, Simon, 'Protest Movements in the 1970s: The Long 1960s'. *Journal of Contemporary History* 43, no. 4 (October 2008): 655–72.

Hall, Stuart. 'Cultural Studies: Two Paradigms'. *Media, Culture and Society* 2, no. 1 (1980): 57–72.

Hall, Stuart. 'Thatcher's Lessons'. *Marxism Today* 11 (March 1988): 20–9.

Hall, Stuart. 'The Meaning of New Times'. In *New Times: The Changing Face of Politics in the 1990s*, edited by Stuart Hall and Martin Jacques, 116–7. London: Verso, 1990.

Hammer, Olav, *Claiming Knowledge: Strategies of Epistemology from Theosophy to the New Age*, Leiden: Brill, 2001.

Hamilton, Guy. 'Guy Hamilton recalls making The Party's Over'. In *The Party's Over*, 7–8. London: BFI, 2010.

Hanegraaff, Wouter J. *New Age Religion and Western Culture: Esotericism in the Mirror of Secular Thought*. Leiden and New York: E.J. Brill, 1996.

Hanegraaff, Wouter J. *Esotericism and the Academy: Rejected Knowledge in Western Culture*. Cambridge: Cambridge University Press, 2012.

Hankins, Barry. *The Second Great Awakening and the Transcendentalists*. Westport, CT: Greenwood Press, 2004.

Hanson, Paul. *The Dawn of Apocalyptic: The Historical and Sociological Roots of Jewish Apocalyptic Eschatology*. 1975. Philadelphia, PA: Fortress Press, 1983.

Harding, Susan. *The Book of Jerry Falwell: Fundamentalist Language and Politics*. Princeton, NJ: Princeton University Press, 2000.

Harvie, Timothy. *Jürgen Moltmann's Ethics of Hope: Eschatological Possibilities for Moral Action*. Furnham: Ashgate, 2009.

Harrison, Andrew. 'Green Gartside: The Brainiest Man in Pop'. *The Guardian*, 22 February 2011, http://www.theguardian.com/music/2011/feb/22/green-gartside-scritti-politti-interview.

Harrison, Brian. *Finding a Role: The United Kingdom 1970–90*. Oxford: Clarendon Press, 2011.

Harrison, Brian. *Seeking a Role: The United Kingdom 1950–7 (The New Oxford History of England)*. Oxford: Clarendon Press, 2011.

Harrison, J.F.C. *The Second Coming: Popular Millenarianism, 1780–1850*. Brunswick: Rutgers University Press, 1979.

Harvey, David Allen. *Beyond Enlightenment: Occultism and Politics in Modern France*. DeKalb: Northern Illinois University Press, 2005.

Havers, Grant N. *Leo Strauss and Anglo-American Democracy: A Conservative Critique*. DeKalb, IL: Nortner Illinois University Press, 2013.

Hayden, Tom. 'Writing the Port Huron Statement'. In *The Sixties: The Decade Remembered Now, by the People Who Lived It Then*, edited by Lynda Rosen Obst, 70–1. New York: Random House/Rolling Stone, 1977.

Heard, Gerald. *The Five Ages of Man: The Psychology of Human History*. New York: The Julian Press, 1963.

Heath, Joseph, and Andrew Potter. *The Rebel Sell: How the Counterculture Became Consumer Culture*. Chichester: Capstone Publishing, 2006.

Hebdidge, Dick, *Subculture: The Meaning of Style*, London: Routledge, 1979.

Heelas, Paul. *The New Age Movement: The Celebration of the Self and the Sacralization of Modernity*. Cambridge, MA: Blackwell, 1996.

Heelas, Paul, et al. *The Spiritual Revolution: Why Religion Is Giving Way to Spirituality*. Oxford: Blackwell, 2005.

Hegel, G.W.F. *The Philosophy of Right*. Translated by T.M. Knox. London and Oxford: Clarendon Press, 1952.

Hegel, G.W.F. *The Philosophy of History*. Translated by J. Sibree. New York: Dover Publications, 1956.

Heindel, Max. *The Message of the Stars*. 1919. Oceanside, CA: The Rosicrucian Fellowship, 1976.

Herbrechtsmeier, William. 'Buddhism and the Definition of Religion: One More Time'. *Journal for the Scientific Study of Religion* 32, no. 1 (1993): 1–18.

Herman, Arthur. *The Idea of Decline in Western History*. New York and London: The Free Press, 1997.

Hesiod. *Works and Days*. Translated by Dorothea Wender. London: Penguin, 1973.

Hewison, Robert. *Too Much: Art and Society in the Sixties, 1960–75*. New York: Oxford University Press, 1987.

Higgins, G. *Anacalypsis, an Attempt to Draw Aside the Veil of the Saitic Isis; or an Inquiry into the Origins of Languages, Nations and Religions*, 2 Vols. London: Res, Orme, Brown, Green and Longman, 1836.

Higgs, John. 'The High Priest and the Great Beast'. *Sub Rosa* 4 (March 2006): 15–23.

Hill, Christopher. *The World Turned Upside Down: Radical Ideas During the English Revolution*. London: Penguin, 1978.

Himmelfarb, Gertrude. 'This Will Hurt'. In *This Will Hurt: The Restoration of Virtue and Civic Order, The Social Affairs Unit*, edited by Digby Anderson, ix–xi. London: The Social Affairs Units, 1995.

Hinckle, Warren. 'Ramparts'. *Oz* 3 (1967): 4–9.

Hitchcock, Mark. *2012: The Bible and the End of the World*. Eugene, OR: Harvest House, 2009.

Hoare, Philip. *England's Lost Eden: Adventures in a Victorian Utopia*. London: Harper Collins, 2005.

Hobbes, Thomas. *Leviathan, or the Matter, Forme, and Power of a Common Wealth Ecclesiastical and Civil*, edited by C.B. MacPherson. Harmondsworth, Middlesex: Penguin, 1968.

Hobsbawm, Eric. *Fractured Time: Culture and Society on the Twentieth Century*. London: Little, Brown, 2013.

Hoffman, Abbie. *Steal This Book*. 1971. Cambridge, MA: De Capo Press, 1996.

Hoffman, Abbie. *Revolution for the Hell of It*. 1968. New York: Avalon Publishing, 2005.

Holmes, John Clellon. 'This Is the Beat Generation'. *The New York Times Magazine*, 16 November 1952, http://www.litkicks.com/Texts/ThisIsBeatGen.html.

Hoopes, John. 'Mayanism Comes of (New) Age'. In *2012: Decoding the Countercultural Apocalypse*, edited by Joseph Gelfer, 38–59. Sheffield: Equinox, 2011.

Hopkins, Jerry, ed. *The Hippie Papers: Notes from the Underground Press*. New York: Signet Books, 1968.

Hopkins, John. 'An Open Letter to Mr Tariq Ali'. *IT*, 19 April–2 May 1968, 11.

Hoskin, Michael, 'Newton and Newtonianism'. In *The Cambridge Concise History of Astronomy*, edited by Michael Hoskin, 130–67. Cambridge: Cambridge University Press, 1999.

Hulanicki, Barbara. *From A to BIBA: The Autobiography of Barbara Hulanicki*. London: V&A Publications, 2008.

Hume, David. 'Of Enthusiasm and Superstition'. In *Selected Essays*, edited by Stephen Copley and Andrew Edgar, 38–43. Oxford: Oxford University Press, 1998.

Hussein, Murtaza. 'The Atlantic Ignores Muslim Intellectuals, Defines "True Islam" as ISIS'. *The Intercept*, 20 February 2015, https://firstlook.org/theintercept/2015/02/20/atlantic-defines-real-islam-says-isis/.

Hutchison, Alice L. *Kenneth Anger*. London: Black Dog Publishing, 2004.

Huxley, Aldous. *Ends and Means*. New York: Harper and Brothers, 1937.

Huxley, Aldous. 'Action and Contemplation'. In *The Divine Within, Selected Writings on Enlightenment*, 185–230. New York: Harper Perennial, 2003.

Huxley, Aldous. *The Doors of Perception and Heaven and Hell*. 1954. London: Vintage Books, 2004.

Huxley, Aldous. *The Perennial Philosophy*. 1954. New York: Harper Perennial, 2004.

Huxley, Aldous. *Brave New World*. Braunschweig: Diesterweg, 2013.

Introvigne, Massimo. 'After the New Age: Is There a Next Age?'. In *New Age Religion and Globalization*, edited by Mikael Rothstein, 61–2. Aarhus: Aarhus University Press, 2001.

Israel, Jonathan I. *Radical Enlightenment: Philosophy and the Making of Modernity, 1650–1750*. Oxford, England: Oxford University Press, 2001.

Israel, Jonathan I. *Revolutionary Ideas: An Intellectual History of the French Revolution from the Rights of Man to Robespierre*. Princeton: Princeton University Press, 2014.

Jackson, Holbrook. *The Eighteen Nineties*. 1913. Harmondsworth: Penguin, 1939.

Jacob, Margaret C. *Living the Enlightenment: Freemasonry and Politics in Eighteenth-Century Europe*. Oxford: Oxford University Press, 1991.

Jameson, Frederic. *Archaeologies of the Future: The Desire Called Utopia and Other Science Fictions*. London: Verso, 2005.

Jameson, Frederic. 'Utopia as Method, or the Uses of the Future'. In *Utopia/Dystopia: Conditions of Historical Possibility*, edited by Michael D. Gordin, Helen Tilley, and Gyan Prakash, 21–44. Princeton: Princeton University Press, 2010.

Januszczak, Waldemar. 'The Cosmic Occultist Who Made It Hip to Be Square'. *Sunday Times*, 'Culture', 7 February 2010, 14–15.

Jenkins, John Major. *The 2012 Story: The Myths, Fallacies, and Truth Behind the Most Intriguing Date in History*. New York: Penguin, 2009.

Jenkins, John Major. 'Approaching 2012: Modern Misconceptions versus Reconstructing Ancient Maya Perspectives'. In *2012: Decoding the Countercultural Apocalypse*, edited by Joseph Gelfer, 163–81. Sheffield: Equinox, 2011.

Johnson, Steve. 'The New Age Movement', http://www.drstevej.com/newage.pdf.

Jonas, Hans. *The Gnostic Religion: The Message of the Alien God and the Beginnings of Christianity*, 2nd edition. Boston: Beacon Press, 1963.

Jones, A.M., ed. The Works of Sir William Jones: with the life of the author by Lord Teignmouth. London, 1807.

Jowitt, Kenneth. *New World Disorder: The Leninist Extinction*. Berkeley: University of California Press, 1992.

Jowitt, Kenneth. 'Rage, Hubris and Regime Change: The Urge to Speed History Along'. *Policy Review* 118 (April–May 2003): 33–41. http://www.hoover.org/research/rage-hubris-and-regime-change.

Jung, C.G. *Psychology of the Unconscious*. New York: Moffat, Yard and Company, 1917, https://archive.org/stream/psychologyuncon00junggoog#page/n0/mode/2up.

Jung, C.G. 'The Sign of the Fishes'. In *Aion, Collected Works*, Vol. 9, part 2, translated by R.F.C. Hull, 71–94. London: Routledge and Kegan Paul, 1959.

Jung, C.G. Preface to *Aion, Collected Works*, Vol. 9, part 2, translated by R.F.C. Hull, x. London: Routledge and Kegan Paul, 1959.

Jung, C.G. 'Flying Saucers: A Modern Myth of Things Seen in the Skies'. In *Civilisation in Transition, Collected Works*, Vol. 10, translated by R.F.C.Hull, 307–433. London: Routledge and Kegan Paul, 1964.

Jung, C.G., ed. 'The Spiritual Problem of Modern Man'. In *Civilisation in Transition, Collected Works*, Vol. 10, translated by R.F.C. Hull, 74–94. London: Routledge and Kegan Paul, 1964.

Jung, C.G. 'Wotan'. In *Civilisation in Transition, Collected Works*, Vol. 10, translated by R.F.C. Hull, 179–93. London: Routledge and Kegan Paul, 1964.

Jung, C.G. 'Archetypes of the Collective Unconscious'. In *The Archetypes and the Collective Unconscious, Collected Works*, Vol. 9, part 1, translated by R.F.C. Hull, 3–41. London: Routledge and Kegan Paul, 1968.

Jung, C.G. *Psychological Types, The Collected Works*, Vol. 6, translated by R.F.C Hull. London: Routledge and Kegan Paul, 1971.

Jung, C.G. 'Psychology and Literature'. In *The Spirit in Man. Art and Literature, Collected Works*, Vol. 15, translated by R.F.C. Hull, para 152. London: Routledge and Kegan Paul, 1971.

Jung, C.G. *Letters 1906–1950*, edited by Gerhard Adler et al. Princeton: Bollingen, 1992.

Jung, C.G. *Modern Man in Search of a Soul*. London: Routledge, 2001.

Jung, Carl, 'Foreword'. In *The I Ching or Book of Changes*, edited by Richard Wilhelm. 1951. 3rd edition, London: Routledge and Kegan Paul, 1968, xxi–xxxix.

Jung, C.G., 'The Psychology of the Child Archetype', In *The Archetypes and the Collective Unconscious, Collected Works*, Vol. 9, part 1, translated by R.F.C. Hull 1959; New York: Princeton University Press, 1969, 289.

Jung, C.G., 'Definitions', *Psychological Types, The Collected Works*, Vol. 6, translated by R.F.C. Hull. London: Routledge and Kegan Paul, 1971. 408–86.

Kampfner, John. *Blair's Wars*. London: The Free Press, 2004.

Kane, Pat. 'In Thrall to New Age Thrills', *Guardian*, section 2, 4 January 1995. 13.

Kant, Immanuel. *Critique of Practical Reason*. Great Books of the Western World 42. London: Encyclopaedia Britannica, 1952.

Kant, Immanuel. *Dreams of a Spirit-Seer*. Translated by Emanuel F. Goerwitz. 1900. Bristol: Theommes Press, 1992.

Kant, Immanuel. 'An Answer to the Question: What Is Enlightenment? (1784)'. In *What Is Enlightenment?: Eighteenth-Century Answers and Twentieth-Century Questions*, edited by James Schmidt, 57–64. Berkeley: University of California, 1996.

Kant, Immanuel. 'Dreams of a Spirit Seer'. In *Kant on Swedenborg: Dreams of a Spirit Seer and Other Writings*, edited by Gregory R. Johnson, 42–57. Westchester, PA: Swedenborg Foundation, 2002.

Katz, David S., and Richard H. Popkin. *Messianic Revolution: Radical Religious Politics to the End of the Second Millennium*. London: Penguin, 1999.

Kemp, Daren. 'The Christaquarians: A Sociology of Christians in the New Age'. PhD thesis, King's College, London, 2003, http://christaquarians.net.

Kemp, Daren. *New Age: A Guide: Alternative Spiritualities from Aquarian Conspiracy to Next Age*. Edinburgh: Edinburgh University Press, 2004.

Kennedy, E.S., and David Pingree. *The Astrological History of Masha'Allah*. Cambridge, MA.: Harvard University Press, 1971.

Kenyon, Timothy. *Utopian Communism and Political Thought in Early Modern England*. London: Pinter, 1989.

Kermode, Frank. *The Sense of an Ending: Studies in the Theory of Fiction with a New Epilogue*. 1966. Oxford: Oxford University Press, 2000.

Kerouac, Jack. *On the Road*. New York: Signet Books, 1958.

Kerouac, Jack. 'The Origins of the Beat Generation'. *Playboy*, June 1969, 31–2, 42, 79.

Kidd, Thomas S. *The Great Awakening: The Roots of Evangelical Christianity in Colonial America*. New Haven, CT: Yale University Press, 2007.

Kielkopf, James. 'What Are the Differences and Similarities Between Neoliberalism and Neoconservatism?', http://www.quora.com/What-are-the-differences-and-similarities-between-neoliberalism-and-neoconservatism.

King, George. *Contacts with the Gods from Space: Pathway to the New Age*. Hollywood, CA: Aetherius Society, 1996.

King, George. *Become a Builder of the New Age*, Kindle edition. 1964. Hollywood, CA: The Aetherius Society, 2014.

Klagge, James. 'Marx's Reams of Freedom and Necessity'. *The Canadian Journal of Philosophy* 16, no. 4 (Dec 1986): 769–72.

Koenig, Peter-Robert. 'Ordo Templi Orientis Phenomenon Birth of a new American O.T.O.: History of the Solar Lodge of the O.T.O. Charles Manson and the Occult', 2011, http://www.parareligion.ch/sunrise/manson.htm, accessed 5 February 2015.

Kramer, Michael J. *The Republic of Rock: Music and Citizenship in the Sixties Counterculture*. Oxford: Oxford University Press, 2013.

Kramer, Samuel. 'Man's Golden Age: A Sumerian Parallel to Genesis XI.1'. *Journal of the American Oriental Society* LXIII (1943): 191–4.

Kripal, Jeffrey J. *Esalen: America and the Religion of No Religion*. Chicago: University of Chicago Press, 2008.

Krishnamurti, J. *Total Freedom: the Essential Krishnamurti*. New York: Harper Collins, 1996.

Kristol, Irving. 'What's Bugging the Students?'. In *The Neoconservative Persuasion: Selected Essays, 1942–2009*, edited by Gertrude Himmelfarb, 117–22. New York: Basic Books, 2011.

Kumar, Krishan. *Utopianism*. Milton Keynes: Open University Press, 1991.

Kumar, Krishan. *Prophecy and Progress: The Sociology of Industrial and Post-Industrial Society*. Harmondsworth, Middlesex: Penguin, 1996.

Kumar, Krishan. 'Utopia and Anti-Utopia in the Twentieth Century'. In *Utopia: The Search for the Ideal in the Western World*, edited by Roland Schaer, Gregory Claeys, and Lyman Tower Sargent, 251–67. New York: New York Public Library/Oxford University Press, 2000.

Lachman, Gary Valentine. *Turn off your Mind: The Mystic Sixties and the Dark Side of the Age of Aquarius*. London: Macmillan, 2001.

Lagon, Mark. 'Memorandum to Opinion Leaders', The Project for the New American Century, 7 January 1999, https://web.archive.org/web/20130609165624/http://www.newamericancentury.org/iraqjan0799.htm.

Landes, Richard. *Heaven on Earth: The Varieties of the Millennial Experience*. Oxford: Oxford University Press, 2011.

Landis, Bill. *Anger: The Unauthorised Biography of Kenneth Anger*. New York: Harper Collins, 1996.

Langman, Lauren. 'Dionysus – Child of Tomorrow: Notes on Post-industrial Youth'. *Youth and Society* 3, no. 1 (1971–2): 80–99.

Larkin, Philip., ed. 'Annus Mirabilis'. In *High Windows*. London: Faber and Faber, 1979.

Larsen, Steen F. 'Remembering Without Experiencing: Memory for Reported Events'. In *Remembering Reconsidered: Ecological and Traditional Approaches to the Study of Memory*, edited by Ulric Neisser and Eugene Winograd, 326–55. New York: Cambridge University Press, 1988.

Latour, Bruno. *We Have Never Been Modern*. 1991. Cambridge, MA: Harvard University Press, 2006.

Lawson, Nigella. 'Astrology and the Need to Believe: Why Are We Going to New Age Cranks for Old-style Cures?'. *Times*, 13 November 1996, 17.

Leary, Timothy. 'To Aldous Huxley', 3 March 1961. http://www.leary.ru/english/letters/?n=04.

Leary, Timothy. 'You Are a God: Act Like One'. *International Times*, 2–15 February 1968, 11.

Leary, Timothy. *Changing My Mind, Among Others: Lifetime Writings*. Englewood Cliffs, NJ: Prentice-Hall, 1982.

Leary, Timothy. *Flashbacks: An Autobiography*. Los Angeles: Jeremy B. Tarcher, 1990.

Leary, Timothy. *High Priest*. Berkeley: Ronin Publishing, 1995.

Leary, Timothy. *The Politics of Ecstasy*. 1968. Oakland: Ronin Publishing, 1998.

Leary, Timothy. *Turn On, Tune In, Drop Out*. 1965. Oakland: Ronin Publishing, 1999.

Leary, Timothy. *Musings on Human Metamorphoses*. Oakland: Ronin Publishing, 2003.

Leary, Timothy. 'Foreword'. In *Counter Culture through the Ages: from Abraham to Acid House*, edited by Ken Goffman and Dan Joy, ix–xi. New York: Villard Books, 2005.

Leary, Timothy. 'How to Change Behaviour'. Presentation at the International Congress of Applied Psychology, Copenhagen, August 1961. In *Timothy Leary: The Harvard Years*, edited by James Penner, 20–37. Rochester, VT: Park Street Press, 2014.

Leary, Timothy. 'To Arthur Koestler', nd., http://www.leary.ru/english/letters/?n=00.

Leary, Timothy, Ralph Metzner, and Richard Alpert. *The Psychedelic Experience*. 1964. London: Penguin, 2008.

Lebel, Jean-Jacques. 'Notes on Political Street Theatre, Parts: 1968, 1969'. In *Artificial Hells: Participatory Art and the Politics of Spectatorship*, edited by Claire Bishop. London: Verso, 2012.

Lebrin, Richard A. *Joseph de Maistre: An Intellectual Militant*. Quebec: McGill University Press, 1988.

Le Cour, Paul. *L'Ère du Verseau*. Paris: Les Editions de L'OmniumLittéraire, 1962.

Lee, Martin A., and Bruce Shlain. *Acid Dreams: The Complete Social History of LSD: the CIA, the Sixties, and Beyond*. New York: Grove Press, 1992.

Lemesurier, Peter. *This New Age Business: The Story of the Ancient and Continuing Quest to Bring Down Heaven on Earth*. Forres: Findhorn Press, 1990.

Lenin, V.I. 'The Theory of Knowledge of Dialectical Materialism and of Empirio-Criticism. III, chap. 3.6 "Freedom and Necessity"', https://www.marxists.org/archive/lenin/works/1908/mec/.

Lenin, Vladimir Ilyich, 'What Is to Be Done?' In *Essential Works of Lenin*. Np: bn publishing 2015, 54–175.

Lentini, Pete. 'The 2012 Milieu? Hybridity, Diversity and Stigmatised Knowledge'. In *2012: Decoding the Countercultural Apocalypse*, edited by Joseph Gelfer, 60–85. Sheffield: Equinox, 2011.

Lévi-Bruhl, Lucien. *How Natives Think*. Translated by Lillian A. Clare. London: George Allen & Unwin, 1926.

Levin, Jack, and James L. Spates. 'Hippie Values: An Analysis of the Underground Press'. *Youth and Society* 2 (1970): 59–73.

Levine, Steve. 'The First American Mehla'. *The San Francisco Oracle*, January 1967. In *The Hippie Papers: Notes from the Underground Press*, edited by Jerry Hopkins, 20–2. New York: Signet Books, 1968.

Lévi-Strauss, Claude. *The Savage Mind*. Chicago: University of Chicago Press, 1966.

Levitas, Ruth. *The Concept of Utopia*. Hemel Hempstead: Allen Lane, 1990.

Levitas, Ruth. 'The Imaginary Reconstitution of Society, or why sociologists and others should take utopia more seriously'. Inaugural Lecture, University of Bristol, 24 October 2005. http://www.bris.ac.uk/spais/files/inaugural.pdf.

Levitas, Ruth. *Utopia as Method: The Imaginary Reconstitution of Society*. London: Palgrave Macmillan, 2013.

Lewis, James R., and J. Gordon Melton. *Perspectives on the New Age*. Albany: State University of New York Press, 1992.

Lind, Michael. *The Next American Nation: The New Nationalism and the Fourth American Revolution*. New York: The Free Press, 1995.

Lind, Michael. 'How Neoconservatives Conquered Washington – and Launched a War', 10 April 2003, http://www.antiwar.com/orig/lind1.html.

Lind, Michael. *Made in Texas: George W. Bush and the Southern Takeover of American Politics*. New York: Basic Books, 2003.

Locke, John. *An Essay Concerning Human Understanding*. London: Penguin, 1997.

Long, A.A. *Stoic Studies*. Cambridge: Cambridge University Press, 1996.

Lovejoy, Arthur O. *The Great Chain of Being*. Cambridge, MA and London: Harvard University Press, 1936.

Low, Anthony. *Aspects of Subjectivity: Society and Individuality from the Middle Ages to Shakespeare and Milton*. Pittsburgh: Duquesne University Press, 2003.

Lucas, Phillip C. 'The New Age Movement and the Pentecostal/Charismatic Revival: Distinct Yet Parallel Phases of a Fourth Great Awakening'. In *Perspectives on the New Age*, edited by James R. Lewis and J. Gordon Melton, 204, 210. Albany: State University of New York Press, 1992.

Lukacher, N., ed. *Time Fetishes: The Secret History of Eternal Recurrence*. London: Duke University Press, 1998.

Lukes, Steven. 'The Grand Dichotomy of the Twentieth Century'. In *The Cambridge History of Twentieth Century Political Thought*, edited by Terence Ball and Richard Bellamy, 602–26. Cambridge: Cambridge University Press, 2003.

Lyell, Charles. *Principles of Geology*. London: Penguin, 1997. 8–21.

Lynch, Gordon. *Understanding Theology and Popular Culture*. Oxford: Blackwell, 2005.

Lyons, Eugene. *Assignment in Utopia*. London: George C. Harrap, 1938.

Machievelli, Niccolo. *The Prince*. Translated by George Bull. Harmondsworth Middlesex: Penguin, 1961.

Mackey, Samson Arnold. *Mythological Astronomy of the Ancients Demonstrated*. Norwich, 1822.

Maffesoli, Michael. *The Time of the Tribes: The Decline of Individualism in Mass Society*. Translated by Don Smith. London: Sage, 1996.

Magee, Glenn Alexander. *Hegel and the Hermetic Tradition*. Ithaca, NY: Cornell University Press, 2001.

Mairet, Philip. *A. R Orage: A Memoir*. London: J.M. Dent & Sons, 1936.

Malthus, Thomas. *An Essay on the Principle of Population*. Harmondsworth: Penguin, 1970.

Manuel, Frank E. *Shapes of Philosophic History*. London: Allen and Unwin, 1965.

Manuel, F.E., and F.P. Manuel. *Utopian Thought in the Western World*. Oxford: Basil Blackwell, 1979.

Marcuse, Herbert. *Five Lectures: Psychoanalysis, Politics and Utopia*. Harmondsworth: Penguin, 1970.

Márquez, Gabriel García. *Strange Pilgrims*. Translated by Edith Grossman. London: Penguin, 2013.

Martin, Arthur. 'Swampy's New Life'. *Daily Mail*, 13 September 2013. http://www.dailymail.co.uk/news/article-2420429/Swampys-new-life-Former-eco-warrior-40-lives-yurt-children-job.html.

Martin, Wallace. *The New Age under Orage: Chapters in English Cultural History*. Manchester: Manchester University Press, 1967.

Martin, Walter. *The New Age Cult*. Minneapolis: Bethany House Publishers, 1989.

Marx, Karl. 'A Contribution to the Critique of Hegel's Philosophy of Right', Introduction. *Deutsch-Französische Jahrbücher* (7 and 10 February 1844). https://www.marxists.org/archive/marx/works/1843/critique-hpr/intro.htm.

Marx, Karl, and Friedrich Engels. *The Communist Manifesto*. 1848. Translated by Gareth Stedman Jones. London: Penguin Books, 1967.

Marx, Karl, and Friedrich Engels, 'The German Ideology'. In *On Historical Materialism*, edited by Karl Marx, Friedrich Engels, and V.I. Lenin, compiled by T. Borodulina, 14–76. Moscow: Progress Publishers, 1972.

Massey, Gerald. *The Natural Genesis*, 4 Vols. London: Williams and Norgate, 1883.

Massey, Gerald. *The Hebrew and Other Creations*. London: Williams and Norgate, 1887.

Matthews, Ian. 'A.R. Orage and the Politics of the New Age'. PhD Thesis, University of London, 2003.

McKay, George. *Senseless Acts of Beauty; Cultures and Resistance since the Sixties*. London and New York: Verso, 1996.

McKay, George, ed. *DiY Culture; Party and Protest in Nineties Britain*. London and New York: Verso, 1998.

McKenna, Terence. *The Archaic Revival*. New York: Harper Collins, 1991.

McKenna, Terence. *True Hallucinations: Being an Account of the Author's Extraordinary Adventures in the Devil's Paradise*. London: Rider, 1994.

McKenna, Terence, and Dennis McKenna. *The Invisible Landscape: Mind, Hallucinogens, and the I Ching*. New York: Harper Collins, 1993.

McMahon, Darrin M. *Enemies of the Enlightenment: The French Counter-Enlightenment and the Making of Modernity*. Oxford: Oxford University Press, 2001.

McNally, Dennis. *A Long Strange Trip: The Inside Story of the Grateful Dead and the Making of Modern America*. London: Corgi, 2003.

Melly, George. *Revolt into Style: The Pop Arts*. London: Faber and Faber, 1970.

Melly, George. *The Observer*, 1 September 1974.

Melton, J. Gordon. 'The Future of the New Age Movement'. In *New Religions and New Religiosity*, edited by Eileen Barker and Margo Warburg, 142–3, 147. Aarhus: Aarhus University Press, 2001.

Melton, J. Gordon, Jerome Clarke, and Aidan A. Kelly. *New Age Almanac*. London and New York: Visible Ink Press, 1991.

Meyer, Christopher. 'Our National Interest Demands the Mother of All U-turns', *The Daily Telegraph*, 23 August 2014, 122.

Meyer, Michael R. 'Rudhyar: Friend, Exemplar and Sage', http://www.khaldea.com/articles/dr_fes.shtml.

Michell, John. 'Centres & lines of the Latent Power in Britain'. *International Times*, 5–20 October 1967, 5.

Michell, John. 'Flying Saucers as a Portent of the Revelation Which will Attend the Opening of the Aquarian Age'. *International Times*, 30 January–12 February 1967, 7.

Michell, John. *The Flying Saucer Vision*. New York: Ace Books, 1967.

Michell, John. *The View Over Atlantis*, revised edition. London: Garnstone Press 1972.

Miles, Barry. *In the Sixties*. London: Jonathan Cape, 2002.

Miles, Barry. *Hippie*. New York: Sterling, 2004.

Miles, Barry. *Jack Kerouac: King of the Beats*. London: Virgin, 2010.

Miles, Barry. *In the Seventies: Adventures in the Counter-Culture*. London: Profile Books, 2011.

Miles, Barry. *Call Me Burroughs: A Life*. New York: Twelve, 2013.

Mill, John Stuart. 'On Liberty'. In *On Liberty and The Subjection of Women*, 7–129. London: Penguin, 2006.

Miller, Elliot. *A Crash Course in the New Age Movement*. Eastbourne: Monarch Publications, 1990.

Miller, Russell. *Bare Faced Messiah: The True Story of L.Ron Hubbard*. London: Sphere Books, 1988.

Mitchell, Joni. 'Woodstock Lyrics'. *Lyricsfreak*, http://www.lyricsfreak.com/j/joni+mitchell/woodstock_20075381.html.

Mitton, Jacqueline. *The Penguin Dictionary of Astronomy*. London: Penguin, 1993.

Momen, Moojan. *An Introduction to Shi'i Islam: The History and Doctrines of Twelver Shi'ism*. Oxford: George Ronald, 1987.

Moore, James. *Gurdjieff: The Anatomy of a Myth*. Shaftsbury: Dorset, 1999.

Moore, John. *Aleister Crowley: A Modern Master*. Oxford: Mandrake, 2009.

More, Thomas. *Utopia*. London: Penguin, 1965.

Morgan, Bill, and David Stanford, eds. *Jack Kerouac and Allen Ginsberg: The Letters*. New York: Penguin, 2011.

Morris, James M., and Andrea L. Kross. *Historical Dictionary of Utopianism*. Lanham, MD: Scarecrow Press, 2004.

Morris, William. *News from Nowhere and Other Writings*. London: Penguin, 2004.

Müller, Max. 'Solar Myths'. *The Nineteenth Century* (December 1885): 900–22.

Myerhoff, Barbara G. 'The Revolution as a Trip: Symbol and Paradox'. *Annals of the American Academy of Political and Social Science* 395, *Students Protest* (May 1971): 105–16.

Nash, George H. 'Forgotten Godfathers: Premature Jewish Conservatives and the Rise of *National Review*'. *American Jewish History* 87, no. 2 (1999): 123–57.

Nation, Stephen. 'Feminine on the Rise'. *Caduceus* 89 (2014): 4–5.

Naylor, Thomas H. 'Neoliberalism: Neoconservatism Without a Smirk'. *The Second Vermont Republic*, 22 March 2010, http://vermontrepublic.org/neoliberalism-neoconservatism-without-a-smirk/.

Nelson, Elizabeth. *The British Counter-Culture, 1966–73: A Study of the Underground Press*. New York: St. Martin's Press, 1989.

Neville, Richard. *Playpower*. London: Jonathan Cape, 1970.

Newport, John P. *The New Age Movement and the Biblical Worldview: Conflict and Dialogue*. Grand Rapids: William B. Eerdmans, 1998.

Newton, Isaac. *The Chronology of Ancient Kingdoms Amended.* 1728. Facsimile edition. London: Histories & Mysteries of Man, 1988.

Newton, Isaac. 'Tabula Smaragdina, Hermetic Trismegistri Philosophorum Patris', Keynes MS 28, in *The Chymistry of Isaac Newton*, King's College Library, Cambridge University, http://webapp1.dlib.indiana.edu/newton/mss/dipl/ALCH00017.

Nicholson, Virginia. *Among the Bohemians: Experiments in Living 1900–1939.* London: Penguin, 2003.

Nietzche, Friedrich, 'Eternal Recurrence'. In *A Nietzsche Reader*, selected and translated by R J. Hollingdale. Harmondsworth and Middlesex: Penguin, 1977.

Nisbet, Robert A. *The Quest for Community.* New York: New York University Press, 1953.

Nuttall, Jeff. *Bomb Culture.* London: Paladin, 1979.

O'Brien, Denis. *Empedocles' Cosmic Cycle: A Reconstruction from the Fragments and Secondary Sources.* Cambridge: Cambridge University Press, 1969.

Obst, Lynda Rosen, ed. *The Sixties: The Decade Remembered Now, By the People Who Lived It Then.* New York: Random House/Rolling Stone, 1977.

Oliphant, John. *Brother Twelve: The Incredible Story of Canada's False Prophet and His Doomed Cult of Gold, Sex and Black Magic.* Toronto: McClelland and Stewart, 1991.

Orage, A.R. *Consciousness: Animal, Human, and Superhuman.* 1907. New York: Samuel Weiser, 1974.

Ortiz, Fernando. *Cuban Counterpoint: Tobacco and Sugar.* Translated by Harriet de Onis. Durham, NC: Duke University Press, 1995.

O'Sullivan, Noel. 'Conservatism'. In *The Cambridge History of Twentieth Century Political Thought*, edited by Terence Ball and Richard Bellamy, 151–64. Cambridge: Cambridge University Press, 2003.

Ouspensky, P.D. *A New Model of the Universe.* 1931. London: Arkana, 1984.

Ouspensky, P.D. *In Search of the Miraculous: Fragments of an Unknown Teaching.* 1949. London: Harvest, 1991.

Ouspensky, P.D. *A Record of Meetings.* London: Arkana, 1992.

Ozouf, Mona. *Festivals of the French Revolution.* Translated by Alan Sheridan. Cambridge, MA: Harvard University Press, 1988.

Pagden, Anthony. *The Enlightenment and Why It Still Matters.* Oxford: Oxford University Press, 2013.

Paine, Thomas. *Common Sense.* London: Penguin, 1986.

Paine, Thomas. 'The Rights of Man'. In *The Thomas Paine Reader*, edited by Michael Foot and Isaac Kramnick, 201–364. London: Penguin, 1987, 2003.

Paine, Thomas. *The Age of Reason.* Mineola, NY: Dover Publications, 2003.

Palmer, Robert, 'Brion Gysin 1916–1986'. In *The Process,* edited by Brion Gysin, vii–xxi. New York: The Overlook Press, 1987.

Parsons, J.W. *Freedom Is a Two-Edged Sword.* Tempe, AZ: New Falcon Publications, 1989.

Partridge, Christopher H. *The Re-Enchantment of the West, Volume II Alternative Spiritualities, Sacralization, Popular Culture, and Occulture.* London: T & T Clark Ltd., 2005.

Pasi, Marco. *Aleister Crowley and the Temptation of Politics.* Durham: Acumen, 2014.

Peck, Abe, 'The Other Convention in Chicago'. In *The Sixties: The Decade Remembered Now, By the People Who Lived It Then*, edited by Lynda Rosen Obst, 260–7. New York: Random House/Rolling Stone, 1977.

Pellegrini, Aldo, 'Xul Solar'. In *Xul Solar*, edited by Mario H. Gradowczyk, 25–50. Buenos Aires: Pan Klub Foundation/ Xul Solar Museum, 1990.

Perry, Charles, 'The Gathering of the Tribes'. In *The Sixties: The Decade Remembered Now, by the People Who Lived It Then*, edited by Lynda Rosen Obst, 188–92. New York: Random House/Rolling Stone, 1977.

Pinchbeck, Daniel. *Breaking Open the Head: A Psychedelic Journey into the Heart of Contemporary Shamanism*. London: Harper Collins, 2004.

Pinchbeck, Daniel. *2012: The Year of the Mayan Prophecy*. New York: Penguin, 2006.

Pinchbeck, Daniel. *2012: The Return of Quetzalcoatl*. New York: Penguin, 2007.

Pinchbeck, Daniel. 'Introduction'. In *The Psychedelic Experience*, edited by Leary, Timothy, Ralph Metzner, and Richard Alpert, iv–xix. 1964. London: Penguin, 2008.

Pingree, David. *The Thousands of Abu Ma'shar*. London: Warburg Institute, 1968.

Pinder, David. *Visions of the City*. Edinburgh: Edinburgh University Press, 2005.

Pittock, Murray G.H. *Inventing and Resisting Britain; Cultural Identities in Britain and Ireland, 1685–1789*. New York: St. Martin's Press, 1997.

Plait, Phil. '2012: The Year Nothing Will Happen', *Discover*, 19 May 2008, http://blogs. discovermagazine.com/badastronomy/2008/05/19/2012-the-year-nothing-will-happen/.

Plato. *Phaedo*. Translated by H.N. Fowler. Cambridge, MA and London: Harvard University Press, 1914.

Plato. *Phaedrus*. Translated by H.N. Fowler. Cambridge, MA and London: Harvard University Press, 1914.

Plato. *Timaeus*. Translated by R.G. Bury. Cambridge, MA, London: Harvard University Press, 1931.

Plato. *Laws*, 2 Vols. Translated by R.G. Bury. Cambridge, MA and London: Harvard University Press, 1934.

Plato. *Republic*, 2 Vols. Translated by Paul Shorey. Cambridge, MA and London: Harvard University Press, 1935.

Polcari, Stephen. 'Contexts, Influences, References'. In *Jackson Pollock et Le Chamanisme*, edited by Mickie Klein, Stephen Polcari, Marc Restellini, and William Rubin, 11–16. Paris, Pinacothèque de Paris, 2008.

Pollard, Sydney, *The Idea of Progress: History and Society*. Harmondsworth: Penguin, 1971.

Pope, Alexander. 'Epitaphs. Intended for Sir Isaac Newton, in Westminster-Abbey, 1730'. In *The Complete Poetical Works of Alexander Pope*, edited by Henry W. Boynton. Boston and New York: Houghton, Mifflin and Company, 1903.

Popper, Karl. *The Open Society and Its Enemies*, 2 Vols. 1945. London and New York: Routledge, 1986 revised edition.

Porter, Roy. *Enlightenment: Britain and the Creation of the Modern World*. London: Penguin, 2000.

Priestley, Joseph. Letters to Members of the New Jerusalem Church, *Formed by Baron Swedenborg*. Birmingham, 1791.

Rado, James, Gerome Ragni, and Galt MacDermot. 'Aquarius'. 1968. http://www. metrolyrics.com/aquarius-lyrics-5th-dimension.html.

Raimondo, Justin. *An Enemy of the State: The Life of Murray N. Rothbard*. Amherst, MA: Prometheus Books, 2000.

Ramstedt, Martin. 'New Age and Business' in 'The New Age Movement and Western Esotericism'. In *Handbook of New Age*, edited by Daren Kemp and James R. Lewis, 186–7. Leiden and Boston: Brill, 2007.

Raskin, Jonah. *For The Hell of It: The Life and Times of Abbie Hoffman*. Berkeley and London: University of California Press, 1988.

Reeves, Marjorie. *The Influence of Prophecy in the Later Middle Ages: A Study of Joachimism*. Oxford: Oxford University Press, 1969.

Reeves, Marjorie. *Joachim of Fiore and the Prophetic Future*. London: SPCK, 1976.

Ringgren, Helmer. 'Akkadian Apocalypses'. In *Apocalypticism in the Mediterranean World and the Near East: Proceedings of the International Colloquium on Apocalypticism, Uppsala, August 12–17*, edited by David Hellholm. Tübingen: J. C. B. Mohr, 1989.

Robb, Thomas. 'The World Ends Tomorrow', http://www.christianidentitychurch.net/world_ends_tomorrow1.htm

Robbins, Thomas, and Susan J. Palmer. *Millennium, Messiahs and Mayhem: Contemporary Apocalyptic Movements*. London: Routledge, 1997.

The Rolling Stones. *The Stones in the Park*. Directed by Leslie Woodhead and Jo Durden-Smith. London: Granada Media, 2001, DVD.

Roszak, Theodore. *The Making of a Counter Culture: Reflections on the Technocratic Society and Its Youthful Opposition*. Garden City, NY: Anchor Books, 1969.

Roszak, Theodore. *Unfinished Animal: The Aquarian Frontier and the Evolution of Consciousness*. London: Faber and Faber, 1976.

Rothbard, Murray N. 'Life in the Old Right'. *Chronicles* (August 1994): 15–19.

Rousseau, Jean-Jacques. *The Confessions*. Translated by J.M. Cohen. Harmondsworth: Penguin, 1953.

Rousseau, Jean-Jacques. *Emile*. Translated by Barbara Foxley. London: J.M. Dent and Sons, 1974.

Rousseau, Jean-Jacques. *A Discourse on Inequality*. Translated by Maurice Cranston. London: Penguin, 1984.

Rousseau, Jean-Jacques. *The Social Contract*. Translated by Maurice Cranston. London: Penguin, 2006.

Royle, Edward. *Robert Owen and the Commencement of the Millennium*. Manchester: Manchester University Press, 1998.

Rubin, Jerry. 'Yippees Are Coming, Coming, Coming to Chicago'. *Oz* 11 (1968): 9–10.

Rudhyar, Dane. *New Mansions for New Men*. New York: Lucis Publishing Company, 1938.

Rudhyar, Dane. *Fire Out of the Stone: A Reinterpretation of the Basic Images of the Christian Tradition*. The Hague: Servire, 1963.

Rudhyar, Dane. *Astrological Timing: The Transition to the New Age*. San Francisco, New York and London: Harper and Row, 1969.

Rudhyar, Dane. *An Astrological Mandala: The Cycle of Transformation and Its 360 Symbolic Phases*. 1972. New York: Vintage Books, 1974.

Rudhyar, Dane. *Occult Preparations for a New Age*. Madras and London: Theosophical Publishing House, 1975.

Rudhyar, Dane. *The Planetarisation of Consciousness*. 1970. New York: Aurora Press,1977.

Russell, D.S. *The Method and Message of Jewish Apocalyptic*. Philadelphia, PA: The Westminster Press, 1964.

Sabine, George H. *The Works of Gerard Winstanley*. Ithaca, NY: Cornell University Press, 1941.

Sampson, Anthony. *Anatomy of Britain*. London: Hodder and Stoughton, 1962.

Sandbrook, Dominic. *State of Emergency, The Way We Were: Britain 1970–1974*. London: Penguin, 2011.

Sanders, Ed. Biographical essay. In *Anthology of American Folk Music*, Vol. 4, Revenant RVM 211, ed. Harry Smith (2000), http://www.harrysmitharchives.com/1_bio/index.html.

Savage, Jon. *England's Dreaming: Sex Pistols and Punk Rock*. London: Faber and Faber, 1991.

Schaffer, Simon. 'Newtonianism'. In *Companion to the History of Modern Science*, edited by R.C. Olby, G.N. Cantor, J.R.R. Christie, and M.J.S. Hodge, 610–26. London and New York: Routledge, 1996.

Scheler, Max. *Ressentiment*. Translated by William H. Holdheim. New York: Noonday, 1973.

Schmidt, James. 'Inventing the Enlightenment: Anti-Jacobins, British Hegelians, and the "Oxford English Dictionary"'. *Journal of the History of Ideas* 64, no. 3 (July 2003): 421–43.

Schmidt, James. 'What Enlightenment Project?'. *Political Theory* 28, no. 6 (2000): 734–57.

Schwartz, Hillel. *The French Prophets: The History of a Millenarian Group in Eighteenth-Century England*. Berkeley and Los Angeles, CA: University of California Press, 1980.

Scott, Charlotte. *Shakespeare's Nature: From Cultivation to Culture*. Oxford: Oxford University Press, 2014.

Scott, Walter, trans. *Hermetica: The Ancient Greek and Latin Writings Which Contain Religious or Philosophic Teachings Ascribed to Hermes Trismegistus*. Vol. 1. Boulder: Shambala, 1982.

Secord, James A. *Victorian Sensation: The Extraordinary Publication, Reception, and Secret Authorship of Vestiges of the Natural History of Creation*. Chicago: University of Chicago Press, 2000.

Segal, Irving. 'A Teacher's Letter to Young People'. In *The Hippie Papers: Notes from the Underground Press*, edited by Jerry Hopkins, 14–16. New York: Signet Books, 1968.

Selver, Paul. *Orage and the New Age Circle*. London: George Allen and Unwin Ltd., 1959.

Sharpe, Eric. *Comparative Religion: A History*. London: Duckworth, 1975.

Shaw, Matthew. *Time and the French Revolution: The Republican Year, 1789 – Year XIV*. Woodbridge: Boydell and Brewer, 2011.

Simmel, Georg. *The Sociology of Georg Simmel*. Translated and edited by Kurt H. Wolff. Glencoe, IL: The Free Press, 1950.

Sitchin, Zecharia, *The End of Days*. New York: William Morrow, 2009.

Sitler, Robert K. 'The 2012 Phenomenon: New Uses for an Ancient Maya Calendar'. In *2012: Decoding the Countercultural Apocalypse*, edited by Joseph Gelfer, 8–22. Sheffield: Equinox, 2011.

Sjöö, Monica. *New Age and Armageddon: The Goddess or the Gurus? Towards a Feminist Vision of the Future*. London: The Women's Press, 1990.

Smart, Ninian. *The Phenomenon of Religion*. London: Macmillan, 1973.

Smith, Adam. *The Wealth of Nations*. Shine Classics, 2014.

Smith, Richard Candida, *Utopia and Dissent: Art, and Poetry, and Politics in California*. Berkeley: University of California Press, 1995.

Smith, Huston. Introduction to Aldous Huxley, *The Divine Within, Selected Writings on Enlightenment*. New York: Harper Perennial, 2003, 1–10.

Sobieszek, Robert A. *Ports of Entry: William S. Burroughs and the Arts*. Los Angeles County Museum of Art: Thames and Hudson, 1996.

South, Stephanie. *2012: Biography of a Time Traveller: the Journey of José Argüelles*. Franklin Lakes: New Page Books, 2009.

Spangler, David. *Festivals in the New Age*. Forres: Findhorn Publications, 1975.

Spangler, David. *Revelation: The Birth of a New Age*. Forres: Findhorn Publications, 1976.

Spangler, David. *Explorations: Emerging Aspects of the New Culture*. Forres: Findhorn Publications, 1980.

Spangler, David. 'Revelation: Birth of a New Age'. In *The New Age: An Anthology of Essential Writings*, edited by William Bloom, 27–30. London: Rider, 1991.

Spangler, David. 'The New Age: The Movement Toward the Divine'. In *New Age Spirituality: An Assessment*, edited by Duncan Sheldon Ferguson, 79–105. Louisville: Westminster/John Knox Press, 1993.

Spangler, David. *A Pilgrim in Aquarius*. Forres: Findhorn Press, 1996.

Spangler, David. *Apprenticed to Spirit: The Education of a Soul*. New York: Penguin, 2011.

Spates, James L. 'Counterculture and Dominant Culture Values: a Cross-National Analysis of the Underground Press and Dominant Culture Magazines'. *American Sociological Review* 41, no. 5 (October 1976): 868–83.

Stanley, Michael W. 'The Relevance of Emanuel Swedenborg's Theological Concepts for the New Age as It Is Envisioned Today'. In *Emanuel Swedenborg: A Continuing Vision*, edited by Robert Larson. New York: Swedenborg Foundation, 1988.

Stanley, Michael W., ed. *Emanuel Swedenborg*. Berkeley, CA: North Atlantic Books, 2003.

Stansill, Peter. 'Psyching in the New Age'. *IT*, 27 February–12 March 1967, 12.

Starhawk. *The Spiral Dance*. New York: Harper and Row, 1979.

Stark, Rodney. 'Atheism, Faith, and the Social Scientific Study of Religion'. *Journal of Contemporary Religion* 14, no. 1 (1999): 41–62.

Starr, Martin P. *The Unknown God: W.T. Smith and the Thelemites*. Bolingbrook: The Teitan Press, 2003.

Stearn, Jess. *Edgard Cayce on the Millennium*. New York: Warner Books, 1998.

Steiner, Rudolf. *World History in the Light of Anthroposophy*. 1950. London: Rudolf Steiner Press, 1977.

Steiner, Rudolf. *An Autobiography*. New York: Steiner Books, 1980.

Steiner, Rudolf. *The Spiritual Beings in the Heavenly Bodies and in the Kingdoms of Nature*. 1951. Vancouver: Steiner Book Centre, 1981.

Steiner, Rudolf. *The Reappearance of Christ in the Etheric*. Spring Valley, NY: Anthroposophic Press, 1983.

Steinfels, Peter. *The Neoconservatives: The Origins of a Movement*. New York: Simon and Schuster, 2014.

Stephenson, Gregory. *The Daybreak Boys: Essays on the Literature of the Beat Generation*. Carbondale: Southern Illinois University Press, 2009.

Stern-Weiner, Jamie. 'What Are Enlightenment Values?' New Left Project, 20 July 2011, http://www.newleftproject.org/index.php/site/article_comments/what_are_enlightenment_values.

Stevens, Jay. *Storming Heaven: LSD and the American Dream*. New York: Harper and Rowe, 1988.

Stevens, Matthew Levi. *The Magical Universe of William S. Burroughs*. Oxford: Mandrake, 2014.

Stone, Jon R. *Expecting Armageddon: Essential Readings in Failed Prophecy*. London: Routledge, 2000.

Stone, Mark Van. 'Maya Prophecies: 2012 and the Problematic Nature of Truth'. In *2012: Decoding the Countercultural Apocalypse*, edited by Joseph Gelfer, 23–37. Sheffield: Equinox, 2011.

Stone, Robert. *Prime Green: Remembering the Sixties*. New York: Harper Perennial, 2007.

Strauss, Leo. *The City and Man*. Based on the 1962 Page-Barbour lectures. 1964. Chicago: University of Chicago Press, 1978.

Stray, Geoff. *Beyond 2012: Catastrophe or Ecstasy: A Complete Guide to End-of-Time Predictions*. Lewis: East Sussex, 2006.

Strinati, Dominic. *An Introduction to Theories of Popular Culture*. London: Routledge, 1995.

Sugrue, Thomas. *The Story of Edgar Cayce*. 1943. Virginia Beach, VA: A.R.E. Press, 1973.

Sutcliffe, Steven J, 'New Age, World Religions and Elementary Forms'. In *New Age Spirituality: Rethinking Religion*, edited by Steven J. Sutcliffe and Ingvild Saelid Gilhus, 17–34. Durham: Acumen, 2013.

Sutcliffe, Steven J., and Ingvild Saelid Gilhus, eds. *New Age Spirituality: Rethinking Religion*. Durham: Acumen, 2013.

Sutcliffe, Stuart. 'Between Apocalypse and Self-realisation: "Nature" as an Index of New Age Spirituality'. In *Nature Religion Today: Paganism in the Modern World*, edited by Joanne Pearson, Richard H. Roberts, and Geoffrey Samuel. Edinburgh: Edinburgh University Press, 1998.

Sutcliffe, Stuart. *Children of the New Age: A History of Spiritual Practices*. London: Routledge, 2003.

Sutton, Matthew Avery. *American Apocalypse: A History of Modern Evangelism*. Cambridge, MA: Harvard University Press, 2014.

Swedenborg, Emanuel. *The Apocalypse Revealed Wherein Are Disclosed the Arcana Foretold Which Have Hitherto Remained Concealed*. English translation of the Latin Edition of 1766 (no date). The Swedenborg Digital Library, http://www.swedenborgdigitallibrary.org/contets/AR.html.

Swedenborg, Emanuel. *The Last Judgment and Babylon Destroyed: All the Predictions in the Book of Revelation Are at This Day Fulfilled from Things Heard and Seen, 1758*. West Chester, PA: Swedenborg Foundation, 2009.

Symonds, John. *The Great Beast: The Life and Magic of Aleister Crowley*. St Albans: Mayflower Books, 1973.

Taves, Annand Michael Kinsella. 'Hiding in Plain Sight: The Organisational Forms of "Unorganised Religion"'. In *New Age Spirituality: Rethinking Religion*, edited by Steven J. Sutcliffe, and Ingvild Saelid Gilhus, 84–98. Durham: Acumen, 2013.

Taylor, Matthew. 'Enlightenment values and the politics of transformation'. *Transformation*, 19 August 2013, https://www.opendemocracy.net/transformation/matthew-taylor/enlightenment-values-and-politics-of-transformation.

Taylor, Robert. *The Diegesis; Being a Discovery of the Origin, Evidences, and Early History of Christianity*. London: Richard Carlile, 1829.

Taylor, Robert. *The Devil's Pulpit: or Astro-theological Sermons*. London: Richard Carlile, 1831.

Teich, Mikuláš, and Roy Porter, 'Introduction' in *Fin de siècle and Its Legacy*, edited by Roy Porter and Mikuláš Teich, 1–9. Cambridge: Cambridge University Press,1990.

Thatcher, Margaret. Interview for *Woman's Own*, 23 September 1987, Margaret Thatcher Foundation, http://www.margaretthatcher.org/document/106689.

Thomas, Keith. *Religion and the Decline of Magic*. Harmondsworth and Middlesex: Peregrine Books, 1971.

Thompson, Damian. *The End of Time: Faith and Fear in the Shadow of the Millennium*. London: Sinclair-Stevenson, 1996.

Thompson, Peter. 'Religion, Utopia and the Metaphysics of Contingency'. In *The Privatization of Hope: Ernst Bloch and the Future of Utopia*, edited by Peter Thompson and Slavoj Žižek, 82–105. London: Duke University Press, 2013.

Thompson, Peter, and Slavoj Žižek, eds. *The Privatization of Hope: Ernst Bloch and the Future of Utopia*. London: Duke University Press, 2013.

Thompson, William Irwin. 'Sixteen Years of the New Age'. In David Spangler and William Irwin Thompson, *Reimagination of the World: A Critique of the New Age, Science, and Popular Culture: The Chinnok Summer Conferences of David Spangler and William Irwin Thompson, July 1988 and 1989*. Santa Fe: Bear & Company, 1991, 17.

Trevelyan, George. 'Spiritual Awakening in our Time'. Lecture given at the Royal Commonwealth Society, November 1972. http://www.wrekintrust.org/downloads/sir_george_spiritual_awakening.pdf.

Trexler, Adam Thomas. 'Modernist Poetics and "New Age" Political Philosophy'. Ph.D Thesis, University of London, 2006.

Trilling, Lionel. *Beyond Culture: Essays in Literature and Learning*. San Diego, CA: Harcourt, 1978.

Tumber, Catherine. *American Feminism and the Birth of New Age Spirituality: Searching for the Higher Self, 1875–1915*. Oxford: Rowman and Littlefield, 2002.

Turgot, Anne-Robert-Jacques. 'A Philosophical Review of the Successive Advances of the Human Mind'. In *Turgot on Progress, Sociology and Economics*, edited by Ronald L. Meek, 41–59. Cambridge: Cambridge University Press, 1991.

Vaïsse, Justin. *Neoconservatism: The Biography of a Movement*. Translated by Arthur Goldhammer. Harvard: Harvard University Press, 2011.

Vardaman, Jerry, and Edwin N. Yamauchi. *Chronos, Kairos, Christos: Nativity and Chronological Studies Presented to Jack Finegan*. Winona Lake, IN: Eisenbrauns, 1989.

Ventura, Patricia. *Neoliberal Culture: Living with American Liberalism*. Farnham: Ashgate, 2012.

Vernon, Roland. *Star in the East: Krishnamurti, the Invention of a Messiah*. London: Constable, 2000.

Versluis, Arthur. *Wisdom's Children: A Christian Esoteric Tradition*. New York: State University of New York Press, 1999.

Virgil. *Georgics*, 2 Vols. Translated by H.R. Fairclough. Cambridge, MA: Harvard University Press, 1916.

Volney, Constantin François. *The Ruins, or a Survey of the Revolutions of Empires*. London, 1795.

Voltaire. *Letters Concerning the English Nation*, London, 1726.

Voltaire. 'The Negro' in *Philosophical Letters. The Works of Voltaire. A Contemporary Version, in 21 vols*. Translated by William E. Fleming. New York: E.R. DuMont, 1901. Kindle Edition.

Von Stuckrad, Kocku. *Western Esotericism: A Brief History of Secret Knowledge*. London: Equinox, 2005.

Wakefield, Dan. 'Erhard's Life After Est'. *Common Boundary*, March/April 1994, http://www.wernererhard.com/boundary.html.

Weaver, Helen. *The Awakener: A Memoir of Kerouac and the Fifties*. San Francisco: City Lights, 2009.

Weber, Max. *From Max Weber: Essays in Sociology*. edited by H.H. Garth and C. Mills Wright, 139. London: Kegan Paul, Trench, Trubner & Co., 1947.

Webster, Charles. *From Paracelsus to Newton: Magic and the Making of Modern Science*. Cambridge: Cambridge University Press, 1982.

Wells, H.G. *A Modern Utopia*. London: J.M. Dent, 1994.

Wertheim, Margaret. *The Pearly Gates of Cyberspace: A History of Space from Dante to the Internet*. New York: W.W. Norton & Company, 1999.

Wessinger, Catherine. 'Millennialism with and without the Mayhem'. In Thomas Robbins and Susan J. Palmer, *Millennium, Messiahs and Mayhem: Contemporary Apocalyptic Movements*, 47–59. London: Routledge, 1999.

White, Hayden. *Metahistory: The Historical Imagination in Nineteenth Century Europe*. Baltimore and London: The Johns Hopkins University Press, 1973.

Whitehead, Alfred North. *Process and Reality*. London: Free Press, 1979.

Whittier, John Greenleaf. *The Supernaturalism of New England*. Norman: University of Oklahoma Press, 1969.

Wilde, Oscar. 'The Soul of Man Under Socialism'. In *De Profundis and Other Writings*, edited by Hesketh Pearson, 19–53. Harmondsworth: Penguin, 1973.

Williams, Raymond. *The Long Revolution*. London: Hogarth Press, 1992.

Willner, John. *The Perfect Horoscope*. New York: Paraview Press, 2001.

Wilson, Bryan. *Magic and the Millennium*. New York: Harper and Row, 1973.

Wintour, Patrick. 'Green Party's Flagship Economic Policy would Hit Poorest Hardest, say Experts'. *The Guardian*, 27 January 2015. http://www.theguardian.com/politics/2015/jan/27/green-party-citizens-income-policy-hits-poor.

Wittgenstein, Ludwig. *The Blue and Brown Books, Preliminary Studies for 'Philosophical Investigations'*. Oxford: Blackwell, 1958.

Wittgenstein, Ludwig. *Philosophical Investigations*. Translated by G.E.M Anscombe, P.M.S Hacker, and Joachim Schulte. Oxford: Wiley-Blackwell, 2009.

Wodehouse, E.A. 'The Order of the Star in the East: Its Outer and Inner Work', from the *Adyar Bulletin* (September 1911). http://www.katinkahesselink.net/his/stareas1.html.

Wolfe, Tom. *The Electric Kool-Aid Acid Test*. 1971. London: Random House, 1989.

Wolin, Richard. *The Seduction of Unreason: The Intellectual Romance with Fascism from Nietzsche to Postmodernism*. Princeton: Princeton University Press, 2006.

Wood, Graeme. 'What ISIS Really Wants'. *The Atlantic Monthly*, March 2015, http://www.theatlantic.com/features/archive/2015/02/what-isis-really-wants/384980/.

Wood, Kelsey. *Žižek: A Reader's Guide*. Oxford: Wiley-Blackwell, 2012.

Wordsworth, William. 'French Revolution'. 1805. In *Poetical Works*, vol. 3, ed. William Knight. London: MacMillan, 1896, http://www.gutenberg.org/files/12383/12383-h/Wordsworth3b.html.

Yablonsky, Lewis. *The Hippie Trip*. New York: Pegasus, 1968.

Yeats, W.B. *A Vision*. 1937. London: MacMillan, 1981.

Yinger, J. Milton. 'Contraculture and Subculture'. *American Sociological Review* 25, no. 5 (October 1960): 625–35.

Yinger, J. Milton. 'A Structural Examination of Religion'. *Journal for the Scientific Study of Religion* 8 (Spring 1969): 88–99.

Yinger, J. Milton. *Countercultures: The Promise and Peril of a World Turned Upside Down*. New York: The Free Press, 1984.

York, Michael. *The Emerging Network: A Sociology of the New Age and Neo-Pagan Movements*. London: Rowman and Littlefield, 1995.

Zeller, Benjamin. *Heaven's Gate: America's UFO Religion*. New York: New York University Press, 2014.

Zimmerman, Rainer E. 'Transforming Utopian into Metopian Systems: Bloch's Principle of Hope Revisited'. In *The Privatization of Hope: Ernst Bloch and the Future of Utopia*, edited by Peter Thompson and Slavoj Žižek, 246–68. London: Duke University Press, 2013.

Žižek, Slavoj. *The Fragile Absolute*. New York: Verso, 2000.

Žižek, Slavoj. *Living in the End Times*. London: Verso, 2011.

Žižek, Slavoj. *The Year of Living Dangerously*. London: Verso, 2012.

Index

Note: Locators with an 'n' denote note numbers.